ANTHONY QUINEY

JOHN LOUGHBOROUGH PEARSON

Published for the Paul Mellon Centre for Studies in British Art by
Yale University Press New Haven and London 1979

FOR LYNN

and for Harriet, Matilda and Augusta
who have lived with 'J.L.P.' almost as
long as they can remember

Designed by Faith Brabenec Hart and set in Monophoto Century Schoolbook.
Printed in Great Britain by BAS Printers Limited, Over Wallop, Hampshire.

Published in Great Britain, Europe, Africa, and Asia (except Japan) by
Yale University Press, Limited, London. Distributed in Australia and New Zealand
by Book & Film Services, Artarmon, N.S.W., Australia; and in Japan by
Harper & Row, Publishers, Tokyo Office.

Library of Congress Cataloguing in Publication Data

Quiney, Anthony, 1935–
  John Loughborough Pearson.

  (Studies in British art)
  Bibliography: p.
  Includes index.
  1. Pearson, John Loughborough, 1817–1897.
2. Architects–England–Biography. I. Series.
NA997.P39Q56 1979   720′.92′4 [B] 79–9832
ISBN 0–300–02253–0

PREFACE

'DOES IT send you on your knees?' This is the question you should ask, Pearson said, when you go into a church; not 'Is this admirable—is it beautiful?' It is a daunting attitude and as a basis for judgement the modern biographer must put it aside, yet never forget it if he is to understand the man and his time. I grew up with the notion that Victorian Gothic was somehow unreal: it lacked credibility; it lacked spirituality. Certainly it would not send you on your knees and could not be compared with the Gothic of the Middle Ages.

Later, studying English architecture under Sir John Summerson's illuminating tuition, I went to see Pearson's masterpiece, St Augustine, Kilburn. The first sight of this church dispelled any misconceptions I had. It did not send me on my knees, but I was immediately taken by its beauty; and I found the complexities of its interior united by over-reaching vaults admirable. Its architecture is one thing; sympathy for the Victorian spirituality which caused this church to be built is harder, though I believe I understand it if only in the same way as I understand Victorian society and its economic basis. My account of this truly great Victorian architect is not therefore illuminated by any special reverence for Victorian religion. I have tried to write an account which is not concerned simply with architectural criticism. However little one may sympathize with them, Victorian attitudes are fascinating and I have tried to show a little of this paradoxical age as a means of understanding one of its most imaginative artists.

After I had seen several of his churches I was asked by the Historic Buildings Board of the Greater London Council to write a report on Pearson's work in London in an attempt to preserve the church of St Peter, Vauxhall, from one of the GLC's road schemes. The scheme died a natural death, but my research continued. A book on Pearson seemed the most natural conclusion to what rapidly became an enthusiastic study. This pursuit was soon discouraged by Sir Nikolaus Pevsner. 'You will never be able to publish a book on him', he told me regretfully when I offered some corrections for *The Buildings of England*. He sweetened the pill by suggesting that I should do a thesis instead, and my first thanks go to him for his continual support for my research and his valuable guidance until the work was complete. My second thanks must go to the Paul Mellon Centre for Studies in British Art whose grant has disproved Sir Nikolaus and made publication of this book possible.

Where my research has been concerned, two people deserve especial mention. Mrs Marion Morgan, Pearson's grand-daughter, played a vital role in preserving the Pearson papers from casual destruction. Since I first went to her some ten years ago she has given me free access to them and appraised my interpretation of them, and she has helped me understand Pearson, despite his deep reticence, with gentle criticism and revealing recollection. Then I must thank Gordon Barnes. His photographs, which appear liberally here, have been of great value to me—even inspiration—and are a testimony to his joy in Pearson's architecture. Often he went ahead of me searching out papers in parish chests, or came behind tying up loose ends. Together we deciphered Pearson's Ledger, especially the often obscure notes at the end of it. His help was crowned with success when he found an aged inhabitant of Nether Wallop who was able to confirm his theory that three untitled photographs from Pearson's collection were of the long-demolished Wallop Lodge, which we had until then only known from accounts in the Ledger.

Of the numerous people who have contributed in particular ways I am indebted to Jill Allibone who shed much light on Pearson's training in Durham and subsequent employment by Salvin; to Susan Beattie who translated Muthesius's *Neuere Kirchliche Baukunst* for me and gave me much information about late Victorian artists and architecture; to Andrew Saint for long discussions on the Victorian architectural profession and lately for a book which, as a model, sets an unattainable standard; and to Bob Weston for drawing many of the plans, elevations and sections which appear here. I should like to thank Malcolm Airs, Timothy Ambrose, John Ashdown, Tony Baggs, J. H. Barratt, Nancy Briggs, Bob Brooker, Neil Burton, Alban Caroe, Hilda Coe, Howard Colvin, Nicholas Cooper and Stephen Croad of the National Monuments Record, Roger Evans, John Gerrard, Henry Howell, Peter Howell, Ted Hubbard, John Hutchinson, Walter Ison, Paul Joyce, Frank Kelsall, Jim Lee, Michael Leppard, Jill Lever of the Royal Institute of British Architects, London, Ginny Messenger who gave me a base from which I could study Pearson's works in the North, Kenneth Mills, John Newman, Brian and Dorothy Payne, John Phillips who is Surveyor of the Fabric of Truro Cathedral, Mark Playford who is Pearson's great-grandson, John Protheroe, Anne Riches, the Mother Superior and Sister Richenda of St Peter's Convent, Woking, John Sambrook, Mark Spurrell, Sir John Summerson, Anthony Symondson, Robert Thorne, Morley Tonkin, Ian Toplis, Martin Weaver, Philip Whitbourn and David Williams for their help; and I must similarly express my thanks to the numerous owners, incumbents, curators, librarians and archivists who have given me their time. Finally I should mention my family's humour and patience—too often they discovered that a journey was being prolonged and a meal delayed by a detour to see a newly discovered Pearson work.

Anthony Quiney,
Blackheath, December 1978.

CONTENTS

Benson and choice of an architect; the site; the plan; the elevation; details; the stone-laying ceremony; controversy over materials; reviews: Muthesius, E. S. Prior, Francis Bond; the cathedral complete

ABBREVIATIONS

THE FOLLOWING abbreviations are used in the List of Plates, in the Notes and in the Catalogue of Works. In the case of periodicals, the year of publication, the volume number and then the page numbers are given, all in Arabic numerals without punctuation unless several separate pages or volumes are quoted together (for example *Builder* vol. 53 (1887), pp. 560, 626 and 657–60 and vol. 54 (1888), pp. 9 and 11 is given as *B* 1887 53 650, 626, 657–60, 1888 54 9, 11). In a few cases there are no volume numbers so the year is followed directly by the page numbers.

A	*The Architect*
AR	*The Architectural Review*
B	*The Builder*
BA	*The British Architect*
BE	N. Pevsner (ed. and unless otherwise stated author): *The Buildings of England*
BN	*The Building News*
Caröe	W. D. Caröe's memoir of Pearson (published anonymously) in the *Journal of the Royal Institute of British Architects* 3rd s. 1897–8 5 113–21
CB	*The Church Builder*
CCE	Church Commissioners for England (formerly Ecclesiastical Commissioners for England) (file)
E	*The Ecclesiologist*
Eastlake	C. L. Eastlake, *A History of the Gothic Revival* (London, 1872)
GLC	Greater London Council
ICBS	Incorporated Church Building Society (file)
Newberry	J. E. Newberry, 'The Work of John L. Pearson R.A.', *The Architectural Review* 1896–7 Vol. I 1–11, 69–82
NMR	National Monuments Record
R.I.B.A.	Royal Institute of British Architects, London
SPAB	Society for the Protection of Ancient Buildings
VCH	*Victoria History of the Counties*

LIST OF PLATES

✿ PROLOGUE

ONE MONDAY evening early in June 1880 a large group of gentlemen assembled at the Royal Institute of British Architects for the last meeting of the session. They elected some new Fellows, listened to a report on the recent architectural examination, and then settled back for the main business of the evening. This was the presentation of the year's Royal Gold Medal. A few knew the recipient well enough, but many were singularly ignorant of him. Well aware of this, John Whichcord, the President, recounted a conversation he had overheard between two architects a day or two before: 'One complained that the Royal Gold Medal was this year to be given to a Mr Pearson, of whom nobody had ever heard, and whom nobody knew; while the other, who had written to a newspaper for information of this Mr Pearson, declared that the Council chose him because he was one of themselves.'[1] The President did not disabuse the two, but had he asked them if they remembered Mr Pearson's churches at Bessborough Gardens and Vauxhall, he was 'quite sure that they would have declared themselves familiar with both. They would have known, notwithstanding the hugeness of London, the church of St Augustine, at Kilburn, and the new church of St John, in Red Lion Square. But the fact is, they had not cared to inquire who the architect of those works was, and he had never, even in these pushing, enterprising days, ostentatiously identified himself with those buildings; or loosened, even for a moment, the old-fashioned bond of modesty and merit.'

That bond has remained unloosed: while Pearson's churches have been much praised, he, the man, is a shadow. His distinguished contemporaries, Scott, Pugin, Butterfield and Street, played leading roles in the Gothic Revival. Pearson did too: his buildings epitomize the main stream of the Revival, phase by phase, as it developed from 1840 until the end of the century; but he almost never wrote publicly about them, and they were largely uncontroversial. They do, nonetheless, bear the stamp of individual genius; and a handful of his churches carry architecture to new heights.

Why was this? Pearson's few known utterances are little help. He was said to be a ready talker, but no one bothered to write down the gist of a single conversation. Only his pupil William Douglas Caröe offered any reason for his master's extraordinary abilities: they amounted to knowledge and diligence, and a true feeling for architecture.[2] Caröe was perceptive, but he worshipped Pearson, the successful Academician and Gold Medallist of the 1880s. He recognized Pearson's early delight in Durham Cathedral and the abbeys of the North; would he, though, have understood the diffident boy assiduously learning his craft in the Durham of the 1830s or the earnest young man studiously building up a practice in Yorkshire in the 1840s? Success,

1. The portrait of Pearson by Walter William Ouless, R.A., exhibited at the Royal Academy in 1889.

artistry, eminence were aspirations natural to Caröe: Pearson hardly gave them a thought.

Nevertheless Caröe was perceptive: he was the first and so far the only writer to appreciate the classical element in Pearson's work. To everyone else Pearson was simply a Gothicist: a Gothicist, simply, he has remained. That evening in 1880 A. J. Beresford Hope, the champion of the Gothic Revival, told the assembly at the R.I.B.A. that he and their medallist had fought

> shoulder to shoulder . . . in the fight for the grand old architecture of the Middle Ages . . . Their friend Mr Pearson was indeed a true and faithful knight. Early in life he paid his vows at the altar of that chaste and beautiful, stern but royally-magnificent virgin, *Ars Gothica*, and to her he had been faithful all his days.

A man of Pearson's diffidence would not disclaim this publicly. If it was necessary for the hero of the moment to have engaged in so righteous a battle for Gothic, then one could not be a turncoat. Not only aesthetics were at stake, morality was too. Only later could Caröe admit that for Pearson style was merely clothing for great architectural ideas; but by then no one heeded him. Pearson had had a good career—better than most—and his age was nearly past. He had certainly been fortunate. He was in tune with the times and never plagued by the doubts which afflicted so many Victorians. He caught the tide and it flowed throughout his long life.

Pearson's career spanned two thirds of the nineteenth century, almost the extent of Queen Victoria's long reign. She gave her name to the age, though it really began a generation before her accession, and embraced the century of peace which lasted from the Battle of Waterloo until the Great War. Peace there was, by modern standards; but there was tumult also: in economic and social affairs especially at the beginning, in imperial affairs later on. Above all, the age was marked by its industrial advances. These were relentlessly pursued by a society which believed in progress for its self-betterment, but simultaneously held to tradition as a sheet-anchor for its values.

The incompatibility of these beliefs was aggravated by the unsteadiness of economic expansion. Every decade between 1815 and the Great Exhibition of 1851 saw a few years of intense economic activity, followed by a deep recession. This led to appalling hardship and social upheaval. Peterloo at the beginning and the rise and fall of Chartism at the end were its most violent manifestations. Sporadic turmoil never erupted into the revolutions which swept the Continent, but the fear that they might spread to Britain was ever present despite political action. The Reform Act, the Factory Acts and the Repeal of the Corn Laws alleviated specific evils and perhaps kept revolution at bay. Other supposed threats were ungodliness and the spread of nonconformity; the official remedy for them was the Church Building Act of 1818, which authorized the building of as many churches as possible out of public funds so that the soul of the working man might be regained for the established church, for his own improvement and for the benefit of the nation.

That Act started Victorian church building on its course. Although many of the new churches were built in the neo-classical style, it was in the rest that the Gothic Revival as applied to ecclesiastical architecture began its development. The style had been used in the seventeenth and eighteenth centuries for churches like the monumental St Mary at Warwick and the playful Shobdon, but those were isolated examples. The new wave of church building encouraged a cheap, thin form of Gothic whose chief features were tall lancet windows and as many stucco pinnacles as the available money would buy. At their worst, these churches were mean boxes, but, in the hands of distinguished architects such as Thomas Rickman, or when there was more money to spare, they showed serious understanding of medieval decoration. At this stage Pearson began his career, assisting the Durham architect Ignatius Bonomi to build cheap Gothic churches, not in fact financed under the Act of 1818, but by Roman Catholics who, as a result of the Relief Act of 1829, were free to worship and build churches.

The first phase of the Gothic Revival culminated in a very high standard of archaeologically correct design, as exemplified by the churches of Pearson and others, largely as a result of Pugin's rhetoric and the artistic reforms instigated by the Cambridge Camden Society in parallel with the liturgical reforms of the Oxford Movement. These were backward looking, an attempt to reassert long-lost values in the face of social change. Nonconformity was not reduced though ungodliness may have been. By the 1850s the success of the reforms showed itself in churches like Pearson's Holy Trinity, Bessborough Gardens, and the forms of worship which large congregations practised there. Simultaneously the nation, now freed from the worst excesses of the economic instability of the post-Waterloo period, could express its vitality and assurance in the Great Exhibition of 1851, and make explicit its desire to expand industry and trade unfettered, and ultimately end poverty. Such were the contradictions of an age in which belief in progress and concern for religion held equal places in men's minds.

The years of economic and social stability that followed—the High Victorian years—produced a new vigorous style of architecture. It was assertive and confident, with, appropriately, raw materials taken from foreign sources. Eclectic and no longer simple re-creations of a past style, its buildings, Pearson's among them, were yet further examples of the manufactures of a fertile and inventive nation.

High Victorian confidence lasted for a generation. Then after about 1870 unchallenged economic expansion was gradually replaced by increasing foreign competition; the British faltered: they no longer had a monopoly of inventiveness even while keeping a monopoly of many markets. Investment abroad stagnated. The quality of education fell behind newly raised standards in France and Germany. There were poor harvests, and cheaply imported corn threatened to ruin agriculture. The problems of Empire, whether in Ireland, Africa or the East, were continually interrupting and confusing social and economic progress at home. These were years of conservatism and retrenchment. The nagging doubts hitherto inherent in Victorian beliefs came to the surface everywhere.

In architecture there was conservatism too, and doubt. What was the role of art in architecture?—in society as a whole for that matter? The problem was faced and discussed exhaustively, but no obvious answer was found. The doubts remained, at least with those honest enough to admit them. Architects exchanged the more overtly foreign elements of the High Victorian style for English ones. For some it was a desire to return to the bedrock of tradition; for others, a demonstration of nationalism. They paid great attention to detailing, and the refined work of the Arts and Crafts Movement took the place of the vigorous but often coarse detail of the generation before. The Movement's philosophy was influential. Its members seemed to be radical in their dislike of academicism, but that was reaction, not true radicalism; more significant for the future was their rejection of any role for industry and its products.

Pearson did not care for their new ways; he remained true to the ideals of his early years. His detailing tended to lapse into mere good taste when it extended far beyond the careful use of mouldings; the massing of his buildings, however, continued in the robust High Victorian tradition; and in his spatial compositions he struck out on his own. In this lies his unique contribution to English nineteenth-century architecture.

The latter part of the nineteenth century might have seen the creation of the long-awaited modern style of architecture, and it is typical of the widespread rejection of radicalism then current that that event had to await the end of the century and took place abroad. This is not to deny the English contribution to architecture: it was held in high esteem; but something else might have been expected from a nation which created the Crystal Palace. The more competent architects were not interested in exploiting its success, and those who most nearly approached the modern style as it ultimately developed, architects like Voysey, strenuously denied that their work was anything but traditional.

Pearson was too old to make radical innovations in the late Victorian period. He kept remarkably up to date, but since his primary work was church building and the whole church-building movement was born to counteract radicalism, the problem of finding a new style fit for an industrial age did not concern him. He did wonders with cheaply manufactured bricks, but his great success was purely architectonic: the creation of churches which explore completely fresh architectural ideas yet stay within the utterly conservative framework of the Gothic Revival.

1 DURHAM

JOHN Loughborough Pearson was born on 5 July 1817. The date is inscribed in the family Bible which records the marriage of his maternal grandparents and nearly two hundred years later the death of his great-grandson in the Second World War.[1]

In 1767 John Loughborough married Elizabeth Wilkinson. Of their ten children, the sixth, Nancy, was born in 1776. In 1794 Nancy, now called Ann as Nancy was thought a frivolous name, married William Pearson who was three years her senior. He was the second son of Thomas Pearson, a well-known local lawyer who came from an established family which once owned property in Durham. William Pearson, a topographical artist, often exhibited at the Royal Academy. He published two books of views: the first, *Rural Beauties*, depicts small churches and cottages in the North West; the second, *Antiquities of Shropshire*, of 1807, has forty views with short descriptions of many of the county's abbeys and castles. The drawings show an appreciation of architectural form which was to be handed down to his youngest son; the texts indicate a desire to record old buildings before their impending destruction.

Like her mother, Ann had many children. Nine were born between 1795 and 1814, including the Ann who died at Truro in 1846, and Sarah who appears with her sister in Pearson's diaries and was to outlive him. In 1817 when she was forty-one Ann Pearson gave birth to her last children, John Loughborough and a twin sister born dead.

The birthplace, surprisingly, seems to have been Brussels. When the census was taken in 1851 and 1861, Pearson gave it as Brussels,[2] and that should be conclusive; but his son Frank stated emphatically that his father had been born in Durham: 'They went to Brussels later.' Maybe no one remembered, and possibly Frank disliked the traditional birthplace because he considered it improper for someone of his father's standing to have been born abroad: it would have made him a foreigner.

If the disagreement existed during Pearson's lifetime, one thing is certain: he would have appeared supremely unconcerned with it. He grew into an unusually reticent man, interested in little but his profession— characteristics praiseworthy in a century which esteemed the virtues of modesty, humility and devotion to duty.

Wherever he may have been born, the young John was brought up in Durham. He had little formal schooling, and there may lie the cause of his reserve. Reserve is at once the defence of the wise and the refuge of the stupid. Self-conscious of his lack of schooling and easily feeling foolish, he may have found wisdom too late to change his manner. Reserve and late development often go hand-in-hand, and he was certainly a late developer.

Pearson regretted his lack of schooling, but did much to make amends for

2. R. W. Billings's view of Durham from his book on the cathedral published in 1843. In the foreground is Robson steam mill; Pearson was to build a house for him on the hillside just to its right.

it. He seems to have been conversant with French and German, and certainly understood French and German architectural books. Probably much of his learning was gained at home, and he must have attended educational classes at Sunday School. During his last two years in Durham, he was a superintendent at the Sunday School in the parish of St Margaret.[3] The perpetual curate there was George Townsend, a canon and prebendary of Durham and a self-styled Tractarian. He was a close friend of Pearson's and probably acted as his mentor. He lent him an encyclopaedia in 1840, and Pearson's diaries for 1841 and 1842 have lists of books which Townsend could have mentioned to him. Townsend entered into a religious controversy with the author of one of them, the prominent Whig Henry Hallam, who wrote a history of European literature and thought which was in Pearson's lists. The subjects of other books in the lists range from geography and travel to philosophy. Lying innocently among long-forgotten tomes on Russia and South America is an account of his travels by Charles Darwin, not yet the dark figure he was to become in Victorian religious circles.[4]

Pearson's lack of general education may be why he published little—so little that it is often said that he wrote nothing. But two articles bearing his initials appeared in the *Church Builder*, one of which describes his church at Appleton-le-Moors in the 1860s.[5] It begins with an account of the life of Joseph Shepherd in whose memory the church was built. The son of an Appleton labourer, Shepherd began as a cabin boy but rapidly rose through honest effort to become a shipowner, and amassed a fortune. Returning to his native village in his old age he wished to make a thank-offering for his life and build a church, parsonage, almshouses and schools, the latter so that others might have what had been denied to him. The tale is typical of the Victorian attitude to life, illustrating self-betterment through honest industry tempered by piety and humility. Pearson's identification with the shipowner and pleasure in participating in building a memorial stand out clearly, perhaps because, while he may have been guided by people like Townsend, he gained much learning through his own efforts.

In 1831 William Pearson placed his son in the office of Ignatius Bonomi. Bonomi is not well known today, but his father Joseph Bonomi, an Italian immigrant, had achieved some fame as a designer of neo-classical country houses. Ignatius Bonomi was County Surveyor and had been practising in Durham for about twenty years. He had built a handful of churches, most of them Roman Catholic, in the plain and thin pre-archaeological Gothic typical of their age; nevertheless some are not undistinguished.

No doubt Pearson had shown an aptitude for drawing before he began his pupillage. By 1836 he had mastered the techniques of drawing elevations, details and perspectives; that October, aged nineteen, he took a boat across the North Sea to Hamburg. There he drew details of a neo-classical house, including mouldings, sections and even an elevation of a doorway especially showing the 'scraper for feet'.[6] Far more significant are drawings of Hamburg Exchange, an ornate renaissance building with an arcaded ground storey (Plate 3). There is a perspective, an elevation of the end bay with notes for making a fair copy of the complete elevation, and some sections and various notes: 'These plinths all different and much obliterated, all these figures are different.' It is a good record, and doubly interesting for the Exchange was destroyed, as he noted, in the great fire of 1842.

Soon Pearson had learnt the craft of architecture, the making of specifications, dealing with tradesmen and craftsmen, surveying and laying out sites, and all the other essential but humdrum duties which go to ensure the efficient building of an architectural design.

What Bonomi taught him of design itself is illustrated by an unfinished manuscript volume which Pearson made in 1840 and called *Studies and Examples of Modern Architecture*. It includes most of Bonomi's current commissions. The first, Christ Church, Battyeford in the West Riding, starts with 'Specifications for all artificers' detailing exactly what work each craftsman is to do. This is followed by a set of drawings: a plan, elevations and section; details of mouldings including bell capitals, water-holding bases and label-stops decorated with masks, details Pearson later used so often that they became characteristic of his style; a large and a small alphabet for the Decalogue 'by Mr. Wailes of N'Castle'; and finally two perspectives in wash (Plate 4). From the even copperplate of the text to the fine lines and delicate colour of the drawings, Pearson showed a quality with pen and brush which far outmatches the commonplace subject. Similar drawings illustrate more churches and chapels; others show Clervaux Castle at Croft in the North Riding and small works including 'Mrs Costobadie's Conservatory', 'Roofing in the chapel yard of Court House at Northallerton for the Dinner for the Agricultural Meeting A.D. 1840 Aug 5', and a charming design for inlaid tiles for the dairy at Lambton Castle in County Durham. Just one public building is included: Bonomi's competition design for the Liverpool Assize Courts; devised as an Italian renaissance palace, it is modish but very pedestrian. If Pearson wanted to emulate his father with this book, he certainly proved his powers of draughtsmanship; if he hoped to use it as a sampler of modern designs in which he had had some hand, then it can be seen only as the naive effort of a provincial architect's assistant.

Correspondence about one of the buildings included in *Studies and Examples* survives in the Chaytor papers. A long series of letters mostly from Bonomi, but a few from Pearson, relate to the building of Clervaux Castle. They show that when Bonomi was away from Durham, Pearson took full responsibility for the progress of the design, suggesting alterations for reasons which are both aesthetic and practical. On 26 February 1840 Pearson wrote to Chaytor, 'I think you will agree with me that the Tower in the principal front projects too much; I would recommend the doing away with the Wall dividing the Billiard room from the Hall by this means we lessen the projection upwards of 5 feet.' Then written around a small sketch-plan (Plate 5), Pearson continued:

> With respect to the Entrance Gateway I would recommend the former plan with a door from the lobby to the Waiting room into the Gateway; this would not only make the Waiting room more comfortable as a Sleeping room, but would also enable the Servant to get to the front door to open it without having to go into the Gateway and open it from the outside.[7]

Pearson was apparently on more friendly terms than one might expect between an architect's assistant and a client from the titled gentry. On 27 April he wrote again to Chaytor explaining more alterations to the plans and excusing himself for not having written before. The letter ends, 'I hope you will accept my apology for my seeming negligence and trusting you may enjoy many returns of the 29th.'[8] There are no more surviving letters from Pearson for over a year until two dated 4 and 31 May 1841 which deal with preparing drawings for tendering, and which builders should be approached. The second letter ends again on a surprising note of affection: 'I have but this to add, how much I am—Dear Sir William—your obedient servant J.L.Pearson.'[9]

3. Hamburg Exchange drawn by
Pearson in October 1836.

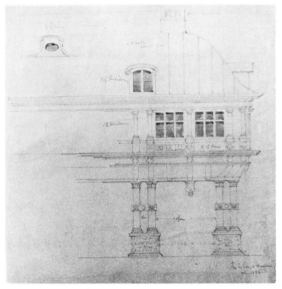

The only other documents relating to this period in Pearson's life are his diaries for 1840, '41 and '42. They are full of items of petty expenditure, and larger ones associated with visits to inspect work in progress at Brancepeth, Croft, St Andrew Auckland and Hartlepool, and a long journey of four days to Scremerston returning by way of Sunderland and Newcastle. Alongside are records of the erratic payment of his salary of forty-four shillings a week, and his rent account for his lodgings in Old Elvet.

Bonomi's house and office were also in Old Elvet, a short way from Durham Cathedral, and Pearson spent every spare hour from office work within its walls; he obtained special permission from the Dean and Chapter to draw the Galilee. Caröe records that, '. . . modest and reticent though he was in all things concerning himself, it was a treat sometimes to hear him speak with all the enthusiasm of youth over his early joy in this great structure'.[10] Pearson similarly made a detailed study of the abbeys and churches of Yorkshire. Caröe was writing from hindsight and knew how much these great medieval buildings contributed to Pearson's mature style, but at the time this study was simply part of a process of self-education.

In the 1830s the Gothic Revival had lost the light-hearted charm of its rococo beginnings but had not yet reached the seriousness of its archaeological phase. While it had received official approval for the new Palace of Westminster, it was no more than an alternative to the much more widespread classical style. Bonomi's churches were Gothic, but Clervaux Castle was Norman, and the Assize Court design was Italian renaissance. There was nothing in Pearson's training which had predetermined his future as a leading Gothic revivalist. The neo-classical style still held sway and the buildings erected in this style were demonstratively the result of deep architectural thought and learning, as opposed to the fancy with which contemporary Gothic buildings were generally designed. Pearson received a knowledge of classical practice as a matter of course, a knowledge which he gained by study and was to extend in London, and which equally, but less obviously, influenced his mature work. There is evidence for his study in tracings which he made of details of classical buildings—the Pantheon, the Doric temple at Segesta and the circular Temple of Vesta at Tivoli among them.[11]

Pearson started with Bonomi at the age of fourteen. Ten years later he left, now grown into a short man who always stood firmly upright. He had thick straight hair parted on the right, and it swept across a high forehead. In later life he had a full beard and moustache, and portraits show that he used reading glasses. The best portrait, by Ouless (Plate 1), shows a man at once authoritative and gentle. This is borne out by his family. They confirm that he was devout; he believed in worship; he believed in prayer. No doubt he held High Church views, but there is nothing to suggest that he was intolerant or priggish. His reticent nature had another side to it: while his relations with Chaytor included genuine affection, with others, especially his fellow architects later, his relations extended further; in the words of George

4. (left) Christ Church, Battyeford, from *Studies and Examples*, 1840.

5. (below) Part of Pearson's letter to Chaytor of 26 February 1840.

6. (bottom) Robson's house of 1842, from the north.

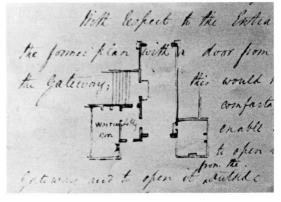

Aitchison, the President of the Royal Institute of British Architects at the time of his death, 'Everybody who knew Mr Pearson must have loved him.'[12]

Pearson's reticent nature had its counterpart. When he strongly cared about something, he would make up his mind and stubbornly hold to his decision. This was often the case later in his life when faced with controversy. It is first apparent in his decision to leave Bonomi, an action described in a letter dated 11 March 1842 from Bonomi to Chaytor: 'Mr Pearson is no longer with me he quitted my employt. very suddenly on being told by me that I had received an offer from a young man whom I had known several years for entering into a partnership which is now about to take place.' Chaytor was upset to lose Pearson and asked Bonomi to offer him the superintendence of the building of Clervaux Castle. Pearson's initial reply seems to have been favourable and it was proposed to ask him to 'specify the amount of salary he wd. deem sufficient'. Forty or fifty shillings was considered to be the rate for clerks of works locally, but Pearson replied asking for a sum 'higher than usual in this part of the country' and that was the end of the matter.[13]

This crisis in Pearson's career probably took place at the end of September 1841, as the last record in his diary of a payment of salary by Bonomi was then. At this time John Dobson's name and address in New Bridge Street, Newcastle, appear. Pearson was clearly acquainted with Dobson, but probably no more than that. Dobson was far more successful than Bonomi, and Pearson may have hoped to work for him. He never did, but instead seems to have tried to set up in practice on his own. Once already he had had work of his own: in April 1841 he 'Received £2. 7. 0. of R. J. Shafto Esq for plans done for him.' In November he made drawings of 'the property belonging to the Corporation and Smith's Charity', and in January 1842 'Received 5/19 of the mayor paid per a/ct for plan of the market place.' This, however, was hardly the way to start a successful practice.

Early in 1842 Pearson designed his first recorded building. On 3 January he got 'instruction to make plans for a house to be built on the north road for Mr Robson'. He worked quickly and on 20 January sent working drawings and specifications to Robson for which he received £5 a month later. The house was built and still survives in North Road (Plate 6).[14] It is a plain but solid late Georgian house of two storeys with single windows flanking a central doorway. It is without pretension, and remarkable only for its similarity to Scott's first building, the vicarage at Wappenham in Northamptonshire which he built for his father nine years before.

Even while he was designing Robson's house, Pearson must have realised that too little work was coming his way, and on 23 January he left Durham for Sunderland to work for George Pickering. Known only for a few churches, Pickering was Anthony Salvin's amanuensis in the North, and it was probably when he was executing work for Salvin at Durham that Pearson met him. The 1842 diary does not indicate how Pearson was employed. At all events he cannot have been satisfied as he only stayed four weeks; on 20 February he 'received from Geo. Pickering for work done for him £3', and the next day left Sunderland for London.

2 &LONDON

PEARSON had made a momentous decision to leave the North, and perhaps wishing to record it especially he noted in his diary on 23 February 1842, 'arrived in London at 4 in the afternoon'. The railway had not yet reached Sunderland, and Pearson must have made the journey by boat. Within a few years, being among the first generation of architects to do so, he could go all over the country by rail, which enabled him to have a large nationwide practice.

At the end of Pearson's diary for 1841 appear Salvin's name and his address in Finchley. Anthony Salvin was born in 1799 and educated in Durham.[1] He lived much of his early life nearby at Brancepeth, which was a noted artistic centre at the time. Possibly Pearson's father was among those attracted there; Pearson himself often went there and would have met Salvin and heard about London.

Salvin first went to London about 1820. His career properly started in the 1830s with commissions for large country houses which established him as the protagonist of the revived Tudor and Elizabethan styles in domestic work. His churches by comparison were undistinguished, but even so he was for a while among the Cambridge Camden Society's favourite architects.

The Society was founded in 1839 ostensibly to promote the study and practice of ecclesiastical architecture; but its real aims were to reintroduce Catholic ritual into the Anglican Church, to control the style of new churches, and to ensure that old churches were suitably restored. Its influence rapidly became widespread, and architects ignored the Society at their peril.

Salvin was a Fellow of the Society of Antiquaries and an early member of the Oxford Society for Promoting the Study of Gothic Architecture. Through these connections and through his work, he was at once conversant with current archaeological knowledge of Gothic architecture and with the increasingly moral criteria which determined the course of the revival of the Gothic style in the 1840s.

Pearson went to see Salvin a fortnight after his arrival in London, and agreed to work for him for 'some weeks'. This extended to six months and, while he was paid only two guineas weekly, it gave him what he had most lacked before—experience of the main stream of English architecture.

Pearson gave no indication in his diary of how he was employed. Luckily a large collection of his drawings survives which sheds some light on this period.[2] Many drawings have undisputed links with Salvin, recording his work from the beginning of his career up to 1848. His important houses of the 1830s—Harlaxton, Methley Hall, Burwarton House, Cowsley Hall, Seaton Carew Parsonage, Scotney Castle, Skutterskelf, Rufford Abbey, Greystoke Castle—and many others are illustrated by plans, some elevations, and many details ranging from porches to chimney-pieces. The drawings greatly helped

7. Tracings from the second volume showing details of a church near Ripon including label-stops in the form of the masks Pearson later used as a signature (right), and the church of St Loup (below right) and Bayeux Cathedral (below left) from Volume III of the Pugins' *Examples of Gothic Architecture*; the early Gothic of Normandy was to be a principal source of Pearson's style after 1870.

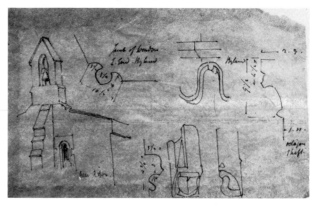

8. (far right) New Hall, Lincoln's Inn: perspective from the south-east, possibly by Pearson who supervised its erection in 1843–4.

Pearson when he designed his own Treberfydd House seven years later.

There are tracings or copies of Gothic designs, for instance Salvin's alterations to the Master's House at Trinity College, Cambridge; his proposed design for the Fitzwilliam Museum; churches at Keswick and Torquay; the additions at Holy Sepulchre, Cambridge, which were sponsored by the Cambridge Camden Society; and an abortive design for a church to be built at Alexandria, a commission which the Society passed on to him. Most significant are drawings of Kilndown church in Kent, which Salvin began in 1839 for Viscount Beresford, and which A. J. Beresford Hope altered to conform with the ideas of the new Cambridge Camden Society. If nothing else, these buildings introduced Pearson to the aims of the Society and the newly defined study of ecclesiology.

Pearson copied whatever took his fancy (Plate 7). As early as April 1833 he had copied measured drawings of Kirby Hall (he was to find inspiration here sixty years later), but most tracings are later. Apart from Salvin's buildings, there are tracings from Vredeman de Vries, and from contemporary works such as C. J. Richardson's *Studies of Old English Mansions*, T. F. Hunt's *Exemplars of Tudor Architecture*, Charles Parker's *Villa Rustica* and Henry Shaw's *Encyclopaedia of Ornament*. These books probably came from Salvin's library, and Pearson, lacking the money to buy them himself, instead traced their numerous plates. In the 1842 diary are noted two books of

Greek Revival designs, Leo von Klenze's *Anweisung zur Architectur des Christlichen Cultus* and Johann Carl Krafft's *Portes cochères et portes d'entrées de maisons et d'édifices publics de Paris*. These, together with several of his drawings and tracings, show that Pearson was studying an alternative to Gothic for churches as well as other types of buildings.

'In early days,' wrote Caröe, describing this collection of Pearson's drawings,

> his education was amplified by numerous careful and accurate sketches, drawn with an excellent line . . . his industry seems to have been untiring, and he drew from every source . . . not a detail of interest escaped him. These drawings . . . exhibit a happily chosen series of designs and details of every possible description, things great and small, artistic and educational, of all styles, English and foreign. Nothing in which an architect should be proficient is omitted.

Pearson eventually acquired a fine library, but at this time he was too poor to make any but occasional purchases. In November he recorded that he had 'bought Gwilt 2/5/-', and in 1841 he had already paid five guineas to subscribe to R. W. Billings's account of Durham Cathedral, although the book was not published until 1843.

Pearson possibly lodged above Salvin's office at 32 Somerset Street, Portman Square. Salvin had lived there himself until his wife's illness had forced him to retire to country air in Finchley. Pearson's low salary may well reflect the provision of free accommodation.

When at last in September his six months with Salvin came to an end, Pearson returned to Durham for 'election day', but stayed in the North only ten days. By the end of October he had 'begun to work for Mr Hardwick at £3. 0. 0. per week' and 'entered into lodgings Seymour Street at 7/- per week'.[3]

Philip Hardwick had just completed designs for a new hall and library for Lincoln's Inn in Holborn (Plate 8). 'I was to assist in the preparation of the drawings for this building for the Surveyors,' Pearson told Wyatt Papworth fifty years later, 'and a hard time I had of it.' Tenders were obtained, and in April 1843 work began. Then, falling ill, 'Mr Hardwick placed the whole thing unreservedly in my hands, and afterwards never interfered with my work . . . I superintended almost daily the building until it was all covered in.'[4]

While the work proceeded, Hardwick's son Philip Charles entered his father's office, but also fell ill and had to recuperate abroad. He had 'little or nothing to do with design' until, probably in 1844, with the carcass completed, he returned to the office. Two months later, Pearson left.

The *Builder* described the New Hall and Library as 'unquestionably one of the most successful buildings of our day'.[5] Eastlake concurred, but thought the carving was 'coldly executed'.[6] Possibly it was designed by Pearson; much of the carving in his own buildings was to be undeniably cold. Those criticisms, on the other hand, cannot be levelled against the fine series of chimney-stacks. Pearson may well have designed them too; in his tracings were many examples to prompt him.

While these years of training and working under Bonomi, Salvin and Hardwick were dominated in architecture by the neo-classical style, albeit in decline, Pearson was ever moving closer to the alternative of Gothic. Yet his studies had been broadly based. Reginald Blomfield later said of him, 'Of classic I think he was simply unconscious.'[7] That is misleading; classic entered Pearson's studies prominently if not equally with Gothic. It was eventually to appear in his own buildings and form one of their principal elements.

Pearson was a near contemporary of Gilbert Scott, who was born in 1811, of Richard Cromwell Carpenter and Augustus Welby Northmore Pugin, both born in 1812, and of William Butterfield, born in 1814. Scott's conversion to Gothic is one of the better-known incidents of his life: 'Pugin's articles excited me almost to fury, and I suddenly found myself like a person awakened from a long feverish dream, which had rendered him unconscious of what was going on about him.'[8] No such thing happened to Pearson; but unlike George Edmund Street, who was born a critical seven years later in 1823, and George Frederick Bodley and William Burges, both born in 1827, he did not grow up with Gothic as an established style.

By 1843 Gothic was in the ascendant. Under Salvin, Pearson had studied its latest forms—Tudor and Elizabethan—for domestic work, and learnt about the Cambridge Camden Society and its part in promoting the style for churches. Assisting Hardwick, he had applied Tudor to a modern building, acclaimed at the time as a notable success. On 20 April 1843 the foundation stone of the New Hall and Library was laid ceremonially. Work advanced rapidly. The New Hall was roofed in the early part of 1844 and the buildings were finished the following year to be formally opened in the presence of Queen Victoria in October 1845.

By that time Pearson had been pursuing his own independent career for two years and was now free to devote to it all his attention. When he came to build his own first large house four years later, he could draw on plenty of experience, practical as well as theoretical, but for churches it was a different matter; in that field he had been involved only in the indifferent. It was with churches that he was to start his independent career, and he had much still to learn. He needed someone to lead him—a new master. The effect of that master was not as melodramatic as it had been on Scott, but the master was the same—Pugin.

3 ✹ THE EAST RIDING

'Let us have an architecture, the arrangements and details of which remind us of our faith and of our country.' This was Pugin's rallying cry expounded in *An Apology for the Revival of Christian Architecture*. 'Such an architecture is to be found in the works of our ancestors, whose noble conceptions and mighty works were originated and perfected under a faith and system, for the most part common to our own.'[1]

It was cant perhaps, but not empty rhetoric. These arguments may have been no more logical than those upholding the ideals of neo-classicism, but they were moralistic: there lay their appeal. Through them and their buildings, Pugin, Scott and the Ecclesiologists achieved overwhelming success in the 1840s converting architects and clergy alike to use only the Gothic style for their churches, and to use it with archaeological correctness, and to restrict its use to the Geometrical Gothic or Middle Pointed of the late thirteenth and early fourteenth centuries when the style had reached the supposed peak of its perfection. Its superiority to Early English or primitive, and to Perpendicular or debased Gothic was, of course, self evident.

'The ancient form and arrangement of the parochial churches, consisting of nave and chancel, should be preserved . . . as in *times past*,' Pugin wrote; and he continued, as though it were an article of faith, 'Galleries are contrary to the intentions of the Anglican church.'[2] Instead there should be fonts, pulpits, lecterns, litany stools, chancel screens, stone altars, frontals, lighted tapers, sedilia, sacred symbols and imagery.

Pearson accepted all this willingly and, judging from his work, studied deeply Pugin's churches as well as his writings.

In May 1843 he applied this study to a perspective of a church which he evidently had some hopes of building.[3] His drawing shows an aisled nave with low transepts, and an aisleless chancel of good size (Plate 9). The sketchy masonry shows that he had heeded Pugin's call for small stones and 'antient irregular joints';[4] and he had learned further lessons: notes on the drawing declare, 'No galleries whatever—. The roofs to be open timber roofs—. . . The whole of the interior of stone. All cement studiously avoided.' This would have put him at the top of Pugin's form; nevertheless it is an ungainly design with an angular steeple like Salvin's at Kilndown, and little advance on those which he had helped Bonomi produce. The best to be said for it is that it has a lively outline.

This church remained a design, but already Pearson was at work on a simpler one, the first of twelve which he built or rebuilt in the opening ten years of his independent career. They show an increasing ability to master medieval forms; and while the first are strikingly dependent on Pugin, the later ones show developing originality and anticipate his mature work. Though he accepted Pugin as his master—who did not in the 1840s?—within a few years he had built churches which Pugin had aspired to but never really

17

9. Unexecuted design for a church, May 1843.

achieved, churches which fulfilled the ideal of the early phase of the Victorian revival of the Gothic style. 'Pearson's nearly perfect fourteenth-century church at Bessborough Gardens . . . summarized it all.'[5]

Here was the foundation of his career as an architect principally of churches rather than of public buildings or private houses. His modesty and reticence prevented him from publicizing his first works, but he was well liked by his clients—some became lifelong friends—and his contacts among the

18

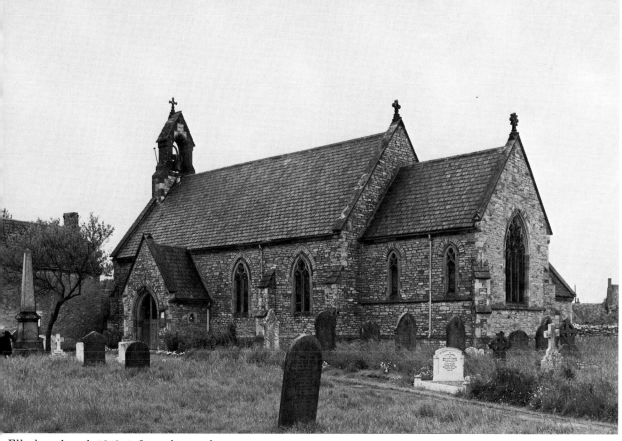

Ellerker chapel, 1843–4, from the south-east.

Ellerker chapel: the interior looking towards the chancel.

12. The Conduit House of 1751 in College Green, Durham; and mask-heads used as label-stops on Pearson's church at Catherston Leweston of 1857–8.

landed gentry and newly appointed Tractarian clergy served him well in the advancement of his career.

His first client was his friend Canon Townsend of Durham. In July 1842 Pearson noted in his diary, 'G. F. Townsend, Brantingham, East Yorkshire.' This was the canon's son who had just been appointed vicar of Brantingham, a living in the patronage of the Dean and Chapter of Durham. Over half the population of the parish lived a mile away in the neighbouring hamlet of Ellerker. The chapel of ease there was very dilapidated through 'neglect and the progress of time',[6] and a Wesleyan chapel had been built nearby only six years before. To provide a decent place of worship and to reassert the authority of the established church, the Townsends had to rebuild the chapel of ease. The canon turned to his protégé and entrusted Pearson with its design.

The design was ready in April; by October work was progressing. The chapel was completed the next summer at a cost of £600, which had paid for a nave and a properly developed chancel with a stone altar raised on three steps, a piscina, sedilia and credence, all according to Pugin's demands (Plate 10). Moreover, Pearson gave it a variety of patterns of correct Middle Pointed tracery. Otherwise, it is a thin building despite the coursing of the stones and the lavish buttressing, both of which obey Pugin's instructions.

20

While praising the 'beautiful construction' of the interior, the *Ecclesiologist* had reservations about the exterior, notably the roof, which was 'scarcely of sufficiently lofty pitch' (it should have been equilateral); but although 'extremely simple', the chapel was, it concluded, 'withal so ecclesiastical and correct in its character that it reflects great credit upon the taste and skill of its architect'.[7]

Circumstance did not allow Pearson to elaborate the design at Ellerker, but, even so, it has a few characteristics of his later churches: for instance the gable crosses, which are mounted on gable cap-blocks decorated with cross gablets, and the elaborate, hammered iron hinges of the nave door. Both show an eye for medieval precedent. More significantly, Pearson took great care with the proportions of the chancel arch (Plate 11). The width of the opening is just half that of the nave, and exactly the same as its height up to the springing of the arch; and the arch has the same centres as the arched braces of the timber roof. From the start, Pearson wanted to achieve that classical harmony which was so opposed to the unresolved, colliding masses which were to be characteristic of Butterfield's and Street's work.

The chapel was noticed by the vicar of Elloughton, a neighbouring parish where the church had collapsed early in 1843; he chose Pearson to rebuild it. The parish chapel of ease at Wauldby also needed rebuilding, and this was paid for by Mrs Anne Raikes of Welton House, a religious woman who, as Lady of the Manor of Welton, was closely involved in the affairs of the parish. Her descendants and their families were responsible for commissioning many of Pearson's important buildings over the next twenty years.

At Elloughton, for the rebuilding of both the church and its chapel of ease at Wauldby, more money was available—in the case of the chapel, nearly £1,000—and Pearson was able to provide more elaborate decoration. Inside both buildings there are pulpits approached by way of passages passing through the chancel wall, a feature which Pugin illustrated in *The Present State of Ecclesiastical Architecture in England*. Wauldby's bellcote is like Pugin's at Warwick Bridge, illustrated in the same place; but the pitch of its roof is much steeper than Pugin's and at the chapel at Ellerker, perhaps in response to the criticisms of the *Ecclesiologist*.

Elloughton church was rebuilt on its old foundations. The most important features to appear for the first time are the masks decorating the corbels supporting the roof braces. Masks decorating medieval corbels and label-stops were described in contemporary books which Pearson would have seen, indeed he had illustrated them in his *Studies and Examples*, but he used them throughout his career to such a degree that they surely had a significance beyond the mere reproduction of medieval decoration. In all likelihood he first came across masks not in medieval churches at all but in the remarkable Gothic Revival Conduit House of 1751 beside Durham Cathedral in College Green (Plate 12). Its parapet is supported by corbels, each of which is prominently carved with a mask like those Pearson was to use a century later. Perhaps he thought of them as a personal link with his home town, and

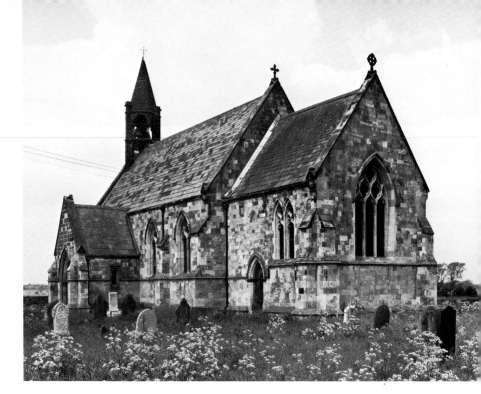

13. (right) St Mary, Ellerton, 1846–8, from the south-east.

14. (below) All Saints, North Ferriby, 1846–8, from the south-east.

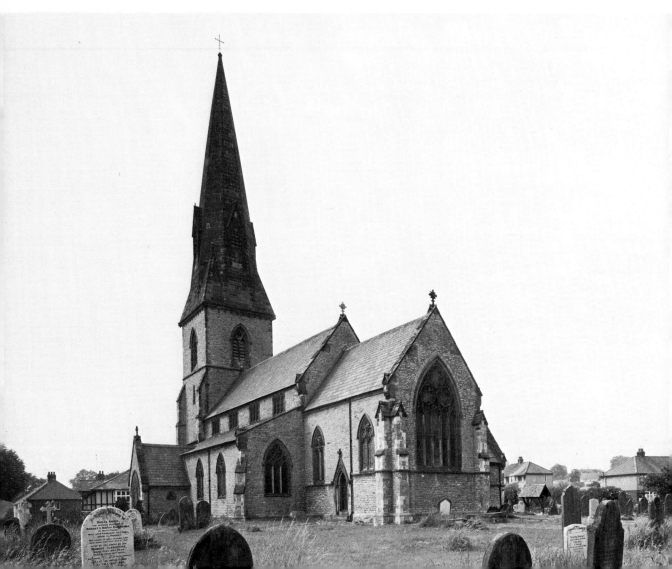

adopted them as a signature to appear even in the most reticent of his designs and the most sensitive of his restorations.

Some fifteen miles to the west of Ellerker and Wauldby, Pearson built a third two-cell church. St Mary, Ellerton, was designed in 1846 and completed early in 1848 (Plate 13). The exterior shows a few modest advances. Like Wauldby, it is finished with finely dressed ashlar. Instead of the windows being accentuated only by voussoirs, they are inset from the face of the wall, so the church at once appears more solid. The reticulated tracery of its east window, commonly used by Pugin and others, was illustrated in Parker's *Glossary of Architecture*; and this may have been the source of the bellcote too, as it is identical to the illustration of one at Shipton Olliffe. Characteristic of Pearson's later churches is the string course which runs unbroken right round the church, binding it together by stepping up to finish sills and over obstacles such as doorways, becoming a hood-mould in the process. No less characteristic is the plan, balanced rather than symmetrical about the longitudinal axis, with a south porch and north vestry.

Pearson designed two more churches in 1846, at North Ferriby (Plate 14), again close to Ellerker in the East Riding, and at Weybridge in Surrey. Quite why he was chosen to design the latter is unclear. William Giffard, the rector, was newly appointed and, being an ambitious Tractarian, needed a new church for the new ritual he would introduce. Supporting the work was one of the church wardens, Dr Spyers, a clergyman who ran a school in Weybridge; he became one of Pearson's closest friends.

North Ferriby and Weybridge churches are twins, although this is obscured by later additions at Weybridge: both have west towers with broached spires, aisled naves with north and south porches, and chancels with north vestries. Churches like these are illustrated in *The Present State of Ecclesiastical Architecture in England*, but the example closest to them in elevation and detail as well as in plan is Pugin's church at Kirkham in Lancashire; Pearson followed its design so closely that he must surely have seen detailed drawings. At Weybridge only the tower is significantly different: its angle buttresses are carried up to the top of the belfry stage to join the broaches of the spire, resulting in an increased verticality which makes the tower appear unpleasantly thin. At North Ferriby the steeple follows Pugin's model closely; the significant difference is not in minor details such as the absence of a string course round the belfry stage or of upper lucarnes in the spire, but in that Pearson gave the spire a marked degree of entasis. All his later spires have entasis; it greatly contributes to their high quality. Here, at the start of his career, it was sufficiently remarkable for a description of how it was set out to appear in the *Builder,* introduced by C. R. Cockerell, who was Professor of Architecture at the Royal Academy and probably the most learned classicist of his day. This spire apart, Weybridge and North Ferriby show Pearson's closest approach to Pugin, an approach which might have been dangerous had all three designs been less impersonal.

Before the end of the 1840s Pearson had met a client who was to lead to his first London church. This was Archdeacon Bentinck, the rector of Sigglesthorne, a parish a few miles on the further side of Beverley from Brantingham. He employed Pearson to restore his church in 1848. Among his acquaintances were the Champernownes of Dartington in Devon who were soon to ask Pearson to rebuild Landscove church and, later, to restore and eventually rebuild Dartington church. Bentinck had more important work for Pearson. He was a canon of Westminster and in that capacity commissioned Pearson in 1849 to build a new church in Bessborough Gardens, a poor part of Westminster. Until then Bentinck was quite unknown to the Ecclesiological Society (as the Cambridge Camden Society had been renamed following its move to London), and, according to its journal, the *Ecclesiologist*, Pearson was 'One of whom we know but little', but, it added, 'that little is all good'.[9] They did not yet count him among their members, nor were they to do so until 1859, when their crusading zeal was on the wane.

Holy Trinity, Bessborough Gardens, was an aisled cruciform church with a central tower and spire (Plate 15). It had a traditional plan, and one already used by Pugin; but Pearson's church was superior to any of Pugin's. In fact, Pugin, a frequent visitor while it was under construction, considered it to be in advance of anything then accomplished by the Gothic Revival.[10] Perhaps he saw it as the fulfilment of the ideals he had not wholly realised himself; at all events he predicted the future success of its architect. Charles Barry admired the church too, and Scott said that it was the finest building of its kind in London—'the best modern specimen of a fourteenth-century English church'.[11] This was generous praise indeed; he had tried to make his own church over the river at Camberwell just that.

Holy Trinity, Bessborough Gardens, was certainly elaborate. The nave arcade had alternating piers, either octagonal or with clusters of four major and four minor shafts; the crossing piers similarly had clusters of shafts, the major ones having fillets (Plate 16). These were types often to reappear in Pearson's mature work. Again characteristically, the church was an exemplar of Geometrical tracery, all the major windows having different patterns. The most obviously impressive feature was its tower and spire rising to 200 feet. Viewing it and Benjamin Ferrey's nearby steeple in Rochester Row, the *Ecclesiologist* hoped that 'London may yet become *la ville des beaux clochers.*'[12]

Holy Trinity's spire was thought to be the most graceful in London, but it was ultimately the liturgical arrangements which gave the most pleasure. 'The crowning merit of this church is the very complete exhibition which it offers of the ritualism of the Prayer Book,' reported the *Ecclesiologist*.

Holy Trinity exhibits every distinctive feature of that system of church arrangements which it has been the constant and primary intention of our pages to advocate, as the embodied mind of the Church of England ... There never was a church more completely built in independence of our

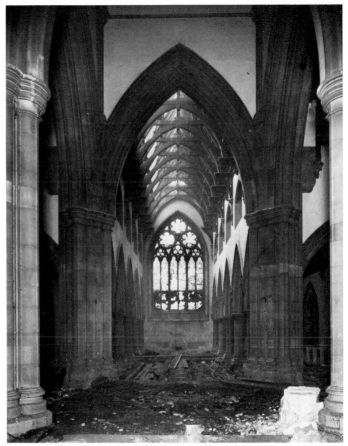

. Pearson's photograph of Holy Trinity,
Bessborough Gardens, 1849–52, from the south-east.

16. Holy Trinity, Bessborough Gardens, looking into the nave
from the crossing, during demolition in the 1950s.

society than this has been: when therefore in this church we behold the
ideas for which we have fought and suffered obloquy so prominently
exhibited, we can indeed thankfully and sincerely offer our *Deo Gratias*.[13]

Even so, the *Ecclesiologist* had reservations. The crossing piers
obstructed the view of the wide chancel, remarkably wider than the nave
because of the awkward site; that was a widespread problem which Pearson
was to solve finally when he abandoned structurally separate chancels and
attendant chancel arches. There was too much carving, 'too finely and too
thinly done'; and, it added, 'we could detect traces of Perpendicular feeling in
the mouldings'.[14] That ultimate sin apart, one can sympathize: despite the
arrangements, the interior lacked the finesse of the exterior.

At the turn of the century, Muthesius admirably summarized the church,
saying that it could not be faulted 'where the handling of forms is concerned';
and, to conclude, 'It could actually be mistaken for an old church; and in
those days that was the greatest praise.'[15]

The carving in Pearson's churches was to improve, but it was never to be
very lively. Always it was to have a subordinate role, and this attitude is
reflected in his support of the Architectural Museum. This was founded in

25

1852 mainly to exhibit specimens and casts of Gothic art and architecture. The intention was that the craftsmen who made what architects designed but who, unlike them, could not afford to travel to see ancient craftsmanship for themselves should be able to study and learn from the exhibits. Not all Gothic architects were enthusiastic: Street thought the museum would encourage copyism, and the carving in some of Pearson's churches would confirm this view. William Morris was to call it 'joyless putty-like imitation that had better have been a plaster cast.'[16]

For a couple of years while Pearson was building up a circle of clients in the East Riding he was still working for Hardwick at Lincoln's Inn. This was fortunate as his salary in the first years of his career must have made up the greater part of his earnings. Before 1846 he probably did not receive fees of more than £100. The combined fees for the churches at Ellerton, North Ferriby and Weybridge, all begun in 1846, may have reached five times that amount, and ensured his existence as an independent architect. For Bentinck's church in Bessborough Gardens he would have received five per cent of its contract cost, again about £500, money which would have entered his account from 1850 onwards. With similar sums coming from work commissioned by one of Mrs Raikes's grandsons in Breconshire, Pearson could at last consider himself affluent and his practice financially secure.

This increasing prosperity is reflected in where he lived. At some time between 1843 and 1846 he left his lodgings and went to live with James Deason, Salvin's former assistant, in Bloomsbury at 31 Keppel Street. This was a boarding house run by Mrs Deason who was probably James Deason's mother. By 1850 Pearson had left there to spend a few months at 20 Suffolk Street and then move into 2 Delahay Street, a Georgian house close to St James's Park. Here he was near the offices of the Ecclesiastical Commissioners; this would save time when submitting plans for approval. More significantly, he would be near Scott's office in Spring Gardens. The neighbourhood was becoming a Mecca for aspiring Gothicists.

His increased affluence allowed him to employ one or more clerks, and for copying drawings and making occasional perspectives he sometimes used an artist. In 1849 he exhibited for the first time at the Royal Academy; two views of his new church at Weybridge appeared under the names of A. Johnson and J. L. Pearson. Johnson may have made the exhibited drawings, but he did not design the church, and his connection with Pearson is obscure.

Details of Pearson's family in the 1840s and '50s are sparse. He helped to support his father with occasional gifts of money until his death in London at the end of 1849. His mother and surviving sisters, one of whom had married a Dutchman, went to live in Holland; his brothers emigrated to America.

Pearson did not become well known through Holy Trinity, Bessborough Gardens, but with it his formal and informal training was complete. Yet he had still to find his own style, and this was to take nearly another twenty years of study, trial and effort. Nevertheless these years saw several masterpieces.

4 ROBERT RAIKES

PEARSON'S first outstanding work was commissioned by Anne Raikes's grandson.[1] He inherited her piety, and in a small way continued the traditions of a family which had the foundation of the Sunday School movement to its credit. The family also had traditions of business and banking: in Hull in the sixteenth century, later in London. The Robert Raikes who returned to Hull and set up there as a banker re-established the family in Yorkshire by marrying Anne, the heiress of Welton House. They had two sons, Thomas who inherited the house, and Robert who went to live at Eastdale, another estate in the parish. They carried on the bank until it failed in 1861.

Robert Raikes of Eastdale employed Pearson, obtaining plans in 1845 for farm buildings; they were never built, and Pearson had not been paid for his work when the family finances collapsed in 1861.[2]

Mrs Raikes was disappointed in her worldly sons, but had great hopes of Thomas's son Robert. In 1837 he went up to Oxford, then the centre of the Tractarian movement, to study at Exeter College. With him was Robert Hippisley; the two fell under the spell of Keble, Newman and Pusey, and on coming down determined to carry the Tractarian revival of ritual worship with them. In 1841 Robert Hippisley married Raikes's sister, and the next year Raikes himself married. His wife was Frances Taunton of Freeland in Oxfordshire, who came from a family sharing his religious views. In 1843 or early 1844 Robert Raikes met his grandmother's young architect; he liked Pearson and he and his wife befriended him. Nearly fifty years later Pearson wrote to congratulate them on their Golden Wedding: 'Will you and Mrs Raikes be kind enough to accept the little old loving cup which I venture to send.'[3] Soon after their first meeting and while Wauldby chapel was rising not far from the family house, Raikes and his wife realised that Pearson was the man who could transform their religious aspirations into architectural reality.

Robert Raikes never took Holy Orders, but Robert Hippisley did.[4] In 1841 he became rector of Stow-on-the-Wold in Gloucestershire. When his grandfather had been rector earlier in the century, the church had fallen into disrepair. At the beginning of 1846 he made use of Raikes's new friend and set about restoring the church, giving Pearson his first work outside the East Riding. Some ten years later he would employ Pearson to build a house, Quar Wood, which was to be his most important domestic work of the 1850s. Meanwhile, in his newly restored church, Hippisley introduced Tractarian ritual, surplices and banners. The parishioners were outraged: they called the enrobed rector 'the Pope's washerwoman', and the monogram IHS which appeared in the chancel they said referred to his grandfather John Hippisley of Stow.

The Raikes family ensured that Pearson's architectural practice was

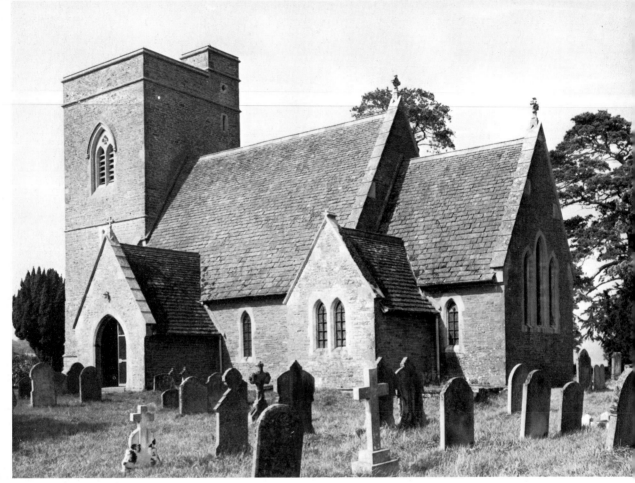

17. Llangasty Talyllyn church, 1848–50, from the south.

soon well established, and from them, financially at least, he received the greater part of his commissions during the first ten years of his career. Robert Raikes was determined to devote himself and his share of the family wealth to religious work. Supported by his wife and her family, he moved to Breconshire where he intended to revive the church by starting a centre of Tractarian worship. In October 1848 he bought Treberfydd, a small estate near Llangorse Lake, and commissioned Pearson to rebuild the local church at Llangasty Talyllyn, add a church school and master's house by it, and then reconstruct Treberfydd House. All this took ten years to accomplish and no pains were spared by Raikes or Pearson on the group of buildings.

At Llangasty Talyllyn, Pearson built a rugged little church exactly in keeping with its mountainous surroundings (Plate 17). The massing, constrained only by pre-existing foundations, depends on severely geometrical shapes. The low, west tower sets the mood for the rest; it is formed of two equal cubes resting on a base equal in height to the parapet which finishes it. The nave and chancel are two similar masses, rectangular solids with

18. (right) Llangasty Talyllyn church: the interior of the chancel.

28

equilateral roofs, the chancel being smaller in each dimension. The south porch and organ chamber are again similar shapes of still smaller sizes. There is little decoration. All the openings have finely dressed, plain chamfers which contrast with the rough, irregularly coursed ashlar. The simplicity of the exterior suggests solidity, and leaves the interrelated parts free to demonstrate the compressed mass of the whole.

The interior is a model of Tractarian taste (Plate 18). In the chancel, from the floor, patterned with ornate tiles, to the walls and roof, with elaborately painted texts and symbols, all the features stipulated by Pugin are there. The process of furnishing and decoration went on for some time. In 1854 Pearson charged £1.14.7 for a silver-plated incense burner, and two years later he charged three guineas for an altar cross.

What the Welsh thought of these is not recorded. At least they showed their indifference by refusing to sell the Tractarian immigrants sufficient land to make the estate pay, and after the family bank's collapse Raikes sadly retreated to England. Happily his descendants reclaimed church and house before their contents were dispersed, and maintain them to this day.

The school at Llangasty Talyllyn, designed to match the church, is an admirable foil to it; Treberfydd House has the same assurance too, and this is surprising until one remembers Pearson's youthful experience in house-building.

The Treberfydd estate included a recently built house to which Pearson began by making a small addition, but eventually he almost entirely rebuilt it (Plate 19). When this happened is unclear. Newberry simply dates the work to 1848; Eastlake says the house was built between 1848 and 1850; and J. R. Bailey gives a building period two years later.[5] The design was probably formulated by or in 1849—W. A. Nesfield's drawings of the garden layout, which can hardly have predated the house, were ready in August 1850. Eastlake adds that 'from time to time further alterations were required until at last nearly the whole of the original house was pulled down.' Despite that, the alterations cannot have been planned piecemeal: the present house is too cohesive. Pearson exhibited a drawing at the Royal Academy in 1851; by then the house had probably reached its present appearance (though an alteration on finished elevations shows the tower built at the south-east corner, and the stable weathercock is dated 1852).

It is similarly unclear how far the shape of the old house determined that of the new. Eastlake says that 'some of the old arrangements of rooms etc., had to be retained, which to some extent interfered with the architect's intentions in design'. That may be, but it is not evident in the main living-rooms, nor that it led to 'a picturesque treatment of the design': the picturesque treatment is carefully organised, not accidental. The arrangement of the servants' quarters alone may reflect real interference by the previous house on the design: the perilous back stairs are hardly planned for convenience. Here, a telling touch is the placing of the housekeeper's bedroom at their foot, to guard the way to the maids' rooms above.

Treberfydd House, 1848–52, from the east.

At Treberfydd Pearson maintained his allegiance to Pugin's principles but could do so with complete individuality. Pugin wrote that a building should not be made picturesque 'by sticking as many ins and outs, ups and downs, about it as possible. The picturesque effect of the ancient buildings results from the ingenious methods by which the old builders overcame local and constructive difficulties.'[6] Raikes no doubt wanted what Pugin would have called an 'English Catholic mansion'. It must be picturesque; but, as Pugin explained, 'An architect should exhibit his skill by turning the difficulties which occur in raising an elevation from a convenient plan into so many picturesque beauties.'

However much the 'local and constructive difficulties' of incorporating the former house taxed him, Pearson produced a convenient plan. An entrance porch in the middle of the north side of the house leads into a spacious staircase hall which divides it from front to back (Plate 20). On the east are the main living-rooms: a pair of linked drawing-rooms with a

31

20. Treberfydd House: the entrance hall.

conservatory beyond, a library (Plate 21) and a billiard-room; on the other side of the hall is the dining-room, with a kind of screens-passage across one end, and beyond is a corridor leading to the kitchens and servants' quarters. This T-shaped plan served him well for the majority of his houses; indeed it was to serve many other Victorian architects equally well.

The plan is reflected by the gabled elevations. The main north front of the house has a square, three-storeyed tower above the entrance porch as its central feature, and around it, the main rooms are disposed in blocks with gables befitting their size. The spirited outline, further enlivened by numerous chimney-stacks, is kept under control by the long horizontal lines of the ridges of the roofs. The chimney-stacks—there are a good dozen—come in all shapes and sizes; they are as much an exemplar of Tudor types as the tracery at Holy Trinity, Bessborough Gardens, was of Geometrical patterns.

Newberry said Treberfydd was 'somewhat after the manner of Haddon Hall or Compton Wynyates'—a happy comparison: Treberfydd belongs to the

1. Treberfydd House: the library.

landscape no less than they do. They were built as a succession of chambers grouped around courtyards, so their massing is looser than Treberfydd's. Pearson's grouping of living-rooms around the hall is tightly controlled with no awkward compromises between the requirement of convenience and picturesque appearance. He carefully contrived Treberfydd's outline to build up towards the centre and to such turning points as the north-east and south-east corners, and only to the west does the house lose itself in the trees with the lower roofs, chimneys and towers of the stables set around a small low courtyard, itself a gem of carefully poised masses.

In these qualities Treberfydd shows its links with Pearson's mature works best. The various parts are well scaled and their components— windows, doorways, copings, and the occasional carving—are indivisibly related both to each other and to the mass of walling in which they are set. Here Pearson shows his sensitivity to materials. The rough dressing and coursing of the locally quarried stone are far superior to Pugin's at

33

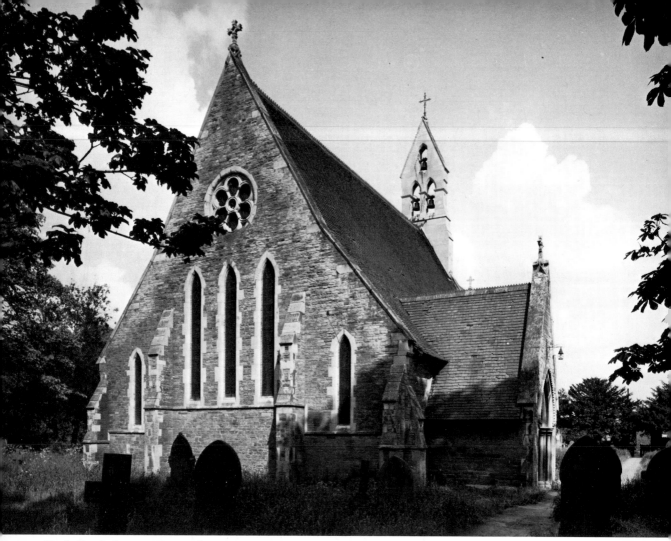

22. St Bartholomew, Eastcroft, 1853–5, from the south-west.

Scarisbrick Hall, which fails in scale both in the relationship of the detailing to the areas it covers, and again in the mechanical quality of its masonry. Pugin praised 'antient irregular joints', but left Pearson to use them.

A better comparison is with Scotney Castle in Kent built by Pearson's master Salvin between 1837 and 1844. Of local stone like Treberfydd, designed in the Tudor style in which Salvin made his name, and planned for convenience as well as for picturesque effect, there is a direct parallel with Treberfydd; yet there is a repetitiousness about its features—windows and gables—which is absent from Treberfydd, and the smoothly dressed, regularly coursed stone shows little feeling for texture. Pearson was better able than Pugin or Salvin to turn theories of design into practice.

Treberfydd's interior fittings, stone chimney-pieces, glazed tiles, the wooden staircase, and patterned leaded windows, all show Pugin's influence; and the drawing-room originally had wallpaper of Pugin's design. The oak furniture, much of which is still in the house, was designed by Pearson, but is strongly reminiscent of Pugin's designs. In 1857 Pearson charged Raikes a

34

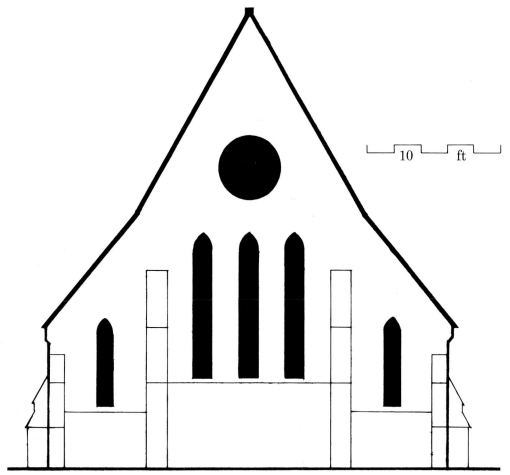

23. St Bartholomew, Eastcroft: west elevation.

nominal commission on the 'cost of papering and painting' and thirty shillings 'Do. upon furnishing Mrs. R's Boudoir.'[7] These are the only surviving accounts, but they show that, as with his churches, Pearson designed not merely the building but the fittings and furniture as well. This included even doorlocks. Many at Treberfydd are handsome pieces of ironwork, and have a strong affinity with his tracings of medieval examples, taken from the Pugins' books. They are all Pearson's design, but the accounts record only one: 'Paid for W.C. door lock and key 18 0.'[8]

In 1857 Pearson provided 'Sketches for Gardener's House.' This is a model rustic cottage which might have been designed thirty years before. It has a single low storey with windows each side of a doorway, all protected by wide eaves, supported by paired wooden posts, forming a continuous loggia. The dominating roof has a gablet at one end, a half hip at the other for variety, and is finished with crested ridge tiles interrupted by a single small stone chimney-stack. The cottage is picturesque enough, but does not have the endearingly exaggerated scale common to its type, as epitomized by Nash at

35

Blaise Hamlet. Even so, it makes a notable link between Nash and the Old English style of the 1870s.

The whole group of buildings at Treberfydd and Llangasty Talyllyn show Pearson's early Victorian phase at its best—a Tractarian Utopia. Had Treberfydd been built for someone of influence or somewhere less remote, Pearson might have established himself as a leading house architect. As it was, he had to wait nearly ten years before he designed another large house, and that was for Hippisley, again a Tractarian. Not until he reached his mature church style in the 1870s did he build houses for clients with no ecclesiastical connections. By then his practice was firmly based on churches, and younger men like Norman Shaw led fashion in house design. Pearson's late houses were fashionable too, remarkably so, but do not compare in importance with his late churches nor with Treberfydd.

Llangasty Talyllyn church was the first where Pearson devised plans and masses more organized than in his earlier designs influenced by Pugin; here he showed an increasing liking for the severity of Early English Gothic. The Champernownes' church at Landscove also has compressed massing, largely

24. Skelton church, from the south-west. From Ewan Christian's monograph.

through the placing of the steeple at the east end of the south aisle, as though a transept. Pearson put towers in the traditional position at the west end of the nave in only a handful of churches thereafter.

Like the first, the last of his early Victorian churches, at Eastoft in the West Riding, is only of two cells but, unlike it, is very tightly organised, especially in mass and elevation (Plates 22 and 23). Its model is the twelfth-century church at Skelton, north of York, which he knew from Ewan Christian's monograph on it.[9] Skelton has both nave, chancel and low aisles, all covered by a single roof with a pitch of about fifty-five degrees, broken in the middle by a bellcote, and on the south by a gabled porch (Plates 24 and 25). For Eastoft, Pearson modified this design by separating the nave from the aisleless chancel and placing a bellcote at their junction on a proper arch. Both nave and chancel have equilateral roofs, but the nave aisles are expressed by the pitch over them being reduced to fifty degrees.

While Skelton is remembered for its unusual shape and its well-preserved ornament, it is Eastoft's massing and proportions, not ornament, which make it memorable. The west façade admirably demonstrates this: it

5. Skelton church: west and east elevations from Ewan Christian's monograph.

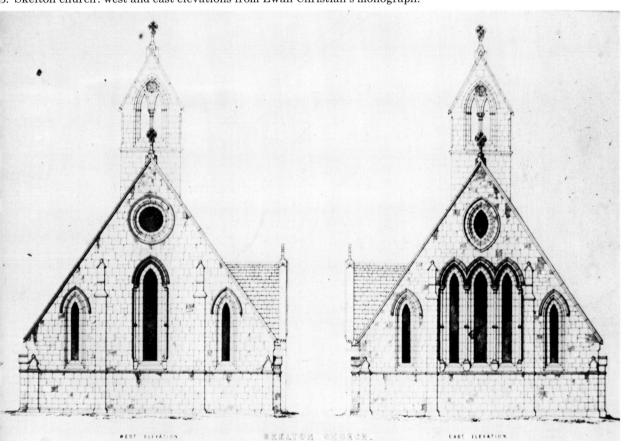

WEST ELEVATION   SKELTON CHURCH.   EAST ELEVATION

exactly fits into a square, the centre of which coincides with the centre of the equilateral triangle on which is based the head of the central lancet; another square, bounded on the sides by the buttresses supporting the nave arcade and beneath, just half its height from the ground, by the string course, reaches the base of the equilateral triangle forming the gable of the nave roof. Pearson interrelated all the parts of the façade into an overlying scheme based on squares, equilateral triangles and circles. What he began in the proportions of the chancel arch at Ellerker came to fruition here. Additionally, while the decoration is severe and restricted to mouldings, the massing is compact but at the same time extremely elegant.

At Appleton-le-Moors, a little further north and ten years later, he built another church of similar type with nave and aisles under one roof, and again with its parts clearly defined in relation to the whole, but there the elegance was replaced by the more vigorous forms of the High Victorian decade. Eastoft comes at the very end of his early Victorian phase—its design was started in August 1853, the month following his first recorded journey to France. The first effects of this visit are apparent in his next church, which was begun seven months later, and open a new phase in his career.

In this first phase, Pearson eventually achieved a standard of design as high as any of his contemporaries. He was strongly influenced by prevailing taste. He neither could nor would avoid it, but he was not overwhelmed by it. At the start, Pugin's churches as much as his writing were foremost in his mind. North Ferriby and Weybridge show how far he would go to educate himself in what he thought were the best examples of Gothic applied to churches. The *Ecclesiologist* called for an adherence to the Middle Pointed style; Pearson obeyed—Holy Trinity, Bessborough Gardens, was the equal of any church—but he began to show an unmistakable liking for the more severe lancet style of the late twelfth and early thirteenth centuries which had been popular in the 1830s. He used lancets at Elloughton and Wauldby in 1844, where they perhaps seem simply old fashioned. At Llangasty Talyllyn, four years later, the lancets were better proportioned and looked forward to his best mature work. By then he had discovered how to do something which eluded many early Victorian architects; namely, he could design buildings largely devoid of ornament and unessential buttressing which looked solid and convincing. This was the result of organised massing and carefully worked-out proportions.

For proportions, he turned again to the decade in which he had trained. From the first chapel at Ellerker, he related parts to each other by a simple geometrical system. Billings put forward the theory that Carlisle Cathedral had been built on a system of geometrical relationships, and later extended this to the churches of County Durham.[10] It was a typical attempt to reconcile classical ideals with the Gothic system and its details. Pearson must have been sympathetic to Billings's theory, practising it tentatively at Ellerker, with confidence at Llangasty Talyllyn and Eastoft; here the quality of design which Caröe so clearly recognized in his master's work is already apparent.

5 ❦ ACTS OF FAITH

OF PEARSON'S early clients none was so influential as Sir Charles Anderson.[1] Anderson was born in 1804, the son of the rector of Lea in Lincolnshire who was also a prebendary of Lincoln. Educated at Oriel College, Oxford, Anderson became a strong Tractarian. In 1840 he published *Ancient Models: Containing some Remarks on Church-Building Addressed to the Laity*, and soon was a prominent member of the Ecclesiological Society. At much the same time he became responsible for the extensive family estates in Lincolnshire and Yorkshire. Probably he knew Raikes and so met Pearson. While he commissioned little from him—the restoration of Lea church and additions to Lea Hall being the sum of it—he appears behind many of Pearson's major works. Anderson probably put forward Pearson's name for the important and difficult restoration of Stow-in-Lindsay church. Certainly Anderson introduced Pearson to his Tractarian friends, for instance Sir George Prevost who employed Pearson to rebuild Stinchcombe church in Gloucestershire. Another Tractarian friend was Robert Gregory who went to London and employed Pearson at Vauxhall on several buildings and ultimately commissioned a new church which marked the last stage in Pearson's attainment of his mature style. Robert Gregory's sister married another of Anderson's Lincolnshire friends, Dr Hannah, who became Warden of Trinity College, Glenalmond, Perthshire. Hannah employed Pearson there, and, becoming Rural Dean of Brighton and Hove, was instrumental in Pearson's building three churches in Sussex. In 1870, probably through Anderson's influence as much as through the example of his restoration of Stow, Pearson was appointed architect to Lincoln Cathedral. Here he met the future Bishop of Truro, and in the cathedral itself found a major source of inspiration for the design of his own cathedral.

At Lea church, Pearson dismantled the decayed Perpendicular chancel window, found indisputable evidence in the rubble for the former existence of a pair of lancets, and reinstated these in 1847–9, using old stones where possible and new for the rest.

'To recover the original scheme of the edifice,' the *Ecclesiologist* advocated, was the true purpose of a 'thorough and Catholick restoration';[2] if that was impossible, then the restored parts, like new churches, should be in the Middle Pointed style. Restorations were to be acts of faith—faith in archaeological findings, and faith in the moral superiority of Middle Pointed. Architects and clergy alike gave churches an appearance in which they believed, not one for which they had incontrovertible proof.

The more honest were to accept Viollet-le-Duc's principles. 'The term Restoration and the thing itself are both modern,' he wrote. 'To restore a building is not to preserve it, to repair, or rebuild it; it is to reinstate it in a condition of completeness which could never have existed at any time.' He recognized that 'absolute principles may lead to absurdities', and offered one guide: a building or part of a building should be restored 'in its own style'.[3]

This Pearson was doing at Lea well before Viollet-le-Duc had written on the subject; by archaeological examination he often tried to discover and to restore exactly the original state which had existed before defacing alterations were made. Sometimes this impoverished the building, if only because what he removed was more interesting than what he reinstated. In other notable cases it was highly successful, a great architectural achievement at little cost to the archaeological evidence of the continuity of the building's history.

The matter is not helped by the ambiguous meaning of the word 'Restoration'. In its widest sense, most of Pearson's early churches were restorations: they restored to their congregations places of worship which had become unsuitable—whether for reasons of decay, size or stylistic propriety. The last was a moral reason, but the others counted as well. The expanding population found many parish churches outgrown by their congregations. So it was that Weybridge church came to be rebuilt. Furthermore, the old church was thought to date from 1500 when religion was in decline, Gothic in its death throes, and 'the erection of churches ... dwindled down into a mere trade'.[4] That was inadmissible. As for decay, the old church had been repaired in 1838, but in 1846 was still 'dilapidated owing to dry rot'.[5] That might have been eradicable, but Giffard's need for a larger church and one in the necessary Middle Pointed style doomed it.

Though its extent is often impossible to determine accurately, decay should not be underestimated. At Elloughton much of the church fell in 1843 before Pearson restored it largely to a new design. The elements had been working away for half a millennium. At Exton in Rutland their work was sudden; in 1843 the church was struck by lightning, the steeple was thrown down and the lightning 'traversed most of the church shattering its walls already in an unsound state from neglect and decay'.[6] Though largely restoring the original design in 1852–4, Pearson gave the church a fine new hammer-beam roof of increased pitch (low-pitched roofs were offensive, too redolent of the Perpendicular style) and rebuilt the chancel with an ornate Decorated east window. It was a conservative restoration, and architecturally the church was arguably improved. It was, though, reinstated to a condition of completeness which had definitely not existed before.

While neglect, decay and poor repair were widespread, they sometimes were mere excuses for enthusiastic parsons to keep up with the general desire to provide proper surroundings for the new forms of ritual and worship. In 1853 Pearson began to rebuild Ashen church in Essex, but the nave was left standing and subsequently repaired; perhaps the chancel could have been repaired too.

Repair was impossible at both Ellerton and North Ferriby; the new structures replaced ruinous churches, one of about 1350 and therefore acceptable, the other of 1240 and rather early for an ecclesiological idealist.

40

St Mary, Stow-in-Lindsay: the
ancel, restored 1850–2, looking east.

27. St Mary, Kirkburn, restored 1856–7, from the south-east.

Both of Pearson's replacements reproduced something of the style of the former ones, and at North Ferriby he used some of the old stones in the new nave arcades. At Stinchcombe, Prevost's old church was 'very dilapidated and very ill built'.[1] That need not be doubted, but, dating from 1526, it was also unacceptably late. In its rubble were stones from an earlier Decorated church, and these determined the style of the new one. Yet, as Pearson recorded, 'The tower and the porch, both of the Perpendicular period, are well built in regular masonry'; and he was quite happy to leave them.

When he had to restore churches drastically, Pearson would reproduce old work if he could find traces of it. Despite the disfavour shown to them, he was highly attracted to the Early English and Norman styles. There are numerous examples of churches which formerly had decayed Perpendicular or later windows which, when taken down, revealed evidence of lancets having been there before. So lancets were put back, using, if possible, some of their stones to justify the choice. Lea church received this treatment. In 1869–70 the 'ugly late Perpendicular' east window of Blechingly church in Surrey was 'returned as near as possible' to 'the original' using reset stones.[8] Much the same happened nearby at Limpsfield, and in 1877 at Hornby in the North Riding. Like Scott, Pearson justified the work by his archaeological investigations, but the wisdom of elevating his discoveries above the more recent but still historical changes which had affected these churches was to become a prime target for the Society for the Protection of Ancient Buildings. What he did was at least better than inserting Geometrical tracery regardless of archaeological evidence, simply on the grounds of moral superiority.

In his defence, Pearson accomplished several triumphs as a result of his

41

archaeological investigations. The earliest was at Stow-in-Lindsay where the church has a Saxon crossing and a Norman chancel. The three-bay chancel had quadripartite rib vaults. In the Middle Ages, the timber roof caught fire and crashed through the vault bringing it down. The rents in the walls where the vault had been torn away were patched, reusing stones from the ribs face-in. The chancel east wall was rebuilt with a Decorated window 'of coarse and heavy character' which by the 1840s was 'in a shattered state'.[9] At a meeting in 1850 of the Archaeological Institute of Lincoln it was decided to restore the church. Sir Charles Anderson, a leading member, must have put forward Pearson as architect. He took down the 'shattered' east wall, and among its stones found four from Norman window arches. These and footings prompted his design for a new wall, a Norman wall reinstated in Viollet-le-Duc's sense, a decade before he wrote on the subject. When the upper stages of the side walls were uncovered, stones from the vaulting arches were revealed. They indicated the curve of the vault and the decoration of the ribs. The only thing in doubt was the order in which the three types of decorative pattern discovered had been applied to the ribs. Pearson's guess was that the most likely order would have been of increasing richness towards the east, and this was adopted (Plate 26).

The restoration was acclaimed locally, and Pearson made an honorary member of the Archaeological Institute of Lincoln as a result. He was to become a member of several other county archaeological societies as a consequence of the research undertaken in the churches he restored. Almost certainly another consequence of Stow was Pearson's election in 1853 as a Fellow of the Society of Antiquaries. He used the initials F.S.A. after his name until he became an Associate of the Royal Academy, but never attended the Antiquaries' meetings. That caused resentment later, but by then the Society were up in arms against his restorations anyway. Had he restored Stow similarly thirty years later, the Society of Antiquaries and the Society for the Protection of Ancient Buildings would no doubt have condemned it for his 'destructive conception of what true restoration means'.[10] The visible evidence of the centuries intervening between the destruction of the chancel vault by fire and its restoration may have been swept away, but the loss of those five hundred years of visible but not particularly significant history is small compared with the visible restoration of the Norman vault. It is an impressive architectural triumph, and at once a substantial archaeological success.

Even before the work at Stow was complete, Pearson was restoring two very decayed and much altered Norman churches in the East Riding for Sir Tatton Sykes, at Garton-on-the-Wolds and Kirkburn (Plate 27). It was the start of what promised to be a fruitful relationship. In each case old stones prompted the design of the new work. At Garton Pearson's decision to keep to the Norman style did not go uncriticized. 'We doubt,' wrote the *Ecclesiologist*, 'whether enough remained to justify this course in preference to the choice of Middle Pointed.'[11]

6 ✥ COLD AND HEAT

THE YEAR in which Holy Trinity, Bessborough Gardens, was begun saw the foundation of another church in London which was to be the most important of its age—All Saints, Margaret Street. Even William Butterfield, its architect, did not realise in 1849 that this church was to overturn the standards of the previous decade. Butterfield attacked established values on three fronts. With its tight planning and wilfully compressed massing, its brightly coloured materials, and the foreign sources of some of its parts, the church was the point of departure for a new generation, leaving architects of the old—men like Ferrey—bewildered. Early in its design, Butterfield abandoned painted decoration as used by Pugin, and substituted coloured materials in its actual construction. This use of colour, constructional polychromy, Butterfield owed to Ruskin, the prophet of the High Victorian style.[1]

More prolific than Pugin, and no less a propagandist, Ruskin first assaulted the standards of the 1840s in *The Seven Lamps of Architecture*, which was published in 1849. Its message was not at once clear, but those who read it discovered one thing: he wanted change; architecture must be expressive and emphatic, or it was nothing.

Among the first habits that a young architect should learn, is that of thinking in shadow, not looking at a design in its miserable liny skeleton; but conceiving it as it will be when the dawn lights it, and the dusk leaves it; when the stones will be hot, and its crannies cool; when the lizards will bask on the one, and the birds build in the other. Let him design with the sense of cold and heat upon him . . . His paper lines and proportions are of no value: all that he has to do must be done by spaces of light and darkness.[2]

Ruskin might have condemned Eastoft for its 'paper lines and proportions' although, inconsistent as always, he praised proportions but declined to define them: 'The man who has eye and intellect will invent beautiful proportions, and cannot help it; but he can no more tell us how to do it than Wordsworth could tell us how to write a sonnet.'[3]

Ruskin's doctrines were moral, yet he chose them for their beauty. Sublimity in architecture, for instance, should be comparable to sublimity in nature. Its characteristics should be

angular and broken lines, vigorous oppositions of light and shadow, and grave, deep, or boldly contrasted colour; and all these are in a still higher degree effective, when by resemblance or association, they remind us of objects on which a true and essential sublimity exists, as of rocks or mountains, or stormy clouds or waves.[4]

Hence High Victorian vigour—but would sublimity necessarily follow? That was left to the individual architect or builder. Ruskin wrote with fervour, was avidly read, widely accepted and as widely misunderstood. The consequences are still so visible that they need no emphasis. Ruskin disclaimed the majority of them. But there were true disciples: the truest was Street, who paid double homage with his book on North Italy, published in 1855,[5] and with his church, St James the Less, Westminster, begun in 1859.

By that time Pearson had begun his studies of French and German Gothic and allowed them full play in Hippisley's house at Quar Wood and in several churches. With these he too paid homage to Ruskin, but less fervently, and not slavishly as he had paid it to Pugin at North Ferriby and Weybridge.

The first signs of being influenced by Ruskin appeared in April 1854 when he completed the design of Devoran church in Cornwall. Although only a few months later than Eastoft, Devoran shows three distinct High Victorian characteristics new to his work: they are the foreign-looking apse, the unusual steeple, and the peculiar junction of the tower and the south porch. These are the direct results of two holidays abroad in 1853, the first recorded continental tours since the one to Hamburg in 1836. The first journey, to Amiens and Beauvais, is recorded in a small sketchbook.[6] At Amiens Cathedral he drew the elevation of 'one bay E side of N transept' (Plate 28), and details, for instance the roof, showing the ridge and noting 'Slates used on the Cath are 8 by about 14.' He drew a section and a ground plan of St Germain, a small aisled church which has an apse rising sheer and unbuttressed from the ground (Plate 28). His last drawing done in Amiens shows an eye for something quite different: he drew the bedstead at his hotel, remarking that it was 'made of walnut (solid) the castor runs in wood grooves laid on the carpet'.

At Beauvais Pearson sketched gables of timber houses, but concerned himself mostly with the cathedral. There are details of tracery, such as the north transept rose, but it is the unexpected and small-scale that attracted his attention: of the twelve pages of drawings of the cathedral, half are of ironwork or bench ends. He drew the church of St Etienne too; and, while there are drawings of the north transept showing the twelfth-century wheel window, one of the earliest known, details of ironwork again strongly occupied his attention (Plate 28).

Pearson's second journey was 'a trip of 20 days up the Rhine and in Belgium at the end of Sep and beginning of Oct 1853'. The first pages of his sketchbook show him crossing Belgium, passing up the Meuse with sketches of Huy and Seraing. Reaching Liège he sketched the cathedral, illustrating an elevation of the nave together with details of the capitals and bases and window tracery; lastly he drew the spire and its finial cross.

At Aachen he made two sketches of the cathedral showing details of ironwork and a window. Possibly on a subsequent occasion but probably at this time he made many more sketches of the building, and these sketches on loose paper were mounted with his tracings. He seems to have been fascinated by the picturesque outline of the building, and as much with the domical roof and the polygonal lateral porches as with the Gothic parts.

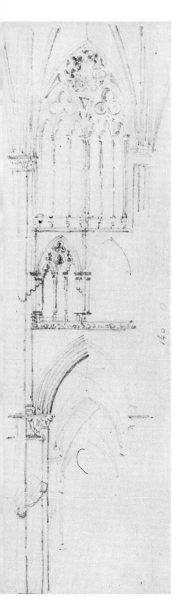

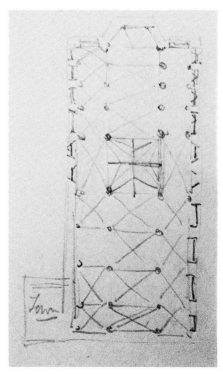

28. Sketches from the trip to northern France in 1853: (far left) elevation of the north transept of Amiens Cathedral; (left) plan of St Germain, Amiens; (below) ironwork on the west door of St Etienne, Beauvais—the ironwork on Pearson's doors was already of a high quality.

29. View of the Lahnstein from the Inn at Stolzenfels, seen in 1853.

30. Oberwesel church, sketched 1853.

From Aachen he went on to Cologne and made several drawings of the still incomplete cathedral. Other sketches show woodwork at St Gereon. From Cologne he went upstream to Koblenz, drawing Drachenfels, Oberwinter, spires at Unkel and Remagen, and details of the fortifications at Ehrenbreitstein on the way.

There is a perspective of the east end of Koblenz Cathedral, showing its round apse and flanking towers. Most drawings, however, show an eye only for the picturesque, like one inscribed: 'View of the Lahnstein from the Inn at Stolzenfels, the castle of Marksburg in the distance' (Plate 29); and in this way, marking his progress up the river, view succeeds view—Rheinstein, Marksburg, St Goar, Rheinfels. Occasionally he must have stopped long enough to draw architectural details such as the pulpit and weathercock at St Goar; and at Oberwesel he had time to climb the hill to the church overlooking the Rhine (Plate 30). He drew details of the rood screen, the reredos, the stalls and some of the windows, and made a plan indicating the

46

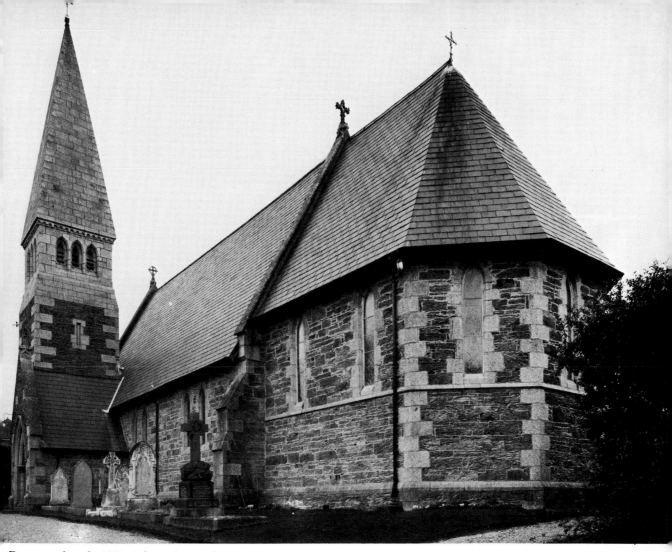

Devoran church, 1854–6, from the south-east.

layout of the vaulting, noting in his sketchbook: '83′ height point of groin.'

Rüdesheim and Mainz completed his journey southwards. He returned from Mainz by way of Brussels. Here he sketched the cathedral and the Hôtel de Ville; and the book ends with views of houses in Antwerp and Cornelis Floris's Town Hall. Among his tracings are further drawings which suggest that Pearson went to Germany on another occasion.[7] They are of Regensburg on the Danube. When they were made is a mystery; the simplest explanation would be that they are indeed tracings, but they are so similar to the sketches made along the Rhine that they were probably drawn on a visit. It is quite clear that Pearson travelled abroad several times, but only meagre clues remain as evidence.

Devoran's semi-octagonal apse, unsupported by buttresses, must be based on examples he had just seen, notably at St Germain in Amiens and the church at Oberwesel (Plate 31). The forerunner of some twenty more, it is emphatic and lacks the finesse of its descendents. Emphatic too, the steeple at

32. Quar Wood, 1856–9: the entrance front as illustrated in Eastlake.

33. Quar Wood: Pearson's drawing of the garden front.

least has a local touch. It is quite unlike any he had designed before. The sheer tower rises up to form a podium for the belfry; this has triple openings on each face; above is a prominent corbel course (the corbels are decorated with characteristic masks) and this carries a heavy pyramidal spire with marked entasis, which gives the impression of crushing the narrower belfry stage. It is typically High Victorian, advocated, at least in spirit, by Ruskin: 'There must be no light-headedness in your noble tower: impregnable foundation, wrathful crest, with visor down, and dark vigilance seen through the clefts of it; not the filigree crown or embroidered cap.'[8]

The same spirit governs the junction of tower and porch. The two are cheek by jowl, the east wall of one doubling as the west wall of the other. Butterfield had done the same at All Saints, Margaret Street, where he had the excuse of a restricted site; at Devoran it is entirely gratuitous.

Devoran church is uncoloured, its irregularly coursed granite walls having the same quality of belonging to the landscape as Llangasty Talyllyn's. Pearson first introduced constructional polychromy at Ashen church where he rebuilt the chancel to a design at last ready in 1856. The walls are banded in red brick and stone; and similarly the window heads have stone voussoirs interspersed with brick. This is a tentative use of colour, and Pearson seems to have been trying to find common ground between the new style and local materials. Always he would have recourse to tradition.

The mid 1850s were not productive years: there were no new churches after Devoran until 1857, and he only executed a few minor domestic works between Treberfydd and Quar Wood, his second great house. Among these was a vicarage built for Robert Gregory close by his church of St Mary the Less in Lambeth. Demolished in the early 1960s, no record of its appearance survives.

In 1855–7 Pearson altered Lea Hall, an early-seventeenth-century house, for Sir Charles Anderson. The works were small, costing only £525. The main architectural feature was the provision of an ungainly stair turret on the south front. Of red brick to match the old work, the turret had in its base a doorway with an arched head, one side of which died into an adjacent block in a way similar to that of Butterfield's entrance porch at All Saints, Margaret Street. The voussoirs of the arch were alternately of red and yellow brick with a red and yellow chequered band above. The third storey of the turret had a similarly chequered band beneath a lead ogee cap. The polychromy and awkward shape showed Pearson's awareness of current trends, just as his hesitating steps towards the High Victorian style are shown at Devoran church.

Quar Wood, the house Pearson built for Hippisley at Stow-on-the-Wold, was completely self-assured. No longer tentatively accepted, the High Victorian style emerges here even more demonstratively than in his church at Scorborough which was soon to follow. He started work in 1856 and on 21 June spent '1 day fixing upon Site for new House' which was immediately followed by 'Preparing design for New House (plan approved)'.[9] The design

49

must have been completed within nine months, as in March 1857 he was '3 days employed resetting out the Site for the House and lines of Terraces and in consequences of mistakes made by Mr Hippisley'.[10] Building continued until 1859, and Pearson charged his commission on the total cost of £8,000 at the end of the year.

In 1954 Quar Wood was altered beyond recognition, and the only record of its former appearance are two drawings, one of the entrance front illustrated in Eastlake (Plate 32), the other of the garden front in the possession of Mrs Morgan (Plate 33). Both were dominated by a massive corner tower which rose to four storeys and contained the main staircase. At its top were an open loggia with pointed openings and blank trefoils in the spandrels and, above, a diapered cornice supporting a steeply pitched saddleback roof which carried a dormer with a heavily corbelled-out, gabled roof, a small lucarne and a tall chimney-stack. Finishing the roof were shaped and polychromatic tiles beneath the crested ridge which ended in finials carrying vanes.

The main feature of the entrance front was a projecting, three-storeyed bay, with a porch in its base and capped by a half-hipped roof. It provided a visual break between the corner tower and a low wing which terminated in a small turret with a hexagonal spire. From here a wall linked the house to a square garden building with a steep pyramidal roof. The garden front, a little less demonstrative, was punctuated by projections and recessions with plentiful gables and half-hipped roofs descending from the corner tower to a single-storey range with gabled attics. The resulting composition was characterized by a series of severely geometrical shapes jostling each other for space under a variety of very steeply pitched roofs which rose diagonally towards the dominating saddleback of the corner tower.

Many of the windows were simply divided by mullions and transoms as at Treberfydd; others, more ecclesiastical, had foiled heads or tracery. Apart from the aggressive dormer in the saddleback, there was little that was unconventional about the details—nothing, that is, like the detailing of E. B. Lamb's and S. S. Teulon's houses.

Eastlake found in Quar Wood 'a freer and less conventional distribution of parts' than at Treberfydd, and 'the saddle-back roof and open loggia of the tower suggest the influence of Continental study'[12]—an understatement if ever there were one. Much the same influence prompted Burges to design his more light-hearted houses, with their equally demonstrative massing. Quar Wood had little polychromy, and the more ornate parts typically were set against large spaces of plain wall. Most characteristically High Victorian was the vigorous massing with its hints of northern France and the Rhineland, rather than wilfully eclectic sources for details. The planning and composition of Quar Wood showed the utmost freedom, yet, as always, the forms and details were within the strict framework of medieval precedent. With Quar Wood Pearson conquered the High Victorian style, but captured no further clients than church builders.

7 ✣ VIGOUR

IN 1856, the year Hippisley commissioned Quar Wood, Pearson burst into activity not to be exceeded until his career reached its zenith twenty years later. The six years from 1857 to 1862 saw the beginning of twelve new churches, many major additions to others, and several new houses as well. If these churches were as accessible and as well known as his later ones are, they would have established him as an eminent High Victorian alongside Butterfield and Street. Despite an element of reticence—a need to control the vigour of the period, rather than abandon himself to it—he accepted all the characteristics of the new style. Constructional polychromy is used sparingly and usually to differentiate structural parts; vigorous decoration appears but is invariably contrasted with plain areas where the eye can rest; while the massing of some of these buildings is occasionally heavy in places, it is not broken by constant collision in an attempt to achieve sublimity at all costs. Pearson was never one of Goodhart-Rendel's rogue architects. 'Ruskin's theories, Butterfield's reforms and Street's sketching holidays, had thrown into the Gothic pot much strong seasoning,' he wrote.[1] Pearson's work in this period was well seasoned, a lot more so than later, and to those who know only his later churches, these come as a surprise. From them emerged his mature style; but they are worth considering in their own light, and they can stand comparison with the best in their time.

The first is Scorborough church in the East Riding, begun in 1857 and finished two years later (Plate 34). The plan is unremarkable: nave and chancel are contained within a single cell, and at the west end is an overwhelmingly tall steeple. This starts by tapering sharply like the podium to the belfry stage at Devoran, but before it has risen far, its upward course is broken by large angle pinnacles and lucarnes which hide the change from square to octagonal in its plan, rather like the pinnacles and gables do on the south-west steeple of Chartres Cathedral. Pearson's main aim seems to have been not the classic beauty of that but the provision of a 'wrathful crest with visor down'.

Both the steeple and the body of the church are decorated with constructional polychromy, though the range of colours is small and applied only in bands or to separate structural parts. Grey bands are set in the pale yellow stone of the exterior, and window shafts are red. The interior (Plate 35) is faced with light grey stone; between the floor and the windows is a band of darker grey, and another at sill level; at the level of the springing of the arches of the window openings there is a band of red, and another beneath the cornice. The shafts inside are of polished black marble. Pearson was unwilling to accept Ruskin's proposition that colour should be independent of form—'They never will, never can be united.'[2]

Carved decoration is restricted to capitals and the cornice finishing the

walls inside. It is French in character, a mass of crockets and foliage, the kind of detail which delighted Ruskin and which Pearson had seen at Amiens and Beauvais; but despite Ruskin he was determined that decoration should be more than ornamental and could fulfil architectural requirements. Like colour, it, too, should not be independent of form; it articulates the interior. Each bay of the nave and chancel is divided from the next by a detached marble shaft supported by a corbel at the same level as, and linked by a band to, the capitals of the nook shafts of the window openings. The division of the nave and chancel is marked only by a pair of shafts similar to those between the bays but rising from the floor. The side walls are finished by an ornate cornice, which breaks forward forming a capital to each of the detached shafts, and continues round the east wall to join the capitals of the nook shafts of the east window, thus binding it to the sides of the chancel.

The *Ecclesiologist* reported that the design showed 'great merit and originality'.[3] Ruskin's influence was by then so pervasive that any sign of foreign study was automatically considered meritorious. No longer was it original, however; indeed Scorborough's originality lies not in the foreign sources of its decoration but in its handling which is chaste and almost classical in its approach to shafts, capitals and cornices, and in the nave and chancel, which are bound together into an indivisible whole with their

34. (left) Scorborough Church, 1857–9, from the north-east.

35. Scorborough church: the interior looking east.

36. St Mary, Dalton Holme: the interior looking east.

junction given just sufficient emphasis to indicate the change in function. Scorborough may be thoroughly High Victorian; by 1857 Pearson had mastered the new fashion, but additionally he could turn it to advantage in his own characteristic way.

He built Scorborough church for James Hall, a local landowner who acted as agent for Lord Hotham of Dalton Hall. As early as 1854 Pearson had met Hotham to examine South Dalton church with a view to enlarging it or building a new one. Nothing was decided, and it was not until after Scorborough church had been started that Hotham, stung into action by Hall's presumption in forestalling him, reconsidered building a new church. Firstly, he had the parish of South Dalton combined with Holme-on-the-

37. (right) St Mary, Dalton Holme, 1858–61, from the north-east.

54

Wolds to form Dalton Holme, and asked Pearson for plans.[4] A design reached tender stage, but it was abandoned and Lord Hotham refused to pay the fee. The church was eventually built to what Pearson described as the 'last design'. The start of work coincided with the Great Eclipse of 15 March 1858. The vicar of Dalton Holme thought this was symbolic: referring to James Hall and his church rising at Scorborough he wrote: 'They say he is "*jealous*" of your church eclipsing his . . . if your Lordship had taken his [Hall's] opinion you would have never built such a "cathedral".'[5] Local gossip had it that Lord Hotham spent his entire fortune in building the church so that there should be nothing for his nephew, his heir, to inherit. This may be only malicious, but Hotham was clearly strange: when his vault was being built within the church, he used to spend long hours on his knees there in the dark.[6] After his death, his nephew lived for little more than a year in which to enjoy what remained of the fortune; yet the family finances cannot have been exhausted and the nephew's brother who succeeded to the title in 1872 spent still more on extending the church.

High Victorian vigour did not necessarily mean to Pearson foreign sources or constructional polychromy. For Lord Hotham's cathedral it was enough to provide a welter of carving and a 200-foot steeple 'planted like an enormous arrow in the breast of the Wold'[7] (Plate 37). With touches of the steeple of St Wulfran at Grantham or perhaps Salisbury's, it is, like the rest of the church, far more English in its detailing than Scorborough, but hardly less High Victorian. The *Ecclesiologist* saw the church as Middle Pointed, strictly English and very ornate;[8] and the *Building News* remarked on its proportions and the richness of its details.[9] This distinguishes the church from his earlier Middle Pointed work: lizards might well bask on its stones and birds build in its crannies; indeed grotesque animals appear liberally in its carved decoration. Comparable to Holy Trinity, Bessborough Gardens, in size, Dalton Holme cost about twice as much, the consequence of expensive materials and vast quantities of fine carved work (Plate 36).

The same intense richness of detail characterizes Pearson's tiny church at Catherston Leweston in Dorset. Smaller even than Ellerker chapel, it cost over four times as much, money spent to provide beautifully finished walls of creamy knapped flint, capped by a frieze, ornately carved with oak, acorn and mulberry. It is hard to imagine more being made of such a limited volume. Like Dalton Holme, the church was not cheap: the tender was for £2,600, an amount which would have paid for all three of his earliest and similar-sized churches. The church pleased: when Pearson sent in his bill for commission he 'Received £200 i.e. £48. 6. 9 over claim.'[10]

Here and at Dalton Holme Pearson gave his attention to far more than lavish detail. Foremost in his mind was proportion. In a letter to Hotham about Dalton Holme's transepts and their effect on the church's proportions, he wrote, 'These additions opening into the nave by side archways have a very

38. Daylesford church, 1859–63 from the south-east.

40. Titsey church: the vestry which the *Ecclesiologist* did not quite admire.

material influence upon both the effect of width and height by adding to the former and taking away from the latter and which it is necessary for me to make due allowance for .'[11] The transepts were not all; the fittings and furnishings, as was usual, were all designed by Pearson, and designed always with the unity of the complete church in mind: 'My wish is to make the church look as well as possible and that the several things in it should bear a proportion to it and to one another and appear to be designed for the positions they are severally placed in.'

At Daylesford, then in Worcestershire, Pearson replaced a Norman church which had been rebuilt in 1816 by Warren Hastings. He incorporated two surviving Norman doorways in his new church and gave the east window such heavy cusping that it must be an allusion to Hastings's Indian career— two references to the past poignant in their disparity.

This Indian touch apart, the church returns to colour and foreign details from Europe, although the cruciform plan is English enough (Plate 38). Once again the steeple is dominant, but unlike the Yorkshire churches not by its height but through its mass. It has a low wide tower and pyramidal spire which, in Ruskin's terminology, is 'massy'; nothing could be further from the elegance of the central steeple at Bessborough Gardens. Large bell openings with tall gables penetrate the junction of tower and spire, to provide the angular, broken lines, the vigorous oppositions of light and shadow, which Ruskin equated with sublimity. The short, French-looking pyramidal spire is decorated with bands of incised pattern; these appear at Salisbury, but Ruskin, in giving this decorative treatment his approval, had preferred to cite foreign examples.[12]

The carving throughout the church, again French, is generally more vigorous than the use of colour, especially outside. The east wall is as ornate as any other Pearson designed. The three lights of the east window rest on a deeply carved band decorated with quatrefoils. The lights are divided by shafts and attached secondary shafts, the latter red; they have capitals with crockets and are linked to a band similarly decorated with stylized vegetation which extends across the width of the chancel to be terminated by grotesque

39. (left) Titsey church, 1859–61: the north wall of the chancel showing the arch opening into the mortuary chapel.

animals. Above the three lights are gables with inset foils, and between these are pinnacles resting on more grotesque animals.

The north vestry lies adjacent to the chancel, divided from it only by a buttress, but its lack of decoration sets it apart. Much the same but with colour rather than with carving happens nearby at North Nibley church, where Pearson rebuilt the east end at about the same time. Again there is contrast: the east wall has coloured bands which stop where the vestry starts.

The interior at Daylesford has less ornate carving and the colour is mild: there are bands of different greys, and the shafts in the crossing and chancel are soft pink and dark grey. This sensitivity is echoed in the detailing, nowhere more than in the newel which rises to the belfry: at the top, the stone newel post branches out forming four pointed arches perpendicular to each other which support the roof of the newel tower; the arches admirably articulate the space where the stair ends and the short passage to the belfry begins. Hardly two feet wide, the spaces are on the smallest possible scale. The care lavished on their design seems out of proportion to the menial and infrequent use of that part of the church, but Pearson seems to have delighted in this paradox—Pugin's desire for truth, but carried to the furthest cranny.

David Verey showed surprise in *The Buildings of England* at Daylesford, and suggested that if Pearson had died immediately after its completion he would be seen very differently;[13] Ian Nairn felt the same about Titsey church in Surrey:

> If Pearson had died in 1867, when he was fifty, he would have been remembered not as a gentle Late Victorian architect, but as a violent Mid-Victorian one. This church lacks the ferocity of buildings like Daylesford in Gloucestershire or Scorborough in the East Riding, but it is crisp and hard in the Butterfieldian sense.[14]

This is really true only of the interior where there is a proud display of constructional polychromy (Plate 39). The local Limpsfield sandstone is enlivened with bands of Bath stone and green Godstone firestone, and the chancel has a multitude of coloured foils and other patterns. Here is the reason for Nairn's reference to Butterfield, but the colouring is mild compared with his and does not disrupt the overall composition.

Nairn was particularly upset by the awkward vestry door set diagonally across a corner behind a thick column (Plate 40). 'Bloody-minded,' he called it; the *Ecclesiologist* was more genteel: 'We do not quite admire the treatment of the sacristy door.'[15] It is surprisingly mannered, the antithesis of the delicacy and logic of the arches over the belfry stairs at Daylesford.

Titsey has the tight planning of Llangasty Talyllyn and Landscove, but unlike Devoran its plan is not particularly foreign.

Uncompromisingly foreign plans return in Pearson's last High Victorian churches. One, Christ Church, Appleton-le-Moors, is his most intense essay in that style; but already at St Peter, Vauxhall, he had designed a church which looked beyond to his late-arriving maturity. By then he had been abroad again.

8 ❦ VAUXHALL

PEARSON'S passport has a visa for France dated 11 August 1855. Perhaps that was just for a holiday: no sketchbook survives and no one remembers one. He went to France again in 1859. The buildings which he saw this time had the utmost influence on his work of the 1870s though some results are visible in the design of Gregory's church at Vauxhall, which was begun on his return.

His passport was stamped at Le Havre on 7 September. The first stage of his journey was to Rouen with stops at Harfleur, Caudebec and St Wandrille where he sketched the church. From here he could have gone to Jumièges; he made no sketches, but photographs of the great abbey church in his collection suggest that he visited it at some time.[2] The next place in the sketchbook is St Martin de Boscherville. The unusual vaulting in the western bay of the nave—a quadripartite rib-vault with two extra ribs springing from the divisions of a tripartite end-wall—is a type which he used at Red Lion Square in 1874 and often again thereafter (Plate 41).

There is every reason why Rouen should have been Pearson's first main objective. It had been well publicised by Ruskin in *The Seven Lamps of Architecture*. The two buildings which Ruskin discussed at length, the cathedral and St Ouen, are those Pearson gave most attention to. He even seems to have looked at them through Ruskin's eyes; his drawings of details, while still typical of him, are of the kind of microcosm which Ruskin most appreciated: foils in gables, leaf ornament, crocket capitals (Plate 42).

From Rouen Pearson went to Louviers. He drew the west door and an elevation of one bay of the nave. Neither is remarkable. The outstanding feature of the church, the late Gothic south porch in which the decoration entirely hides the structural elements of the design, is the kind of thing which Ruskin would have condemned out of hand. Pearson did not draw it.

From Evreux he turned westwards to Lisieux and Caen, where he found buildings which were to have the profoundest influence on his mature style. At Lisieux he drew details of the gallery and west window and, more important, a perspective of the north-west tower, a tower very like many of his own later ones. The only building which he drew at Caen was St Etienne (Plate 43). The ten pages of sketches of it immediately show the *rapport* which he felt with the church. He took from it liberally—its western spires, its eastern turrets, and, inside, its foiled triforium balustrade and nave vaulting—and made these his own. The Doge's Palace was 'the central building' of Ruskin's world;[3] St Etienne was Pearson's.

He travelled on to Bayeux and Coutances. All the while his sketches show things which had delighted Ruskin: foliated cornices and capitals, tracery, and stained glass, three sketches of which are coloured.

Pearson left Normandy and travelled south to Le Mans where he drew several details of foliated capitals in the cathedral. He then went on to Chartres, but strangely only sketched the church of St Pierre. Perhaps he felt

41. The western bays of the nave of the church at St Martin de Boscherville showing the pair of extra ribs springing from the divisions of the tripartite end wall.

that he could learn more from studying a church of a similar size to those he was building himself than from a large cathedral.

Apart from sketchbooks recording his travels, Pearson collected photographs, and two volumes of these give an idea of his extensive knowledge of European architecture. France is well covered. Some photographs are of buildings during restoration. For instance, Notre Dame in Paris appears without the flèche over the crossing, and the flying buttresses at the east end are in course of construction, suggesting that the photograph was taken late in the 1850s; but while this and other photographs can be roughly dated, they are only slender evidence that Pearson visited Paris or anywhere else at any particular time. The photographs such as those of Reims Cathedral before the restoration of Viollet-le-Duc and again of the 1850s are a fascinating record of French architecture, and demonstrate Pearson's wide acquaintance with it from Avioth in the east to Quimper in the west, from Soissons in the north to St Gilles du Gard in the south.

Apart from France, the photographs show that Pearson had visited, or at least was familiar with, the buildings of several other countries. There are a few photographs of Belgian churches and even fewer of Germany: Ulm Cathedral, and three views of old houses in the Römerberg and Judengasse in Frankfurt-am-Main, two of which are dated 1878. There are several undated photographs of Spain: apart from two views of Burgos Cathedral, they are all of buildings in the south—Barcelona, Salamanca, Seville, Tarragona and Valencia.

Like all the best architects in the 1850s, Pearson needed to widen his

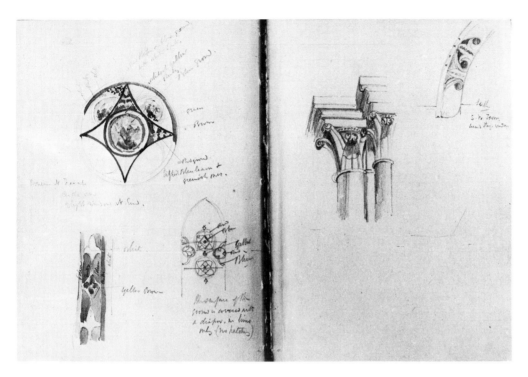

42. Details of stained glass and capitals in Rouen Cathedral, drawn 1859.

43. St Etienne, Caen: part of the interior of the central lantern, 1859.

horizons by studying foreign architecture. His journey to France in 1853 had an immediate effect on his style though the results were undigested. The later journeys had a more profound influence, and his studies in Normandy were indispensible to the formation of his mature style. Even as late as an Italian visit in 1874—he was 57 at the time—he found inspiration which he would put to good use in both novel plans and rich decoration.

As do all architects of genius, he took from what he saw and made it his own. In the last analysis, his debt to Normandy was as great as to Yorkshire and the North. The medieval churches of these two regions were the corner-stones of his style.

When Sir Charles Anderson's friend Robert Gregory took up the incumbency of St Mary the Less in Lambeth, he asked Pearson to design a church in Vauxhall. It was to have the most far-reaching consequences on the course of his career, becoming the prototype of his later town churches. This and other work commissioned by Gregory introduced him to the architectural problems of Victorian society in a wider context than did his country churches for the landed gentry, Tractarian clergy and their sympathizers.[4]

Following the closure of Vauxhall Gardens, this part of Lambeth was

44. The schools at Vauxhall before the church was built, as shown in the *Builder* 1860 18 497; the boys' and girls' schools are to the left, the master's house over the gateway and the art school to the right with the soup kitchen beyond.

rapidly overrun by slums and noxious industries. The parish of St Mary the Less, from which Vauxhall was later divided, had a population of fifteen thousand: many received parochial relief;[5] fewer than ninety were assessed for tax, and more than a quarter of these were publicans.[6] Gregory attacked these social evils with not just religious remedies but social ones too.

His church, built in cheap Commissioners' Gothic by Francis Bedford in the late 1820s, had aisles added to each side to accommodate schools; they were small, quite inadequate for the needs of the parish and had fallen into disuse. The church itself had not been touched in the ten years prior to Gregory's arrival, and services were ill attended.

His first acts were to reopen the school under a trained mistress, and refurbish the church under Pearson's superintendence, providing heating and new, free seats to be reserved for the poor. Gregory was determined to live among his parishioners. Pearson designed a vicarage for him; built between 1854 and 1856, it cost £1,780.

These only provided a base for Gregory's efforts. What he wanted was a Victorian equivalent of a modern social centre: a large new church, and schools for children and apprentices. Religious instruction and the teaching

. The chapel at St Peter's Home, Kilburn, 1867–9.

of trade skills were thought to be the surest way of combating poverty: the one giving the will to work, the other the means. This was the genesis of St Peter, Vauxhall, both the church and the schools built around it.

The schools were the first to be started (Plate 44). Their foundation stone was laid in 1860 by the young Prince of Wales acting as Duke of Cornwall (much of the parish was the Duchy's estate); it was his first public engagement. The schools were built at the rear of the future church with large rooms on each floor, the boys being on the ground floor with the girls above; they had separate playgrounds too. There was still enough space for a master's house and, to the rear, an art school and a soup kitchen.

In many ways the art school was the most important part of Gregory's scheme. Vauxhall contained two large factories, Doulton's pottery works and Maudslay's steam-engine factory. Doulton's required designers and artists, and Maudslay's required draughtsmen. By training artists and by teaching Maudslay's mechanics to draw, Gregory hoped to give his poor parishioners the opportunity of bettering themselves. The schools were opened in 1861 and used both during the day and for evening classes.

During the 1870s and '80s they achieved great renown and many leading sculptors were trained there under Jules Dalou and then W. S. Frith.[7] Among them were George Tinworth, who became well known for his pottery designs manufactured by Doulton's and who was to make a terra-cotta panel for Truro Cathedral; and George Frampton, who, like Frith, was to work for Pearson at the Astor Estate Office. Another was Walter William Ouless, the portrait painter. He came from Jersey and spent a year at the school before graduating to the Royal Academy Schools in 1865. Pearson designed a studio for him at 12 Bryanston Square; and he painted Pearson's portrait which was exhibited at the Royal Academy in 1889 (Plate 1); it was thought to be 'a speaking likeness' and shows that Ouless was trustworthy and sympathetic with a high degree of technical skill.[8]

The soup kitchen was designed to double as a cookery school. It was a failure and so was converted into a large schoolroom for boys, their original accommodation being given over to infants. A room above was used for manufacturing army clothing; in the evening it became a club, and it was probably here that religious instruction, the other side of Gregory's plans to alleviate the poverty of the district, was given to parishioners. Describing it, the *Builder* exactly catches the atmosphere of the times:

> There are meetings held in the district, to which the poor can come in their working clothes, and when they are sufficiently instructed to value the privileges of worship, they attend the hearty congregational services in the church, which are not such as to attract strangers from a distance, but suited to the needs of the parishioners.[9]

Gregory produced a supply of teachers by including an orphanage on the site; it was for the daughters of clergymen and professional men, who were apprenticed as pupil-teachers, their salaries going towards their maintenance.

. The west end of St Peter, Vauxhall, flanked by the orphanage on the left and the vicarage on the right, 1862–4.

The schools were not free; sixpence a week was charged for each child, but this was too much for the poorer parishioners, especially those from the part called Salamanca. Gregory wanted a school for them where he need charge only a penny. Pearson made various designs between 1861 and 1865 and finally a cheaper one which was built in 1866. The Salamanca Schools were L-shaped and had an open plan, the boys and girls being at opposite ends. They were closed only in 1960.

One of the leading benefactors of St Peter, Vauxhall, was Benjamin Lancaster, a close friend of the first vicar.[10] Just before the church was begun, Lancaster's wife started a home for the sick in a house in Brompton Square. Accommodation was restricted and so the Lancasters moved to a big house in Kilburn, turning to Pearson to adapt it and add a chapel (Plate 45). It was named St Peter's Home.

To tend the sick, Mrs Lancaster founded a nursing order of sisters run on the lines of a lay convent. The founding of lay orders in those days caused much controversy. Strong objections were raised against the training of nursing sisters who entered as novices and, having completed their novitiate, took Holy Vows before going out into the world to nurse. Many of the poor

67

women from Vauxhall who had become novitiates had previously been prostitutes. The home not only took them in, but worse, it also took in their unfortunate offspring. Archbishop Benson, who had formerly been the first Bishop of Truro, condemned Mrs Lancaster out of hand: 'Her method of receiving illegitimate children, sum down, no questions asked, entirely taken charge of for life, is facilitating vice.'[11]

St Peter's Home sheltered sick in four wards; three doctors attended them with nineteen permanent staff and several lay novices. So great were the demands on the home that the adjacent house was leased and linked to it, and in 1873 there were a hundred sleeping under its roofs. Still the criticism continued. Rumour had it that the children taken in 'no questions asked' by Mrs Lancaster were over-harshly punished and for some misdemeanours were even locked up in cages.[12]

In spite of it all, the home flourished: novices were trained and went all over the world; a mission was sent to Korea and stayed until the war in 1950; convalescent homes were set up as the numbers at Kilburn increased. In 1882, soon after Mrs Lancaster died, Benjamin Lancaster gave the money to build a new home for incurables in her memory near Woking in Surrey. Here Pearson designed a new building rather than adapted an old, and in the summer before he died he was asked to add a chapel, his last important design. It was built under the supervision of his son, whose connection with the home continued for a further thirty years.

It was not until 1860 that Gregory asked Pearson to design his long-desired new church in Vauxhall. Completed by November, the plans were too expensive to build and had to be modified and shorn of much carved ornament. In this form the church was eventually built in 1863–4, the furnishing and decoration, which were never completed, continuing several years more (Plate 46). Unchanged was the essential element of the original, the interior space, which depends for its treatment on the plan, the proportions and the use of vaulting throughout. Pearson broke new ground with each of these, and brought them together with fanatical consistency. The reduction in ornament makes them all the more telling.

For these qualities, St Peter, Vauxhall, is the prototype of Pearson's great town churches of the 1870s and '80s, and so of the first importance among his works. It is important as well in the development of Victorian church architecture in a wider context, providing the model for many cheap town churches built during the remainder of the nineteenth century.

Previously the plans of Pearson's churches, Devoran excepted, had been traditionally English. Vauxhall has a Romanesque plan. A western narthex leads into an aisled nave and chancel with a semi-circular apse. To provide for contemporary usage, rather than apses the south aisle ends in an organ chamber, and two extra bays added to the outside of the last two bays of the north aisle house a morning chapel. Lacking transepts, west towers and entrance porches, this is Italian Romanesque rather than English, French or German, and the position of the unbuilt tower almost detached against the

47. St Peter, Vauxhall. The elevation of the original design of 1860 shows a church loaded with vigorous decoration (the plan changed less, only the west entrances being different).

48. St Peter, Vauxhall: the apse.

north aisle would also have been Italian. Italian companiles were Ruskin's ideal; towers, he said, 'shall seem to stand, and shall verily stand, in their own strength; not by help of buttresses nor artful balancings on this side and on that'.[13]

The year before, 1859, Street had designed an almost detached campanile for St James the Less, and made it the most Italian of his career. Typically Pearson's steeple shows a more wary acceptance of Ruskin: its details are English and it remains attached to the church, at least at its base.

The internal elevations of the church, Newberry said, were English too,

69

and based on the abbeys Pearson knew from his youth. The nave arcade has cylindrical piers carrying drop-arches, a blank triforium (from Tintern Abbey), and a clerestory with paired lancets and circular lights above; the chancel, more French, has paired openings in the triforium and single lancets in the clerestory (Plate 49). Although the apse has no arcade, its upper parts are like the twelfth-century apses at Sens, Vézelay, Chartres or the French-designed Canterbury.

The exterior of the apse differs from the interior principally in the triforium openings being treated as parts of a tall ground storey which rises unsupported by ambulatory or buttresses and unbroken by band-courses or mouldings to the level of the sills of the clerestory windows (Plate 48). In comparison with the French character of the interior, this is Italian. The *Ecclesiologist* was reminded of Murano though San Abbondio at Como is a better comparison.[14] Vauxhall's apse, unlike Italian apses, is a continuation of the chancel. That is typically French, more logical, and exactly what one would expect from Pearson.

The exterior again differs from the interior in having no lateral divisions between the windows, neither shafting like the interior nor buttresses. Pugin recommended buttresses to give a feeling of strength and solidity[15]—everyone used them. Ruskin was most scathing about it:

> In most modern Gothic, the architects evidently consider buttresses as convenient breaks of blank surface, and general apologies for deadness of wall. They stand for ideas, and I think are supposed to have something of the odour of sanctity about them; otherwise one hardly sees why a warehouse seventy feet high should have nothing of the kind, and a chapel, which one can just get into with one's hat off, should have a bunch of them at every corner.[16]

Vauxhall's apse is fifty feet high and has to take the thrust of the vaults, so (warehouses notwithstanding) buttresses might seem to be a structural necessity. At Stow, a dozen years before, Pearson had proved he could convert the outward thrust of a vault downward through the use of a *tas de charge*, and dispense with buttresses. Now he did it in his own first great vaulted church.

According to Ruskin, strongly projecting buttresses are northern in character. They allow reduced wall space and increased window space; in the south, windows are small, so there is no need for projecting buttresses. Ruskin's prejudices naturally favoured the southern type:

> Both are noble in their place; the northern decidedly most scientific, or at least involving the greatest display of science, the Italian the calmest and purest; this having in it the sublimity of a calm heaven or a windless noon, the other that of a mountain flank tormented by the north wind, and withering into grisly furrows of alternate chasm and crag.[17]

Had Street read this when he liberally applied buttresses to the apse of St

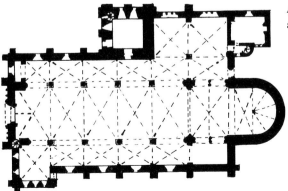

49. St Peter, Vauxhall: the interior looking east,
and plan.

50 ft

James the Less? They cannot be fulfilling a constructional need as great as their size would suggest, and are evidence of his endless desire for massy vigour. Pearson's apse may be calm and pure; its uncluttered form stands for nothing so much as mass.

As executed, St Peter, Vauxhall, looks very different from what was first planned. The west end shows this most. Instead of large square corner buttresses rising up into turrets and a small central buttress acting principally as a break between the windows, all three are the same, rising only to the height of the west windows, but projecting boldly to embrace a narthex at their base. The west windows, along with all the others, lost their cusping, resulting in plate tracery which is very like that at Bourges Cathedral.

The principal result of these modifications was to leave the church composed of severely geometrical masses and shapes. 'The change from the easy grace of Holy Trinity to the baldness and almost brutality of St Peter's is startling,' *The Times* reflected.[18] Brutalism, the style of the 1960s, is considered to have had a founding father in Butterfield—the word is seldom associated with Pearson. His brutalism at Vauxhall was caused by lack of money, not by a wilful desire to startle, nor to be self-consciously innovating. It was simply, as the *Architect* noted, 'an excellent example of a brick church for a district where economy must be supreme'.[19]

The church cost a mere £8,000, a third of the cost of Dalton Holme. In this modified form, it inspired James Brooks in his design of St Chad, Nichols Square, Shoreditch, which was built five years afterwards. Its windows have similar plate tracery; its west end is similarly treated with a narthex, double windows above and a wheel window in the gable; the east end has a similar rounded apse rising unbuttressed from the ground, a feature which Brooks exploited by placing an echoing chapel adjacent on the south.

Had Vauxhall been built to the original design, the interior would have been similar in many respects to Dalton Holme—well proportioned and highly enriched with much carved decoration and a little colour. Without most of the decoration, its unusual spaciousness is immediately apparent (Plate 49). This is partly the result of the vaulting—above all, the church has been remembered for that. 'The speciality of the church is its groined roof,' the *Ecclesiologist* wrote; 'this feature gives this fine design unusual importance'.[20] Muthesius called it 'a milestone in that it is the first church of modern times to have a vault with brick infilling between masonry ribs'.[21]

As he pointed out, vaulting is unusual in English churches and even cathedrals are not vaulted as matter of course. Even so, Vauxhall was not the first nineteenth-century parish church to be vaulted; forty years before, St Luke, Chelsea, had been vaulted in stone; and Street was already employing vaults with stone ribs and brick cells for the chancel of St James the Less. These were expensive churches. Vaulting in this extremely cheap church was all the more impressive, despite Pearson's claim that he could build a vault nearly as cheaply as any other type of roof.

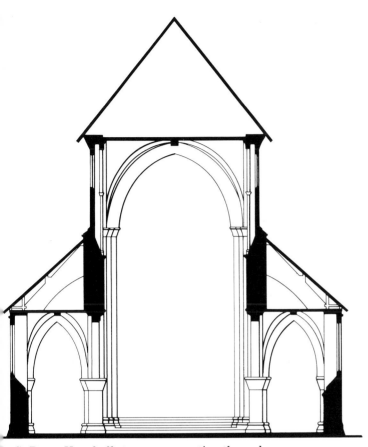

). St Peter, Vauxhall: transverse section through nave.

51. St Peter, Vauxhall: elevation of nave.

At Vauxhall the nave has four bays of quadripartite rib-vaulting but the western bay is quinquepartite, the fifth rib bisecting the west wall and carrying the thrust of the vault down to the central buttress. This type is fairly common in aisles (it appears in the choir aisles of Canterbury and Lincoln Cathedrals), but is unusual in a major end wall, one of the few instances being at St Cross, Winchester. This form of vault often appears again in Pearson's churches where end walls have central buttresses separating two windows, and has the effect, like the vault of an apse, of bringing a succession of quadripartite bays to a less abrupt halt at the end wall.

The division between nave and chancel at Vauxhall is marked only by an arch of greater projection with more orders than the rest; it hardly interrupts the progression of the bays towards the east end of the church. The choir bay has a sexpartite vault because it is longer than individual nave bays, and possibly to emphasize its different use. The sanctuary is covered by a narrow bay of quadripartite vaulting and the apse has five cells. Perhaps coincidentally, this vaulting sequence is exactly the same as in the late-twelfth-century church of St Leu d'Esserent, north of Paris.

73

The cells of the vaults which Pearson had replaced during his restoration of Stow had been coursed in the French fashion, the voutains being tapered so that the courses could rise between the ribs to meet in a clean edge at the crown. An advantage of using shaped voutains is that they can be made thinner and lighter (important at Stow to keep the loading of the new vault on the old walls to a minimum). If the voutains are common bricks, then the English pattern of vaulting must be used in which the voutains rise in parallel courses and meet at the crown diagonally.

Pearson emphasized the parallel courses by inserting courses of red brick among the yellow to make star patterns, like those formed by tiercerons in a star-vault, but lacking projection they do not obscure the vault's structural logic.

The vaulting gives the church its overwhelming French character. The proportions of Vauxhall recall a French source too. One obvious difference between French and English Gothic cathedrals is that, as the style developed, French ones became increasingly high, rising to the soaring proportions of Amiens and Beauvais which are three and more times as high as they are wide, whereas English cathedrals more usually rely for their effect on great length. At Sens the proportions are much lower than in other French Gothic cathedrals, and the soaring effect is replaced by one of unusual tranquillity. The ratio of the width across the nave between the piers of the main arcade, and their height up to the springing of the ribs is $1:1.6$. This ratio is the Golden Section, a ratio not associated so much with Gothic as with renaissance architecture. Its visual harmony, recognized since antiquity, became as characteristic of Pearson's churches as the stylistic sources of their details.

The Golden Section governs many of the proportions at Vauxhall. The most clearly observable use is, just as at Sens, in the ratio of the width across the church between the piers and their height up to the springing of the vaulting ribs (Plate 50). In the nave bays the Golden Section governs the ratio of the lengths of the wall ribs and the transverse arches, a ratio made explicit on plan by the angle of the diagonal ribs.

The Golden Section appears again in the ratio of the height of the nave piers from the bottom of their bases to the top of their capitals, and the distance between one pier and the next; and in the proportions of the triforium and clerestory taken bay by bay together from the string course above the main arcade to the crown of the vault (Plate 51). Indeed many of the individual parts—string courses, shafts and openings—are placed in such a way that they enclose rectangular areas, the sides of which have this classical ratio.

It is typical that Pearson should fuse this essentially classical element into his reinterpretation of the Gothic style. It is the key to understanding the effortless dignity of his interiors.

Pearson's first London church, Holy Trinity, had been a qualified

52. Christ Church, Appleton-le-Moors, 1863–5, from the south-west.

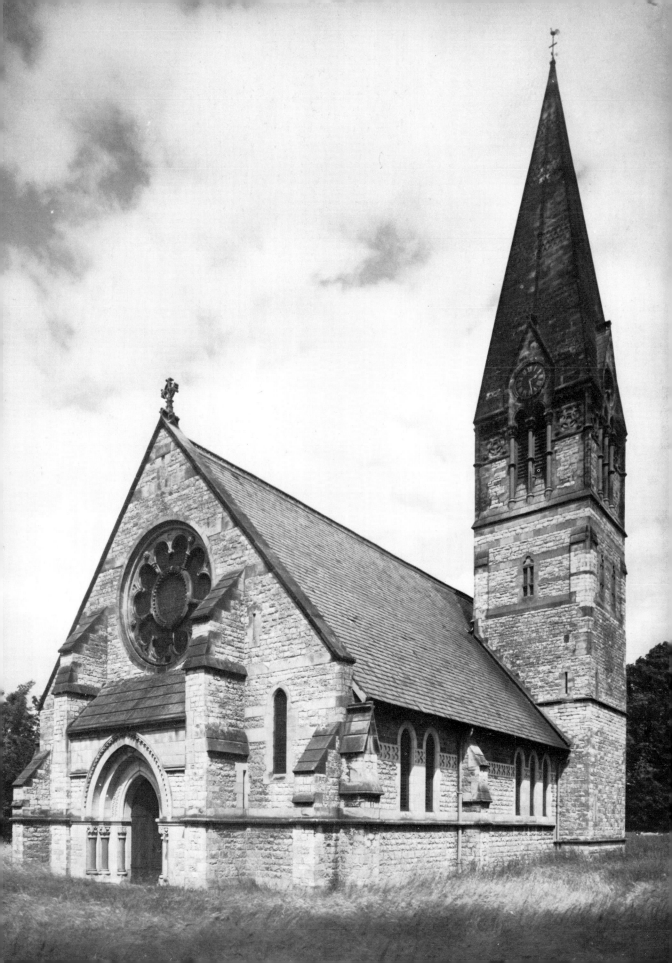

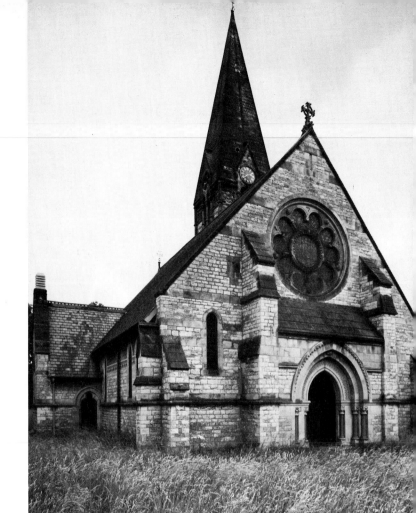

53. Christ Church, Appleton-le-Moors, from the north-west.

54. Christ Church, Appleton-le-Moors: capital of a nave pier.

55. Freeland church, 1866–9: view into apse.

success; St Peter, Vauxhall, was welcomed almost without any qualification. The *Ecclesiologist* thought it was first class, and concluded: 'We have seldom had a more important design—or one more satisfactory—than this before us';[22] and the *Building News* said the church showed 'wonderful results by the use of the very simplest materials . . . few recent designs show more marked or well applied originality'.[23]

Impressed by the spaciousness of the church, Eastlake commented:

It was perhaps when the rage for foreign Gothic was at its height that a building was begun in London, which, from its size, the nature of its construction, and the masterlike skill of its design, deserves especial mention. The church of St Peter's, Vauxhall, is not only an excellent example of Mr Pearson's originality in design, but may be fairly described as one of the most successful instances of modern ecclesiastical architecture in London.[24]

Muthesius thought the church of the utmost significance not just for its vaults but for the simplicity of its forms which gave the interior an overwhelming solemnity: 'in short, this church, like scarcely any other, is

76

harmonious,' he wrote; 'the importance of this building lies far more in its simple grandeur, through which it became a pattern for future development and in which it anticipated the best qualities of English church architecture.'[25]

St Peter, Vauxhall, is overshadowed by its successors. Without it, they could never have been designed.

Its immediate successor, however, was Christ Church at Appleton-le-Moors in the North Riding. Designed in 1862–3, it is a small, unvaulted version of Vauxhall, half the size of its predecessor, but with a similar compact plan. In elevation it is less similar; the apse is like Vauxhall's but other features come from Skelton church, the source for Eastoft. The nave and aisles are covered by a single roof just like the one at Skelton which Pearson adapted for Eastoft, this time without a change of pitch (Plate 53). The nave is lit by a large wheel-window in the west wall, and, with a timber roof as well, the effect of the interior is quite different from Vauxhall as a result. Under the wheel is a narrow narthex between the buttresses supporting the nave arcade, possibly a reinterpretation on a small scale of the west end of the nearby Byland Abbey.

Appleton has the great advantage of a completed tower (Plate 52); it shows how Italian Vauxhall would have appeared, because of its position. In design it is quite different, being square and capped with a short Pyramidal spire, a tall version of the tower at Daylesford. There is a harmony between the proportions of the bottom stage of the tower and the apse beside it which suggests that they are both based on the Golden Section.

The plan is Romanesque, and the interior decoration is equally early in style. 'The tie-beam roof, the rounded apse, with its open arcade and decorative painting, the severe and primitive foliage of the carved capitals and the square-edged arches which they carry,' Eastlake described as 'the earliest and severest type of French Gothic, with an admixture of details almost Byzantine in character.'[26]

Colour and carving are restricted. The capitals Ruskin would have classified as 'Organic form dominant',[27] so they are pure white as he advised, to let their carving speak for itself (Plate 54). They stand out strongly against the mild colours of the bare walls above and the rich red incised work in the chancel. For the rest, the church is severely plain.

Despite its similarities, Appleton church is worlds away from Eastoft; it is emphatically expressive where the other is elegantly persuasive. In his mature churches yet to come, these two opposed elements were to be fused.

While Appleton church was being built, Pearson was commissioned by the Raikses and Tauntons to build a new church at Freeland in Oxfordshire, which turned out to be his last High Victorian design. Like Appleton and Vauxhall, it has an unbuttressed apse, and the tower is placed against one side of the chancel near the junction with the nave. The apse is low, but its vaulted interior makes it look like Vauxhall on a tiny scale, and the decoration is similar, with a painted band below the lancet windows (Plate 55). The saddleback tower is a reminder of Butterfield's at St Matthias, Stoke Newington; Bodley had just built a couple at Scarborough in the North Riding and Selsley in Gloucestershire, and perhaps Pearson felt that he should do a pair too—this one and another at Over Wallop in Hampshire.

These churches make a surprising contribution to High Victorian Gothic—surprising for being so different from Pearson's late style. They lack its restraint; yet by High Victorian standards they are restrained even if they do not lack the vigour of their period. Henceforward his churches never lacked vigour. Their importance is no less because he later advanced so far beyond their High Victorian style. Both this and his early phase were periods of development, the first influenced by Pugin, the second by Ruskin, and while they must be seen as necessary steps in the attainment of his mature style, some of his churches of both these periods are among the best of their time. No other Victorian architect made so great a contribution to the Gothic Revival from its beginnings to a final achievement like Pearson's. His High Victorian churches are thus the more fascinating; they cannot be dismissed for being immature or untypical.

9 WORK AND MARRIAGE

PEARSON's methods of work, especially between 1854 and 1866, are recorded in great detail through the survival of a single ledger[1] (Plate 56). At the most superficial level it shows that as he obtained more work an increasing amount of his time was spent travelling to discuss designs, to inspect and to lay out sites, to explain plans to vestry meetings, to obtain contracts from builders, and to supervise work in progress; and sometimes he would go to the services when his churches were consecrated.

With the railway complete between London and York, he could make the larger part of the journey to the East Riding by rail, but even so it was followed by a lengthy coach ride. To save time and expense when he was going far from London, he would visit several sites at one time. In September 1857 he spent over a week in Yorkshire; travelling up on a Monday he reached Scorborough on Tuesday; on Thursday he was at Kirkburn; on Friday he examined the site at Dalton Holme and visited Garton-on-the-Wolds; next day he went to Whitwell-on-the-Hill where he stayed for a long weekend. He returned to London on the following Wednesday, and before the day was over he had written a letter about Dalton Holme to Lord Hotham. The next day, Thursday, is unrecorded but he must have set out from London again, for he spent Friday and Saturday at Treberfydd. This incessant travelling is characteristic of the years recorded by the ledger; for Pearson it was as much a part of his work as designing and drawing, though it would have exhausted many others. This Yorkshire visit and its sequel to Treberfydd were an essential part of building up his practice. The work at Whitwell-on-the-Hill in the end was unproductive, but at Scorborough and Dalton Holme he had two highly lucrative commissions.

Few journeys were less productive than one taken in 1858.[2] On 16 December he 'left town by night train . . . to visit Mr Garrett to survey his parsonage at Paul [Cornwall] and to take measurements of same and grounds for Alterations and enlarging'; next day he 'arrived late at night', and then spent three days surveying; on 21 December he 'returned to Town by early morning train from Penzance got home 5 o/c 22nd. Time 5 days.' For this he charged fifteen guineas for time and £8. 16. 0 for expenses. Two months later he had made plans for the extensions thus adding a further £50 to Garrett's bill. Garrett's finances were not up to paying for this, let alone the work, and eventually in August 1860 Pearson received a cheque 'to satisfy claim & stop further suit—£35. 0. 0'.

Pearson charged for his travelling expenses as an addition to his fees, which were usually five per cent. If he had to spend an unusual amount of time on a job or if designs were abortive, he charged for his time. The twelve guineas which he charged, but never received from, Robert Raikes of Eastdale, were for ten days work, a daily rate of about twenty-five shillings.

By the early 1850s he had increased this to three guineas; from 1864 he charged four guineas; and from 1866, five guineas.

It was unusual for clients to fail to pay him, even for designs which were never built, but occasionally he had to wait a long time for his money, often a year or two rather than months. It is easy to see why, although Raikes and Bentinck were commissioning expensive works as early as 1848, he was not in a position to set up his own office until 1850 or 1851.

Some of Pearson's early work was hardly architectural. In 1851 he charged £3. 8. 6 for his 'Expenses down and up' to West Molesey in Surrey and 'One day's time Surveying the Church & advising as to dry rot.' He was not paid until four years later.[3]

As his practice grew there was no longer need to accept onerous and unrewarding commissions of this kind. Even so, he reported on the work of other architects to the Incorporated Church Building Society to which he was a consulting architect from 1860 until his death. In 1860 he charged a mere five guineas for travelling and one day's work to survey St Briavel's church in Gloucestershire, and the next year five guineas each for surveys of three more churches in the West.[4] It is hardly surprising, although not entirely for the reason given, that later he 'ceased on account of increasing years to take an active part' in the Society's work.[5]

One surveying job stands out: between 1 and 5 October 1861 he travelled to Holderness to make a 'Survey of the Churches of Garton & Tunstall, Winestead, Welwick, Skeffling, Easington, Humbleton, Sproatley, Preston, Burstwick & Burton Pidsea, Halsham, Sunk Island, Humpton [Holmpton], Hollym, Rimswell, Ottringham, Paul [Paull] and Hedon and to report on each separately.'[6] If nothing else, it was a feat to travel round nineteen churches in five days and make even a cursory examination of them. He charged just short of £50 and this sum presumably included only minor expenses, if any, as he was staying at Dalton Holme before and after.

An analysis of Pearson's accounts between 1854 and 1866 shows that his annual travelling expenses usually amounted to about £100. In 1855 they were at a minimum of £43, and only once did they exceed £200; that was in 1861 when his charges for commission and time reached a maximum of £1,764. These are a better quantitive guide to his activity. Before 1857 commission and time usually amounted to between £200 and £250 annually, but in 1855, when he eventually charged commission for Eastoft and Stinchcombe churches and a few other relatively expensive buildings, these charges came to just short of £600. The years 1857 and 1858 saw a great increase in activity and the charges were for £878 and £1,295. Although he was no less busy in 1859 and 1860 his charges fell back to around £400. After the fruitful year of 1861 when he charged Lord Hotham over £1,000 for Dalton Holme bringing the total up to £1,764, his charges for commission and time again fell back, but their general tendency was to increase and the last three years of the ledger show an annual average of around £1,100.

Pearson's bills were not settled immediately although a few clients like

56. Page 93 from Pearson's surviving ledger showing sundry expenses in connection with St Peter, Vauxhall, and finally the charge of £400 commission on its cost of £8,003. 7. 2.

Lord Hotham paid £100 'in anticipation' of work proceeding before Pearson sent in his account. The result was for his income to lag behind the accomplishment of the work which had earned it. At the same time it was not subject to quite such extreme variation. In the mid 1850s he annually received an average of £250. Between 1856 and 1858 his income rose progressively from rather less than £500 to a peak of well over £1,200, and then from 1859 to 1862 it rose again from a trough of below £600 to a new peak of £1,600. For the remaining four years covered by the ledger, although fluctuating, his gross earnings averaged about £1,000 each year.

This pattern in Pearson's accounts must have continued throughout the 1860s and '70s, peaks following troughs, but all the time the tendency was for the amount and the value of his work to increase. The seventies brought him commissions for churches costing well over £10,000, and the fees for each were at least £500. At the end of the seventies he was appointed architect for

Truro and for that could expect to be rewarded with a fee of at least four times as much. In the event the appointment made him rich. The modest affluence which he gained in the fifties was transformed by numerous commissions which resulted from Truro. He became architect in charge of several cathedrals, and what he received for restoring them often amounted to as much as he received for building his own most expensive churches.

What proportion of Pearson's gross income was consumed by the costs of running his office is unknown. His clerks and his manager would have been paid wages possibly amounting to a few hundred pounds a year. Added to this were the costs of drawing materials, postage and accommodation. His office was in his own home, but even so he had to pay for heating, lighting and ground rent. None of these amounts nor any details of his office expenses are given in the ledger.

Pearson's last big patrons in the East Riding were the Sykeses of Sledmere, the most important landed family in the county.[7] One of them had been a partner in the Hull bank which eventually brought down the Raikeses. Another was Lord of the Manor of Brantingham, the parish where Pearson started his career; the daughter of this Sykes married into the Hothams. Another married into a North Wales family, the Davies Cookes of Gwysaney, who employed Pearson in Flintshire. Sir Tatton Sykes, the fourth Baronet, Deputy Lieutenant of the East Riding, and High Sheriff, had extensive estates on which he bred bloodstock and reared sheep on a large scale. He was equally successful in business and sport, and loved boxing. None of these activities prevented him from supporting the religious life of the county. While his younger brother, typically of landed families, held two livings, being rector of both Hilston and Roos, Sir Tatton was patron of four. Between 1856 and his death in 1863 he employed Pearson to restore the churches at Bishop Wilton, Garton-on-the-Wolds and Kirkburn, and to rebuild Hilston church.

Pearson's career was founded in the East Riding. His earliest patrons lived or had connections there, and for them he built eight new churches and restored ten more during the first twenty years of his career. In 1857 came the first signs of competition when he made various designs for a new church to be built for a young heiress, Louisa Haigh, and her guardian and stepfather, Arthur Stephens, at Whitwell-on-the-Hill. A design to cost £5,000 was

> prepared according to instructions, approved [and] subsequently aban-
> doned ... Design No 2 also prepared according to instructions upon
> reduced Scale, approved of, working drawings prepared for tender, the cost
> not to exceed 3500£ ... Design No 3 in Norman style upon still further
> reduced Scale approved & working drawings partly prepared. Cost not to
> exceed 2500£.[8]

In 1858 Miss Haigh came of age and inherited Whitwell Hall; she sent her stepfather packing, married Sir Edmund Lechmere of Malvern, dismissed Pearson and called in Street in his place. Street had already worked for

Lechmere. His design for the church, Gothic not Norman, and costing well over £2,500, was built; he was at the beginning of a very successful career. Pearson sent in a bill for £258 for his trouble but settled for £200.

Though Street was a rival, the two were on sufficiently good terms to travel abroad together and Pearson supported Street when the architectural examination question was being discussed at the R.I.B.A. in 1861. Street proposed an amendment that the examination should be open to 'any person', not just British subjects. Pearson seconded the motion but it was not carried.[9] Perhaps he was prompted by his own supposed foreign birth.

Street was just one of the architects whom Pearson counted as friends rather than mere acquaintances. He preferred their society to any other, though his relationship with his fellow architects is not well recorded.

The Architectural Museum was where Pearson met many of his early architect friends; like Scott's office, it was near his home in Delahay Street. He knew Scott before the museum was founded, but while Scott counted him a friend, Pearson probably stood in awe of the great man, at least at the beginning. In November 1858 he wrote to congratulate Scott 'with unfeigned delight' when he was given the commission to design the new government offices in Whitehall. Scott would naturally produce a Gothic design, and Pearson was pleased for his sake, 'not so much for the addition it makes to your practice as for the complete acknowledgement of those talents we all admire and of that style of architecture we conceive most fitting and which we all serve.'[10] An acknowledgement of Scott's talents it may have been, but not of his style. When Palmerston presented his terms—an Italianate design or no commission—and a delegation was formed in his support, Scott 'tried to get up a counter address, but the Gothic architects did not come forward'. Pearson, though, was among the dozen or so 'who exerted themselves in the most generous way, and willingly signed'.[11] Palmerston eventually won the Battle of the Styles. Scott thoroughly compromised his principles, but his reputation survived and so did Gothic. He did not forget his allies and often thereafter gave Pearson help.

Pearson and Burges knew each other well at least as early as 1855, and seem to have shared a mutual friend in Ewan Christian. Once—when is not recorded though it was probably after 1874—they went abroad together along with George Devey and Street. The party set out from Dunkerque for a tour of France, Belgium and Holland. They were an ill-assorted crowd: Pearson, diffident, pious, hard working; Street, authoritarian, equally pious, ceaselessly active; Devey, an Irvingite, keen on designing carriages and tackle for the horses he loved to drive; and Burges, rich and working only when he wanted, irreligious and—worse—accustomed to taking opium.

While Pearson may have been only acquainted with John Dobson, he seems to have been on far better terms with Dobson's son-in-law Sydney Smirke. Smirke was a generation older than Pearson and had a wide-ranging career during which he filled numerous Establishment posts. If his buildings were not quite first rate, he certainly knew how to succeed. He may have known Pearson from the 1840s when Dobson's name appears in Pearson's diary and certainly would have done later through the R.I.B.A. and the Royal Academy, yet his only recorded personal connection with Pearson is posthumous: Pearson designed his tomb in Trinity Cemetery at Tunbridge Wells.

In 1848 C. R. Cockerell took some interest in the spire of Pearson's church at North Ferriby; in 1849 or '50 when his church in Bessborough Gardens was under construction, it was admired by Barry, Pugin and Scott, yet their memoirs do not mention it. Pearson may have known Barry and Pugin well but must have strongly felt himself their junior in ability as well as years. After Pugin's death, he served on the working committee of the Pugin Travelling Fund, and donated two guineas as a memorial to him; and in May 1860 he attended Barry's funeral in Westminster Abbey.

Pearson registered as a member of the Institute of British Architects in 1834, the year of its foundation. Not until 1860 did he become a full Fellow of the Royal Institute as it now had become. In 1862 he served on one of its committees; this was for the 'Conservation of Antient Monuments and Remains', and he joined Scott, Street, Digby Wyatt, Burges, Ewan Christian, Salvin and several others engaged in restoring churches. The same year he was a member of the Council which chose Salvin as the Royal Gold Medalist for 1863.

Ewan Christian was an old friend.[12] Pearson had subscribed to his book on Skelton church, which was published in 1846. Christian was three years older than Pearson and, like him, designed and restored many churches; but little of his immense output shows imagination. He became architect to the Ecclesiastical Commissioners and so was in continual contact with Pearson.

Christian was an extremely devout man, and ran a Sunday School in Hampstead where he had made his home. It was probably there that Pearson met his cousin Jemima Christian, on a visit to London from her home in the Isle of Man.

A ring marks 28 October in Jemima's diary for 1861, and the family assume that on that day they became engaged.[13] Pearson was aged forty-four; Jemima, thirty-two. Like him, she did not record personal matters in her diary, even their wedding day is unmarked; but folded in the back is a cutting from a paper headed 'Hints on the Duties of Married Life, by the late Bishop of Calcutta.'

It is a pity that Jemima did not mark her wedding, for it is incorrectly recorded in the family Bible as 4 June 1862, a typical example of the family's inattention to personal matters. The marriage certificate clearly states the date as 5 June. They were married in Hampstead parish church by Dr Spyers, Pearson's friend from Weybridge.

For a wedding present, Ewan Christian gave his cousin Jemima a book, *The Resolutions of Mary Christian upon the day of her Marriage*.[14] Their ancestor wrote it in 1740, when she married a future Bishop of Carlisle. His career, according to the introduction to the book, was blessed by his wife's goodness. The book must have greatly appealed to the Victorian mind with its insistence on humility and devotion as wifely virtues; today it seems a forbidding present from a forbidding cousin.

Pearson took Jemima back to his home at 22 Harley Street, St Marylebone. He had moved there from Delahay Street in 1855 or 1856, transferring his small office at the same time. The house, one of a terrace built about 1770 on the Portland estate, had three main storeys with a basement and attic. There was a spacious hall with a fine staircase which had a rail supported by elegant iron balusters wrought into a lyre pattern. Pearson probably used the ground floor for his office and lived on the first and second floors; the servants would have lived in the attic and worked in the basement.

On 14 January 1864 the Pearsons had a son, Frank Loughborough, the only child born to them. This was to be of the utmost importance to Pearson, ensuring that his practice should have a successor, and one who would faithfully complete many of his buildings. In September there are three weeks empty in his surviving ledger, and perhaps Pearson took Jemima and the infant Frank on holiday. If he did so, it was for the last time; early in the following year Jemima contracted typhoid fever, and on 25 March she died.

The cause seems to have been unknown to her son and certainly Frank's children were unaware of it; they were told that Jemima had died of cancer. The suspicion is that, just as it may not have been proper for someone of Pearson's standing to have been born abroad, so it may not have been proper for his wife to have died of so common a disease as typhoid fever.

Jemima's death was the great tragedy in Pearson's life. It devastated him. It devastated his practice. Work ceased.

A week after her death he visited Spyers at Wallop Lodge, his country home in Hampshire. Spyers may have offered him the consolations of friendship and religion. With great sense he offered him the consolation of work; he wanted further alterations made to Wallop Lodge. In the end Pearson largely remodelled it, but it was a lengthy process coaxing him back to life. For a month or two he made practically no professional visits, and their number only slowly returned to normal as the summer progressed and turned to autumn. Even then a large proportion were to Wallop Lodge or to Halstain House, the school run by Spyers in Weybridge.

The interruption in his work was not without effect. The most grievous blow was in the North. Sir Tatton Sykes, the fifth Baronet, having succeeded his father, asked Pearson to design some cottages at Sledmere and schools at Bishop Wilton. In 1865 he commissioned from him two new churches, one to be built at Wansford, the other at Thixendale. Pearson made designs and put them out to tender. The design for Wansford, which has recently come to light at Sledmere, was like Scorborough but with a central tower. It should have pleased Sykes as it would his father, but either it did not or Pearson worked too slowly for him. He changed his mind, and on 26 October Pearson received a cheque for £458. 17. 6, the total amount of his claim for all the projected buildings. He was in effect paid off.[15] The two churches were subsequently built to Street's designs.

> He had the satisfaction of finding the Master of Sledmere a client who was as anxious as he could have been himself, not only to give every village a building where the people could meet for public worship, but such a building as should, by the purity and beauty of its architecture and the completeness of its arrangements, insensibly affect for good those who were gathered together within its walls.[16]

Pearson's aims were no doubt identical to Street's, but from then on the East Riding was effectively Street's territory, not Pearson's.

Pearson's failure in Yorkshire might have had a disastrous effect on his career. He lost commissions to build four churches, and to rebuild or restore six more. He never built another church in the East Riding again. Fortunately there were friends offering support. Robert Raikes's brother-in-law William Taunton of Freeland Lodge had already used Pearson near his estate to restore Minister Lovell church; now, supported—and perhaps prompted—by Raikes, he commissioned the church at Freeland and then a parsonage and school to be built next door; Gregory's needs in Vauxhall were not yet satisfied; and there was 'dear Doctor Spyers'.

As for the infant Frank, he was brought up on the Isle of Man by Jemima's unmarried, elder sister, Sarah Christian, in a conventionally strict Victorian way. They lived with a married sister Hannah Moore at Cronkbourne, the Moore's family house. Pearson bequeathed a £60 annuity to Sarah, as he did to his own surviving sister. Frank stayed on the Isle of Man until about 1871 when he was seven years old. He was then sent to school to be under Spyers at Halstain House. No doubt religious instruction was well to the fore, and Frank could soon recite all the Collects by heart; but he never became devout like his father.

Spyers was not without humanity. It was the rule that all school meals must be finished. Frank hated fat, and when his fellow pupils rose from the table, he was often left sitting before an unfinished plate. After a moment Spyers would come back into the dining-room, pour out some of his beer and give it to Frank to help him wash down the offending morsels.

Nor was Pearson a forbidding or a distant father, and he wanted Frank to have the good education which he lacked. When Frank was twelve he took him down to Winchester where the two stayed in a hotel while Frank took an examination for the College. In the evening they played cricket together in the hotel courtyard to relax. Frank won an exhibition and Pearson was rewarded.

Two years after Jemima's death Pearson moved to 46 Harley Street. Here he designed many of his great works, from St Augustine, Kilburn, to Truro Cathedral. The house accommodated not only him and his assistants and clerks, but a resident staff of three, Frank in the holidays, and very often visitors.

10 ❧VERNACULAR REVIVAL

JEMIMA's death and the ensuing hiatus in Pearson's work coincided with a marked change in his style. The vigour of his High Victorian period was subsequently modified by a sensitivity which is characteristically late Victorian. The long, empty, spring and summer days of 1865 left him to brood about the design of churches. He could reflect upon the thirty-five years spent to accomplish his masterpiece at Vauxhall—paradoxically still a masterpiece despite its reduction to the barest shell of his first scheme. Its plainness, perhaps, he saw reflecting his own diffidence; certainly he came to see it as a point of departure, one which would lead to Kilburn in five years' time. Yet this may be too reasoned: these developments were already foreshadowed in the easier and more modest climate of house design.

Even before Quar Wood, in fact simultaneously with his work for Sir Charles Anderson at Lea Hall, Pearson built a small parsonage at Braintree in Essex (Plate 57). He made two abortive designs and a third in 1855 which was built. The parsonage is a plain two-storeyed house, built in red brick, with black brick diapering to the upper floor of a type then appearing in Butterfield's houses. The outline of the parsonage reflects its L-shaped plan: an entrance on the west opens into a hall; ahead and on its right are reception-rooms, down a corridor on the left are service-rooms. The west elevation has a projecting block for the entrance and the whole is gabled. The continuity of the elevation once again is maintained by the ridge of the main roof which extends from one end to the other. All this can be seen in larger format at Treberfydd; otherwise the house is stylistically utterly self-effacing, indeed like Butterfield's contemporary houses which similarly depend on vernacular tradition. Pearson was to develop the vernacular tradition further than any other of his generation.

In the decade which followed Quar Wood, Pearson designed a few more houses. All but one were vicarages with the restraint of Braintree Parsonage. Two in Yorkshire, at Broomfleet and Appleton-le-Moors, date from 1861 and 1862. Both are of local materials enlivened with a few dark bands and diapering. Broomfleet Vicarage was built to a revised design; an early design had a porch in a two-storeyed block with a half-hipped roof a little like Quar Wood's (Plate 58), but this was omitted in the executed version, an L-shaped building with a large, mullioned and transomed window lighting the staircase. Paul Thompson notes Butterfield's influence in 'the spare brick diaper, the small-scale window frames and the complex hipped roof'.[1] The roof is hardly complex, but the vicarage is like Butterfield's contemporary cottages at Kirby Muxloe in Leicestershire. How far Pearson's exploration of the vernacular tradition was prompted by Butterfield or was a parallel development is open to question. The latter is more likely. His interest in the subject was stronger than Butterfield's and he took it much further. At all

57. Broomfleet vicarage, church and schools as first designed in 1861; only the church was built as shown; a sch[ool]
was eventually built further away by someone else.

58. Braintree parsonage, 1853–5: entrance front.

SOUTH ELEVATION

59. Ayot vicarage, designed in 1866: entrance front.

events, designs based on local vernacular tradition rather than formal style were widespread among Victorian architects. Pearson did not publicize his, and knowledge of some of them is the result of the lucky survival of his second ledger. It is tantalising to imagine how many similar works may survive unknown. Their inconspicuousness does not help.

Another vicarage design, for Ayot St Peter in Hertfordshire, was completed in 1866 (Plate 59). Larger and more conspicuous than the earlier ones, its sole ecclesiastical touch is the pointed arch of the entrance. Unlike Broomfleet, it has a complicated layout of roofs and there is some mild polychromy. Pearson was insistent that it should be mild: 'The bands of colour on the elevations are to be header courses in which the darkest headers are to be used,' he wrote in the specification; 'they are to be picked out from the rest of the bricks used as facers and are not to be blackened or coloured in any way but are merely to be the darkest headers in the bulk of the bricks used.'[2] Here is true late Victorian sensitivity.

From 1860 until at least 1871 Pearson transformed Wallop Lodge for Doctor Spyers (Plate 60). Though demolished in 1915, its appearance is known from three of Pearson's photographs. By Jemima's death only £214 had been spent, partly on the private chapel; in 1866 he charged commission on a further £1,100, so most work must have taken place by then, and there was still an outstanding sum on Spyers's account in 1871. The house is haphazard, so much so that Pearson must have kept far more of the original house than at Treberfydd. He added a few features from Quar Wood, such as a two-storeyed entrance block with a half-hipped roof; and there were similar details too: shaped roof tiles, crested ridge tiles and finials. The house was faced in local

89

60. Wallop Lodge: view *c.* 1870 from the south-east as shown in one of Pearson's photographs.

flint, with horizontal brick bands and diapering as well as quoining, far less mild than at Ayot St Peter, and more like Butterfield's domestic work of the period. There was some of Quar Wood's assertiveness, for instance in a large semi-circular bow, rather like a church apse, and the chapel had a dominating pyramidal spire which was probably Pearson's. Quar Wood was uncompromisingly High Victorian, but Wallop Lodge seems to have hesitated between that and the vernacular tradition, and ended up an awkward mess.

A far more likeable progeny of Quar Wood are the schools in Lambeth, completed for Gregory in 1861. The *Ecclesiologist* described them as 'well-ordered and picturesque';[3] indeed their massing is lively but not overcrowded with jostling shapes; and there is the same effortless sense of scale which is found in the stable yard at Treberfydd (Plate 44).

Pearson found the High Victorian style inappropriate for country schools. When in 1863 he designed a school to be built at Appleton-le-Moors, he gave it a large east window with plate tracery and a bellcote very like his early one at Ellerton.

The adjacent master's house, designed in 1863 though not built until 1865, is notable for having a wing with a jettied and half-timbered upper storey. Pugin published many drawings of timber-framed houses; these Pearson knew and copied, and he drew examples he had seen for himself. Some of Butterfield's small houses, such as Alvechurch Rectory in Worcestershire of 1855, are extensively half-timbered in a thin, awkward way; but the key influence was Pearson's friend George Devey. His half-timbered cottages, especially those at Penshurst in Kent of the 1850s, influenced Shaw and Eden Nesfield and through them a whole generation.[4] Vernacular buildings had attracted topographical artists for a long while, two of whom, J. S. Cotman and J. D. Harding, had trained Devey as a water colourist. Pearson's interest in vernacular buildings was probably aroused by his father whose *Rural Beauties* shows that humble buildings could be as inspiring as Durham Cathedral.

Though not part of it, Pearson maintained his connections with the Brancepeth circle through Salvin and William Nesfield who was in Salvin's office during Pearson's time there, and later designed Treberfydd's gardens. His son Eden Nesfield had trained like Devey under Harding. In 1862 Eden Nesfield and Shaw visited Penshurst, saw Devey's work and made a tour of the half-timbered and tile-hung houses of the Weald. In 1863–4 Shaw built his first half-timbered cottage, the Bailiff's Lodge at Bromley Palace in Kent. It was almost exactly contemporary with Pearson's schoolmaster's house at Appleton. Shaw's lodge was the predecessor of his great half-timbered houses—Leyswood, Grims Dyke, Cragside and several others. By the time the first of them was begun, Pearson had already designed his first half-timbered house, the remarkable Roundwyck House at Kirdford in Sussex. Shaw's houses, with the vertical accents of their close studding, tall gables and magnificent chimney-stacks, are full of High Victorian vigour; Roundwyck is relaxed and gentle.

Designed and built between 1868 and 1870, it is a small country house the size of Quar Wood (Plates 61 and 62). Like Treberfydd it emerged from a previous building; Eastlake said 'it was first intended only for a farmhouse, but afterwards expanded into a small residence in connection with the farm.'[5]

Its planning is like Treberfydd's: an entrance on the west opens into a hall; on its south are the reception-rooms, on the north the service rooms; and further north these lead into the farmyard. Again recalling Treberfydd are the large windows divided by stone mullions and transoms and the numerous gables and long roof ridges broken only by many varied, tall chimney-stacks. The houses, too, share a feeling for local material; to quote Eastlake again: 'This house is treated in a very picturesque manner, and the local materials used—viz. stone, brick, tiles, and oak timber—are ingeniously intermixed in the design.'

The stone ground storey turns to brick for the servants' quarters and farm buildings; the upper storey is half-timbered, its gables at the front dominated by a magnificent chimney-stack on a stone plinth. Without Shaw's

61. Roundwyck House, 1868–70: view from the south-east as shown in Pearson's photograph.

vertiginous proportions, its effect comes from its massiveness; and in this, it performs the same aesthetic function as Quar Wood's entrance block. The entrance at Roundwyck has a porch, the most delightful feature of the elevation: fitting into the re-entrant angle made by a projecting bay, it has a rounded tent roof supported on wooden arches carried by a pair of posts; stone steps curve down from it to the driveway.

The elevations are full of easy variety, pulled together by the roofs and released again by the several stacks. To the south is a stone, two-storeyed polygonal bay, with a parapet originally, and large windows opening around it on both storeys. It is only a short step to the three bays which Voysey gave to Broadleys at Cartmell Fell in Lancashire in 1898.

Unlike Treberfydd, Roundwyck had neither formal garden nor landscaping. On the south is a terrace; here and elsewhere are flowerbeds and trees; then fields stretch away to the woodlands of the Sussex Weald. It is a perfect setting for such a house.

Determined to accredit styles, Eastlake called Treberfydd 'Manorial Gothic',[5] and Quar Wood 'Early 14th century'; Roundwyck he labelled 'Late 13th century',[8] even more nonsensically than when William Morris applied the term to Red House, which Philip Webb built for him. 'Old English', as Nesfield described his cottages at Hampton-in-Ardern, or 'Vernacular

Roundwyck House: from the east (above) and west.

63. Crowton vicarage under construction 1872–4, viewed from the south-east.

64. Freeland church, vicarage and school, designed 1865–6 for the Raikeses and Tauntons, and completed unlike the scheme at Broomfleet, from a photograph of a painting in Pearson's collection.

65. Clifton vicarage, York, 1878–9: entrance front from the west.

66. Whitwell parsonage, 1885: garden front from the south.

Revival' are far better terms. They leave style suitably vague and suggest the seemingly accretive nature of the houses they describe. Accretive Roundwyck is, but only in being built onto a former house as Treberfydd was; like Treberfydd again, its design is carefully contrived, not, as it appears, the result of happy accident.

In one important way Roundwyck House differs from Shaw's contemporary half-timbered houses: it completely lacks their High Victorian melodrama. It is so free and light that it could have been designed many decades later.

Pearson built several more houses in the sensitive vernacular idiom of Roundwyck. Most are vicarages. Crowton Vicarage in Cheshire, begun in 1871, had many of Roundwyck's features on a small scale, with half-timbering based on Chester models and used with more thought for structural function than at Roundwyck (Plate 63). Half-timbering appears on wings of the contemporary vicarage and school at Freeland with more assurance than at Appleton (Plate 64). At Clifton Vicarage, built in 1878–9 on the outskirts of York, tile-hanging was substituted for half-timbering (Plate 65). The vicarage exhibits many other Old English features normally associated with Shaw and Nesfield such as plaster covings and thick glazing bars to windows, as well as tall chimney-stacks. It pays passing respects to the emerging 'Queen Anne' style; so does Spurfield, built at Exminster in Devon a decade later. It is a heavy house composed of severely geometrical shapes only slightly relieved by Old English tile-hanging, half-timbering and plaster coving.

Perhaps Pearson's finest small house is Whitwell Parsonage in Derbyshire, of 1885 (Plate 66). He chose to build it not only from good local stone but from stone salvaged from a previous building on the site, and oak from a local barn was used for chimney-pieces. The projecting gabled entrance block with its pointed arch is a single early Victorian feature to stress its ecclesiastical role. The garden front is freely designed with a magnificent tall chimney-stack rising from the ground at the east and a series of well-grouped windows in bays along the rest of the elevation. The dominating roof, starting by the tall stack, sweeps to a long hip at the west. It anticipates some of Voysey's best houses. Largely through its homogeneous material the house has an admirable dateless quality extending beyond Roundwyck's Old English.

11 ✠ KILBURN

THE PRINCIPAL requirement of early Victorian Gothic was that it be correct, of High Victorian that it be vigorous. Pugin inspired the first style, Ruskin the second. If late Victorian Gothic can be evoked by a single word, then it is sensitive. Who inspired that? No single name can be readily found. Partly the new style was a reaction against the slavish copying of the first and the restless expressionism of the second. If there were prophets at all, they were Pugin and Ruskin again, but interpreted by a new generation.

Prominent in that generation was George Frederick Bodley. In 1860–1 he was persuaded to modify his foreign-looking design for All Saints, Cambridge, partly to make it more acceptable to the old-fashioned taste of his clients. They may have seen his new design as a welcome return to the taste of the 1840s, but it displays Bodley's meticulous care for decoration. That was new. The church is one of the earliest to be decorated by artists of the future Arts and Crafts Movement: Ford Madox Brown, Burne-Jones and William Morris.

Morris was a protagonist of the late Victorian style, in theory through his published attitudes to design and restoration, and in practice through his artwork and furnishings. In the 1850s he had worked with such prominent late Victorian architects as Philip Webb, Norman Shaw and John Dando Sedding in Street's office. It was here that the late Victorian style was born.

Street said, 'three-fourths of the poetry of building lies in its minor details',[1] echoing Ruskin's belief that buildings should give employment to all kinds of craftsmen. 'This is the glory of Gothic architecture, that every jot and tittle, every point and niche of it, affords room, fuel, and focus for individual fire.'[2]

Pearson's attitude was exactly opposite: the architect should control builders and craftsmen; the fire should be his. Ruskin and the Arts and Crafts Movement struggled to eliminate this attitude, and return to the conditions of building in the Middle Ages. In practice it proved romantic nonsense; but architects did at least become more sensitive to the various skills of craftsmen. Bodley's All Saints, Cambridge, led to such treasure houses as Sedding's Holy Trinity, Chelsea, a church which was intended to be 'a field in which the first workers in each art and craft should unite in doing their best'.[3]

It was expensive, so expensive that it was never finished as planned. Without money for lavish detail, would sensitivity be of any avail? St Peter, Vauxhall, provided an answer. It showed that sensitivity could be obtained with cheap materials; that fine proportions might be a substitute for lavish ornament; that, above all, a feeling for space might overcome all other deficiencies. Despite Street and Ruskin, ornament is less specially architectural than space. No Victorian architect created more complex combinations of spaces than did Pearson. On occasion they are truly baroque in their

97

ambiguity; at other times, often interrelated in the same building, they achieve a classical calm. It is in his ability to design spaces, rather than to decorate surfaces, that Pearson shows the sensitivity characteristic of the late Victorian period. Here lies the essence of his unique contribution to Victorian architecture.

In lesser churches, he displayed his sensitivity in their massing and detailing. Sometimes that was enough to provide sparkle if not fire; but he became increasingly busy towards the end of his life and some of his works designed then are 'ecclesiastical and correct' but not one jot more.

67. (left) St John, Sutton Veny, 1866–8, from the south-east.

68. St John, Sutton Veny: looking into the chancel from the nave.

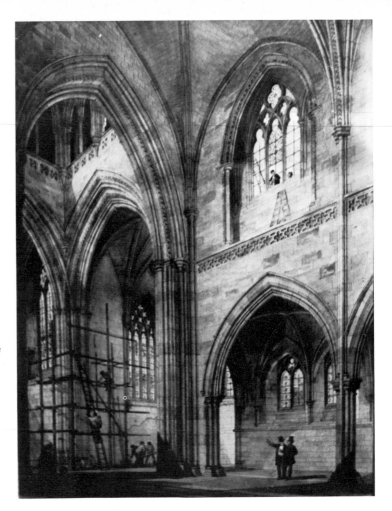

69. Pearson's perspective of the nave and crossing of Wentworth church under construction, exhibited at the Royal Academy in 1875.

70. (far right) Wentworth church, 1872–7: the interior looking towards the chancel.

The change from High to late Victorian in Pearson's work first appears at his church at Sutton Veny in Wiltshire (Plate 67); it looks back to the Middle Pointed style in a way comparable to Bodley's Cambridge church. The design closely followed Freeland's. In November 1865 Pearson went to Sutton Veny to inspect the site; he went again in the following January, and on 23 April was 'directed to make a new design'. A fortnight later it was done and on 7 May he 'Set out Ch.'; it was complete in 1868.[4]

Like Holy Trinity, Bessborough Gardens, Sutton Veny has a traditional cruciform plan, and the massing and detailing are similar, with a prominent central steeple and conspicuous Decorated tracery. Beresford Hope said of Holy Trinity that it was a pity that Pearson had not given them 'a second and better edition of that church'.[5] He evidently did not know Sutton Veny.

This improved quality distinguishes Sutton Veny both from the earlier church and from early Victorian Gothic in general. The choir and sanctuary vaults have star patterns like those at Vauxhall, but they are marked as much by the changing texture of their stone as by its colour (Plate 68). Constructional polychromy is largely absent, and seldom appears again. Of rich carving there is practically none.

The nave walls rise to the roof unadorned, showing Pearson's willingness to forgo decoration and let well-laid ashlar speak for itself. The arcade is supported on round piers, again like Vauxhall; on the other hand, the capitals are not highly carved but bell-shaped, having an undecorated drip-mould section which Ruskin would have disliked; the crossing piers are similar. They are typical of Pearson's work thereafter. In many late Victorian churches, the capitals are omitted, leaving arches to die into their supporting piers. Pearson always retained capitals in order to differentiate pier and arch, and to define the exact proportions of the openings they span. The capitals and the water-holding bases which go with them are his translation of a classical order into Gothic; untranslated is their purpose.

A year after work began at Sutton Veny, Pearson went to Wentworth in the West Riding with a view to restoring the old church for Lord Fitzwilliam, but a new church was built instead. Progress was slow: the design was not completed until 1872, and the church was only finished in 1877 (Plate 69). It is similar to Sutton Veny, but it is slightly larger and has a clerestory where Sutton Veny has none; most importantly it is vaulted throughout (Plate 70).

Unlike Vauxhall and Sutton Veny which have cylindrical piers

71. Thurstaston church, 1883–6, from the south.

unrelated to the vaulting shafts above, Wentworth has composite piers with four major shafts carrying the main arcade and the transverse arches of the vaulting, and four minor shafts carrying the diagonal ribs. This logical use of shafting again becomes characteristic. Inside, the colour of the yellow Darfield stone is unrelieved except by the fine stained glass by Kempe and by Clayton and Bell, and by the chancel's elaborate marble mosaic floor. It is among the first to show the influence of an Italian visit in 1874. For the rest, the church is an essay in the Middle Pointed style—correctly, vigorously and sensitively applied, but no more.

The trouble was that the church lacked the intensity of Pearson's recent work. It was, as the *Builder* said, 'a design which it is scarcely possible to distinguish from Late Gothic',[6] but scholarship now was no longer enough.

Despite that, Pearson continually returned to the Middle Pointed style of the 1840s for his country churches. Crowton in Cheshire of 1869–70 and Porton in Wiltshire of 1876–7 are two which might be contemporaries of Ellerker or Ellerton except for their solid appearance and sensitive detailing. More expensive churches such as Thurstaston in Cheshire, while outwardly correct, have real fire within (Plates 71 and 72). Thurstaston's three nave bays lead through a tripartite traceried screen, which rises right up to the vaulting, into a chancel, which is divided into a nearly square single-bay choir and a slightly larger and higher sanctuary of two narrow bays. There is

72. (right) Thurstaston church: the interior showing the nave seen through the screen from the chancel.

102

a continual feeling of movement; but the parts are firmly unified by the vaults, and despite the size—less than seventy feet by twenty feet—the effect is not of the restlessness of the High Victorian period but of remarkable spaciousness.

Pearson reached the summit of his artistic achievement with three churches: St Augustine, Kilburn; St John, Red Lion Square, in Holborn; and St Michael, Croydon. The first two are masterpieces (sadly, was a masterpiece, in the case of Red Lion Square); masterpieces of complexity resolved by the unifying effect of their vaulting; the latter is calmer but has its complexities too. In these churches is the vocabulary of much of the remainder of Pearson's work, work which was to include nearly twenty fine churches or chapels built in as many years. With these autumnal flowers of the Gothic Revival, his genius at last attained its full expression.

St Augustine, Kilburn, was built for Richard Carr Kirkpatrick. He was the first chaplain of the Lancasters' St Peter's Home, and a strong Tractarian and curate at Kilburn parish church. When a new vicar of immovable low-church views was appointed and clearly would not compromise with his curate, Kirkpatrick walked out with much of the wealthy congregation and formed a separate District where Tractarian worship could be continued. Pearson owed the commission to Lancaster who strongly recommended him to the building committee, which was also considering Street (who was thought to be too busy to give proper attention to the work), Brooks and Withers.

Pearson had begun planning the new church by June 1870. The site was

73. (left) St Augustine, Kilburn, from the south-west; the steeple was completed in 1897.

74. St Etienne, Caen, from the south-east.

procured in the following month, and before the end of the year its main features had been designed. A temporary, iron church was first erected. In July 1871 the foundation stone was laid, and there was a procession in which Pearson, the building committee and the contractor marched, singing, 'We march, we march to victory.'[7]

Pearson had designed a noble church. Sombrely coloured by dark red brick with Bath stone dressings, it is typical of his late town churches, and has lively massing dominated by a soaring spire (Plate 73). Its design, with tall gabled lucarnes and corner spirelets, is inspired by the thirteenth-century spires of St Etienne at Caen (Plate 74). These rest on corbel tables running round the entire perimeter of the earlier towers and appear top-heavy. Pearson's spire, which is placed on its tower with the corbelling stopping well short of the corners so that the lines made by the angles of the tower pass unbroken across their junction with the spire, is perfectly proportioned, and seems to be an inevitable continuation of the tower. The tower is also Norman French, and resembles the north-west tower of Lisieux Cathedral.

Perhaps the most similar steeple in Normandy is at Bernières, Calvados, though it is more squat. Pearson probably knew it well. Street, too, must have known it; his steeple at St Saviour, Eastbourne in Sussex, designed about three years earlier than Kilburn, is of the same type, but less elegant, and recalls the vigorous outline and detached position of the one at St James the Less. Street provided the cradle for late Victorian Gothic but did not grow far into the style himself.

The spire of Kilburn is the model for many more Pearson designed, but, apart from three at Truro, few were completed. St John, Red Lion Square, was to have had a similar spire and a tower pierced by similar bell openings; but in other respects it was the most Italianate of Pearson's mature designs (Plate 75). Canted to the main axis of the church and almost entirely detached (only one corner met the outer wall of the outer aisle), its position 'standing in its own strength' was obviously influenced by Ruskin, and the tower's details would have had an Italian touch. It was designed to rise plain and sheer with only shallow buttresses to give it support up to the three tiers of paired bell openings; their details were French, but this arrangement was Italian.

Though in a similar detached position against the south aisle, the Croydon tower, by distinction, would have had an English look, with tapering corner buttresses becoming set back as they rose, and three tall bell openings on each face. The Bordesley tower would have been similar though more ornate, and tabernacles were to have replaced the corner spirelets. The plainest of all, at Cullercoats, was in fact completed. Like the planned tower of St John, Upper Norwood, it is placed over the south transept. It has paired bell openings and the broached spire has tall lucarnes but no corner spirelets. This simplicity of form shows to perfection what Pearson began at North Ferriby forty years before.

75. St John, Red Lion Square: Pearson's perspective exhibited at the Royal Academy in 1878.

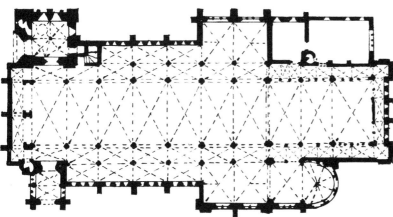

76. (facing page) St Augustine, Kilburn: Pearson's perspective of the interior looking east, exhibited at the Royal Academy in 1871.

77. St Augustine, Kilburn: the interior looking east, and plan.

50   ft

In a postscript to a letter to Scott dated 23 January 1871 Pearson had written, 'I am going to build a brick church at Kilburn and all groined but on an exciting new plan.'[8] Though this is largely masked outside, there is a hint at the west end. The sources for its features are characteristically an amalgam of English and Norman French. The rose window in the west end, a plate tracery quatrefoil surrounded by radiating trefoiled openings, is French; but its disposition over a row of lancets with, beneath, a shallow narthex with a cat-slide roof is reminiscent of Byland Abbey. What Pearson designed in the starkest simplicity for Appleton-le-Moors is here used again in a façade of great subtlety. The rose is recessed behind an arch as if the walls and vault of the nave had been allowed to progress outwards beyond it by half a bay. The gabled arch with its lower parts filled by the narthex is like the central arch of the west front of Peterborough Cathedral. On the other hand, the turrets which flank the arch are pure Norman French, from St Etienne, Caen.

The west end at Kilburn is a masterly essay in projection and recession. Progressing from the tower to its attached stairway, to its porch, to the rose window and the lancets beneath in the west end of the body of the church, to the relieving arch above them supporting the gable end of the roof, to the corner turrets and the narthex between them, plane projects upon plane. None of these forms the main west wall of the church; indeed the wall is never defined. The style of the parts is early Gothic; the projection of one beyond the next is late Gothic: the interior of Prior Crauden's chapel at Ely of about 1325 has just such a treatment of the surfaces of its walls; every feature projects from or is recessed into the wall plane in such a way that the principal plane is undefined. The wall itself is solid, but at Kilburn the exterior planes are carried through overlapping one another to the interior. That is more characteristic of baroque than Gothic architecture.

The base of the tower contains the main entrance to the church; through its vaulted interior, the aisle on the north side of the westernmost bay of the nave is reached. From here can be seen a continuous progression of quadripartite vaulted bays reaching eastwards with a flood of light from a hidden source falling across the screen dividing nave from chancel. The interior seems remarkably spacious, and it is not immediately apparent that the width of the nave is only about twenty-eight feet. The church seems higher, too, than its modest fifty-eight feet, and similarly its length is deceptive. Nothing, in fact, is quite what it appears at first sight: a number of ambiguities suggest an interior of greater size than its actual dimensions.

The lack of a clearly defined west wall is just one example. On its inner face a pair of arches similar to those of the nave arcade carry two superimposed arcades set well before the plane of the rose window at the top. Behind the arches is an apparently large, poorly lit space which, in fact, is only the same width as the aisles, a bare ten feet. The lower of the two arcades above is similarly poorly lit, but behind it a second row of arches is discernible and a further space beyond. These spaces are only about four or five feet wide, but that is not evident from below. The upper arcade stands before the five lancets beneath the rose window; the space between it and the lancets, made explicit by the good illumination from them, adds to the illusion that the dark and secretive spaces below may be much larger than they are.

The equal nave and chancel are divided only by steps and an arcaded screen; there is no chancel arch (Plate 76). They are surrounded by a continuous aisle with a gallery above, which runs down both sides of the church and across the east and west ends. The nave has outer aisles opening at the east into transepts, north and south, which are separated from the nave by the galleries over the inner aisles, carried across them on bridges.

The plan is unusual, and quite unexpected from outside (Plate 77). While the outer aisles of the nave are visible, the inner aisles are hidden, because the clerestory wall is supported not by the main arcade, but by the arcade between the inner and outer nave aisles (Plate 78). The church has, as Pearson told Scott, 'a gallery all round treated as a triforium and clerestory combined'.[9] This was not purely architectural as has often been thought, but designed for the use of the young girls during their novitiate at St Peter's Home.

Above the main arcade is a tall second arcade framing each bay of this clerestory, and this is joined to the clerestory wall by buttress walls. The late thirteenth-century Albi Cathedral has interior buttresses like this; Pearson had a photograph of the cathedral showing them (Plate 79). In spatial terms, they simplify and clarify the interior by bringing together the spaces which were formerly divided in typical Gothic cathedrals. The main arcade becomes attached to the exterior curtain wall by the buttresses, causing the aisles to disappear, the vestigial spaces which they occupied becoming recesses for chapels.

In Pearson's design the purpose is not to simplify or to clarify, but the opposite: it is to give the illusion of great size. Unlike at Albi, the internal buttresses at Kilburn are supported on the transverse arches of the inner aisle—the Albi system applies only above the level of the main arcade. The lower storey is conventional. Because the plane of the clerestory wall is not that of the main arcade but recessed from it by the width of the inner aisle, the nave seems to be wider by the width of the inner aisle than its actual dimensions.

If Pearson was consciously using the internal buttressing of Albi, he may have been inspired by a further source: St Barbara at Kutná Hora (Kuttenberg) in Bohemia. A hall church with inner aisles supporting a gallery, and outer, exterior aisles, it differs from Kilburn in section principally in having two sets of flying buttresses, not internal ones. Pearson later knew the church from Grueber's book on Bohemian churches where a section is illustrated; but whether he knew it before he designed Kilburn is an open question.[10]

In the internal elevations of normal Gothic churches the arches of the main arcade, triforium if there is one, and the vaulting are all clearly defined not only by their height but also by their relative importance. In a few cases this does not follow. At Oxford Cathedral and Romsey Abbey the main arcade embraces both the aisles and the gallery; there is a lower subsidiary arcade over the aisles—the normal relative importance of the two arcades is reversed. At Rouen Cathedral there is a lower arcade carrying a gallery constructed in conjunction with intended aisles much lower than those eventually built, for which a higher main arcade was added. Pearson knew these unusual examples just as he knew Albi, which too has arches dividing the chapel spaces in the ground storey from the clerestory. At Kilburn (Plate 80), because the main arcade is low and the aisles beyond are poorly lit in comparison with the clerestory bays, and because the upper arcade framing the clerestory is nearly as high as the nave vaulting, it is possible to mistake the upper arcade for the main one, as though this were a form of hall church with tall aisles blocked by the buttress walls between the bays. This must have been Pearson's intention: commenting on his drawing of the interior of the church, both the *Architect* and the *Building News* noted that the aisles were 'of equal height with the nave and opening into it by lofty arches'.[11]

The ambiguity between the aisles and the galleries above (themselves aisles) is echoed by a further ambiguity between gallery and clerestory. Pearson combined the two, but at an even higher level, just below the wall arches of the nave vault, he added a further vestigial clerestory with small openings. It gives the illusion of increasing the nave's height without compromising the illusion of width. It is a balancing feat of genius.

Moreover there is an illusion of great length. In part, this stems from the dissolved wall plane at the west end which is reflected in simpler form at the east. The effect is increased by the end walls rising to a greater height than the transverse arches spanning the body of the church; the vaulting of the two end bays has to rise to accommodate their increased height. This is unusual in medieval practice, although there are comparisons in the polygonal apse of the Palatine chapel at Aachen, which cants outwards before turning round the east end, and again in the great canted east window of Gloucester Cathedral; both produce similar spatial effects by slightly different means.

The effect of length at Kilburn is undoubtedly increased by the continuity between nave and chancel, a continuity which depends on the transepts being isolated from the nave by the galleries which are thrown across the openings to the transepts on bridges (Plate 81). From the west end the transepts are quite hidden. The *Architect* missed them, and noted 'a long unbroken nave of eight or nine bays . . . without transepts'.[12]

Pisa Cathedral or St Mark's at Venice might be the source of the bridges obscuring the transepts; but it is just as likely that Pearson was influenced by the strainer arches which cross the openings into the transepts at Salisbury Cathedral. His arches are, by distinction, a continuation of the arches of the nave arcade, and the bridges have two bays to match the two of the transepts. Central piers rise free of internal buttress walls through the bridges to

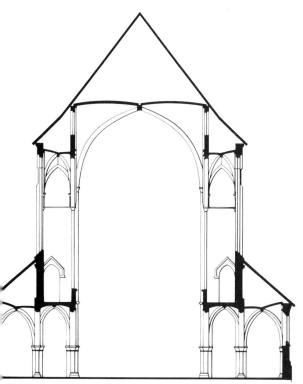

St Augustine, Kilburn: section through nave.

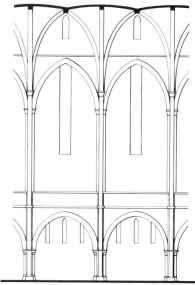

⊓⊓⊓⊓⊔ 10 ft

80. St Augustine, Kilburn:
elevation of nave.

81. St Augustine, Kilburn: the interior showing the bridge
across the openings into the north transept and part of the
chancel screen.

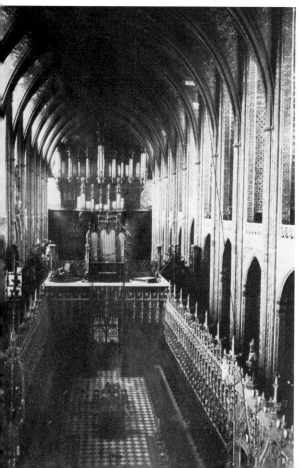

Pearson's photograph of Albi Cathedral.

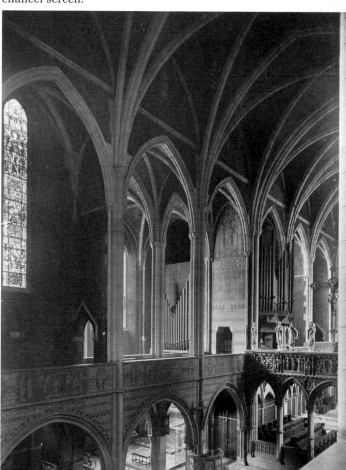

support the continuing upper arcade and the arches of the nave vault. These tall free-standing piers have an English source in the central piers of the Chapel of the Nine Altars at Fountains Abbey, which support two arches over the entrance to the transeptal chapels in just the same way. The similarity goes further: they all have four major shafts grouped cardinally round the central core and four diagonal ones, and they have water-holding bases and bell-shaped capitals.

The Kilburn transepts were criticised for being of little congregational value,[13] but they let a great influx of light fall on the chancel screen. Pearson similarly lit the high altar at Truro with a pair of eastern transepts.

The complications of Kilburn's design may seem excessive, but they are not obtrusive. The design is full of dramatic tension, yet the parts are welded together by the vaulting. The ambiguities of the separate features are almost baroque in character, but the features themselves are strictly based on medieval precedent. They achieve the effect of making the church seem vast when in fact its size is only typical of many suburban parish churches.

Henry-Russell Hitchcock sees Pearson at Kilburn starting 'a new line of vast plain churches';[14] words which reflect Muthesius who saw it as one of the largest of modern times.[15] Pearson achieved the effect he sought.

Kilburn was acclaimed: 'The church is a work of genius,' wrote the *Church Builder*;[16] 'It has about the noblest interior in London,' the *Architect* stated;[17] and the *Building News* repeated the point, finding it 'unsurpassed'.[18] Muthesius thought the interior 'solemnly church-like and sublime'; he was no less gripped by the 'picturesque and at the same time majestic'[19] exterior. Pevsner describes St Augustine as 'One of the best churches of its date in the whole of England, a proud, honest, upright achievement ... The spatial composition is original and wholly successful.'[20]

Pearson proved here that he was now the complete master of space: he could fashion extraordinarily complex volumes, and through the vaults above could resolve and unite them into one grand whole. In this, he accomplished something seldom found in English architecture, and perhaps not so successfully since the time of Hawksmoor and Vanbrugh.

Almost immediately after St Augustine was designed Bodley began his own church dedicated to St Augustine—at Pendlebury in Lancashire. He too used the internal buttressing of Albi, but to achieve an effect like that of the original. He pierced the buttresses to allow a passage through them much as Pearson did at gallery level at Kilburn, but Pendlebury has no galleries and only one high arcade which embraces the recessed clerestory; above is a wooden barrel vault. At eighty feet the church is much higher than Kilburn, and this together with the simplicity of the interior accounts for its clarity and purity. Thereafter many architects, notably Leonard Stokes, took up Albi's internal buttressing, but most followed Bodley and few approached the spatial complexity of Kilburn. The only architect perhaps to do so was Basil Champneys, and surprisingly not in a church at all but in the reading room of his John Rylands Library in Manchester of 1890–9.

12 ✠ RED LION SQUARE AND CROYDON

THE MONTH after Pearson attended the ceremony to lay Kilburn's foundation stone, he went to France. His passport was stamped at Etretat on 31 August. There was no resulting sketchbook, and probably this was just a holiday in the country he loved best. There was one last working tour. It was to Italy. Inside his sketchbook cover he wrote, 'A tour of about three weeks in April 1874.'[1]

Much of the tour was hurried, and it was presumably made by rail. He started in Turin, sketching brick cornices, stairways and an arcaded gallery. In Genoa he visited the cathedral and drew details of the nave arcade and sketched the tower and its octagonal dome. There is a large plan of the seventeenth-century Palazzo Durazzo showing the layout of some of its rooms and its staircase. Two days later he was in Pisa drawing shafts with bases and capitals (Plate 82). Next day he arrived in Siena and sketched a plan of the octagonal part of the cathedral, drawing with it a section of one of the piers. A brief stop in Orvieto followed and on 20 April he arrived in Rome.

He may have stayed there five days. Although he cannot have been in any of the towns on the route for more than a few hours, he had covered thirty-three pages of his sketchbook; in Rome he covered a further twenty-five. Above all he was attracted by marble pavements, classical and medieval (Plate 83). He drew the floors of the Pantheon and San Clemente, and drew a plan of the baldachino in the latter. There are sketches of the pavements in the Sistine Chapel, Sta Maria del Popolo, the Baths of Caracalla, Sta Maria della Pace and Sta Maria Aracoeli, where the pulpits caught his attention as well. It seems that he completely avoided the great renaissance and baroque churches and palaces of Rome and never approached St Peter's; none were sketched. On his return, however, he did visit the Palazzo Farnese and drew a detail of a staircase, noting '10 × 5 rise'; it is impossible to guess why he was attracted by this detail.

Continuing south from Rome Pearson reached Naples and stayed four days, perhaps more. Many of his drawings there are of tombs rather than the churches such as Sta Chiara and San Giovanni a Carbonara in which he found them (Plate 84). Ruskin's influence is visible in his notes of the colours of the marbles used in their construction. During his stay he took a boat across the Bay of Naples to see Capri and Sorrento, and the trip is recorded by two views.

His return journey through Italy appears to have been more rushed. He stopped a night at Assisi and made sketches showing ironwork. He presumably saw the frescoes in the churches and a photograph of them is included in his collection. Back at Orvieto he drew more ironwork before

82. Pearson's sketch of a capital in Pisa Cathedral, 1874.

travelling on. Nearly all the rest of the sketches are of Florence. They include a tomb in the Duomo and the pavement in the baptistery. He climbed up to San Miniato and drew details of the crypt chapel. Back in the city he continued sketching at Sta Croce, Or San Michele and San Lorenzo (Plate 85). The book ends with a sketch of a grille in Milan Cathedral.

Pearson did not visit Lombardy or the Veneto on this occasion, nor Sicily; however, he had many photographs from these parts and may well have been there at some time. These photographs are not all of medieval subjects: Juvarra's Palazzo Madama at Turin. Brunelleschi's Pazzi Chapel and the Cancelleria in Rome are a few examples of what he collected, the latter being especially notable, as the Golden Section governs many of the proportions of its façade; but the majority of the photographs are of medieval churches or inlaid marble floors. One building appears of which Ruskin would have thoroughly disapproved, the Certosa at Pavia; but others would have redeemed Pearson, especially the many views and details of churches in Verona and Venice and, above all, the Doge's Palace and St Mark's.

Through his visits and by studying photographs he became thoroughly acquainted with European medieval architecture. His expanding library completed this knowledge. When St Hugh's apse was uncovered at Lincoln Cathedral during his restoration, he noted that several French churches and

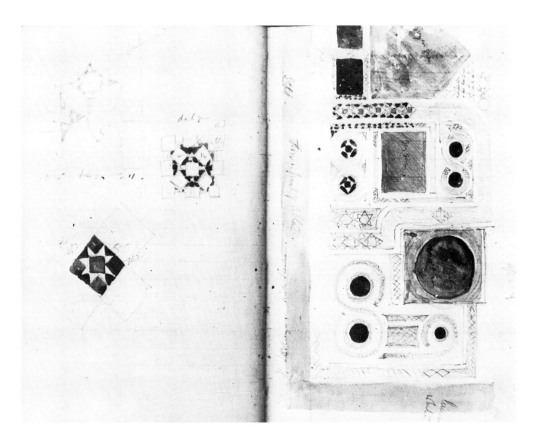

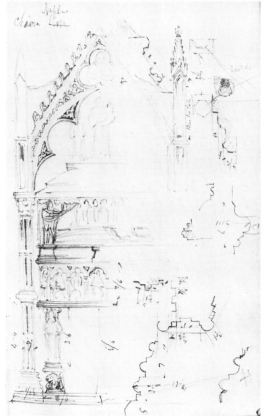

83. Marble floor before the altar in San Lorenzo fuori le Mura, Rome, drawn and painted 1874.

84. Annotated sketch of a tomb in Santa Chiara, Naples, 1874.

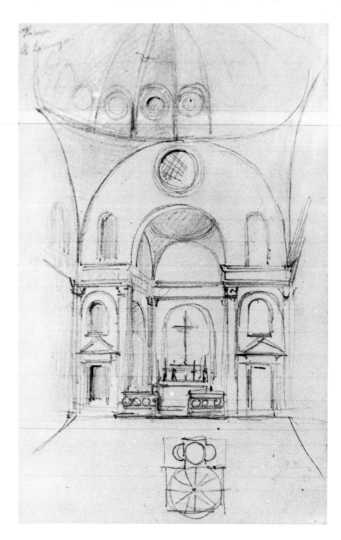

85. Brunelleschi's Old
Sacristy in San Lorenzo,
Florence; Pearson must
have felt an affinity with its
proportions in this
demonstration of his
awareness of classical
architecture.

cathedrals illustrated by Viollet-le-Duc in the first volume of the *Dictionnaire*, notably at Chartres, Fontevrault, Nevers and Vignory-sur-Marne, 'offer several curious parallels to the Lincoln arrangement',[2] and he found more at Hohenfurth, Strakonic, Humpolec and Frauenthal, which were all illustrated in Bernhard Grueber's *Die Kunst des Mittelalters in Böhmen*.

Pearson's Italian experiences immediately inspired him when, on his return, he started the design of St John, Red Lion Square, in Holborn, for William Webber. The placing of the tower was just one example. At Kilburn he was given an easy, open site. At Red Lion Square it was the opposite, restricted and awkward. On a corner of the square, the site became progressively narrower from west to east, and a terrace of houses encroached at the west end of the south side. To complicate matters, the site was to provide for not only the church but also a clergy house and parish room as well as the usual vestries.

On the open east side, Pearson placed the chancel with a morning chapel on its south side and, balancing it, a tall clergy house on the north; the parish room and vestries were in a crypt beneath the chancel (Plate 87). This gave space for a chancel only twenty feet wide. Westward the site opened out only to become constricted again by the terrace. At this widest part was the junction between nave and chancel, and Pearson put the tower with an entrance to the south alongside the street just before the terrace. The entrance led into an outer aisle screened from the inner aisle so that one had to move westwards to gain access to the inner aisle and the nave itself. To accommodate the required numbers, the nave had to be made as big as possible, and since it could not extend far to the west, Pearson made it wide, twice the width of the chancel—in fact, as wide as the chancel and its aisles together.

In solving the problem of joining the wide nave to the narrow chancel, he characteristically found ideas in medieval buildings and reworked them to his own advantage. He turned his back on any solution typical of many a preaching box in which the chancel would be a small, more-or-less unrelated space tacked onto a big nave; he turned his back on a solution recently exploited by Street, first in St Philip and St James at Oxford and then at Eastbourne and St John, Vassal Road, Lambeth, in which the easternmost nave bay is canted inwards to meet a narrower chancel, a solution which produced an untidy junction between the two parts even though it did relate their spaces in an off-hand way.

Though Pearson rejected Street's solution, it may have been through Street that he found inspiration. In his account of Spanish Gothic, Street described Gerona Cathedral.[3] It has a typically French aisled choir with apse, ambulatory and radiating chapels. Guillermo Boffiy's aisleless nave, built over a century later, is as wide as the chancel and its aisles together. The nave vault springs from the same level as the vault of the chancel and has the same curvature, but, being about twice the width of the chancel, its crown rises to about twice the height above the springing. The only concession which Boffiy made to the design of the earlier east parts was to continue the triforium openings into his own work as a link between old and new.

Another source of inspiration was Sta Croce at Florence which Pearson had just visited. Like Gerona Cathedral, Sta Croce has a nave as wide as both chancel and aisles; but there is little conformity in design between the parts. Like Pearson's design, the nave is arcaded and has aisles, and there are single, tall clerestory lights adjacent to the springing of the chancel arch, very like the ones at Red Lion Square.

What he took he made his own, just as at Kilburn; once again calculated ambiguities entered the design to provide characteristic illusions of space (Plate 86). On plan the nave arcade continued into the chancel space as the outer arcade of the chancel aisles, apparently to become lost in darkness; but at the same time the arcade stepped one bay inward at the junction of nave and chancel and then continued down the chancel sides, separating it from its aisles. It made the chancel look as though it had been placed in a larger room, or even telescoped into it. Had Pearson seen Sta Maria in Via Lata on his visit to Rome of 1874, and noted Pietro da Cortona's façade, the interior of which

86. St John, Red Lion Square, 1874–8: photograph from Pearson's collection of the interior looking towards the chancel.

87. St John, Red Lion Square: plan (the vaulting shown in the outer aisles and in the tower is conjectural).

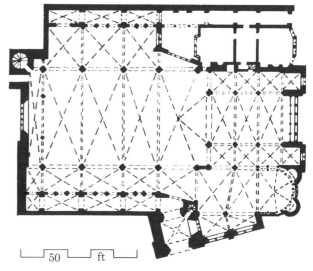

50 ft

has two rows of columns running along its width which appear to run on beyond the apsidal ends as if the apses had been telescoped into its space, he would have found an uncompromisingly baroque parallel to his own Gothic church.

Apart from the continuation of the triforium openings and the similar proportions of the chancel and nave vaults at Gerona, Boffiy made no further attempt at linking his nave to the older parts. Pearson continued the chancel triforium openings (tribune openings, really, as there was a gallery behind) on the east wall of the nave beside the chancel arch and then on its side walls.

That provided as much continuity as the arcade below, but what really united the chancel and nave was the vaulting. Without altering the height of the crown of the vaulting Pearson simply raised the height of its springing in the chancel and increased the verticality of its proportions. It was not enough to give to nave and chancel vaults rising to the same height; in order to link the two parts more firmly he used a form of vault which he had seen in the westernmost bays of St Etienne, Caen, and the church at St Martin de Boscherville (Plate 41). The vault is quadripartite with two extra ribs added to one side to spring from the divisions of a tripartite wall. Pearson used just such a vault in the easternmost bay of the nave at Red Lion Square. The diagonal ribs sprang normally from shafts which rose from the main arcade. The two extra ribs sprang from shafts attached to the chancel arch, and tied it and the chancel vaulting to the nave vaulting; in this way the spaces of nave and chancel were totally unified. The chancel arch, dramatically framed at the east end of the nave, had the proportions of the Golden Section. The interplay of spaces was baroque in character, the opening between the two purely classical; yet the means of achieving all this was medieval: partly late thirteenth-century Italian, partly fifteenth-century Spanish, partly twelfth-century Norman French. Pearson's composition transcended them all.

The detailing of the church, it goes without saying, was medieval too, and had its sources in the north of England and in Normandy. The tall lancets which Pearson had used from the early days of his career and which he had recently used at Kilburn, appeared again at Red Lion Square. The wide nave clerestory bays had pairs of them. The east end of the chancel had a magnificent array of two tiers of five lancets, the taller upper tier being graduated in height; they are like the two tiers at the west end of Ripon Cathedral.

The church was well received by the professional journals: 'Here is some original treatment of Gothic at all events,' commented the *Builder*, and other journals agreed.[4] They noted the skilful handling of the awkward site but none remarked on the junction of nave and chancel. Muthesius did say that the arrangement of the piers 'produces a special effect of the most picturesque kind', but he did not comment on the vaulting. He concluded: 'This church displays all the master's remarkable characteristics and the handling of detail that is unique to him.'[5]

St John, Red Lion Square, was built between 1875 and 1878, all except for

121

tower and spire. In the early years of the present century Frank Pearson added a small, vaulted, apsidal baptistery to the west end, but otherwise the church remained unchanged until it was hit by a stick of bombs in an air raid in 1941, and after temporary patching up was demolished. Traffic flows over its site now.

With Kilburn, Red Lion Square deserves a special place in Pearson's work because the main complexities of design appeared in the body of the church, and the side chapel was comparatively simple; in each case he designed an apsidal chamber attached to the side of the chancel with an intervening aisle. The bodies of his great town churches designed afterwards are more restrained, and complexities are reserved instead for these side chapels and their junctions with transepts and chancel aisles.

The first instance of this is at St Michael, Croydon. He was asked to provide a design in 1876 and it was exhibited the next year at the Royal Academy, but lack of funds delayed building until 1880–1. The steeple was left a stump.

The church is cruciform with a nave of five bays, the western bay serving as a baptistery and narthex with entrances on each side and a gallery supported on three arches thrown across its western half. The chancel, the same width as nave and crossing, is a little like Vauxhall, having a long bay for the choir, followed by a short bay and a semi-circular apse containing the sanctuary. The chancel is surrounded by a narrow passage aisle, reminiscent of the one in the crypt of Ste Chapelle at Paris; it is less than half the width of the nave aisles, and runs round the apse as an ambulatory more in word than deed. A small, square chapel opens off the north transept, a larger one off the south transept.

The interior elevation as well as the chancel is like Vauxhall (Plate 88); but the three storeys of the nave continue unchanged into the chancel, and the vertical members have priority over the horizontal members: vertical shafts rise from the ground to support the vaulting as at Wentworth, and break across the string courses defining the bottom of the blank triforium stage.

As at Vauxhall, the Golden Section determines the proportions of much of the interior, notably the cross section of nave and chancel, and the length and width of nave bays. These proportions give the church its overwhelming feeling of classical calm, a calm which is reinforced by the detailing.

This consists of nothing but mouldings. Gone are the vigorous and assertive carved capitals of Vauxhall. The shafts have water-holding bases and bell-shaped capitals, and in the chancel the only added enrichment is the nailhead on the ribs of the vaulting.

There is, even so, an increasing richness towards the east in the vistas produced by the arcades around the chancel. Contributing most are the shafts and spaces of the two chapels in the angles between chancel and transepts. The northern chapel is comparatively simple, but the southern one has the baroque spatial qualities which appear in the bodies of Kilburn and Red Lion

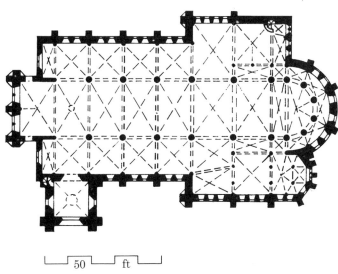

88. St Michael, Croydon, built 1880–1: the interior looking east, and plan.

50 ft

Square, but which here are restricted to this one part. The chapel has two bays. Its nave bay is covered by a single quadripartite vault; nothing apparently could be simpler. However, it is approached through a triple arcade formed by a large central arch and subsidiary side arches which suggest aisles, and this suggestion is strengthened by a similar triple arcade between the chapel nave and chancel. The nave is far too small to have real aisles divided from it by a longitudinal arcade, but the illusion was strong enough for *The Buildings of England* to describe the chapel as having 'itself a nave and aisles'.[6] The illusion is maintained by its apsidal chancel. The apse is in the form of five sides of an octagon and has a vault with six ribs to match. The eastern three sides of the vault are not supported on the end walls of the chapel but on arches carried by the side walls and two slim piers between. These are in line with the piers of the arcades at each end of the chapel nave, so the feeling of the chapel having aisles extends throughout its length. Beyond the arches round the east end of the apse is a further tiny space before the end wall, and this too is vaulted with a quadripartite vault, some seven feet by eight feet in size, flanked by a pair of lozenge-shaped vaults which each has a single rib across its shorter axis. It is only in these extra three cells beyond the apse that the tripartite transverse section suggesting aisles, and expressed so far only by the triple arcades, comes to be expressed finally in the vaulting. The whole chapel occupies a space of only about thirty-five feet by fifteen feet, yet Pearson was able to achieve so great a feeling of space as to create the illusion of a church within a church. It is comparable to the chancel at Red Lion Square, which appears as though placed within a larger church; but at Croydon the chapel is really in miniature, 'a spatial toy worthy of Soane',[7] or, to pursue the baroque allusion, worthy of Guarini.

None of this exacted comment from the architectural press. The journals looked simply at the main body of the church, the *Architect* finding it 'a very original design . . . full of marks of that feeling for proportion and detail in which Mr Pearson is never wanting';[8] and the *Builder* seeing 'real architectural genius in this design', and concluding that it was 'something quite out of the common run without any oddity or straining after novelty'.[9] Certainly the design of the south chapel is unstrained; but it has novelty or nothing.

These three great town churches brought Pearson to the climax of his career. More still were to come, churches in which he exploited a wide variety of ideas, using Gothic principles to produce a whole new range of spaces, but he had now established his style. Spatially it was based on a balance of complexity and serenity, some parts often having their germ in the fourteenth century, the proportions using the Golden Section. The detailing came from Normandy and the abbeys of Northern England with decoration severely restricted to well-tried mouldings. Despite his age—he was now sixty— Pearson had much still to build, and the principles of design which he had now throughly worked out were to serve him well through the last successful twenty years of his remarkably long life.

13 ✸ THE OFFICE

As PEARSON's practice expanded during the 1870s he came increasingly to rely on assistants. Luckily it was in his nature to do this, unlike Street who worked himself into an early grave despite an office full of budding architects who would have shared his burden had they been given the chance. Pearson had learnt the need to delegate as early as the 1840s when he employed clerks and artists to help with drawings.[1] In the 1850s he was permanently employing clerks. They mostly worked in the office but occasionally they would make surveys. In 1856 Pearson charged for extra copies of plans which his clerk had made, and the next year when he surveyed Braintree church he also charged for 'Clerks time 5 days plotting the Same. £5 5 0.'[2] By 1861 Pearson had doubled the daily rate for clerks' time to two guineas, though how far these charges were related to their wages is unclear.

As early as 1865, if not before, Pearson's office was managed by John Codd.[3] He perfectly understood his master, and none could have served with greater loyalty. Codd was a trained architect in his own right who had been elected a member of the Architectural Association in 1863, and was an Associate of the Royal Institute of British Architects. He attended to the administrative side of the practice, taking drawings of churches to the Ecclesiastical Commissioners and to the Incorporated Church Building Society for approval, and ironing out difficulties with clients. He dealt with great quantities of Pearson's correspondence as well as much important architectural work.

When Pearson was working on St Peter's Home in Kilburn, he was 'often to be seen in the new building, and Mr John Codd, his head clerk, gave us every moment he could spare'.[4] He continued to do so until his death in 1910, and after Pearson died designed a chapel for the home. In 1882 Codd's son and daughter caught typhoid fever, and were nursed back to health in the home by one of the sisters as Codd was 'very badly off and could not afford a nurse'.[5] Pearson no doubt paid Codd the standard rate for his work and that was not much. It is evidence not so much of Pearson's meanness as of his unawareness of money and his own increasing wealth. In 1885, twelve years before his death, he made his will and bequeathed to his 'valued and faithful assistant John Codd £300' and hoped that his son would continue to employ him. This was a good legacy but a tiny fraction of Pearson's estate at the time of his death.

In 1891 Codd independently designed just one important building, Bentley church in the West Riding; 'a remarkably competent design' according to Pevsner, and one which shows his employer's characteristic style without being a slavish copy.[6]

John Codd must have had a romantic disposition. In 1890 he published a book of poems: *A Legend of the Middle Ages and other Songs of the Past and*

Present.[7] It was dedicated to Sir Charles Anderson, now an old man who had ceased to play a part in Pearson's career many years before, but who was still remembered with deep affection. Lines like the following are unsurprising:

> On entering the archway, he stood 'neath a dome,
> Which outrivalled the glories of Petra or Rome,
> A single stone, stretched o'er a vault such as man
> In art's boldest flights ne'er attempted to span.
> High above, in the dim light, the fancy could trace
> Broken fragments of bosses, and weird-like, the grace
> Of columns and groin-ribs which seemed to entwine,
> As though Nature had reared the first medieval shrine.

The poems may be derivative, but Codd had both a wide vocabulary and feeling for the rhythm of words. His continual theme is love, and not always the idealized love which might be expected of a devout church architect's assistant.

> I love my Love with a loving love,
> A love as loving as love can be;
> And my Love loves me with a loving love,
> For she is a loving love to me.

> I would that my Love were a little bird
> To carol and warble from spray to spray:
> The sweetest music that ever I heard
> Were discord when matched with my Love's sweet lay.

Equally indispensable was another of Pearson's valued and faithful servants, his clerk of works, James Bubb. His father, a tile-layer, had worked at Bessborough Gardens, and perhaps James Bubb assisted his father laying tiles in the church at Titsey.[8] He began working for Pearson in the late 1850s and was clerk of works for some of his best churches, including Red Lion Square, and for Truro Cathedral. When a controversy arose over the material of which the cathedral should be built, Bubb visited every quarry in Cornwall to report on its resources. He built the crypt of the cathedral, and, when he suddenly died in 1882 of typhoid fever, his funeral, which Pearson attended, was held beside the corner stone. Bubb, 'this genial and efficient craftsman', was succeeded by Robert Swain, who had just completed work on Pearson's church at Upper Norwood. He did much to publicize the work at Truro in order to raise funds for its continuation.

From the late 1860s Pearson was assisted by many architects, serving as articled pupils or looking for experience and secure employment. Few achieved national stature, though many had successful careers, and they were indispensable to Pearson as his practice expanded. Among the earliest was William Lieper (1839–1916) who was in Pearson's office about 1870. He had a successful career in Scotland. His Camphill church in Glasgow has a steeple of exactly the same type as Kilburn's; and the body of the church also

126

89. Pearson
photographed in 1874. An
engraving of it appeared
in the *Graphic* for 9 May
1874 illustrating an
article on new Associates
of the Royal Academy.

has motives taken from Pearson's best churches, including groups of tall
lancets and other Early English details.

Another architect brought Pearson as much work as assistance. This was
his friend Charles Buckeridge.[9] He was born in 1832 or '33, was probably a
pupil of Scott's, and later superintended works for him in Oxford. Buckeridge
built up a practice of his own there and soon was busy restoring churches in
the dioceses of Oxford and Llandaff. In 1869 he came to London, but his
expectations were cut short by his early death in 1873. All his current work
was passed on to Pearson and faithfully executed by him largely as
Buckeridge had intended, some of it years after, with only minor revisions.

After his death, Buckeridge's son, John Hingeston, became Pearson's
pupil until 1879, and later assisted him. In 1886 he emigrated to Australia.
Pearson had just designed a cathedral for William Webber who had left Red
Lion Square to be Bishop of Brisbane. Pearson and Benson, now Archbishop
of Canterbury, recommended Hingeston Buckeridge to Webber, proposing
that he should execute the cathedral. It was premature: as yet there was no
money for it. Buckeridge in the meantime was able to build up a large practice

127

without help, and was far more successful than his father. Another son, Charles Edgar, assisted Pearson for a short while. He showed a marked talent for painting reredoses, but death also brought his career to an early end.

Charles Buckeridge had an assistant, Matthew Holding, who worked under him on the design of Caerphilly church in Glamorgan. When Buckeridge died, Holding moved to Pearson's office where he assisted with the execution of the design and some of the remainder of Buckeridge's outstanding commissions. Holding admired and absorbed much of Pearson's style; his own churches in Northampton clearly reflect his indebtedness: not only are they vaulted in part, but they also share many of the thirteenth-century characteristics of Pearson's mature work.

Pearson did not establish an office which trained a great line of architects, unlike Scott and Street. While they lived, he was always in the second line. Modesty was the keynote. It was a modest part he took in the affairs of the R.I.B.A., even as a member of its Council. In 1874 he deputized for Street whose wife had just died, receiving for him the Royal Gold Medal. Scott, who as President presented it, described Pearson as Street's 'valued friend and ours' and hoped that 'the time would come when Mr Pearson would receive the medal otherwise than as the deputy of another'.[10]

These were not idle words. Scott had always tried to help his friend. In January 1871 Pearson wrote to offer his wishes for Scott's return to health: 'be careful not to work so hard. There is a limit to man's powers. He may not discover it for many years but a time will come when it becomes necessary to husband his strength.'[11] Pearson continued by telling Scott about the amount of work involved at Lincoln now that he was Architect to the Cathedral, and asking advice: 'I am uncertain at what rate to charge for my time. What would you advise? I have seldom if ever charged more than 5 gns: a day. Ought I do you think to charge more considering all the circumstances?' Scott's reply is lost, but Pearson seems to have continued charging at five guineas.[12]

The letter ends with a postscript of excruciating modesty in which he begged Scott's support at the Royal Academy where his name had been put up with Digby Wyatt's and Burges's to become an Associate. 'I am afraid that I am but little known among painters and,' he justly grumbled, 'I fancy that they know but little of architecture generally and don't even know who to vote for.' He had failed the previous year, and failed again this time. Few had heard of John Loughborough Pearson.

Success came in 1874 (Plate 89). It was none too early. In 1880, following his acclaim as architect of Truro Cathedral, he was made a full Academician. He took an active interest in the Academy, exhibiting some three dozen drawings from 1849 until the year of his death. At least twice he was responsible for the hanging of the architectural section of the Summer Exhibition,[13] and he was a visitor to the Junior School of Architecture.[14] Street had revived the school and most of London's articled pupils attended classes there. Doubtless Pearson was aware of his duty to them, but duty is not inspiration and the latter they seldom got.

14 ✤ LINCOLN

In 1870 Pearson was appointed Architect to Lincoln Cathedral. It was an important step, both towards Truro, as Kilburn, Red Lion Square and Croydon were, and towards the controversial restorations of the last dozen years of his life, which, more than his own buildings, brought him to public notice.

Early in his career Pearson restored buildings by taking them down and rebuilding them stone by stone, as nearly as possible as they were before. Later he marked individual stones to enable him to reset them exactly in their former positions. Riccall church in the East Riding was closed in 1862 having become dangerous.[1] The chancel immediately received unsympathetic treatment from Ewan Christian acting for the Ecclesiastical Commissioners;[2] but that left the nave arcade tottering under the weight of the dilapidated clerestory, and the tower, which was founded on rotten logs, split on all sides. In 1864–5 Pearson took it down, marking the stones for eventual replacement, and similarly took down the clerestory and south aisle wall, except for its ornate doorway.

This was shored up and gradually pushed upright. The piers were at all angles, but firm enough. Believing that they could nevertheless bear the weight of the rebuilt arcade and clerestory, Pearson left them as a reminder of the state of the church before he restored it. So they remain today (Plate 90). The rest he rebuilt, adding a new porch to protect the Norman doorway. All this was in replica, and more: it was nearly all built of the same stones replaced in their original positions. The work was expensive: it cost over £3,000. A new nave and west tower might have cost no more, but despite their Perpendicular style the old ones were thought more valuable than new. Indeed the church retains a strong architectural and archaeological interest, which is usually lacking after such thorough restoration. Few would be prepared to call it 'a lie from beginning to end', and its superiority to Ewan Christian's facile Decorated chancel is readily apparent.

This is the best side of Pearson's restoration work. Humdrum churches received seemingly casual treatment in the name of ecclesiological propriety. Braintree church in Essex, restored between 1856 and 1867, was, according to Pearson's report, in poor repair. Worse were the furnishings: 'The W end of the south aisle is used as a school room of two storeys . . . The whole is seated with high deal pews, five feet high, steps lead up to galleries, the pulpit is in the centre of the chancel arch supported over the aisle by irons fixed to the seats on either side.'[3] The school was removed, the furniture replaced, and the galleries thrown out. The work cost more than the restoration at Riccall, indeed it was hardly less drastic, but the results are poles apart. Even so, the *Building News* called it 'rescuing the church'.[4]

Hemsworth church in the West Riding suffered similar rescue. It was a poor church. In 1812–13, nearly £600 had been spent 'repairing and

90. (below) Riccall church: view of the south side of the nave following Pearson's restoration of 1864–5.

91. (bottom) Steetley chapel, restored 1880, from the south.

92. (right) St Mary, Lastingham: the interior showing Pearson's vault, completed 1879, to complement the eleventh-century vault of the crypt.

beautifying' it, the work being done by village tradesmen without an architect, and in 1841 the vicar repaired the chancel, had all the openings renewed, the Lady Chapel recased, and a north vestry built.[5] In 1865 Pearson rebuilt the tower, south aisle and porch; he took down the clerestory and put in a new roof spanning both nave and aisles; he made new piers for the north arcade to match those of the south; he scraped the interior and lowered the floors, covering them with Minton's tiles, and added new fittings. Ecclesiological propriety may have been satisfied, but the *Ecclesiologist* of all journals described the work as 'destruction framed by the hand of the nineteenth-century Restoring Angel'.[6] The article was written by James Fowler, one of the first to attack this kind of restoration publicly. Hemsworth may have been a poor church; Pearson left it a poorer one — 1865 was a bad year, and his heart was not in the work.

Scraping, removing pews and galleries, refurnishing: these were things which Pearson did on many occasions, though in at least one case, his restoration of Westmill church in Hertfordshire, he confined himself to repairs; box pews and galleries were allowed to remain, but ten years later they were swept away by someone else.

Until late in the nineteenth century untouched medieval churches were not rare, and unless they were of outstanding architectural interest there were few to argue that they should not be adapted for modern ritual. Georgian fittings were thought less of than Victorian varnished pitch-pine ones are today. But while much was lost in the course of Pearson's restorations, much was gained. The archaeological reconstruction of Stow on the one hand, and the drastic but careful preservation through rebuilding of Riccall on the other, were works of great distinction.

The problems of restoration generally present a dilemma and lead to opposed voices among those who feel the need to express principled criticism. At Steetley in Derbyshire conservative repair was enough (Plate 91). The nave had been decayed and roofless for a century. Restoration had been proposed for some time, and not without opposition. It centred around the notion that this was 'a monstrous piece of vandalism to a picturesque and romantic ruin'.[7] 'Fears of utilitarian vandalism' became so strong that George Edward Mason who had commissioned Pearson had to protest that the work was recommended by the British Archaeological Association and 'Mr Pearson is well known as a careful restorer.'[8] The porch had suffered most: the entrance was damaged, and its gable ruinous. In 1880 Pearson rebuilt the gable, unearthed the bases of the outer order of colonettes and provided new shafts for them. Several stones were found lying around the site; they came from the porch, and where possible were replaced. The restoration could not have been more sensitive, and archaeological interpolations were few.

There were more at Hythe church in Kent. The builders of the thirteenth-century chancel had intended to raise a vault, but left it with only the springers and a transverse arch formed against the east wall. Pearson restored the chancel in 1886–8, and feeling strong sympathy for its fine Early

English detailing completed the three bays of quadripartite vaulting. The church gains immeasurably even though its history has been falsified. No one spoke against that. His vault at Lastingham in the North Riding added during his restoration of 1880 is a complete falsification, yet Pevsner describes it as 'a sensitive, appreciative and ... courageous job' (Plate 92).[9] Architectural propriety was ever dearer to Pearson than the accidents of the past. He was after all, an architect.

That is not to deny that he could be careful and sensitive. His repairs to Swimbridge church in Devon of 1878–80 are an illustration. 'The whole of the windows excepting three in the North Aisle wall are new,' he reported, 'and I am informed are exact reproductions of old ones which they have replaced. I very much regret however that these windows have been dealt with, for they might otherwise have been restored in a more conservative way and with more of the old character in the workmanship.'[10] His own conservative repairs maintained that character, and the restoration of the splendid fifteenth-century rood screen leaving much worn wood could not have been better done. The other lavish fittings, especially the post-Reformation font, would have appalled many of Pearson's generation and been swept away, but, aware of their rarity and craftsmanship, he determined to keep them.

The restoration of Lincoln Cathedral began in a conservative way too. His report of 1874 emphasized the south-west tower, which was unstable. The pressure of the tower on the Norman work below had caused severe fractures in the masonry, and although the front was well founded on rock, it needed to be tied to keep it from splitting apart, and the fractures needed to be filled. 'It is curious,' Pearson wrote, 'to note upon how little masonry the western towers stand at the level of the upper gallery of the western front.' He proposed a course of repair, concluding, 'Lincoln now stands alone amongst the Cathedrals in that as yet nothing has been done towards a thorough restoration'; that, he said, should be 'careful and conservative'.[11]

The Dean and Chapter did nothing. Pearson's report of 1875 listed proposals for the whole church. The west front needed attention at a possible cost of between £8,000 and £10,000, and general repairs to stonework might cost over £50,000. At the same time, he suggested restoring the western spires which had been removed many years before.[12] Not surprisingly the Dean and Chapter were in no mood to consider that.

Instead, with so much money at stake, they called for a second opinion, and, with Pearson's approval, asked W. H. Barlow, the engineer who had designed the celebrated train shed at St Pancras Station. He approved Pearson's proposals: it was inadvisable to restore the verticality of the west front, but it must be secured, especially to support the south-west tower.[13] The Dean and Chapter were convinced. Work began and continued until the end of 1880. The façade was tied together, and the newel inside the southwest corner reinforced to bear the weight of the tower which had been so inconsequently built over it. Apart from minor repairs, this concluded the work. It was careful and conservative, and sufficed for fifty years. Pearson's wish to improve on what he found was quickly forgotten.

15 ✠ TRURO

NOTHING brought success to Pearson's career so much as Truro Cathedral.[1] As everyone pointed out, no new cathedral had been built in England for the Anglican faith since St Paul's, and that was only a replacement; otherwise one had to look back to the Middle Ages. Even so, this success was tempered by his diffidence and by declining interest in church building. The cathedral, too, lacked the final touch of genius he had given to his last three town churches.

Plenty of explanations can be found for this. There was a vociferous building committee to be satisfied, and, more formidable, there was Bishop Benson.[2] His over-riding requirement was to have a cathedral; not a large church, certainly not an enlarged parish church, but a cathedral which should look like a cathedral in a traditional sense, and serve an ancient faith with revived forms of worship in a revived ancient see.

As long before as 1847 the first attempt had been made to revive the See of Cornwall. It was a drawn-out process, and only in 1876 was the Bishopric of Truro Bill passed by Parliament. In 1877 Edward White Benson was appointed as first bishop. He came to Truro from Lincoln where he had been chancellor and chaplain to the bishop, and, no doubt, acquainted with Pearson.

A scheme of enlargement of Truro parish church was prepared by a local architect, J.P. St Aubyn,[3] but Bishop Benson was determined that Truro should have a new cathedral to rival the achievements of the Middle Ages. In 1878 he formed an executive committee with powers to obtain an architect by means of a competition limited to Bodley, Burges, Pearson, R. P. Pullan, St Aubyn, John Oldrid Scott and Street.

Bodley, Burges and Street were well-established architects and John Oldrid Scott, whose father, Sir Gilbert Scott, had died only weeks before, was to inherit some of his father's position. Street, although seven years younger than Pearson, was the best known among them, and had achieved additional fame as the architect of the Royal Courts of Justice. With Henry Clutton, Burges had won the Lille Cathedral competition, and later he had built St Finn Barr's Cathedral at Cork in Ireland. Bodley had never built a cathedral but, quietly and modestly like Pearson, had built many fine churches and established a good reputation. Pullan was the least known of all; he had designed some churches and had also entered the Lille Cathedral competition. St Aubyn, rather better known, had built churches in the West Country, Essex and London.

From as early as the Royal Exchange competition of 1839, competitions had proved to be a poor way of obtaining a design, inevitably stirring up general controversy, and resentment among the losers.[4] The Government Offices competition provided the occasion for the Battle of the Styles; and the New Law Courts competition of 1866–7 was no less punctuated by controversy even though style was not an issue. All but one of the architects selected to provide competing designs for Truro Cathedral expressed strong disapproval of so dignified a work being degraded by submission to competition. The committee bowed to this, amended its conditions and decided to allow the seven architects the choice of submitting drawings or photographs of their executed cathedrals or large churches instead of producing a design.

The change in the terms of the competition reduced the chances of a recurrence of the fiasco which led to the adoption of Street's design for the Law Courts; the choice would be between architects, not designs which might or might not be executed. Nevertheless, Pullan and St Aubyn sent in designs; J. M. Brydon sent in a design even though he was not one of the architects invited to compete;[5] and a design by James Hicks was illustrated in the *Building News* but not sent to the committee.[6]

Even Bodley sent in a design.[7] He believed he had made certain of winning by entering a complete set of drawings with numerous alternatives on fly-leaves. His office thought them better omitted as likely to confuse the committee. His cathedral was to include two towers over the transepts, like Exeter, and two bays of the old parish church as a Lady Chapel. Together with this, Bodley sent a perspective of his newly erected church at Hoar Cross in Staffordshire. Hoar Cross church has a truly cathedral-like crossing tower and chancel, the tower being reminiscent of Durham Cathedral; and the sumptuous vaulted chancel has decorations as fine as they are rich.

Of the remaining architects, Burges sent his designs for Lille, Edinburgh and Cork Cathedrals of which only the latter had been built; Street sent his design for Christ Church Cathedral, Dublin, and the design of his nearly completed nave for Bristol Cathedral; and Oldrid Scott sent drawings of a few parish churches and his father's Edinburgh Cathedral which he had helped to build.

Pearson sent no design, but sent drawings of his recent churches: Freeland, Wentworth, Kilburn, Red Lion Square and Croydon. The executive committee cast seven votes for him, the remaining four going to Bodley. The two architects were recommended to the general committee which, under Benson, formally adopted Pearson as the winning architect. For Bodley it was the greatest disappointment of his life.

Accepting his appointment, Pearson said with characteristic modesty:

> I shall have very great pleasure indeed in undertaking the work at Truro. At the same time, I much fear that I may not be able to realise all that may be expected of me, and all that I myself would desire. I feel it is a great privilege to have to design and build such a work and I had scarcely dared to hope that the chance of doing so would ever come to my lot . . . I can only say that I will endeavour to do my best, with the means you may anticipate being able to lay out upon it.[8]

93. Truro Cathedral from the south-east in 1895, showing St Mary's aisle, preserved from the old parish church.

134

95. The abbey of Jumièges: the west front.

The design posed several problems. The site in the lowest part of the town was small and difficult, and hemmed in by houses. Occupying most of the east part was the parish church which the building committee assumed would be swept away; the tower was only a hundred years old and the rest including the Perpendicular east end was in a very poor state of repair.[9] Nonetheless, the newly formed Society for the Protection of Ancient Buildings appealed against its destruction. Despite that, the general opinion was that Pearson should not 'cripple his design' merely for the sake of antiquity.[10]

Nevertheless he decided to keep the south chancel aisle of the old church: it was the best preserved part and architecturally most interesting; it would serve for parochial services and private prayer, much as his side chapels served in his recent town churches, as well as being a reminder of the old church (Plate 93). The bishop and building committee called it 'tinkering up rotten stones', but Pearson said he would 'grieve beyond anything if it were done away with', arguing that it would cost as much to build a new chapel as to restore the old aisle.[11] In fact it cost more than he anticipated, but everyone was so pleased with the result that they only praised him. It gave the cathedral its one stroke of genius.

The constricted site for the new cathedral would only allow a building the size of Ripon or Rochester Cathedrals; and, being in a valley surrounded by houses, this was not an auspicious beginning for a design intended to dominate the town. English cathedrals are characteristically expansive in design, gaining their monumentality from great length rather than from great height. That was impossible at Truro. Worse, Cornish churches—low, unvaulted and seldom with spires—offered no help at all.

94. (left) Truro Cathedral from the north-east.

137

96. Truro Cathedral: Pearson's perspective from the south-west, exhibited at the Royal Academy in 1880.

97. Truro Cathedral: the plan of 1878–9 (omitting the cloister and chapter house) based on one given in Newber₁ which, significantly, does not show the nave angled; this was introduced only when its construction was begun.

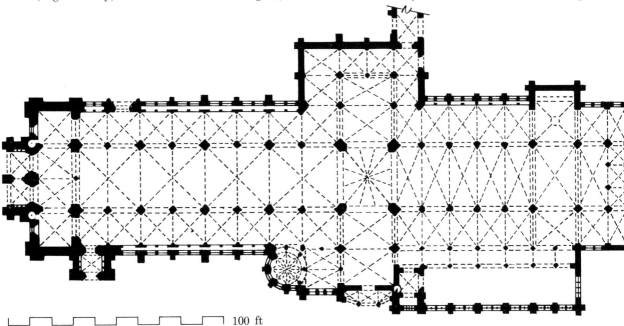

100 ft

To achieve a monumentality to rival the Middle Ages, Pearson had to build upwards. He must look to France. There was no other choice. Subsequently, he was criticised for planting an alien building on Cornish soil. It may not be Cornish, but despite its partly French plan and details, it is not altogether alien. The cathedral is cruciform with two sets of transepts; there are twin towers at the west end, a larger central tower over the main crossing, and a square east end. The main source of these features is Lincoln Cathedral; that would please Bishop Benson, if not Cornishmen. Pearson reworked Lincoln's plan, reducing its size, making it tighter by lessening the projection of the transepts and removing other excrescences, and giving it a conciseness which is characteristically French. That was to please himself.

The tall towers and spires leap upwards to dominate the town; like Kilburn's their inspiration comes from Normandy (Plate 94). The west towers of St Etienne, Caen, overwhelm the west front of the abbey; at Lincoln, by contrast, they rise behind the curtain wall like 'prisoners looking over the bars of their cage'.[12] In the best Gothic designs, the towers are assimilated into the west front without losing their ascendancy. Pearson sought to incorporate his towers in such a way that they would not overwhelm the front but would neither be masked by it. Perhaps he was inspired by the Abbey of Jumièges where the west end of the nave projects a little forward of its flanking towers, thus avoiding the dominating effect of their great height (Plate 95). At Truro (Plate 96), the section of the nave and its vault is expressed by the relieving arch over the rose window just as at Kilburn, and, similarly, the end wall of the nave is flanked by two turrets of Norman French pattern, which stand before the inner corners of the towers, reducing their otherwise overwhelming effect, and preparing the way for them rather than obscuring them (as do, for instance, the turrets which rise up the outer corners of the west towers at Coutances).

The east end of Truro, by distinction, is uncompromisingly English, being based on the north transept of Whitby Abbey. Both have tiers of triple lancets, the central ones being subtly larger, and a rose window above the gable, all set between buttresses which rise up to octagonal turrets.

The cathedral neatly fits into the southern part of its site with roads close against each end and the south side. On the small amount of spare land remaining to the north Pearson planned a small lop-sided cloister like Salisbury's and an octagonal chapter house, neither of which has been built (Plate 97).

The axes of nave and choir are slightly angled; there is ample medieval precedent for this, but the reason is to overcome the constraints of the site and to allow for the retained aisle of the old parish church. This aisle, now known as St Mary's aisle, determines the plan of the east parts. It lies on the lowest part of the site, its floor being well below the nave floor and even lower still than the floor of the choir. The problem was to buttress the choir on the south side without interfering with the continuity of the spaces between it and St Mary's aisle. To the north, the thrust of the vaults is taken down by buttresses from the clerestory over and across the vault of the north aisle, and then by further buttresses down its outer wall to the ground. These last buttresses had to be omitted on the south as they would have cut through the space between the south choir aisle and St Mary's aisle. The thrust from the choir vault is taken down across the south aisle vault as it is on the north, and then it is taken by massive transverse arches carried over an outer aisle before St Mary's aisle by the piers of arcades which separate it from the neighbouring aisles. It is an ingenious and successful solution, and it provides a characteristic vista of shafts and vaulted spaces to enrich the east end (Plate 98).

The nave elevation is of three storeys: arcade, tribune and clerestory (Plate 99). The arcade storey and the clerestory are equal in height; the tribune is just half this height. The various parts of the elevation fall within a grid of squares, so relating them to each other in a classical rather than a Gothic manner.

The width of each pair of nave bays, that is from one major pier to the next, is the same as the height of the ground storey up to the string course defining it and dividing it from the tribune. The square so formed is vertically divided by the minor pier and similarly horizontally divided into equal halves by the line of the tops of the capitals of the arcade piers and the springing of the arches. Thus each double bay of the ground storey is made up of one large square divided horizontally and vertically into four equal small squares. Another equal small square embraces a single bay of the tribune. A large square similar to those of the main arcade delineates a double bay of the clerestory. Like the double bays of the main arcade, the clerestory can be divided vertically and horizontally into four small squares, the horizontal divisions being the springing of the arches of the pairs of clerestory lancets and the springing of the transverse bisecting arch of the sexpartite vaulting, and the vertical divisions being the shafts supporting the bisecting arches of the sexpartite rib-vault.

While the elevation of the nave is delineated by this series of squares, the transverse section of the cathedral is characteristically based on the Golden Section. The height of the springing of both the transverse arches of nave and aisles are determined by it, and so too are the positions of many of the features of the east and west walls.

Truro demonstrates Pearson's ideal Gothic interior harmonized by classical proportions. Simple mouldings locate and differentiate the various elements of the design rather than adorn it, and piers and shafts demonstrate the structural logic of the Gothic system.

Apart from the unvaulted St Mary's aisle, much of the cathedral has quadripartite rib-vaults. The exception is the nave, which has sexpartite vaults, a logical but archaic covering to the major and minor piers of its arcade. It comes from Pearson's beloved Caen (and numerous other places with early Gothic vaults). The double nave bays are nearly square, being slightly wider than long, and it may be that he wished to retard and soften the pace from bay to bay, which would have been quick and staccato had the bays been given identical piers and quadripartite vaults; such vaults would have been over twice as wide as long. Perhaps, given the relatively short nave (little over 125 feet compared with over 200 feet at Lincoln), he did not wish to make the feeling of progression from bay to bay too urgent; but equally possibly he wished to perpetuate the dissolving effect on the individual bays of Lincoln's tierceron vaults, but chose to do so with vaults whose ribs have a structural rather than a decorative function (Plate 102). If nothing else, they would happily remind Benson of the vaults of Lincoln's transepts.

The crossing has a twelve-part vault, the three cells in each quadrant echoing the triple openings on each face of the tower. The vault again shows Pearson's preference for the logical use of ribs rather than for the web of liernes and tiercerons which covers the crossing vault of Lincoln Cathedral.

In the re-entrant angle between the south nave aisle and the west aisle of the south transept, Pearson placed a circular baptistery with double openings into it from each of these aisles. The openings in the nave aisles are a continuation of the arcaded outer wall; the openings in the transept aisle reflect those in the transept arcade opposite. In this way he established

Truro Cathedral: view towards St Mary's aisle from
e south transept.

99. Truro Cathedral: the interior of the nave looking west.

continuity between the aisles and the baptistery. The central piers of the two pairs of openings double within the baptistery as two of eight piers which rise at regular intervals round its walls to support its vault. The pattern of the vault is like the apse vault at Pershore Abbey. From each of its eight piers ribs rise to a central boss dividing the vault into eight cells; a further eight short ribs radiate from the central boss following the ridges of the cells to meet at smaller bosses the junctions of pairs of tiercerons rising from the eight piers. The ribs, decorated with nailhead, form a rich eight-pointed star. The functional separation of the baptistery is established by the richness of its marble floor, of the font itself and its cover suspended from the central boss, all glowing with warm colours; yet the baptistery is no mere excrescence, but seems to be a logical growth from the aisles to which it is attached. Its architectural richness outshines the east end.

Pearson intended that the high altar and its reredos should be the focus of attention inside the cathedral (Plate 100). 'Upon the design of this,' he explained in 1886,

> I have devoted a considerable amount of time and study for upon this feature I rely more than upon any other for giving dignity to the general design of the interior of the Cathedral, it being the centre and culminating point of the choir. I propose to execute it in the finest Bath stone so that it shall have the effect of being part and parcel of the building.[13]

To heighten the effect, the reredos is brought into prominence by the flood of light falling on it from the eastern transept windows, much as the chancel screen is highlighted by the transepts at Kilburn. The reredos is unfinished and its square effect is not what Pearson intended; that is a pity. Also a pity is the dull carving by Nathaniel Hitch of Pearson's hierarchical design.

Through illness, Pearson's plans were shown in an unfinished state to the building committee in May 1879; they were completed in June some ten months after his selection, and were accepted on 4 August. Benson was pleased and thought that the new cathedral would rank among the noblest in the land 'for grace, for religiousness, for simplicity'.[14] Four drawings were exhibited at the Royal Academy in 1880 and their appearance coincided with the stone-laying ceremony. The design was generally praised, praised for its 'perfection', 'purity' and 'majestic severity'. The *Building News* said Truro was 'equal to anything which this gifted architect has yet produced and we question if any other living architect would have produced a more suitable and masterly design.' The central tower and spire it described as 'the grand apex to the bounding outlines'.[15]

The foundation stone was laid on 20 May, according to *The Times*, 'with princely state, with religious solemnity, with mystic ceremony, and with a pomp and glitter almost barbaric in its splendour'.[16] Pearson was already used to ceremonies like this even if it was the most splendid he ever attended.

100. Truro Cathedral: Pearson's photograph of the choir seen from the crossing.

101. Pearson's photograph of Truro Cathedral showing the east parts from the south as they were completed in 1887; the scaffolding is just being removed from St Mary's tower.

He would join processions and hymn singing with good heart, but not what *The Times* called 'mystic ceremony'. The Prince of Wales laid the stone in his capacity as Duke of Cornwall. Beforehand he had told Bishop Benson that, as Grand Master of 'an ancient fraternity which from its earliest days had been identified with all that is beautiful and grand in architecture',[17] he would like the traditional masonic symbolism included in the ceremony. The idea appealed to the Lord Lieutenant of Cornwall, Lord Mount Edgcumbe, who was not only chairman of the Cathedral Building Committee but Provincial Grand Master as well. So the Prince insisted that Pearson be made a freemason before the main ceremony. He had to submit to this with whatever grace he could summon. His discomfort was aggravated because the Prince was assisted by the architect and prominent freemason John Gibson who was the designer of a few churches for assorted noncomformists and of some well-known banks. Perhaps Pearson forgave him, he was a fellow server on the Council of the R.I.B.A., but the Prince was another matter; Pearson stubbornly resisted the Prince's wishes thirteen years later when they were next thrown together. As for freemasonry, he ignored it.

The day's ceremonies were at last completed and James Bubb started to lay out the foundations. Almost immediately there was trouble. Although it had been suggested that the cathedral should be built in local granite, Pearson had designed it to be in Bath stone because it was easier to dress and carve. Opposition to the use of Bath stone grew. It was a Cornish building: of Cornish stone it should be built. In May 1881 Pearson conceded that part at least might be of granite, and showed how the cost would increase as more

144

was used.[18] A committee was set up to investigate the matter. In August a meeting tried to resolve the problem, but it was not until October that, with Pearson's report on Cornish quarries together with estimates for the cathedral built with various combinations, a decision was reached.[19] The cathedral was to have Carnsew granite for its exterior ashlar, with Box-ground (or at Pearson's discretion Doulting) for dressings, and the interior was to have St Stephen's granite as ashlar and Bath dressings.

This was a compromise, and as far as the interior went, unobjectionable. For the exterior, the choice of granite for the ashlar and the softer Box-ground for the carved work, much of which projects, was bad, as the hard and impervious granite would throw rainwater on the softer stone leading to its early erosion. This has indeed happened and some dressed and carved stone has weathered badly.

On 3 November 1887 the completed east parts together with the crossing, the stump of the central tower clear of the roofline, both transepts and two bays of the nave with the baptistery were consecrated (Plate 101). Benson— now Primate— was highly pleased with the new cathedral: it was 'far finer and purer than we dared to hope'.[20] The architectural press generally praised it and the *Builder* said of the junction of St Mary's aisle with the new work that 'a more happy instance of making an architectural beauty out of a constructive difficulty has seldom been seen: it is a thing done in a true architectural spirit.'[21] The decoration and the fittings were another matter. Sumptuous they might be, but many critics thought them commonplace: there was too much of the 'ecclesiastical art-furniture shop'.[22]

A more serious criticism had been voiced as early as 1882. While the design shows 'Pearson at his best . . . the most complete master of reproduced Gothic architecture since the death of Scott', the *Builder* saw 'not a new thought in the design; it is simply a Mediaeval cathedral over again.'[23]

That, of course, is what Benson wanted, but it has been the basis of all adverse criticism ever since. Muthesius saw in the cathedral the seeds of the general failure of Victorian architecture to achieve modernity: 'To him who seeks the link between modern works and the present day which must come out of a healthy cultural situation, this building can hardly count as the climax of a life's work, a life's work moreover of the richness of Pearson's.' Truro may be 'powerful' and 'magnificent', but even so it

> requires for the uninitiated an explanation that this is a new work and that it is not the plan of an old English cathedral . . . When the old master-builders had to make do with a nave span of $28\frac{1}{2}$ feet in a structure the size and importance of Truro, it was imperfections of technique that dictated it. To imitate this to the letter today, as happened at Truro, is an embarrassment and shows a lack of independence which would have been tolerated in no earlier age.

At Red Lion Square Pearson had vaulted a span of forty feet in a remarkably free design which exploited a difficult site. The site at Truro imposed its restrictions: the cathedral could be no longer, and given his chosen plan and desire exactly to regulate its proportions, the width was thus determined. Size for its own sake was of no account—even to produce greater monumentality.

Deferring to Benson, Pearson was unwilling to depart as far from precedent as he had done in his recent churches. As the *Builder* noted, 'Mr Pearson is really at his best in some of his smaller churches, rather than in this mere resuscitation of the architecture of the past.'[25] That is partly true, but hard. Pearson was not merely resuscitating the past; as in his recent churches, he was reusing it in new combinations, here to create an ideal.

This was not apparent to most critics. E. S. Prior wrote condescendingly that Truro was 'a not unworthy representation of the ambitions of and faculties of the nineteenth-century architect. It has an expression of culture, and here and there some invention of design.'[26] Prior's own buildings, especially his church at Roker in County Durham, are full of invention of a very personal kind; but he never built a cathedral.

With more justification he criticised Pearson's 'flagrant misuse of opportunity' in not giving Truro 'a generous local expression from the rough dressed granite', but bringing in its place 'the cheese-cut Bath stone of commerce—the mildest vehicle of jerry-building ambition'. Prior rightly saw the cause of this:

> Pearson, as a nineteenth-century architect was held tight in the chains of his professional status. Having learnt his Lincoln Cathedral . . . he could only use a stone in which the Lincoln detail could be worked. The popular and successful architect was obliged to repeat himself and give his clients what they had been trained to expect.

Here lies the crux of the matter; despite Muthesius, Truro does embody the spirit of its time, its strengths and weaknesses. In essence the whole nineteenth-century church-building movement was backward looking, academic yet romantic. If historicism can be accepted, Truro is a *tour de force*. If it cannot, three or four hundred years of architecture stand dismissed.

Prior had more—too much—to say about resuscitating the past:

> By Pearson the life of Gothic is revived as a drama in acts. One sees the whole style of 'Early English', its pauses and phases one by one. Though in Truro quire built straight away, they succeed one another as if a century were fancied between the scenes; as if masons worked and grew old and their children learned a new craft in the wings of the theatre.

Francis Bond expanded on this:

> The crypt is in the massive style of the latter years of the twelfth century; the choir is supposed to have been commenced in the early years of the thirteenth century; but since . . . the aisle windows are lancets, while those of the clerestory have early plate-tracery, we are to imagine that the upper part of the choir was not finished before the middle of the century.[27]

. Truro Cathedral: nave vault.

So he goes on. It is all convincing stuff, but misses the point. Pearson was not playing archaeological games. The crypt may appear older in style than the clerestory, but the reason is propriety. Who would design an elevation which increases in massiveness and decreases in decoration as it rises? One might as well accuse the first builders to set an Ionic Order on a Doric, and a Corinthian on the Ionic, of attempting to suggest that several decades passed between the erection of their three storeys.

Bond makes strange reading today. 'There is real interest in tracing the meanders of Mr Pearson's scholarship,' he says,

> Because it is but a reproduction of the planning, construction, and detail of a bygone age, it does not follow that the design is unjustifiable or uninteresting. Mr Pearson was just as much at liberty to reproduce at Truro a thirteenth-century type of ecclesiastical architecture, as Alberti and Brunelleschi to resuscitate the art of Imperial Rome at Mantua and Florence for the edification, instruction, and delight of mankind.

Did he really mean to honour Pearson by comparing him with Alberti and Brunelleschi? In the early years of this century it seemed that revivalism was about to give way to the long-awaited modern style, and the real trouble with

147

Truro was that it belonged to the last, dying years of revivalism, just as Brunelleschi's Foundling Hospital belonged to the first.

Bond's verdict on Truro was prejudiced by his hopes for Liverpool, a cathedral which he thought would break out of the constraints of revivalism. Truro, he wrote, was 'admirably adapted for the ritual of the Church of England as it was in the thirteenth century'. In fact it was admirably adapted for the revived ritual of the Oxford Movement which Benson was anxious to foster. Liverpool would be thoroughly modern:

> In design as well as in plan, the cathedral is a revulsion from the 'Imitative Gothic' which has been the vogue for more than half a century, and which found final expression in Truro cathedral; Liverpool cathedral cannot be labelled as 'Early English' or 'Decorated' or 'Perpendicular'; it is none of them . . . it can hardly be doubted, however, that its vastness of scale, the free handling of the masses, the depths of its shadow effects, the stern sobriety of the exterior, and the general absence of frippery, will make it one of the most grave, solemn, and monumental buildings of Christendom.[28]

High hopes! The cathedral is certainly impressive for its vast scale, that above all things; but it is 'Gothic' and in its way 'imitative'. It no longer appears as the antithesis of Truro. Perhaps through its vastness lies one failing which at least cannot be levelled at Truro. Truro was complete within thirty years: after seventy Liverpool was not.

Truro is a compromise. For that one can blame Pearson's response to a formidable client and the impress of his times. If Benson shares the responsibility for the cathedral being the shape it is, at least he could not have found a better architect to fulfil his desires: neither one with greater knowledge to produce such a design, nor one to accept his client's wishes with such sympathy. Without Benson, the cathedral would not have been started; without him and his successors it would not have been finished. They and Pearson's design inspired the desire to complete the building, a desire which coaxed money from the inhabitants of a poor county and led to a resumption of work in 1897, sooner than many expected.

By October 1898 the foundations of the nave had been laid. In 1903 it was complete and blessed, and the crossing tower was raised. In 1910 the addition of the west towers brought the building of the cathedral to a close. In 1935 one bay of the cloister was added, but thirty years later Pearson's designs for the rest and for the chapter house were abandoned.

The nave, the *Builder* said ungenerously, 'adds little but completion'.[29] An ideal architecture needs completion. Completion, too, expresses the certainties of the Victorian age. Characteristics of all three phases of its revival of the Gothic style are there too—in its archaeological correctness, in the bold massing and bounding outline of its exterior, and finally in its proportions and the subtle inter-relation of the spaces around the baptistery and around St Mary's aisle. Pearson was at his best in his churches; yet, despite all, Truro Cathedral is a qualified masterpiece.

16 ❦ SUCCESS

IN THE nine years which elapsed between Pearson's appointment at Truro and the completion of its east parts, he designed fourteen new churches. It was an astonishing feat for a man in his sixties who had not previously been prolific. Even as he lived through his seventies his output hardly fell, and right up to the last months of his life he brought forth designs which had all his best qualities but were nonetheless fresh and original.

Almost as soon as Truro was started, came the design of St John, Upper Norwood, Surrey; the plans are dated November 1878 but no work was done until 1881 when, just three years after the foundation stone was laid, the first bricks were placed upon it. A year later the chancel with two bays of the nave was dedicated and in April 1887 the church, completed except for its steeple, was consecrated by Archbishop Benson.

The nave has five bays, the western one containing a complicated arrangement of entrances with inner and outer vestibules, flanking an enclosed baptistery, leading from an exterior narthex. The cruciform plan is typical of Pearson, but the church is unusually wide (Plate 103). The nave bays are twice as wide as long, and as wide as they are high up to the springing of the vaulting arches—a much lower proportion than the Golden Section. This is partly offset by a tall clerestory, which is set in deep reveals with a gallery below.

The east end of the church is dominated by two tiers of five lancets, skilfully graduated in width, which fill the upper part of the east wall (Plate 104). Set before them, another wall rises above the reredos and contains identical but unglazed openings. Each space between the openings in the two walls is ceiled by its own quadripartite vault. This architectural enrichment of the east end is continued in the vaulting of the east bay. Like the eastern nave bay at Red Lion Square, it is a quadripartite vault with two extra ribs; these spring from shafts running up between the outer two and the central three lancets. This produces a richer effect at the east end and more tightly binds the unusually wide east wall to the vaulting, yet it softens the eastern boundary of the chancel by obscuring the planes of the two walls.

Following hard on Upper Norwood, the design of St Alban at Bordesley, Birmingham, was complete early in 1879 and the church was started almost immediately, the foundation stone being laid at the beginning of 1880; the church was opened the following year.

Perhaps needing to conserve his energy, Pearson made Bordesley very similar to Croydon. The two have almost identical plans with practically the same dimensions (Plate 105). That is not to say that Bordesley does not have a separate personality; it has an original arrangement of entrances in the western bay of the nave, and its south chapel is differently treated. It lies immediately next to the chancel with no intervening aisle. A single bay with a

103. St John, Upper
Norwood, designed
1878: view of the
interior, 1881–7,
looking east, and
plan.

104. (facing page)
St John, Upper
Norwood: east bay of
the chancel.

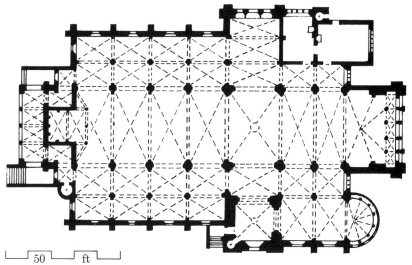

50 ft

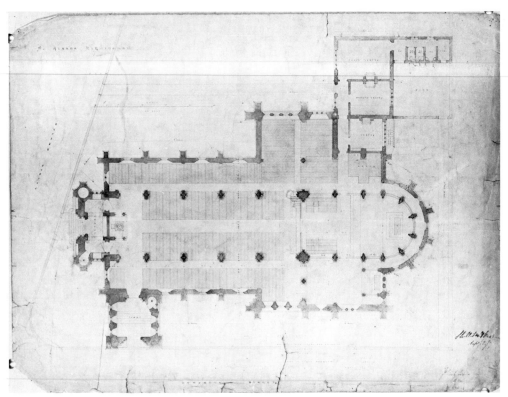

105. St Alban, Bordesley, 1879–81: plan.

quadripartite rib vault represents its nave and another suffices for its chancel. The eastern cell of the chancel vault, though, has two extra ribs springing from the piers of a triple-arched, screen across the eastern side; it is again just like the vault at the east end of the nave at Red Lion Square. At Bordesley the vault ties the three arches firmly into the space of the chapel's chancel bay. Beyond the central arch of the arcade is a further tiny square bay acting as a canopy for the altar; it has its own tiny quadripartite vault and a three-light window in its east wall. The bay is flanked by two side bays similar in size and these suggest aisles otherwise unexpressed in the chapel. The south bay stops in a single-light window; the north bay opens into the narrow ambulatory round the apse. The chapel is more tightly united to the body of the church than its counterpart at Croydon, but its planning is not quite so complex.

Making up for this is the arrangement of the western entrances, a development of design of Upper Norwood. The nave projects by one bay to the west of its aisles, and at ground level is transversely divided into three. The central section forms an external vestibule and is entered from a large gabled west door. In its side walls, two further doorways lead into the side sections of the west nave bay, which form inner vestibules on each side. All three spaces are roofed at low level by quadripartite vaults, and above them is a gallery, just as at Croydon and Upper Norwood. Within the church, just beyond the

152

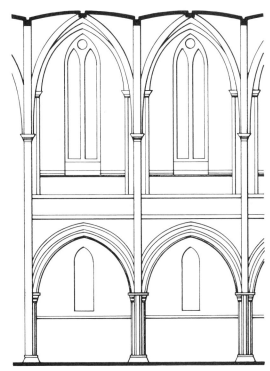

⊔⊔⊔⊔⊔⊔ 10 ft

106. St Alban, Bordesley: the interior looking east.

107. St Alban, Bordesley: interior elevation of nave.

central outer vestibule and still covered by the gallery, is the font. This arrangement of entrances and—symbolically close—the font became as typical as his treatment of the side chapels.

The interior of Bordesley is like Croydon, but while the latter has three storeys with a blank triforium, Bordesley's triforium, like Upper Norwood's, has shrunk to a mere passage with a parapet pierced by quatrefoils beneath the clerestory windows which are in deep reveals (Plate 106). That is of less note than the characteristic use of the Golden Section to govern many of the proportions, notably in the cross section, the plan of the nave bays and many elevational features such as the width and height of the clerestory (Plate 107).

At the end of the century the *Builder* could describe the church as 'the finest piece of architecture that Birmingham has to show; severe in style, noble in proportion and with almost the dignity and spaciousness of a small cathedral'.[1]

Much the same could be said of three more churches which followed in 1882 and 1883: St George, Cullercoats, Northumberland; St Agnes, Sefton Park, in Liverpool; and St Stephen, Bournemouth.

The design of Cullercoats church was ready by 1881 and it was built in 1882–4 (Plate 108). Its severe and simple plan, outline and massing, and detailing are matched by its exposed position facing the North Sea; its local sandstone and sparse carving show what might well have sufficed at Truro.

153

The church is cruciform and only the nave has aisles; there are no complexities anywhere, no side chapels, no vistas of columns, and the ingenious but simple arrangements of the western entrances renders projecting porches unnecessary. The westernmost aisle bays are open to the outside and protect entrances giving access to each side of the west nave bay, which has the usual gallery across it. The font is simply placed between the two entrances before the start of the gangway up the nave between the benches.

The nave is of three storeys, and like Vauxhall has an arcade supported by cylindrical piers, a blank triforium, and a clerestory taller than Vauxhall's with windows with plate tracery set in deep reveals (Plate 109). The arches of the quadripartite vaulting spring from shafts with bases set on the capitals of the main arcade, for which there is an appropriate northern precedent in Whitby Abbey. The individual proportions differ from those at Vauxhall, but it seems that they are set out in a similar way using the Golden Section. The three-storeyed elevation extends into the chancel, the ground-storey arcade becoming blind as there is no ambulatory, again as at Vauxhall, but the apse is polygonal, not semi-circular.

While there are no vistas of piers and spaces beyond, there is a subtle effect of perspective within the church as its width and height slightly decrease first between the nave and crossing, and then between crossing and sanctuary. The nave and crossing have quadripartite vaults. The two bays of

108. Pearson's photograph of Cullercoats church, 1881–4, seen from the south-east.

109. Cullercoats church: the interior looking east.

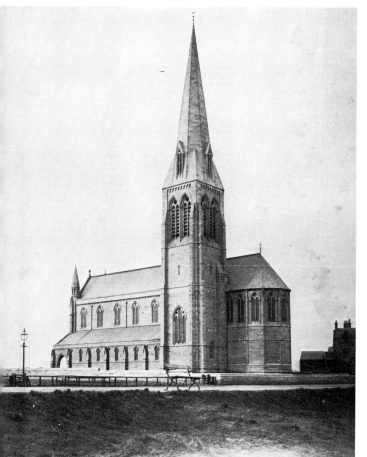

the sanctuary have a single octopartite vault, a transverse rib bisecting the vault in order to accommodate the two-bay treatment of the side elevations, and a ridge rib linking the east crossing arch with the boss from which radiate the six ribs of the apse. Pearson very seldom used ridge ribs, and here it serves the aesthetic purpose of giving continuity to the sanctuary.

Through its simplicity and proportions, the interior has an almost archaically classical feeling. So does the exterior, partly because of its symmetrical plan. Only at the crossing is the symmetry broken, and broken in the most emphatic way by the tall steeple over the south transept.

Similarly emphatic is the tall apse rising from the ground—sheer, unbuttressed and undecorated except for narrow shafts and string courses marking the divisions between bays and storeys. The lower storeys are blank; in the clerestory the lights are linked by narrow blind arches to the vertical shafts giving a horizontal continuity to this stage. The east end seems designed primarily to withstand the weather. It may have the purity which Ruskin saw in unbuttressed types, but in no way does it suggest the 'sublimity of a calm heaven or a windless noon'.

All the wall surfaces are clearly defined; all baroque feeling for space is purged from the design. It is the antithesis of Kilburn. The classical simplicity of the interior and the plainness of the exterior with the single bold emphasis of the steeple are an ideal creation, 'noble, honest, earnest, yet a little cold';[2] such is the nature of ideals.

Pearson's plans for St Agnes, Sefton Park, were completed by the end of 1882 and building began the next year, to be finished in 1885. The church has many of the characteristics of Cullercoats, notably its symmetry; but its similarities are obscured by several differences (Plate 110). Most important of these are its western transepts, additional to eastern ones; then transepts, chancel and apse are all aisled, and, with an attached chapel, there is a return to the characteristic vistas of piers and partly hidden spaces of the earlier churches; and, finally, the tower is replaced by a *flèche* over the eastern crossing, and turrets in the re-entrant angles of transepts and chancel (Plate 111).

The west front of Sefton Park shows most the similarities between the two, being framed by buttresses and having windows with the same tracery. Again from Cullercoats are the open porches in the aisle ends each side of the nave; but continuity of the west end with the rest of the church is immediately broken by the western transepts. They form a kind of large narthex with a baptistery in the northern arm.

There is a similar though simpler arrangement at All Saints, Torre, Torquay, Devon, which Pearson designed at much the same time. Both Torre and Sefton Park have four-bay naves. At Sefton Park the piers of the arcade, as at Cullercoats, are cylindrical with no attached shafts, but they support only one further storey, the blank triforium of Cullercoats having shrunk at Sefton Park to a parapet like Bordesley's for the passage which runs below the clerestory.

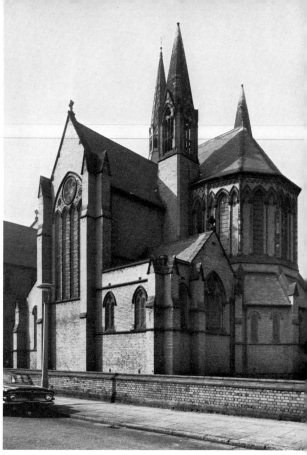

110. St Agnes, Sefton Park, 1882–5: seen from the north-west.

111. St Agnes, Sefton Park: the east end seen from the south-east.

The main crossing, as at Cullercoats, contains the choir, and the sanctuary follows in the apsidal east end. A sexpartite vault covers it, and its eastern transverse arch cants outwards to meet the boss from which radiate the ribs of the apse vault, a more economical link between the two than the ridge rib at Cullercoats.

The internal vistas at the east end, so lacking at Cullercoats, are as rich as at Croydon or Bordesley. The side chapel has a nave and chancel with a square end, each of a single bay and both complete with aisles. Just as at Bordesley, the aisle on the north side doubles as the south chancel aisle and leads into the ambulatory. There is another fine vista in the main north transept under the octagon which carries the organ gallery (Plate 112). It has eight peripheral piers, all of black marble, supporting a vault similar to the one in the baptistery at Truro, but the ribs, instead of radiating from a central boss, spring from a central pier. The pattern is like Pearson's unexecuted design for the Truro chapter house, but at Sefton Park the side arches are open and linked to the north wall of the transept by further piers and ribs.

As with most of his best churches, Sefton Park is built of local materials. The exterior is faced with red Ruabon brick and has red Runcorn sandstone

112. (right) St Agnes, Sefton Park: the organ gallery seen from the north aisle.

156

dressings; their effect could hardly be more different from the dark Northumberland sandstone of Cullercoats. The harsh brick, though suggesting Waterhouse more than Pearson, does not diminish the design. The *Building News* described the church as 'one of Mr Pearson's finest works',[3] and today it is recognized as 'the noblest church in Liverpool',[4] in *The Buildings of England*. Similarly, 'the finest church in Bournemouth'[5] is St Stephen, which Pearson designed between 1881 and 1883; the west end unusually was begun first and opened in 1885, the east end not being built until 1896–8, and the tower (without its spire) following only in 1907–8.

The apse is the finest Pearson ever designed, the massing and spaces suavely balanced, yet full of fire. Over the crossing there is a *flèche* as at Sefton Park; similarly in the re-entrant angles between transepts and chancel rise a pair of turrets (Plate 113). At the east end the polygonal apse rises sheer from the ground with no visible ambulatory, just as at Cullercoats, but it is buttressed and the pitch of its roof increases some way up, suggesting that the simple exterior may hide a complex interior.

This is the chief glory of the church. It has a double treatment similar to the side elevation at Kilburn. The ground storey has an ambulatory passage, which, bay by bay, is crossed at the level of the arches of the main arcade by narrow arches bearing a pierced parapet like that running beneath the

113. (left) St Stephen, Bournemouth, designed 1881–3, completed 1898, seen from south-east.

. St Stephen, Bournemouth: the interior looking east.

115. St Stephen, Bournemouth: the apse seen from the south transept.

116. St Hilda, Darlington, 1887–8, from the south-west.

clerestory. There is no ceiling to the ambulatory at this level, and its outer wall rises up to contain the clerestory windows which are in the form of triple lancets. They are seen from the body of the church through tall pointed arches above the main arcade (Plate 114). Unlike Kilburn, where the piers carrying the arches above the main arcade are linked to the clerestory wall by internal buttresses, the piers of the apse at Bournemouth are only linked to the outer wall by the narrow arches thrown across the ambulatory passage. The thrust of the vaulting is taken down by high vaults over the ambulatory at the top of the clerestory wall and then transferred to the shallow exterior buttresses. The internal piers over the main arcade are very slender, and with the clerestory windows being much larger than they could have been had they been pierced through the narrower gap between the main arches, the apse is extraordinarily light and airy (Plate 115). The detailing, typically of Pearson, is thirteenth-century English and French; the spatial effect, however, is like that of the fifteenth-century apse of St Lorenz at Nuremburg, although it is much more tightly controlled at Bournemouth by the structural function of the vaulting ribs.

This is not mere resuscitation of medieval forms, but true Gothic in its

117. (right) St Mary, Chute Forest, 1870–5: the interior looking east.

160

full spirit of creativity. Muthesius's complaints of perpetuating 'imperfections of technique' and 'lack of independence' are completely negated by it.

Taking into account Pearson's age (he was approaching seventy when the first part of St Stephen, Bournemouth, was finished), his heavy commitments to cathedral restorations and the declining requirement for new parish churches towards the end of the nineteenth century, it is remarkable that he continued to produce fine new designs at all during the last ten years of his life. Despite his modesty, his fame was such that he was an obvious choice for would-be clients who wanted the best. If they provided him with an attractive commission, they got the best from him. For his part, he tried not to accept too much work.[6] In the mid 1880s he used a local architect, C. H. Chorley, to help him execute Headingley church. Once at least, through lack of time, he refused a small commission.[7] Otherwise, perhaps because he had neither time nor interest, or perhaps because he gave the work to an assistant, his clients sometimes got humdrum designs. His churches at Winnington in Cheshire and Treharris in Glamorgan have little to suggest that they were designed by the foremost church architect of their time; clearly they were cheap. St Mark, Barnet Vale, Hertfordshire, is one of several where funds were so restricted that only part was completed. For St Hilda, Darlington, County Durham, funds again were severely limited. At least that was recognized at the start, and in 1887 the church was designed to seat five hundred and twenty at a cost of a mere £4,500. The site did not help, tapering from west to east; but Pearson took advantage of this to provide an aisled nave, unaisled chancel, and north chapel, the last squeezed in with its sides canted inwards towards the east. The church is of plain, local brick with a minimum of stone dressings and a wooden roof with tie-beams. The chancel arch appears to be based on the Golden Section, and, together with the characteristic side chapel providing views from the nave and chancel, this gives the church a quality which raises it quite out of the ordinary. Even its poverty-stricken exterior has a fine feeling for massing; and its tall elements, and plain, strong, geometrically-shaped brick walls, shorn of ornament, suggest that the church could have been built by a twentieth-century Gothic Revivalist well after the First World War (Plate 116). It is the extreme example of what Pearson called 'my cheap churches'.[8] Others, less extreme, at Sturton-by-Stow in Lincolnshire, Hove and St Leonard's in Sussex and Hambleton in the West Riding similarly look forward to the present century. Despite their bareness, the best side of Pearson's architectural personality is there.

These cheap churches invariably have wooden roofs, though for some enough money was forthcoming at least for a vaulted side chapel. In the 1880s Pearson built a few expensive churches with wooden roofs resting on stone transverse arches, an uncharacteristic departure. His first roof like this appears in the aisles at Sutton Veny; his first church completely roofed this way at Chute Forest in Wiltshire, four years later in 1870 (Plate 117). Spanning nave and chancel are three brick transverse arches, as appear in

162

118. All Saints, Hove, 1889–1901: the interior looking east.

Italian Romanesque churches. Pearson, though, probably first saw such arches in the choir galleries of Durham Cathedral.

He first used them on a large scale at St Michael, Headingley, Leeds, where he was rebuilding R. D. Chantrell's church of 1838. The designs were made in 1882, and the church was built between 1884 and 1886 using some of Chantrell's foundations and walls. From the west, the transverse arches appear in perspective as a series of gradually diminishing frames for the east wall. They give, said the *Builder*, 'a very monumental look to the interior'.[9]

Between 1889 and 1895 Pearson rebuilt St John, Redhill, Surrey, which had been built in 1842 by James Knowles senior and had had aisles added in 1860 by Robert Hesketh, a local architect. Pearson left the aisles and replaced Knowles's nave and chancel with a vaulted chancel and a nave with a wooden roof resting on stone transverse arches carried by new shafts attached to Hesketh's arcade. Once again the arches provide a series of frames for the chancel as seen from the west entrance, and the effect is increased by the chancel being a little lower and narrower than the nave.

The type reached perfection at All Saints, Hove, Sussex (Plate 118). Here there were no restrictions imposed by a previous building, and financial limitations were few, at least at the beginning. Designed in 1887–9, the west parts were built by 1891, and the east to his slightly modified design followed in 1898–1901, after his death.

Hove is Pearson's largest parish church. Without recourse to galleries it can seat thirteen hundred. Its forty-foot nave is Pearson's widest. With a length of 160 feet it approaches Truro. Its final cost, about £40,000, makes it his most expensive church.

Because of its fine windows by Clayton and Bell, it is dark. The roof is practically invisible, adding an air of mystery which would be absent with a more visible vault. Though the transverse arches tend to separate the bays from each other, the bay-by-bay division is softened by the nave piers whose clustered shafts subtly change in outline as one progresses eastwards. It is like moving through a succession of frames formed by the nearer shafts of the piers and the lower mouldings on the soffits of the transverse arches, the only parts to catch the light.

The chancel, too, appears as a final frame for the altar and the triple window above. Narrower than the nave, it is connected to it in a quite different way from Red Lion Square. It has three bays, two for the choir and a third for the sanctuary. The two choir bays are as wide as the nave, but the chancel arch and the piers dividing the two bays are as narrow as the sanctuary and project into the choir as internal buttresses. The height of these piers related to the space between them is, as one would expect, based on the Golden Section. As the final frames for the east end, all attention falls on them. The effect is increased by the lighting: the choir has small clerestory windows; the sanctuary large ones which flood the high altar with the only concentration of light in the whole church.

Of all the square east ends in Pearson's churches, this suggests the greatest concentration of thought: subtle perspective effects, dramatic lighting, intricately inter-related spaces, ideal proportions. Here, said Goodhart-Rendel, Pearson 'gave of his best'; the chancel, he continued, 'is as nearly perfect as can be; nothing lovelier than the triplet of two-light windows (the middle one most subtly made slightly broader than the others) has been achieved since the days of Alan de Walsingham.'[10]

He had just one criticism:

The rest of the building is scarcely less excellent save for one blemish, incomprehensible in a work of Pearson's of all men. The body of the church has no vault. All this richness of moulded ashlar, this glory of fine craftsmanship depends for its preservation upon a covering of perishable burnable timber. Pearson, whose surpassing skill in the design of vaulting marks him out from among his contemporaries has here been content to let money be lavished upon non-essentials when the great need of the building was unsupplied.

Reappraising the church, Sir John Summerson takes no exception to the lack of vaulting; the nave piers and the layout of the chancel favourably attract his attention, and he describes the church as 'a masterpiece . . . a work of extraordinary subtlety'.[11]

17 ACCLAIM AND ANGUISH

Scott never lived to see it, but, as he had hoped, Pearson was eventually awarded the Royal Gold Medal of the R.I.B.A. He had already won a gold medal in 1878 at the Paris International Exhibition where he had shown several drawings including a sheet of designs for church towers; and in the same year, along with many others, he was made a Knight of the Legion of Honour. The next year he won a bronze medal at the Sydney International Exhibition.[1] These were little compared with the R.I.B.A. Gold Medal, which was presented to him in 1880 in recognition of his success at Truro. More, the President, John Whichcord, presented it 'as a tribute not only of just admiration for the noble works of architecture which you have designed, but also of sincere respect for your professional and private virtues'.[2]

Pearson was greeted with continued and hearty applause, and replied to the President's eulogy with evident difficulty:

> I have never felt more embarrassed in my life, or more unable to express my thoughts and feelings, than at the present moment. I know not how to thank you sufficiently for having paid this great compliment to me . . . and I hope you will be content to accept my simple thanks, and to believe that they are accompanied by very deep and very warm feelings . . . I owe my heartfelt thanks for the complimentary way in which you have received me this evening, which will ever be implanted in my recollection. I shall never forget it. It is something to have worked for, and to have attained, and it is something never to be forgotten.

Pearson was expressing the truth, for 'silently and perseveringly, a proud and an enviable position had been surely attained'. At last this was recognized, and on 27 November he was made a full Royal Academician.

It was a year of acclaim. Anguish followed: 1881 took a grim toll of architects; for Pearson the year became sadder as it grew longer. He had not had so distressing a time since his wife died. On 7 March his life-long colleague William Nesfield died. Five days later came the death of his old friend and comforter Dr Spyers. In April Burges died; he was not yet sixty.[3] And Pearson had further disturbances to contend with.

On 10 May he moved from 46 Harley Street where he had lived for fourteen years, and went to 13 Mansfield Street.[4] He did not involve himself in the actual move, and spent the day at Truro attending a building committee. His new house, fine and spacious, was built early in the 1770s to the designs of Robert Adam. Alone of his houses it survives and his residence and death there are recorded by a London County Council blue plaque which also commemorates Sir Edwin Lutyens in the present century. It is paradoxical that like so many of the great Gothic architects of the nineteenth century Pearson should have lived in a Georgian house. Not only that, but he designed and had made furniture for it. In 1869 he had designed a Gothic bookcase; of pitch pine, its place should be a vestry and its contents hymn books and tracts. The finely and richly inlaid cabinets which came from Mansfield Street are utterly different and would look nowhere better than in an Adam interior.[5]

Three months after the move Pearson left the sad shores of England for a rest.[6] On 6 August Street had written in his diary: 'Went to see the doctor being troubled a little with headache; he puts it down to overwork and wants me to go to the Baths of St Gervais.' Pearson decided to go with him and together they submitted to daily baths. After ten days Ewan Christian joined them, but by then Street had had enough; he went off to climb in the Alps and look at buildings before returning to join the others who had now moved on to Aix-les-Bains.

Street's health was not to improve, and as the autumn advanced it steadily deteriorated. December came. On the 14th Decimus Burton died: he was a relic of a past age. On the 17th Salvin died. He was old too, but for Pearson it was a wrench. The next day came Street's death. Like Burges, he was not sixty. The profession reeled under this last and most grievous blow. More funerals and the sickbed claimed Pearson; it was a black end to a miserable year.

If 1882 had nothing else to offer, there was at least work. Pearson had never had so many major churches being built. That in itself brought further fears. He was sixty-five, an age when he might consider his advice to Scott ten years before and husband his strength. There was little hope of that, and he had still to provide for the continuation of his practice.

The answer lay in his son. Frank had been a good pupil at Winchester and hoped to go up to Cambridge, eventually to become a civil engineer. But Pearson insisted that he should train to become an architect. He did not begrudge his son three years at University; but more pressing matters decided against it. With the east parts of Truro begun and with no immediate prospect of the cathedral being finished in his lifetime, he felt, rightly, that the best way of ensuring its ultimate completion was the training of the one person who might accept the task of doing the work after his death. Frank had regrets, but, having inherited his father's character, he considered it to be his duty, and faithfully and modestly accepted it.

18 ✣ PUPILS AND PRINCIPLES

WHEN Frank went into his father's office he sat beside Caröe, and the two were kept under Pearson's constant instruction.[1] Truro Cathedral was well under way and they were entrusted with making detailed drawings. Frank, straight from Winchester and with less experience, was the tracing clerk.

Born in 1857, William Douglas Caröe was the son of the Danish consul in Liverpool; going down from Trinity College, Cambridge, he spent a year in the office of E. B. Kirby, the architect of several Roman Catholic churches in the North-West, before becoming articled to Pearson. After working on the Truro drawings Caröe helped when Pearson was examined by a Select Committee enquiring into the restoration of Westminster Hall by measuring the old work and searching the Print Room of the British Museum and private collections for old views of the building.

Caröe was pushing where the Pearsons were reticent. He could be overbearing and rather grand—not for him the Pearsons' modesty.[2] He later persuaded Pearson to propose him for membership of the Athenaeum Club; Frank would have liked to have become a member too, but his father, not recognizing this, and not considering the club to be of assistance to an architectural career, did not put forward Frank's name.[3]

There was rivalry between Caröe and Frank Pearson, but it never spoiled their close friendship formed as they trained together. At Cambridge Caröe had been a good oarsman and had only just failed to make the Boat Race crew. He and Frank bought a boat in Oxford and at weekends rowed it in stages back to London. Frank took to sailing and became a keen yachtsman.

In the late 1880s Caröe began his own career; he started by working in the evenings, but soon Pearson allowed him half the day for his own commissions.[4] He became well known for his archaeological insight into buildings, one result of his training under Pearson. Another was his good structural knowledge; his cathedral restorations rivalled Pearson's without attracting the same controversy. When Ewan Christian died in 1895 he was to succeed him as architect to the Ecclesiastical Commissioners and design their offices in Millbank. In 1895, too, he entered a limited competition for a church at Exeter which was assessed by James Brooks. Caröe, who sent detailed drawings and an accurately costed specification, won the competition, and his design was built.[5] The church, St David's, is 'one of his finest achievements', according to Pevsner, and 'the only church of the last 100 years at Exeter to stand up against the cathedral'.[6] It is a remarkably independent design, and only the tall aisles, mere passages through the buttresses, may owe their existence to Pearson.

Caröe, living until 1938, became like Pearson an octogenarian. So did another assistant, John Ernest Newberry (1862–1950), who wrote an account of Pearson's career in the first number of the *Architectural Review*.

He was articled to an obscure architect, E. Hide, and studied at the Royal Academy Schools before becoming Pearson's assistant.[7] He exhibited a design for a church in Pearson's best Early English style at the Royal Academy in 1891.[8] After Pearson's death he became an assistant architect at the Admiralty, and later was in partnership with Francis Hugh Greenaway. The churches which they designed together show as much of the influence of the Arts and Crafts Movement as they do of Pearson.

Edward Appleby Robson was in the office in 1890; he is really only remembered as the son of the London School Board architect E. R. Robson. They shared with Pearson a Durham background. The young Robson designed a vicarage to go with Pearson's church at Upper Norwood; it was undistinguished, and was demolished in the late 1960s. Other assistants were Sidney Caulfield, Arthur Caldwell, G. B. Carvill and A. D. Sharpe. Caulfield worked on Truro; Carvill was a member of the Architectural Association, and may later have assisted Caröe.[9]

When Pearson rebuilt Westminster Abbey's north transept, Sharpe helped search for old views to provide evidence of its original state. He became Frank Pearson's assistant and stayed with him until Frank retired at the outbreak of the Second World War. One of his final acts was to help empty the office and send all the papers for salvage. Luckily Frank's daughter Marion interrupted them and was able to rescue some of the papers, including six volumes of tracings which were shown to her as 'examples of your grandfather's industry', before they were to be thrown out.

Several architects who were not Pearson's assistants were clearly influenced by him. Arthur Cawston's churches show this, none more than the vaulted, Early English St Philip, Stepney. Cawston admired Pearson's work and wrote a letter to the *Builder* in praise of Pearson's completion of the north transept of Westminster Abbey.[10] Henry Jervis, too, was clearly influenced by Pearson and must have had St John, Red Lion Square, in mind when he designed his St Augustine, Lynton Road, in Bermondsey in 1875.

Pearson's influence is very evident in Scotland. He built little there, Ayr church being his only major work, but long before it was built Scottish architects had seen his work in the architectural journals. James Sellars's Bullhaven church in Glasgow of 1877 owes much to Pearson; so does J. J. Burnet's and J. A. Campbell's Barony church of 1886 in the same city. The junction of its nave and chancel is very similar to the junction at Red Lion Square and there are other strong stylistic similarities. Pearson chose their design in a competition which he assessed, even though it did not strictly conform with the stipulations laid down.

Pearson's assistants and the other architects influenced by him could never be said to have formed a school. His smaller, cheaper churches such as those at Sturton-by-Stow and Hambleton became models for many small, suburban churches built in this century but generally Pearson developed his style of Gothic to its limits, and later architects were forced to go in a different direction.

Pearson's attitude of self-effacing perseverance towards his work was recognised by Caröe, who irritated Frank Pearson with his often expressed view that the architect was above all an artist. For Pearson, architecture was firstly a profession in which one should try to excel. An architect should satisfy his clients, and without denying the artistic nature of his work Pearson went to great pains to do this.

He was devout and a strong churchman; this gave him the justification for his career. Consequently he would not build churches for any but Anglicans. His churches included all the features required for Tractarian liturgy: stone altar tables, altar crosses, reredoses, altar rails, sedilia, chancel rails or screens, lecterns, litany stools; aesthetic effect should reinforce the religious effect of these features. Benson recalled that 'Mr Pearson said that the question to ask oneself on entering a church was not "is this admirable—is it beautiful?" but "Does it send you on your knees?" '[11]

The biographer of Bishop Wilkinson, Benson's successor at Truro, embroidered on this:

Before he could put pen to paper or even begin to imagine what sort of a building he should design he made his communion . . . Mr Wilkinson had the opportunity of praying with Mr Pearson then and there . . . It was under such influence as his that Pearson was able to design such a building as to draw from the Archbishop, when the choir was consecrated, the remark that it was a most spiritual building.[12]

It is natural that the Truro clergy should believe that religious inspiration was the prime ingredient of Pearson's success, but Caröe was more helpful in identifying it as 'a genuine feeling for architecture, backed by irrepressible diligence'. However, Pearson's feelings were attuned to those of his clients: when he was shown round his newly completed church at Croydon he said with great feeling, 'This is a place for real worship.'[13]

This attitude led Pearson to prefer to provide properly finished, dignified designs even though they might cost too much to be immediately built in their entirety, rather than to provide poverty-stricken designs which could be quickly completed but would be incapable of improvement later if more money became available. Although his church at Vauxhall was to have been built in stages, money was forthcoming to complete all of it, excepting the tower and some of the decoration, in one campaign; but from the time of Kilburn onwards two or more campaigns were needed to complete many of his large town churches. This is the reason why the towers of so few of them were finished; the towers being the last parts to receive attention. St Alban, Bordesley, is a noteworthy example. In 1865 two priests, James and Thomas Pollock, set up a mission there, and soon realised that they would need a large church.[14] In 1871 a temporary church was opened. They obtained a design for a permanent church from Butterfield, but it would have cost three times the amount they had suggested to him. They decided to build Butterfield's chancel and add a temporary, iron nave; but Butterfield declined to allow

119. Pearson's statue on Truro Cathedral's
south porch.

120. Truro Cathedral: Pearson's outline
perspective from the south-east.

that. The Pollocks therefore turned to Pearson, asking him to provide a design on which they could spend £7,000 to build part. Pearson replied: 'I am quite ready to carry out the Church divided in any way', so the east parts were planned to be built for £7,000, and the rest left for later. However, the Pollocks had only £4,000 on offer, and some of that seems not to have materialized, for when the whole church was eventually built the debt on it amounted to £14,000. How it was paid off makes harrowing reading, but this policy of building in stages did give Pearson the opportunity of building many of his finest interiors.[15]

Caröe records that in Pearson's procedure 'The plan always received the first and fullest consideration.' It helps to explain how Pearson achieved a feeling for space in his later churches which surpassed the work of all his contemporaries. It is appropriate that his statue on the south porch of Truro Cathedral shows him holding a plan of the cathedral rather than a perspective or model of it (Plate 119). It is on plan that space, that most special quality of architecture, depends.

'In general design,' Caröe continued, Pearson 'aimed first at form, covering both proportion and contour, and no matter how simple or how rich the detail of the design, these qualities of proportion and outline always held the first place, and are to be found equally prominent in whole buildings, in their parts, and in their details.' This is admirably demonstrated by a perspective drawing of Truro Cathedral which Pearson made without showing any detail and only including the windows of the east bay of the chancel, the rest of the building being left blank (Plate 120).

As for proportion, Carvill recalled Pearson tersely answering a journalist's question about the design of his steeples by saying that if it looked too short he would raise it, and if too high he would lower it.[16] That sounds haphazard, but Pearson could trust his eye, and despite this answer his proportions are invariably fully worked out.

The relationship of parts to the whole was never left to chance. One of the most characteristic features of his late churches is his treatment of morning chapels; they are like miniature churches completely integrated into the whole, and giving additional scale to the rest of the building.

The detailing of Pearson's churches may never be considered among the best of its kind. In some of his late churches the sculpture is lifeless, and seemingly designed to the standards of the 1840s. On the other hand it has an undeniably hierarchical quality, and admirably conforms with the overall architectural concept. Like many Victorian architects Pearson generally designed the furniture and fittings of his churches himself, and often extended this to include altar frontals and vestments. There are fine examples of these at Kilburn, Croydon and Shrewsbury.

Reacting against his overall control, the *Builder* urged, with Pearson in mind, that architects should 'study architecture and leave the designing of sculpture to sculptors'.[17] Perhaps Pearson's late churches where sculpture is kept to a minimum and the stonework decorated only with mouldings are the

most pleasing. He was unable to progress beyond the lively carved decoration in the churches of his middle period and produce work comparable to the best of the Arts and Crafts Movement (Plate 121). If he could not break with tradition, some of his carving is of fine quality and extremely lavish, especially in his church at Hove, and in the Astor estate office, his last domestic work.

121. (left) The reredos of St Peter, Vauxhall, carved by Messrs Poole of Westminster and with mosaics by Salviati of Venice; it is the most vigorously alive example of all Pearson's carved work.

122. Astor Estate Office: four panels by Frampton, which did not please Frank Pearson, of figures from the Arthurian legend.

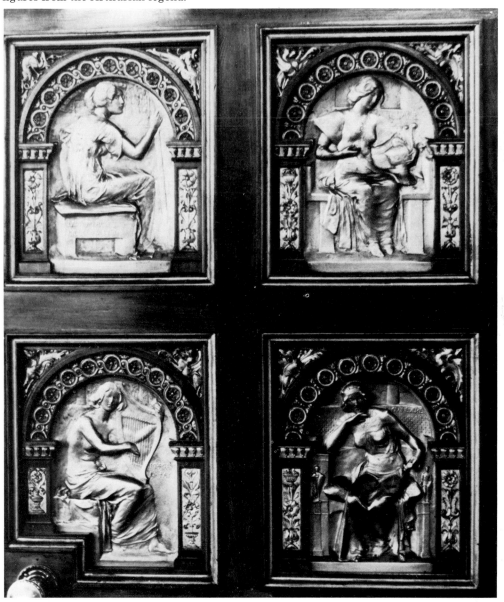

Frank Pearson probably reflected his father in his irritation with sculptors as opposed to carvers—artists, that is, as opposed to craftsmen. The sculptor Sir George Frampton made the panels in the door of the Great Hall at the Astor estate office, which Frank Pearson helped his father to build and to decorate (Plate 122). Some of Frampton's carving did not please, and Frank asked that it should be altered.[18] Frampton made perfunctory alterations with which Frank had to be satisfied; but, he grumbled, a carver would have scrapped the work and begun again. The Pearsons no doubt agreed with Ruskin: the architect's business is to dispense with the aid of perfect sculptors; he should 'devise such a system of ornament as shall be capable of execution by uninventive and even unintelligent workmen ... Giotto may design a campanile, but he cannot carve it.'[19]

So Pearson turned to Thomas Nicholls, Nathaniel Hitch and Harry Hems. Nicholls certainly produced more interesting carving for other architects; for Pearson his work is competent. Perhaps that is enough. At all events Pearson's churches must be judged as architecture rather than as repositories of works of art.

There is a parallel in Pearson's attitude towards the design of stained glass. He at first employed William Wailes of Newcastle to make stained glass, presumably because he had got used to dealing with him when he was training with Bonomi. Wailes produced glass of variable quality, and his stained glass for Pearson's church in Bessborough Gardens was unexceptional: 'Why is it that Mr Wailes's work is always a lottery?' asked the *Ecclesiologist*.[20] Later Pearson preferred other makers, and no longer employed Wailes even at churches where he had done previous work. He ruled out William Morris on the grounds that he usually failed to conform with the architectural character of a church and, surprisingly, that his work was more in keeping with buildings of a classical design. He presumably disliked Burne-Jones and other designers of the Arts and Crafts Movement for similar reasons. He warily approved of C. E. Kempe, wishing that he would submit his designs for approval.[21] Otherwise he liked John Powell, whose designs were carried out by Hardman and Company, and, above all, Clayton and Bell. Much of the glass in Pearson's churches is good, well above the average, and his desire that it should conform with the architectural character of his churches does not seem to have inhibited its design in the same way as it inhibited the carving in them.

Pearson's attitude to carved decoration is often thought to have extended to building materials and his use of them. There is no doubt that he was occasionally led into unhappy compromises. He designed Truro Cathedral to be built from Bath stone because, being a cathedral, it had to be enriched with plenty of carved decoration—the ease of carving Bath stone combined with its good weathering qualities and plentiful supply made it an almost unavoidable choice. But local critics demanded that the cathedral be built of local material. That meant granite, which was not in good supply and was far too hard to be easily carved. It could only be used for the plain ashlar and the carved parts of Truro were completed in Bath stone as originally planned; it was by no means a good compromise.

Pearson's work both on the north transept of Westminster Abbey and on Westminster Hall were criticised for the harsh stone employed, Chilmark for the one, Ketton for the other. Pearson was hoping to guard against the corrosive effects of London's atmosphere, and in that he was only as successful as other architects have been.

He excelled in the use of cheap materials, as is demonstrated by his brick, town churches from the time of Vauxhall on. He was happy to see the brick interiors of his churches painted, despite Ruskin's warning: 'I have most assuredly never yet seen a painted building, ancient or modern, which seemed to me quite right.'[22] Some of his early churches, such as Llangasty Tallylyn, had simple stencilled painting, but the chapel of St Peter's Home and the churches at Vauxhall and Kilburn had more elaborate schemes like those he later had seen at Assisi. The Clayton and Bell painting at Kilburn cannot stand comparison with Cimabue's or Giotto's frescoes—Ruskin was right to conclude that 'The architect has no right . . . to require of us a picture of Titian's in order to complete his design'[23]—but it adds a glowing warmth to the church, which is lacking in its hierarchical sculpture.

When Pearson was allowed a free hand and had no reason to carve much of the surfaces of his buildings, his genuine sensitivity to materials stands out. This is evident in many of his churches, but it shows more in his houses; Treberfydd and Whitwell Rectory are two examples of his happy use of local materials.

Pearson was no less successful with expensive materials. After his visit to Italy in 1874 he often made extensive use of marble for floors. Typical of several is the floor he designed for the choir of Bristol Cathedral: Archbishop Benson thought it 'lovely and bright', but it made him 'afraid of stepping through it'.[24] Rare materials were used without stint in his work for Astor, and their effect is grandly sumptuous.

In his late churches carved areas contrast strongly with plain areas; it is one of the characteristics which show how much he was influenced by the abbeys of the North. The carved parts in these churches are usually in the form of mouldings, sometimes enriched with dogtooth, and invariably with medieval precedent. Their harmony with his architectural concept is the greatest legacy of his years under Pugin's influence.

Equally characteristic is the care which he took with the plain ashlar. This was noted by Cawston who singled out the varied masons' work, and the stone courses of differing sizes and dressings. He had heard it said that Pearson 'insists on employing some left-handed masons'.[25] That may or may not be true; it was not recorded by Newberry who had much to say about Pearson's finishing of stonework:

It is not rubbed perfectly smooth and set with very fine joints in the usual manner. His custom is to have the stone 'dressed' on the face with a chisel,

123. Shillitoe at work on Truro Cathedral *c*. September 1882; in the foreground is the masons' yard with a derrick o the right; behind, the arches of the choir arcade are complete and a second derrick is employed to lift stones up to f the spandrels.

the joints are kept wider and set and pointed with a darker coloured mortar, thus accentuating the fact of the fabric being built up of separate stones. This treatment gives interest to a perfectly plain piece of walling, the surface having what is known among painters as 'quality'.

Early in his career Pearson put his buildings out to tender just as Bonomi did before him. Consequently they were usually built by local contractors, and although some often recur in one area it is evidence only of their ability to put in the lowest tender. For instance, Simpson and Malone of Hull worked on the churches at Bishop Burton, Kirkburn and Woolley. Pearson was no doubt satisfied with their work, but they gained the three contracts because they were competitive. In the eighties and nineties, however, four contractors appear so often that Pearson must have chosen them firstly for their reliability and quality of work. Cornish and Gaymer of North Walsham,

176

Norfolk, and Thompson of Peterborough both worked for Pearson in Kent as well as in their home counties; Luscombe of Exeter worked in Cambridge as well as Devon; but above all the name of John Shillitoe stands out, not just because he built Truro Cathedral, but because Pearson employed him more than any other contractor, and throughout the country from Lancashire and Yorkshire down to Sussex and Hampshire.

Pearson first used Shillitoe early in the 1870s when he was in partnership with his brother-in-law, Morgan, to build Moss church in the West Riding which Pearson executed for Charles Buckeridge. Shillitoe and Morgan came from the nearby village of Campsall. Pearson used them again at Skipwith and York. In the early eighties they built churches in Birmingham, Liverpool and Surrey, and in December 1881 Shillitoe who had by then left his partner was appointed contractor to build the first part of Truro Cathedral. The contract was based on a schedule of rates. Critics held that this led to the cathedral costing more than it should have done.[26] Shillitoe brought 150 tons of scaffolding down by sea and employed a pair of tall derricks (Plate 123). At the other end of the scale, he allowed the youngest son of Bishop Benson to help the masons, 'to the delight of his spiritual and temporal father'.[27]

It is recorded at least once that Pearson chose Shillitoe to build a church even though his tender was not the lowest. In 1884 the building committee of Silverhill church in Hastings, Sussex, were prepared to contract with Shillitoe provided that he charged less than £6,000. That was too optimistic; an increased offer was made, but simultaneously local builders were allowed to tender in competition. Eventually Shillitoe's tender of £8,100 was accepted even though another builder had put in a tender of £90 less. The latter complained of favouritism and asked for an explanation but never got one.[28] The explanation is clear: Pearson trusted Shillitoe, and both expected and obtained good work from him until his death in 1891.[29]

All in all, the picture which emerges of Pearson's office is one of ceaseless industry and quiet efficiency. There are no vivid accounts of it as there are of Scott's and Street's offices. No doubt it was dull rather than sparkling, established procedures being a prerequisite to the accomplishment of Pearson's designs. Nevertheless, the office was illuminated by his warmth, and his assistants were happy to work there; they recognised the quality of his work and the esteem in which his profession held him.

Pearson lived increasingly for his work. He became very reticent about his private affairs and cared little for society. Only his fellow artists and his club, the Athenaeum, attracted him.[30] In this society he was known as 'a ready talker with a ready smile and a keen sense of humour'.[31] He was held in high regard for 'his kindness of heart, his amiability of temper, his courage, his vigour of mind and uprightness'. Cosmo Monkhouse thought he was 'cheerful and kindly, a thorough gentleman in feeling and manners',[32] and Caröe agreed. He found it 'quite impossible to overrate the charm of Mr Pearson's personal presence and character'; he was 'a fine type, in short, of a courtly English gentleman'.

Apart from his work, his architectural library and his professional friends, Pearson had one other interest: the collection of pictures and *objets d'art*. [33] He acquired sketches—many of which were romantic landscapes—from fellow Academicians. In 1893 Thomas Somerscales exhibited *Corvette shortening sail to pick up a shipwrecked crew* at the Royal Academy. Before the exhibition was officially open, Pearson saw the picture and determined to have it. After he had negotiated its purchase from Somerscales, he was told that the Prince of Wales had seen it in the exhibition and wanted to buy it, and so he was asked to release the picture. He stubbornly refused and insisted on keeping it. Pearson's family think his consequent disfavour with the Royal Family may have ruined his chances of obtaining a knighthood, but at least he had his revenge for being made a freemason before Truro's foundation stone was laid. The picture was eventually given to Lancing College in memory of his great-grandson, a bomber pilot killed in the Second World War, who was educated there.

Starting his career when he did, and becoming an architect of churches rather than public buildings, it was inevitable that Pearson should design in the Gothic style. The moralistic attitude towards style which existed in his early years made it certain that he should be condemned when he strayed only so far as the Norman style. With Beresford Hope publicly calling him a 'faithful knight' dedicated to '*Ars Gothica*' amid general approval, it is no wonder that Pearson did not publicize his use of the classical Golden Section in his churches. Beresford Hope and he had survived the Battle of the Styles and seen the triumph of Gothic, however short lived. Beresford Hope's last years were threatened by a new style which at least in secular buildings was rapidly displacing Gothic: 'the smirks and leers and romps of naughty "Queen Anne"'. By 1880 'she was to be seen everywhere frisking, caracolling, and gambading about, saying, "You know I am 'Free Classical'!"' 'More free than welcome,' Beresford Hope added darkly. 'Mr. Pearson had had the courage to resist the blandishments of "Queen Anne", and they welcomed him for it.'[34]

Pearson may have been Beresford Hope's champion of Gothic, but his was a romantic picture, and not entirely true. Despite Pearson's love of Durham Cathedral, the Northern abbeys and the churches of Normandy, there was more for him in architecture than either Gothic or style. Caröe was firmly and rightly convinced that for Pearson 'style was but the clothing of great architectural ideas', and his 'scholarship and inexhaustible knowledge of tradition were the means only towards the expression of such ideas'. That in his later years he cherished the ambition to design a great classical or renaissance building is not as surprising as it was to Reginald Blomfield. 'Had such an opportunity offered,' Caröe concluded, 'there can be no doubt that we should have had from his remarkable sense for proportion and composition, from his intimate knowledge of detail, a building as full of refinement, character, and repose as the best of those in that medieval manner which he made peculiarly his own.'

19 ✥ LAST HOUSES

PEARSON's Vernacular Revival houses represent one side of his late Victorian domestic work, a side whose origins can be traced back to his early work at Treberfydd and Braintree. The other side is represented by houses in a far more marked style, not Gothic but Elizabethan or Jacobean, if not quite naughty 'Queen Anne'. This was a far cry from the mechanical Elizabethan of the 1830s and '40s, though Pearson may have felt its roots then in such buildings as Salvin's extravagant Harlaxton Hall and in the books he had studied in his youth.

Lechlade Manor House in Gloucestershire, the first in the style, was designed in 1871–2 (Plate 124). An innovating feature of Elizabethan country houses was their symmetry; in their early Victorian revival this conflicted with the desire for a picturesque outline. Pearson made only the garden front of Lechlade symmetrical, with two projecting blocks with canted bays to their first two storeys flanking a recessed block with a semi-circular bay. For the rest, the composition is balanced rather than symmetrical, and, as at Treberfydd, this was a consequence of its well-considered planning.

Outer and inner porches lead through a vestibule to a wide hall extending the whole width of the house. Opening from it on the eastern symmetrical garden side are the three principal rooms, the library flanked by the drawing-room and the dining-room. The billiard-room, kept apart as a male preserve, is entered from the vestibule or from a garden door. The principal staircase occupies one end of the hall, and the back stairs for the servants leads out of the other end beside a passage to extensive kitchens and service-rooms.

These are subordinated to the main part of the house by being lower and almost detached. Contrived like a coach-house and stabling round a courtyard, they too are skilfully planned. The male and female servants had separate quarters over the rooms in which they worked, and reached them only by their own stairs; these join the back stairs of the house so that any room could be quickly serviced although at the cost of some climbing. The nannies had most climbing to do: the extensive nurseries were in the third storey so that children could be neither seen nor heard.

Lechlade Manor House is larger and more massive than Treberfydd. Its massiveness is offset by a series of carefully placed towers and shaped gables; the juxtaposition of the tall main part of the house and the low servants' quarters to the side is very attractive even if their stylistic dress is commonplace.

In 1878 Pearson began to plan the remodelling of Westwood House at Sydenham in South London for Henry Littleton, the chairman of Novello's, the music publishers. In 1868 he had employed Pearson on small works at their premises in Dean Street, though why he chose him is unknown. Ten

179

124. Lechlade Manor House, 1872–3: garden front,
and plan.

125. (facing page) All Saints' Vicarage, Hove,
1882–3; the best of Pearson's red brick Gothic
houses for the clergy.

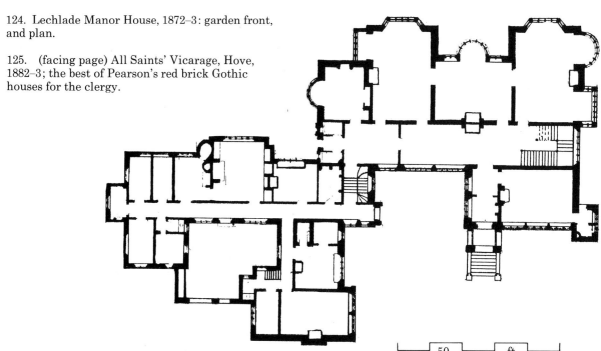

50   ft

years later came this one large commission which was executed in 1880–1. Littleton entertained many celebrated musicians there—Liszt and Dvorak were the best known—and some played for his friends in the sumptuous music-room which Pearson designed. The relationship between architect and client flourished, as with the Raikeses, and in 1891 Frank Pearson married Littleton's grand-daughter Cecilia.

Littleton insisted that the design of what was to be almost a new house should be in the French renaissance style (Plate 126),[1] which had been revived in Paris at the Louvre in the 1850s and became popular in England in the following decades. Although superficially in this style, Westwood's roots can be traced back to the French of Quar Wood. The house has been demolished, but surviving drawings and photographs give a good idea of its exterior. Both elevations were symmetrical—a new departure for Pearson—and several bays and tourelles finished with separate roofs added a liveliness to the massive outline of the building under its large hipped roof, giving it its predominantly French character.

The details, above all the ornate window frames and gables, the mannerist pilasters and panels decorated with arabesques (all in cut and rubbed brick) were as much English as French; and a ground-storey loggia on the garden front had arcades strongly reminiscent of Wren's Fountain Court at Hampton Court with blank arches and, beneath, open subsidiary basket arches.

Westwood House had seventeen bedrooms, a handsome music-room, and presumably many reception-rooms. The music-room, the only room of which an illustration survives, was lavishly panelled, and the ceiling had carved joists. The ends were screened by a pair of detached Corinthian columns bearing heavy cross beams.

The *Builder* called the house late Elizabethan;[2] Newberry, though, said it was in the style of 'old French chateaux'. The bays, tourelles and gables, and the conical and pyramidal roofs could certainly have come from the Loire, but they are the offspring of Quar Wood. It was Westwood's symmetry and consequent regular massing which made the difference.

The *Building News* more specifically described the house as in the style of François Ier, and thought it showed Pearson to be 'a master of Renaissance design'.[3] Despite its High Victorian parentage, the house was, it said, 'without restlessness'; an allusion to the overall sensitivity of the composition. While not overtly in the 'Queen Anne' style, it had some of its traits, especially as they were to be applied to the new schools just being started for the London School Board. J. J. Stevenson's Red House in Paddington of 1870–1 was probably the first London house in the 'Queen Anne' style. He encouraged his partner E. R. Robson, the School Board's architect, to use the 'Queen Anne' style for their schools.[4] Pearson knew Robson, and must have known how his schools would develop. Many of Westwood's features—its symmetry, its large windows, its outline enlivened by turrets and gables, its decoration in cut brick—were all to be found in the Board schools of the 1880s.

. Westwood House: drawings of entrance front (above) and garden front, exhibited at the Royal Academy in 1880.

Pearson's last essays in the Elizabethan and Jacobean styles were for Emmanuel and Sidney Sussex Colleges at Cambridge. Emmanuel House at the former was built between 1892 and 1894; it is irregular with projecting bays, shaped gables and battlements; a competent solid building with good massing. His work at Sidney Sussex is more extensive. The designs of 1890 were to include a handsome Jacobean chapel which was never built, and a range to the north of the Hall which was. Part of this range is regularly planned with pairs of bows executed in stone, strongly reminiscent of those at Kirby Hall, and brick sections finished with shaped gables between; beneath, a projecting arcade with basket arches runs along the entire length. The junction with the older parts of the college is happily handled with irregular, projecting bays on each side and a passage leading from the arcade through the body of the building to the opposite side. Pearson knew Kirby Hall from his youth, and must have been well aware that it had inspired T. G. Jackson's Jacobean buildings in Oxford. The *Builder* thought it charming;[5] the *Building News* found it 'undoubtedly dignified', but was rightly concerned that 'propriety is not always a sufficient substitute for interest and "go"'.[6]

This lack of freedom is most evident in Pearson's town vicarages and clergy houses. Generally of red brick with Bath stone dressings, and often gabled (Plate 125), a suitable ecclesiastical appearance comes from their prominent trefoiled windows. This will do for vicarages beside his red brick churches, as at Red Lion Square and the Catholic Apostolic church, but otherwise they seem unwelcoming. None compare with Whitwell Rectory.

Mark Girouard concludes that Pearson's country houses 'in style and treatment form a curiously varied mixture'.[7] Pearson's churches fall into three distinct groups: early, High and late Victorian. To a less marked extent his houses do too. Treberfydd, Quar Wood and Westwood House have respective parallels in the churches at Llangasty Talyllyn, Daylesford and Hove. Had he built more houses, these parallels might be clearer and their variety more explicable. Despite building only a few, he kept up to date throughout his career. This was not just a matter of style. He was sympathetic to local materials and vernacular traditions of house building from the time of Treberfydd on; and Roundwyck and Whitwell Rectory show a truly late Victorian sensitivity to the vernacular. With clients like Littleton at an early stage in his career Pearson might have become a great house builder. Though imaginatively planned, his late houses do not have the spatial characteristics of his late churches, nor can they show his particular blend of the early Gothic of Normandy and the North of England, so it is hard to relate them directly to the products of his genius. However, Pearson gave his houses the same vigour as he gave his churches; and, when given the occasional opportunity, he could be as fresh and stimulating as house architects fifteen and twenty years his junior.

20 ❧ THE SOCIETY
FOR THE PROTECTION
OF ANCIENT BUILDINGS

In 1878 Pearson's career as a church restorer was greatly affected by three events: Scott died, leaving him to succeed to much restoration work; chosen as architect for Truro Cathedral, he gained great publicity, and soon had several cathedrals entrusted to his care; and, lastly, the Society for the Protection of Ancient Buildings, founded the year before by William Morris, published its first annual report, which challenged the whole philosophy of restoration and attacked individual works with as much spirit as the *Ecclesiologist* had vetted new churches thirty years before.

Nearly as long ago as that, Ruskin had cried out against restoration:

It means the most total destruction which a building can suffer: a destruction out of which no remnants can be gathered: a destruction accompanied with false description of the thing destroyed ... it is *impossible*, as impossible as to raise the dead, to restore anything that has ever been great or beautiful in architecture.[1]

Architects believed they could raise the dead; for him, it was 'a lie from beginning to end. You may make a model of a building as you may of a corpse, and your model may have the shell of the old walls within it as your cast might have the skeleton, with what advantage I neither see nor care; but the building is destroyed.'[2]

Architects and clergy cast this from their minds, but occasionally felt uneasy. Even Scott, the most inveterate of restorers, had attacked unscrupulous restoration in his book *A Plea for the Faithful Restoration of our Ancient Churches*, but his written principles were hardly less ambiguous than those implied by his own works.[3]

It was his proposed restoration of Tewkesbury Abbey that set Morris to write to the *Athenaeum* proposing an association to protect it and other ancient buildings from destruction.[4] Within months it had been formed; its aim, said Morris, was to stop 'the destruction and falsification of our ancient monuments ... not their bodies merely'; and, he continued, 'Our enemies are the enemies of the works of all styles alike, ignorant destruction and pedantic reconstruction.'[5] His were fighting words, and while the SPAB hoped to persuade, it recognized that it would have to attack as well. It did this with vigour, and during the 1880s transformed the easy climate in which restoration had been previously pursued into one of bitter controversy.

Pearson, who already had restored fifty churches, found his aims and methods unceasingly questioned; soon he came to be mistrusted by the SPAB, becoming its prime enemy, and opinions of his capabilities diverged; they remain the same today. That he went so far to meet the objections of the SPAB illustrates the fundamental care which he lavished on worthy buildings. Before he could have become acceptable to the Society, he would have had to care for less worthy buildings as well, and be less willing to accept the requirements of ecclesiological propriety. When he restored East Farleigh church in Kent—clearly one which did not greatly impress him—he reported: 'to give more dignity to the East end I propose to raise the window and as the tracery is of poor design and is modern, I have introduced a new window of the same date as that of the North of the Chancel.'[6] By 'date' Pearson meant style, an unfortunate confusion where the philosophy of restoration is concerned; and his unspecific use of 'modern' suggests nothing so much as a slipshod attitude to history. Perhaps it was not that, but it infuriated his critics. What concerned him most was to make the church 'a very effective building'. Ecclesiological requirements came first.

'He invariably gave the fullest consideration to the points of view urged against him,' Caröe recorded, 'and satisfied himself whether they were worthy or not of his attention; but he was not to be drawn into public controversy.' That was left to his clients and would-be supporters who joined battle without hesitation. It saddened him that he should be brought to public notice through these controversies rather than through his own buildings.

The major controversies were invariably over cathedrals. Where churches were concerned, Pearson went on as before, not unmolested by the SPAB; indeed in every year from 1878 it adversely commented on some restoration of his. The big guns were kept for the cathedrals. They fired first at Peterborough, and there they fired last.

In 1874 Scott had found that the cathedral's central tower was in a parlous condition and needed repair. No money was forthcoming; no work was done. In July 1882 Pearson examined the cathedral and said that the tower was dangerous. Still nothing was done. Then at the very end of the year it cracked and started to move. Pearson was called from London by telegraph. He repeated what he had said in July. The tower was unsafe. Now it was moving. The position was desperate. The south-east pier was bulging and might soon collapse. Few needed reminding of what had happened at Chichester when the central tower had come crashing down into the cathedral. In January Thompson, Scott's former contractor, brought two steam engines to the site to assist in taking down the tower, stone by stone, each numbered for eventual replacement. At the end of February Pearson presented his proposals for rebuilding. The cause of the trouble was that the piers supporting the crossing and tower were ill founded and poorly constructed; their rubble core had turned to dust and was no longer bonded to the ashlar. There were two courses of action. The crossing arches could be supported by centring while the piers below were rebuilt on strong concrete foundations. When this was done, the stonework of the arches could be repaired and the tower rebuilt. The alternative was to take down and rebuild

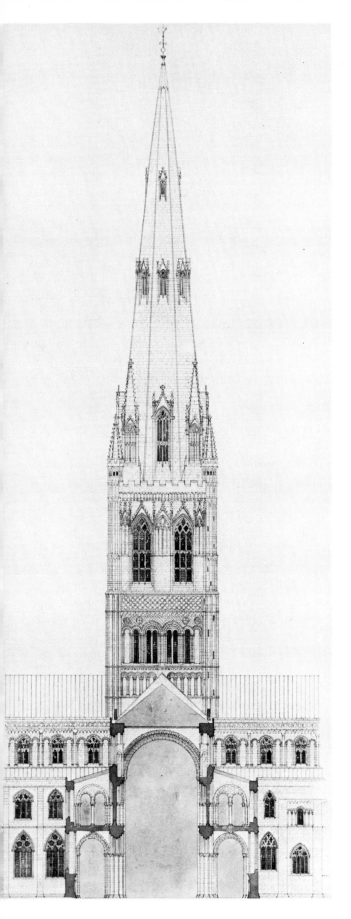

127. Peterborough Cathedral: the crossing showing (left) Pearson's design for rebuilding, including raised tower and spire, exhibited at the Royal Academy in 1885; and (below) one of the rebuilt Norman arches (at bottom) and to left and right the rebuilt fourteenth-century arches.

the whole lot. This would cost £5,000 less, he estimated, a saving of some forty per cent. The Dean and Chapter, loath to spend anything on a timely restoration, now, not surprisingly, chose the cheaper course: take it all down, marking the stones, and rebuild. The SPAB considered that the other course had not received enough attention: 'it might, possibly, have been more expensive . . . [but] well worth while to spend the extra sum required to treat it in a conservative manner'.[7] It did, however, approve marking the stones.

Pearson, watching the demolition, noted that the east and west arches had been rebuilt in the fourteenth century, and, unlike the Norman ones, were pointed, thus spoiling the unity of design. At the same time the tower had been lowered and lightened, and a stage of arcading above the arches had been removed. Used as rubble inside the fourteenth-century arches were the carved stones which provided evidence for this. The capitals of the piers below the fourteenth-century arches had been cut from the previous Norman capitals turned face-in.

In August 1884 Pearson proposed to restore the two Norman arches, thus re-establishing unity of design, and to build a higher tower with the reinstated Norman arcade, for which he designed a spire in his best thirteenth-century style. These proposals caused uproar. The Dean supported them, the Chapter was against them. So was the Bishop, but the money came from the restoration committee, and that body supported the Dean. Rebuilding stopped. The Dean enlisted the support of Sir Edmund Beckett (later Lord Grimthorpe) who was restoring St Alban's Abbey at his own expense, a work widely criticised then and now. He wrote many ill-tempered letters to *The Times* which prompted E. A. Freeman, an Oxford professor and a medievalist, to counterattack, calling Pearson's spire 'a monstrosity', which it certainly was not, and putting forward a design of his own which was unbuildable.[8]

Order was only restored in April 1885 when Archbishop Benson was appointed to arbitrate. He had resigned from the SPAB but was still sympathetic to its tenets. Finding that the restoration committee had been improperly set up, he dismissed it and appointed a new one. As for the restoration, the old work, he decided, should be reinstated exactly as it had been; 'it was more consistent with continuity of historical tradition'.[9] The antagonists were pacified; the SPAB was consoled: 'We have escaped the misfortune of a nineteenth century addition to Peterborough and that is the greatest gain'[10] (Plate 127).

It is sad that Pearson's fine spire was so readily dismissed; it would have been a handsome addition to the cathedral, even though his proposals for the tower were less acceptable. It never had a chance. Money was poured into the rebuilding and refitting of the choir. For lack of funds, work came temporarily to a halt in 1887, and when all was complete in 1890, it had cost nearly £32,000.

Pearson's scheme for restoring Westminster Hall brought about an illuminating confrontation with the SPAB because it took place in formal surroundings, not in the press.[11] In 1882 Street's Law Courts were completed, and the former courts, an accretion of buildings on the west side of Westminster Hall, were demolished, leaving the side bare. Barry's plans for completing the Houses of Parliament had been abandoned nearly twenty years before, and there were now no proposals for the newly cleared site. Pearson was asked by the Office of Works, without any clear instructions, simply to restore the west side of the hall.

He found that the lower part of the west wall largely consisted of Norman masonry belonging to the original building. On individual stones was a fine series of well-preserved masons' marks, which were likely to deteriorate rapidly if they long remained exposed to the smoky atmosphere. The upper part of the wall had been rebuilt at the end of the fourteenth century, when Hugh Herland's great hammerbeam roof was constructed. This had necessitated buttressing the wall with flyers, which had now been exposed. Pearson's archaeological examination showed that there had been a cloister under them; the foundations of its outer wall were found and the height was clearly indicated by marks on the returns of the buttresses.

He reported his discoveries, and suggested that a restoration of the cloister would give adequate protection for the remains of the Norman wall, and make an appropriate finish to the west side of the hall; this pleased the Office of Works, which told him that many uses could be found for any rooms he might provide in the new structure.

He then designed a two-storeyed cloister with a wide arcade on the ground storey and rooms above lighted by pairs of Decorated windows to each bay. An embattled parapet finished the wall, which had details appropriate to the period when it was built suggested by drawings of the original by Wren and others which Pearson had discovered.

His plans were completed by April 1884, and then subjected to the scrutiny of a Select Parliamentary Committee which examined witnesses including establishment architects who generally supported Pearson's plans, and members of the SPAB who opposed them. Pearson's attitude as a restorer and the SPAB's view of buildings as archaeological documents were brought into sharp conflict. Pearson's archaeological findings were not seriously questioned; the points at issue were: how far would he be restoring what had previously existed, and was that an appropriate thing to do.

On the first point it was immediately clear that all that was known with certainty was the position and height of the cloister wall; its fenestration was uncertain. However, Pearson argued, 'The height is a restoration; the section of the mouldings of the parapet is a restoration; the two-light windows are a restoration; Sir Christopher Wren shows them in his plan as having two lights all the way along.'[12] He admitted he had adapted the fenestration, and had to agree with Somers Clarke, who spoke for the Society of Antiquaries and the SPAB, that much of his design was imaginary. Somers Clarke had the grace to say that no architect could have done more than Pearson to recreate the original wall; but that was not the point. He was confusing archaeological certainty with archaeological possibility. Even if his restoration were justified, it would be a sham. J. J. Stevenson said it was bad modern Gothic as well; something more in keeping with the present should be built. Surprisingly he suggested a black-and-white, timber wall of a type one could find in Chester. It might be incongruous, but no one would mistake it for fourteenth-century work. The illogicality of this was not questioned, nor was he asked why this proposed wall should appear more modern and less likely to be mistaken for medieval work than Pearson's. As for its incongruity, that was a source of conflict; and none could do better than J. T. Micklethwaite when asked whether the new work should harmonize with the old: 'Architecturally it should, but not pseudo-archaeologically.'[13] How that might be done, he did not say, and there lay the dilemma.

The only humour in the drawn-out proceedings came when William Morris was examined.[14] He did not know whether it was necessary to protect the flying buttresses, but if it was, thought the protection should be of the simplest kind. 'Most stone walls I have seen built at the present day are a great deal better than they are when they have got the architectural additions to them. A piece of architecture may be ugly; a stone wall cannot be.' The addition must be 'obviously modern'; but he, too, did not say how. He recommended that if Pearson's cloister wall were built, to avoid confusion, it should bear the inscription: 'This building was built in such-and-such year of the reign of Queen Victoria, and was done by such-and-such a gentleman, and it pretends to be old, and is not.' Shaw Lefevre, the committee chairman, asked him if the inscription on his own proposed construction should read: 'This was erected in the reign of Queen Victoria; does not pretend to be old', to which Morris replied that it should read: 'Certain stupid people having injured the flank of the Hall, we were obliged to put up this utilitarian business here in order to preserve the thing from rapid decay.'

General support for Pearson's proposed restoration was given by Arthur Blomfield, James Brooks, Ewan Christian, John Oldrid Scott and Alfred Waterhouse. The committee took their advice. Poor Charles Barry's desire that his father's scheme be completed was ignored. A minority report was based on the evidence of Somers Clarke, J. T. Micklethwaite, J. J. Stevenson and William Morris. The remaining points to be decided were: should the cloister wall be as high as Pearson proposed, since, despite the archaeological authenticity of its height, it might unpleasantly obscure the flying buttresses; and should Pearson's recommendation for raising the towers at the north end of the hall be adopted. Sensibly these were not, and eventually a lower cloister wall was built to an alternative design by Pearson, which he had been asked to produce, but did not favour. It has less archaeological justification, and its architectural wisdom was immediately questioned, even though it allowed a more extensive view of the flying buttresses. It would have been better as Pearson first designed it, but at least it is congruous.

Morris's proposals for an inscription were not pursued. It is easy to sympathize with his off-hand comments, but his radical attitudes did not endear him to those concerned with restoration; they, right wing by nature, were bound to distrust the intrusions of one so openly embracing socialism. The issues—restored use and architectural propriety on the one hand, and, on the other, archaeological continuity maintained by conservative repair—hardened and allowed no room for compromise. It was ironical that the radicals sought to conserve, the conservatives to alter radically.

At Westminster Abbey where Pearson inherited from Scott the unfinished project to rebuild the façade of the north transept, he earned the undying enmity of the SPAB, becoming in their eyes the greatest destroyer of all. Originally built in the thirteenth century, the transept had a new porch added in the late fourteenth century which was replaced in the eighteenth. The rest 'had to a large extent disappeared under a layer of alterations',[15] the most notable being those of William Dickinson working under Wren between 1719 and 1722 when the tracery of the great rose window was rebuilt as a 'daisy',[16] and filled with enamelled glass designed by Sir James Thornhill. During the nineteenth century Wyatt, Blore and then Scott had done works which, according to Morris, were 'well meant, ill-conceived, and disastrous pieces of repair of various degrees of stupidity'.[17]

In Scott's defence, his study of the Abbey was thorough: few knew more of its history and architecture. It is hard to support the SPAB in condemning his restoration of the Chapter House to a fair representation of the original; it has more architectural propriety than it previously had archaeological interest as a muniment store. The north transept, though, could have served as it stood. Sadly he persuaded the Dean and Chapter that restoring its medieval appearance would enhance the Abbey, and they became enthusiastic. He began with the porches, and in taking them down found missing features which confirmed his view of the original design. As always he found what he sought.

Scott lived to begin his porches, then died, leaving them to be continued by his son John Oldrid. When Pearson succeeded to the surveyorship of the Abbey, the north transept could have been left with just the porches completed, but the authorities wanted the work continued and Pearson was ready to do it.

He asked Burges's advice about published accounts of the building. Burges replied, sending a list of books 'which really treat it completely', among them being R. Widmore's *An Enquiry into the First Foundation of Westminster Abbey*, 'the most trustworthy book of all', and J. P. Neale's *Westminster Abbey*, 'the best book for illustrations and general infotn.'[18] Pearson and his assistant Sharpe scoured topographical collections for views showing the transept before the alterations, the principal one being Hollar's view of 1654, which predated Wren's work.[19] Morris called it a 'curious nondescript engraving'—more a criticism of Hollar's artistry than what he showed. This and Pearson's own archaeological investigations during the removal of the old stonework determined the new design.

He wanted to build it in Ketton stone, but felt obliged to continue as Scott had begun with Chilmark, less attractive and no better able to withstand London's smoky atmosphere. That was criticised, and so was the decoration. 'The result is most unsatisfactory,' wrote Morris. It is 'another example of the dead-alive office work of the modern restoring architect, overflowing with surface knowledge of the medieval in every detail but devoid of historic sympathy and true historical knowledge.'[20]

Pearson's restoration included returning the arcaded passage below the rose window to its assumed thirteenth-century design as suggested by Hollar, and rebuilding the buttresses, the projection of which had been reduced by Dickinson in 1719–22, again to the assumed original. The most controversial part was destroying the 'daisy' window and designing another, based on the one shown by Hollar, but adapted to take the enamelled glass (Plate 128). The glass has radiating figures, and so that they might fit the new tracery, they had to be shortened at the feet. Had Pearson 'intended to have new glass but was then forced to keep the old?' asked the *Builder*.[21] It is probable.

128. Westminster Abbey: north transept: P. E. Masey's perspective of Pearson's design executed in the 1880s.

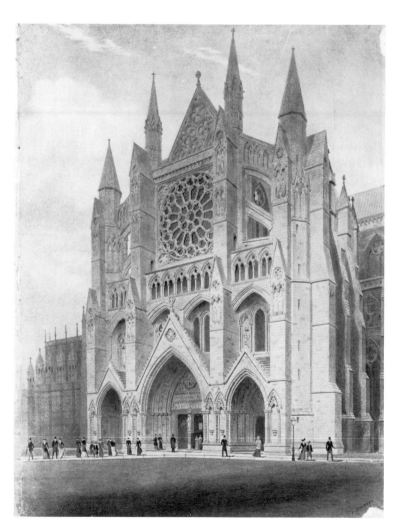

The SPAB condemned the new tracery for its specious archaeological 'correctness' which required the old glass to be 'cut up and mangled after a most strange and barbarous fashion'.[22] W. R. Lethaby, who was later surveyor to the Abbey, called Pearson's 'scientific restoration' of the façade 'all false', and noted that in the old rose there had been large foiled circles in the upper spandrels to light the roof above the vaulting; now they were 'blank and blind and foolish'.[23]

Even the *Builder* called the adaptation of the glass 'an incredible piece of bungling'.[24] Later that was forgotten; Pearson's transept was 'an exceptionally fine example of what must be called restoration . . . completely in the true spirit and feeling of Medieval architecture',[25] and the *Building News* agreed: 'He has inspired his work with an interest and a living character which contributes in no small degree to the unqualified success of the whole thing.'[26]

Maurice Adams poured scorn on the SPAB and their like. 'The upper part of this transept was the beautiful design of J. L. Pearson,' he wrote.

> It is difficult to understand the cult of the anti-repairist, but a painter-friend, a 'whole-hogger', as they say, in anti-everything, confided his opinion that it would have been better to have built a plain stock-brick wall, if this front really did need repairing, and that would have better expressed, as I understand him, the speechless poetry of modern architectural capabilities.[27]

Today it is hard to judge the north transept as architecture. Were it part of Truro Cathedral it could be praised, but the history of its construction must unfortunately be taken into account. Pearson may be excused for completing Scott's scheme, for completing what the Dean and Chapter were resolved to complete, for making a real and scholarly attempt to reproduce the original design. He may be excused for paying scanty regard, as all previous generations of architects had done, to an earlier but recent building; that he did it more drastically than had been done before was only a matter of degree. To the SPAB they were just excuses and entirely unacceptable. Morris described Hawksmoor's west towers as 'monuments of the incapacity of the seventeenth and eighteenth century architects to understand the work of their forefathers'.[28] Pearson's north transept façade is that and more; not only did he ignore all the past but the thirteenth century, but he destroyed it as well. There lies his reputation.

That Pearson executed simple repairs to the Abbey is forgotten. He replaced decayed stonework on the south side of the choir, and repaired the clerestory walls and buttresses of the east limb including the flying buttresses and shafts supporting them. Some of this was to eighteenth-century parts, but, notwithstanding that, they were allowed to remain, and no attempt at restoration to an original condition was made. The repairs were condemned by the SPAB for removing medieval masonry, but it could hardly have been left. Similar repairs have continued ever since.

Pearson has been called the last of the restorers, his successor the first of the repairers. Certainly nothing like the restoration of the north transept has been attempted again, but with the recent removal of the medieval roof a valuable piece of fine medieval joinery has been destroyed. That is not repair, and can only be called restoration in the loosest sense of the word.

Pearson continued to anger the SPAB. At Lincoln, his repair of the cloister was castigated by Somers Clarke.

> The open walls towards the garth had soon after their erection swung over a little. They had been supported by small intermediate buttresses, examples of the skill with which our forefathers could make even a prop an object not unpleasing to look upon. Mr Pearson has restored the cloister and restored away the intermediate buttresses so that this page of history is carefully removed.[29]

Another proposal provoked an outcry which led to the SPAB scoring its only major victory over him. The fourth side of the cloister had been destroyed in the fifteenth century and remained ruinous until 1674 when Wren built a library there. An influential landowner called Shuttleworth, already an open-handed benefactor of the cathedral, wanted to extend the close. As part of the scheme, he persuaded the Dean and Chapter that it would be desirable to remove Wren's library and rebuild it on part of the new open space. Pearson said that this could be done, and in its place he could restore the fourth arm of the cloister to match the remaining three. These proposals were made public in 1892, and, supported by the Society of Antiquaries, the SPAB immediately protested. The Dean replied that he and the Chapter were acting under the strongly expressed opinion of their highly competent architect, and they had no doubt that his judgement was right; the library was to be re-erected, not destroyed. That might have been, but, as the SPAB claimed, a historical fact was to be destroyed. The scheme was consequently shelved, and Pearson turned his attention to the north-west tower which was causing anxiety. The correspondence in the *Builder* started by Somers Clarke who had wished that Pearson 'had been more anxious to preserve and repair rather than "to restore" and build up sham antiquities' making our churches 'the cold, lifeless, unhistoric edifices most of them have become',[30] degenerated into a tiresome discussion of Scott's abilities as a restorer and Grimthorpe's as a destroyer.

Of all the controversies between Pearson and the SPAB and the Society of Antiquaries, the last was the most bitter and futile.[31] Even while Pearson was presenting his proposals for the restoration of the central tower of Peterborough Cathedral, the west front was known to be in poor repair (Plate 129). In 1892 a stone fell from it; in March 1895 a gale brought down four pinnacles, and the Dean feared that the whole front might be insecure. Morris wrote to say that the front should be preserved at all costs, and no attempt be made to pull it all down and rebuild it. Would-be subscribers to a repair fund should be told what was intended, and he concluded: 'The front "restored"

194

129. The west front of Peterborough Cathedral in 1968, seventy-two years after Sir Charles Read said it would 'never again be seen'.

would be of no value; we want it preserved.'[32] The *Builder* gave him partial support: there should be 'no "restoration" frolics', but it thought that the whole front might have to come down; and that while an engineer should be associated with Pearson, he was in fact the best architect for the job; 'his restoration of the crossing piers is unassailable'.[33]

In May Pearson reported that the piers carrying the great arches of the front had from an early date leant outwards; the fourteenth-century porch was probably inserted to help stabilise them, and, later, ties were put in. He reported again in February 1896 that the north gable was in the worst condition, and by September had reached the conclusion that it must be taken down, with the possibility that the central gable might also need to be dismantled. The trouble, as at Lincoln, resulted from towers having been built on parts insufficiently strong to bear them; they rested on the vaults of the two outer arches, which were improperly constructed in the first place with an ashlar facing now quite detached from a rubble core turned to dust. Thus the arches were crushed and cracking, and the gables bulging.

In April the Society of Antiquaries wrote to the Dean and Chapter suggesting that there was a better way of repairing the front than the one proposed by Pearson; and that it should be underpinned. This was about to be done anyway, but the real trouble was in the upper parts, not the foundations. The Society wrote again asking for time to prepare a specification of the work which it proposed, and in December members visited the cathedral. Although

195

they were not allowed up the scaffolding, they concluded that the north gable did not need taking down; it was without a blemish and the trouble was internal.

The antagonism spilled over into the press. The *Builder* added its flame to the wrath exposed by the correspondence columns of *The Times* simply by reporting it:[34] the various letters showed the absurd pass to which things had come when people with no knowledge of building construction thought themselves privileged to offer their opinions in the most dogmatic and dictatorial way, and regarded the Dean and Chapter as guilty of a crime because they refused to accept these opinions. The *Builder* singled out Sir Charles Robinson and Miss Octavia Hill for 'declaiming in sublime wrath against the wickedness of meddling with the ancient front . . . it may be doubted whether there are any two more totally incompetent to give an opinion on a question of building structure . . . [it] is not worth the paper it is printed on'; and then, against the easiest target of all:

> that blustering busybody, Lord Grimthorpe, of course must put his word in a letter the main object of which, as usual, is to glorify himself and to assert the superiority of his ridiculous disfigurement of St Albans . . . nothing could do more to ferment a prejudice against Mr Pearson . . . than the announcement that Lord Grimthorpe sided with him.

The controversy continued unabated; and Sir Charles Read, the secretary of the Society of Antiquaries, was reported as saying that the west front of Peterborough 'will never again be seen'.[35] *Punch* found cynical humour in the events:

> An Architectural Settlement. First Man (eminent in painting, literature or science): 'What a controversy about Peterborough Cathedral! Do you know anything about architecture? I don't.' Second Man (ditto): 'Nothing whatever and I've never been within twenty miles of Peterborough.' First Man: 'Nor have I. Then let us go at once and sign a memorial to the Dean and Chapter asking them not to let anybody do anything.' (*Exeunt* excitedly.)[36]

It was not inaction which the Society of Antiquaries and the SPAB wanted. The two drew up a specification outlining how they would repair the front, and offered to repair the north gable free of charge. They asked for the time and opportunity to put their proposals in more detail. However, just before Christmas 1896, the Dean and Chapter decided to ignore them and authorized Pearson to proceed with his restoration. As for the proposals, they were brushed aside:

> We should be guilty of most culpable neglect of duty were we to allow any hazardous experiments to be made on so important an example of Early English architecture as the west front of the Cathedral, of which we are the duly-appointed guardians, and for the safety and preservation of which we, and we alone, are responsible.[37]

The *Builder*, of course, supported them: 'They have had wholesale abuse heaped upon them in public prints. If they had yielded . . . they would have been absolutely false to the trust reposed in them.'[38]

Early in January 1897 Pearson began work, but the Society of Antiquaries and 'their henchmen' of the SPAB battled on and published their specification and a statement of their action since the controversy arose. They complained that Pearson had underpinned the front in May 1896 only after they had recommended it in their April letter. The taking down of the gable was quite unjustified as it was possible to tunnel into the core from behind, remove the defective rubble, and replace it with concrete. In this way the gable could be preserved from the destruction proposed by Pearson and now begun. They further complained that they had not been allowed on the scaffolding, and so had been unable to inspect the front closely.

The Dean and Chapter ignored them, but the *Builder* did not let the matter go. It dismissed this 'latest phase in the futile agitation' as 'colossal in its impertinence';[39] the signatories were distinguished only by youth and inexperience, and belonged to a party (J. J. Stevenson excepted) which refused to belong to the R.I.B.A.[40] Their fetish was non-disturbance of the visible work; their panacea, underpinning and recoring from behind working upwards. That, commented the *Builder* with much truth, could not be done with defective work above. The scheme, in short, was lunacy, and it poured scorn on the two societies for inviting the Dean and Chapter

> to dismiss their architect, the man admittedly of the first experience in England in dealing with large medieval structures, and to put the work instead into the hands of those of whose experience they know nothing, and at the same time to lose from the work their contractor, who stands first in experience in such work, because he regards the proposed method as one which is unsafe not only to the building but to the lives of his workmen.[41]

Pearson felt the attacks on him acutely, but remained silent. Although the Council of the R.I.B.A. refused to do so officially, nearly all its members signed a letter in support of Pearson.[42] The work progressed. The north gable and the arch beneath were taken down, the stones being marked as they were removed. In March rebuilding began. The arch required two new stones, and of the gable's two thousand and six, all but a hundred and seventy were repositioned. In July the *Builder* reported that all the stones were back in the positions they had occupied before, and that was the best possible comment on the ridiculous storm of indignation. 'It is to be hoped,' it continued, 'that the authors of this clamour that "the west front is about to be destroyed" will have the honesty to withdraw.'[43] Its own part in the clamour it viewed with self-righteousness, and it congratulated the Dean and Chapter and Pearson on the successful completion of an anxious and difficult piece of work, carried out 'in the face of an unexampled storm of archaeological bigotry and intolerance'. To this victory cry came two partially conciliatory letters from E. S. Prior and J. Micklethwaite saying that they held no personal

197

animosity for Pearson, but only for those who preferred a smart new copy to a genuine work of art; and then, at last, the adversaries put away their pens.

The controversy now seems to have been out of proportion to the occasion. Perhaps the action of the two societies instilled caution; perhaps their specified method of repair might have worked, though it is doubtful. Pearson's method of repair did work and has visibly continued to work. It was not unduly harsh. The west front was not destroyed. What one sees today is not a smart new copy, and certainly no restoration like the north transept of Westminster Abbey.

The tragedy was that Pearson could not be trusted. Although he had always been capable of sensitive repairs even when drastic work was required, he was condemned for wanting to improve on history for the sake of architectural propriety. To antiquarians, and to the *Antiquary* in particular, he had been brought up in 'the old school of ecclesiastical "restorers" who considered that if you pulled down an old building and erected a copy of it you were preserving the old work. Mr Pearson seemed unable to shake off this exploded and destructive conception of what true restoration means.'[44]

Sadly this was sometimes true, but not really true of his restoration of Peterborough's west front. If it was true of his proposed restoration of the crossing, it was less true of what he did. If the stones of a cracked and crumbling building about to fall are taken down, numbered and put back with the damage repaired, is that really erecting a copy? It is a matter of opinion. No repaired building can be what it was beforehand, and is bound to lose a little. When Pearson was sympathetic to a building, he kept that little to a minimum. Where buildings were 'modern' or had few features of architectural interest, he trod dangerous ground to make them 'effective'.

Peter Ferriday describes the recasing of the Westminster Abbey north transept as absurd and pointless, and the proposal to move Wren's Lincoln library a 'really wicked scheme'.[45] Misguided Pearson may have been, but never malevolent. Even so, for the *Athenaeum*, 'No building was safe in his hands.'[46]

Caröe on the other hand called Pearson 'one of the most learned, tender, and skilful of those whose lot it has been to preserve many of our most cherished monuments of antiquity'. Here speaks the architect. Unlike the antiquarian, he has to contend with clients and keep buildings in use. It is easy to prefer the SPAB's view, but the dilemma remains. Cathedrals have now become national monuments, centres for tourism as much as religious worship, and, though they still need drastic repairs, controversy has moved on to stately homes, houses, railway stations, warehouses, and industrial and commercial buildings, where continued use conflicts more sharply with their original form. Lastly, there is the acute problem of redundant churches.

Archbishop Benson may have the last words. He crystallized the contradictions and ambiguities of the matter after the reopening of Bristol Cathedral in 1895. 'In the restoration,' he wrote, 'I recognize Pearson's tender hand which makes things new yet leaves them looking old.'[47]

21 THE LAST DECADE

THE PUBLICITY which surrounded Pearson's appointment as architect of Truro ensured that he inherited the position of England's leading church architect, a position which had become vacant with Scott's death and which Street was too busy and too tired to fill before his own death. His practice expanded accordingly. With reliable assistants he was able to contain the extra work until he died in his eighty-first year, without it overwhelming him. With Street's death in 1881, and with Butterfield pursuing out-of-date High-Victorian ideals, the more adaptable and more slowly developing Pearson, now at the height of his creativity, reached the summit of his profession.

Perhaps it was because he felt that this involved him in certain duties, perhaps because the Truro competition had been unusually successful for its time, or perhaps only because Ewan Christian persuaded him—whatever the reason, he entered a competition just once again. In 1884 one hundred and one architects sent in portfolios of work to the Liverpool Cathedral Building Committee headed by their consulting architect, Ewan Christian. Pearson was among them. Christian recommended twelve architects including Pearson for further consideration; and along with Bodley, Brooks and William Emerson he was asked to submit a sketch design before they made their final choice. Pearson began one but in 1885 injured his right hand and with so much other work withdrew. Poor Emerson won the competition but never had the satisfaction of seeing his cathedral started as the chosen site was abandoned.

Pearson's other executed cathedral was designed for William Webber, formerly the vicar of Red Lion Square, who was consecrated Bishop of Brisbane, Australia, in 1885. In 1887 he returned to England both to commission Pearson to design a cathedral for him and to raise money for it. He did not insist on a cathedral to rival medieval ones; nor was there a committee requiring at the last minute an indigenous design. Webber had already obtained one masterpiece from Pearson. He was confident of getting another.

A design was ready by February 1889 (Plate 130), but Webber was less successful in raising money to pay for building it. Work only began on the east parts of the cathedral early in this century when Frank Pearson made minor modifications, mostly to reduce the amount of decoration. Later he extensively modified the design of the nave and west towers; the latter have not been built yet. The original plan was for a cruciform church with a wide nave of nearly thirty-five feet, and double aisles, apse and ambulatory, short transepts about half way along the length of the building, and an apsidal side chapel on the north (Plate 131). Apart from the central and west towers, the compact plan is more like those of some of Pearson's churches, though the ambulatory is not just a passage, but wide enough to fulfil its purpose.

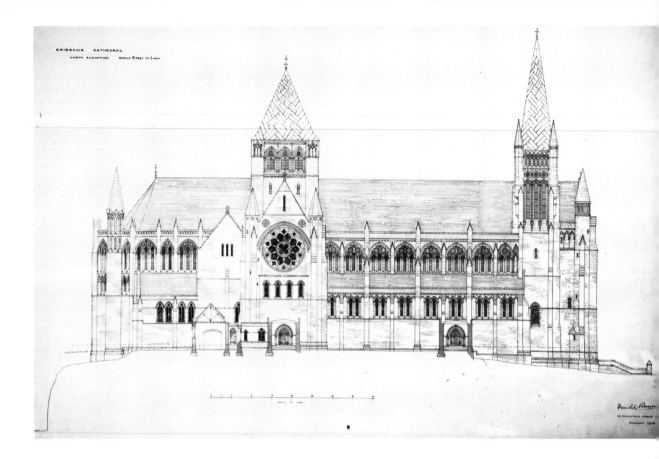

130. Brisbane Cathedral: the north elevation as modified by Frank Pearson in 1908; the nave has been lengthened, lancets of the transept have been exchanged for a rose and details of the east end simplified.

131. Brisbane Cathedral: plan (the square east chapel was later omitted).

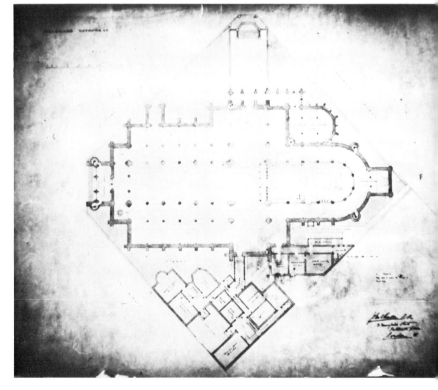

Truro Cathedral expresses Pearson's ideal of classic Gothic, combining elements from Lincoln and Normandy. Brisbane, like Kilburn, is spatially more intricate. The apse, probably inspired by Barcelona Cathedral, has very tall, slender piers supporting a high arcade which leaves only enough room beneath the wall arches of the vaulting for small quatrefoil clerestory lights (Plate 132). The three-storeyed ambulatory wall is treated as though it were the main wall. Brisbane has a hot climate, and like Street for his Crimea Memorial church, Pearson gave the cathedral narrow windows high up and a blank ground storey to keep out the sun (Plate 133). The apse and the high altar within it are lit by the clerestory windows in the outer wall, which are placed so high that they leave the ambulatory floor comparatively dark. Thus the ambulatory seems to be separated from the apse at ground level, but, higher up, the slender piers provide only a weakly defined spatial barrier between the two. In this Pearson achieved the same ambiguity and interpenetration of spaces as there is in the side elevation of Kilburn.

The exterior of the apse, with much of his father's decoration omitted by Frank Pearson, rises plain and supported only by shallow buttresses and stair turrets. Though much broader, there is a touch of Albi in it; for Ruskin, propriety would have been well served in its undoubted southern character.

Brisbane Cathedral was planned to have a nave like Truro's with sexpartite vaulting rising from major and minor piers, and an entrance between tall west towers. Pearson did not make a definitive design for the west front. An elevation of 1889 shows the end of the nave projecting clear of the towers as at Truro, with an entrance in a narthex. In 1897 he drew an impressively fine perspective considering his eighty years (Plate 134); here the towers are closer to the end of the nave, with the upper part of the west wall, as in many of his later churches, supported by a relieving arch which continues the line of the interior cross arches. The towers have massive buttresses, their strong vertical lines carrying on into corner turrets set before pyramidal spires.

With its apse based on Barcelona, Brisbane Cathedral is typical of some of Pearson's late churches where Catalan models inspired him to achieve subtle interpenetrations of spaces. As opposed to the more classical Truro, Brisbane is the fulfilment on a monumental scale of his feeling for the baroque.

The cathedral has never had the publicity—or criticism—which came to Truro. It was too far away and built too late. Those who have seen the two declare Brisbane the finer building. Having more of Pearson's churches in its design, this is easy to understand. Its historicism is worn more lightly; with less carved decoration, partly Frank Pearson's contribution, the strong accents of its powerful design stand out more sharply; its exciting spaces are more readily assimilable than exact proportions. Brisbane Cathedral is less an ideal creation, and at once more expressive. In short, the two cathedrals, on opposite sides of the globe, represent opposite facets of Pearson's genius.

The last ten years of Pearson's life saw little diminution of his output;

132. Brisbane Cathedral: the interior of the apse (above), and the interior looking east.

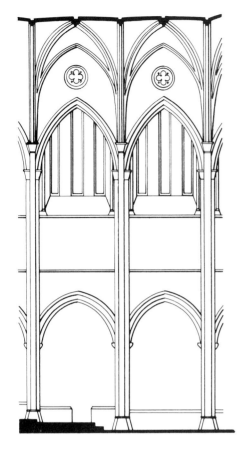

⎍⎍⎍⎍⎍⎍ 10 ft

133. Brisbane Cathedral: choir elevation.

134. Brisbane Cathedral: perspective from the south-west, of 1897.

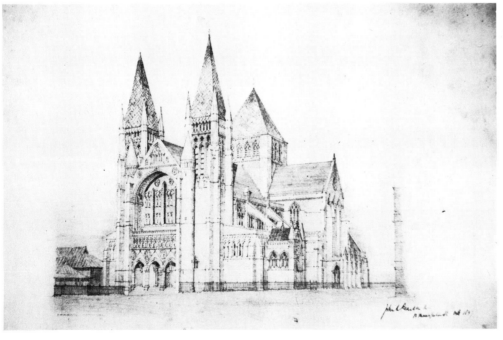

135. St John, Friern Barnet, 1890–1, from the east.

there were nearly twenty new churches. Among these, South Ascot church in Berkshire is memorable for its baptistery, an octagonal vaulted chamber set astride the south aisle wall. St Theodore, Port Talbot, Glamorgan, has quadripartite rib-vaults for all but nave and transepts; it is of his classic type with Early English detail and ornament consisting almost entirely of mouldings. Perhaps Pearson saw in the location of this, his largest Welsh church, a reason to provide a Celtic touch with a typically Breton turret over the chancel arch.

Two of these last twenty churches stand out because, like the great churches of the 1870s and early '80s, they are vaulted throughout. The earlier, St John, Friern Barnet, Middlesex, was designed in 1889, and the east parts were finished in 1891. The nave was built in 1901 by Frank Pearson, and the west end completed to his modified design in 1911.

The church was built for Frederick Hall, a former chaplain of St Peter's Home and curate of St Augustine, Kilburn. In 1888 he had visited the ruins of

204

Heisterbach abbey above the Rhine south of Bonn, and he asked Pearson to base his design on it. So Friern Barnet has a semi-circular apse with prominent flying buttresses and, inside, it is supported by paired circular piers (Plates 135 and 136). These features are absorbed into a characteristic design: the apsidal chancel is joined to an aisled nave of equal width; southwards is a chapel, also with an apse; and to the north are vestries and an

136. St John, Friern Barnet: the interior looking east.

organ chamber planned to have a tower built over them. In elevation there is the severity of Cullercoats, but the blank panels of the triforium are omitted giving the church lower proportions. The width and height of the cross arches are equal as at Upper Norwood; the church would consequently appear rather low, but for the tall clerestory lights rising right up into the vaults to practically the level of the ridge. The chancel arch barely projects, and the internal space is very simple and, unlike Cullercoats, uninterrupted by transepts. In its final form, the nave was built one bay longer than planned, and Frank Pearson gave it western transepts incorporating entrances on each side and a central space for the font. He retained his father's plan for the vault for the western bay, a quadripartite rib-vault with the now familiar pair of extra ribs springing from tripartite divisions in the end wall. The vault softens the termination of the west end and reflects the form of the apse at the east.

The second of these two vaulted churches, the Catholic Apostolic Church, Maida Avenue, Paddington, was built in the first few years of the 1890s. The details have not been disclosed by its proprietors; a pity, as it is the only English church which Pearson built for clients outside the established Anglican faith. It is the last of the type begun by St Michael, Croydon (Plate 137). The apsidal south chapel has minute aisles and an ambulatory separated from the body of the chapel by tall clustered shafts; it is a church within a church, yet differently planned from all the others Pearson had designed before (Plate 138). An extremely narrow further aisle separates it from the chancel, and here are the typical vistas of shafts and spaces with which he so loved to enrich the east ends of his churches.

There is an unusual though again typical arrangement of entrances and baptistery at the west end (Plate 139). The apsidal baptistery is centrally placed under a gallery built across the west end of the nave, and projects outwards beyond the building. The side walls of the nave project, too, by a complete bay beyond the west wall, and terminate in turrets between which an arch is carried across, at the same height as the nave vault inside the church, to support a decorated arcade and the roof gable. The west wall appears in a far deeper recess than at Truro. At ground level this recess is nearly but not quite filled by the projecting baptistery, which appears to be joined to the projecting nave walls by a passage which in its turn extends beyond the nave on either side as an open arcaded loggia, containing the entrance lobbies, to link the body of the church to the base of the otherwise detached tower on the south and to the caretaker's house on the north. The deep central recess is based on the central arch of the west front of Peterborough Cathedral; Pearson tried to avoid the peculiar effect of the Peterborough galilee squeezed into the central opening, but the projecting baptistery, which takes its place, looks as if it is about to be swallowed by the yawning jaws of the recessed end of the main body of the church. Hawksmoor would have enjoyed that.

The Catholic Apostolic Church is the last of Pearson's great vaulted

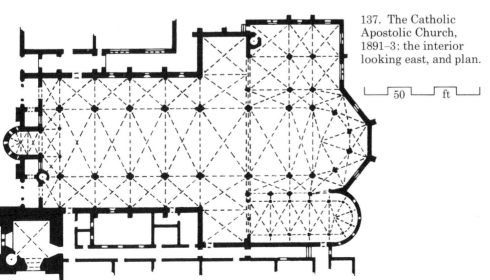

137. The Catholic Apostolic Church, 1891–3: the interior looking east, and plan.

50 ft

town churches, though by no means the last of his great vaulted buildings; he designed several large vaulted chapels which show his feeling for proportion and space no less than his churches do. One of them was his last completed design.

The earliest one, designed in 1885 for St Mary's Convent at Wantage in Berkshire, was built in 1887–9. From outside it appears to be an aisleless building with a square east end. This simplicity is echoed in the finely proportioned, vaulted interior. Only the sanctuary is not immediately comprehensible. Its east wall has triple openings in the form of an arcade; its quadripartite vault characteristically having two extra ribs on the east side springing from the arcade's divisions (Plate 140). Beyond the arcade are three small semi-octagonal spaces, the central one, a little wider than those flanking it, acting as a canopy for the altar. Each of these spaces has a vault with the same rib pattern in miniature as that of the eastern bay—four ribs and two extra ones springing from the east side—and ends with a lancet in a groined recess. Instead of the east end coming to an abrupt end, the space is thus split into three and gradually constricted. At first sight the termination appears to be apsidal; its actual form is only slowly revealed as one progresses eastwards, and not finally clear until it is possible to see into the three vaulted

138. (left) The Catholic Apostolic Church: the south chapel seen from the south transept.

139. The Catholic Apostolic Church from the south-west, the caretaker's house to the left and the stump of the tower to the right.

recesses beyond the triple arcade. The resulting spatial effect is intricate, but the repetition of the vaulting pattern unites the three small spaces to the body of the chapel, and their logical relationship is firmly established.

As Surveyor to Westminster Abbey, Pearson was involved in making designs for chapels to house the monuments of national worthies which were increasingly filling up the Abbey. Between 1888 and 1892 he made a series of designs for three proposed sites. The most acceptable of these was to the south of Henry VII's Chapel and east of the Chapter House. It had the advantage of being in an architecturally prominent position facing onto Old Palace Yard, and so not only could the chapel house monuments but it could itself be monumental. On the other hand access from the Abbey would have to be by way of confusing corridors carried under the flying buttresses of the Chapter House, and the chapel would not appear to be part of the Abbey. Pearson's various proposals all have projecting apsidal side or end chapels to each bay. A perspective shows a cruciform building rather higher than the Chapter House with double aisles running from west to east across the transept ends[1] (Plate 141). The ornament is in the Decorated style to contrast with Henry VII's Chapel: such a site required rich decoration, Pearson no doubt believed, but his fine drawing suggests 'too much cheese-cut Bath stone'. Nevertheless the chapel's massing is skilful, and the interior with its walls curving round successive apses, with its arcades of paired shafts, and presumably with all the spaces vaulted, would have been characteristic of him at his most exciting, yet unlike any of his church interiors.

The second proposed site was where the old refectory had stood on the south side of the cloister. Although not part of the Abbey church, it was part of its former buildings. However, there were difficulties with lighting and the proposed chapel would be unpleasantly close to Ashburnham House, it would interfere with the remains of the refectory, and, finally, it would be hidden from view with little of its exterior visible. Here Pearson proposed a long hall with much the same plan as the former refectory (Plate 142). Its side walls were to be arcaded and have internal buttressing, so that each bay would provide a frame for large free-standing monuments. The ornamental detail was again to be in the Decorated style, with Geometrical tracery for the windows, and a vault with a ridge rib, tiercerons and liernes, like the nearby cloister vault; the eleventh-century remains of the refectory wall including the blank arcade with plain block capitals were to be retained in the lower levels of the chapel.

The third site was on the north side of the nave where it was proposed to add an outer aisle as a monumental chapel. Such a building would certainly appear to be part of the Abbey, and there were no buildings in the way of this project, but being the only uncluttered part of the Abbey it was immediately objectionable. Pearson's proposals for a chapel here are not illustrated, but he described alternative treatments:

140. The chapel of St Mary's Convent, Wantage, 1887–9, showing the interior looking east.

141. Project for a monumental chapel for a site to the south of Henry VII's Chapel, 1892.

One of these takes the form of an additional aisle to the nave, with chapels attached for the display of monuments and with communications leading to it from the west end of the nave and from the north transept . . . It will be readily understood how all the recesses between the great buttresses and other recesses provided in the plan would lend themselves to the arrangement and display of the monuments . . . My second plan takes the form of a double cloister glazed on both sides, enclosing a garth with approaches from the Abbey similar to the previous scheme. The four sides towards the garth I propose to divide into chapels, by transverse walls, and recesses formed by the great buttresses of the nave would be available as before.[3]

Any of these chapels would have caused an uproar, especially from the Society for the Protection of Ancient Buildings, and it is probably just as well that none was built.[4] Pearson had plenty to do in less controversial surroundings.

In the first years of the 1890s he designed another chapel quite unlike any other before. It was for the Protestant cemetery of Ta Braxia at Floriana, just outside Valetta, Malta, and completed by 1896 for Lord Stanmore as a memorial to his wife, her tomb being placed under a canopy on the outside of

212

2. Project for a monumental chapel to be built on the site of Westminster Abbey's ancient refectory: the interior as illustrated in the *Builder* 1890 59 491.

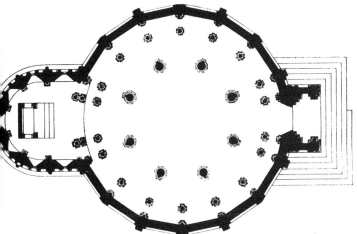

143. (facing page) Ta Braxia cemetery chapel, *c.* 1894: view from west.

144. Ta Braxia cemetery chapel: Pearson's photograph of the interior, and plan.

50   ft

145. The Astor Estate Office, 1892–5, from the south.

the apse (Plate 143). The chapel is sixteen-sided; around a central dome on an octagonal drum are double aisles, eight cylindrical piers separating the inner one from the octagonal centre, the piers being doubled between the aisles except for the bays opening into the west entrance and the apsidal chancel (Plate 144). The details of the chapel, like its plan, are Italian Romanesque, even Byzantine. The vaulted interior, the double aisles with their proliferation of shafts and vaulting ribs, and the contrast between the brightly lit central space and the dark aisles are all typical of Pearson. Frank Pearson played some part in designing the chapel; it can be seen as the precursor of his Romanesque churches at Madrid and at Cap d'Antibes, but despite its unusual plan and style, his father's hand is strongly evident.

The Byzantine style was all the vogue in the 1890s, reaching a climax with Francis Bentley's Westminster Cathedral, commissioned in 1894. Pearson first introduced elements of Byzantine origin into his detailing in the 1860s: Vauxhall has a single capital in the north chapel which is a pure example of this style. After his visit to Italy in 1874, he occasionally turned again to the style for details. The Ta Braxia chapel shows how well he could adopt new fashions for whole buildings when the occasion demanded, but still keep his architectural ideals intact.

Pearson's last domestic work catches reflections from his entire career.

146. (right) The Astor Estate Office: one of the oriels.

216

His client was William Waldorf Astor. He wanted an eminent architect, and Pearson was as eminent as any. To have chosen a church architect might seem strange and Pearson was indeed reluctant to work for Astor, yet it was a fruitful choice. Astor had inherited a vast fortune in America, and on the strength of it finally settled in England. Here he built up a newspaper empire and indulged his love of European history and literature in various building works at his town and country homes in Carlton House Terrace and at Cliveden respectively. These were undertaken by Pearson. No one was so different from his early clients as Astor, yet he wanted the same thing—historicism. His romantic attachment to the past, perhaps even his need to identify with the culture of Europe's past, are comparable to the Tractarians' desire to have churches reminding them of their ancient faith. This attachment found architectural fulfilment in the miniature palace which Pearson designed in 1892–3 and completed in 1895 as his Estate Office in Temple Gardens overlooking the Thames (Plate 145).

The exterior is in an ornate Tudor style executed in finely carved Portland stone. Around the large, mullioned and transomed windows is much enrichment with linenfold and arabesques. A frieze with triglyphs and Tudor roses in the metopes runs round the building, giving way above oriel windows to bands of more arabesque, and over all is a cornice punctuated with grotesques (Plate 146). It is lavish yet free.

147. The Astor Estate Office: inner hall and staircase.

148. The Astor Estate Office: the gallery.

The planning is clear. A hall leads into a staircase compartment with an upper-storey gallery with the main rooms opening off it, a great hall taking up all of one side. All the main rooms have opulent decoration, much being designed by Frank Pearson and executed by well-known carvers and sculptors. Only the best was good enough for Astor. The inner hall has cedar-panelled walls and a fine, geometrically patterned floor of marble, jasper, porphyry and onyx, like the chancel floors which followed Pearson's visit to Rome (Plate 147). The ornate staircase has newel posts supporting carved figures by Thomas Nicholls representing the chief characters from *The Three Musketeers* (Astor's favourite book). The gallery above carries yet more carved figures by Nicholls, and in a frieze are eighty-two characters from Shakespeare (Plate 148).

The library is full of richly carved panelling (Plate 149); and originally contained a great marble chimney-piece carved by W. S. Frith, bearing the names of the Astor family. The major room is in the form of a great medieval hall, with a hammerbeam roof recalling the one Pearson helped to build in the New Hall of Lincoln's Inn, fifty years before (Plate 150). The plan differs from medieval precedent, for each end is a mirror-image of the other, and the main entrance is from the centre of one side. Instead of high and low ends, there are two large openings with basket arches, with elaborate cedarwood chimney-pieces in ingle-nooks on one side, and large stained-glass windows on the

149. The Astor Estate Office: the library.

150. The Astor Estate Office: the great hall.

other. The stained glass is by Clayton and Bell representing Swiss landscapes at sunrise at the east end and sunset at the west. Once again there is rich panelling and arcading, here filled with carved gilded plaques, Astor's *Who's Who in History*: Alfred the Great and Bismarck, Fair Rosamund and Anne Boleyn keep unlikely company with Voltaire.

Pevsner calls the Astor Estate Office a 'perfect gem of its kind', and notes its early Elizabethan style 'treated with great finesse, and nowhere with slavishly copied elements'.[5] Pearson gave Astor a building truly Edwardian in its splendour; yet it is obviously backward-looking. How much Pugin would have admired it, and how much he would have welcomed an opportunity to have built just such a building for a wealthy client fifty years before! The Astor Estate Office is reminiscent of Scarisbrick Hall, though Pearson was grave where Pugin had been brittle. It is as if Pearson had made concrete one of Pugin's idealised inns: the south front has memories of Pugin's illustrations of The George at Glastonbury and The Angel Inn at Grantham. No less than Pugin, how much Burges would have enjoyed the interior with its schemes of historical and legendary heroes! He would have designed a more light-hearted toy; yet grave though it is, Pearson's work is a toy. It is more substantial than, say, Strawberry Hill, but it was designed for much the same reason: as an extravaganza to entertain. It does so with all the opulence and sensitivity of the last decade of the century. The Revival had turned full circle.

Pearson's architectural career lasted for sixty-six busy years. Although details of his health are sparse, he must have had a good constitution to stand up to the gruelling programme of travelling, visiting, office work and designing which continued to the end of his life with little respite. His holidays were not always regular, but as he grew older he tried at least to take a break in the autumn: he knew how to relax, and how to delegate.

He was ill early in 1887 and stayed at home while the weather remained cold; he was ill again in 1888 and 1892, and Codd had to attend meetings away from London in his place. It is impossible to know how grave these illnesses were; now in his seventies, he may simply have made slight indispositions the excuse for not making arduous train journeys.

In the winter of 1894 he was ill again, and although the attack may have been mild, there is no doubt of its effect; in a letter excusing his employer, Codd wrote, 'Mr Pearson is better and has gone away for a change, he does not regain his strength so rapidly as could be wished.'[6]

Plans were delayed; meetings missed. But though the effect of ill health on his work during the last twenty years of his life was undeniable, it was practically negligible. Apart from failing to complete designs for Liverpool Cathedral, all was accomplished. With the great series of churches designed while he was in his sixties only gradually falling off in number but not at all in quality as he approached his eightieth year, and with the incessant problems of restorations of cathedrals and numerous churches, he had never been busier in his life.

. The Woking Convent chapel, 1898–1900: the interior king east.

152. Woking Convent chapel: the interior of the apse.

Luckily he was helped by his son who, after his marriage, lived next door to him. Frank Pearson had a deep understanding of his father's methods of work, and he willingly and sympathetically interpreted his father's wishes. He took on a major part in designing the fittings of the Astor estate office, and he probably played an extensive part in designing other buildings too. All Pearson wanted when he insisted that Frank should follow his own profession was utterly fulfilled. During the 1890s Frank began practising on his own account, and first exhibited at the Royal Academy in 1891. His houses evolved from the Jacobean of his father's Lechlade and Westwood; one of his churches took All Saints, Hove, as its point of departure; others developed the revived Byzantine style.

During the 1890s Frank and Cecilia Pearson had four daughters; the third, Marion, now Mrs Morgan, was christened at St Augustine, Kilburn, then complete but for its steeple. She was born just too late to have any personal memories of her grandfather, but in treasuring all that was told to her of him as well as safeguarding many of his papers, she has done more than anyone else in keeping his memory alive.

On 28 January 1897 Pearson went down to Woking to have preliminary

221

discussions about a new chapel for St Peter's Convent which he had built a dozen years before for his old client, Benjamin Lancaster. The discussions centred on the required size, the proposed site and the money available. In March he told the committee of Sisters for whom he was doing the work that the dimensions must be reduced to fit the site and their purse. In June he took his designs to Woking and on 7 July they were accepted; contract drawings were prepared and in November Pearson sent tenders, the one put in by Luscombe, his contractor at Bristol, being accepted for £8,945.

Building was to start immediately and the formal cutting of the first sod was planned for 17 December; but six days beforehand Pearson died. Work was postponed. With Frank Pearson in charge, the foundation-stone was at last laid on 9 July 1898, and the completed chapel was dedicated just two years later.

Unlike the chapel at Wantage, Woking Covent chapel is aisled, and has the section of a hall church. The aisles stop before the east end which terminates in an impressive apse rising unbuttressed from the ground like Vauxhall's (Plate 151). The bay before the apse narrows towards the east, and opening off each side is a further apse, a little smaller than the east one. Outside, the chapel has a lobed appearance, the plan and elevation with its three tall apses rising to the roof suggesting a Byzantine or an Early Christian, centrally planned church. Inside, the effect is quite different. From the west end, the chapel appears to terminate simply in a single apse. Moving east, one sees further spaces, slowly revealing themselves on each side, with light flooding through to illuminate a baldachino. Finally, when the east is reached, the form of the side spaces is clear: apses with vaults similar to that of the slightly bigger eastern one. They are like tall, round, radiating chapels opening off a polygonal apse without the usual ambulatory—a nice ambiguity. The dual function of the side spaces to provide extra light and to form diagonal spaces at first mysterious and only slowly revealed is as fine as anything Pearson had done before, yet quite new (Plate 152).

The chapel has a crypt under its east end, which has a similar plan, except that it is arcaded with shafts supporting the floor above, thus forming narrow aisles. Here the excellent ornament designed by Frank Pearson is all Byzantine in style, both the carved capitals and the wall surfaces which are partly faced in patterned marbles, partly in mosaic. He designed the baldachino in the main chapel too, though it is very similar to his father's at Peterborough Cathedral, which is inspired by the one at Sta Maria in Cosmedin in Rome.

The vaulting, the mouldings, and the form of the tall lancets are all early Gothic, typical of Pearson; the basis of the plan—part late Gothic, part early Christian—is not like anything he had used before, but its spatial function has all the drama one expects from him. Even in the last months of his life, he continued to find inexhaustible inspiration in the buildings of the past, and could absorb what he wanted, to make fresh designs which have all his best qualities: a unique feeling for mass, proportion and space, above all for unity.

✒ EPILOGUE

PEARSON was working right up to the end. 'Mr Pearson may be said almost to have died in harness,' recorded the *Builder*, 'and those who were acquainted with his sturdy figure and appearance would never have guessed that he was over eighty years of age. It is not often that we hear of an architect keeping up the active exercise of his art, and apparently the full interest in it, through so long a life.'[1] In November 1897, apart from proposals for Chichester, Wakefield and Perth Cathedrals, he was attending to working drawings for the chapel at Woking and obtaining tenders for its execution. The decision to finish the nave of Truro had been made and that required attention. He knew he could never live to see the cathedral completed, and early in December he told his daughter-in-law Cecilia, 'You will never see it finished either.'[2] He was wrong. His apparent despondency was caused by ill health. On 2 or 3 December he had suffered an intestinal obstruction; an operation was performed four days later, but he lacked the strength to recover from it. He had one last satisfaction: Frank told him that Kilburn's spire was finished. At 1.15 in the morning of Saturday, 11 December 1897, he died at his home in Mansfield Street. Asthenia—general weakness—was certified as the cause of death.

His death was reported the same day in *The Times*. A day or two later it was announced at the Royal Institute of British Architects 'with evident emotion', emotion felt for the loss of a friend and the most eminent of its elder fellows.[3]

The Queen sent a message of sympathy, and letters of condolence came from former clients: the Earl of Mount Edgcumbe, Earl Fitzwilliam, Lord Stanmore, Lord Hotham, and others with a more modest position in society. Many of Pearson's old friends and patrons were long dead: George Townsend, Archdeacon Bentinck, Dr Spyers, and William Taunton; they had been more recently followed to the grave by Sir Charles Anderson, Sir George Prevost, Benjamin Lancaster, and Archbishop Benson.

Pearson was buried in Westminster Abbey at noon at 16 December.[4] His pall-bearers included the Presidents of the Royal Academy and the Royal Institute of British Architects, the second Bishop of Truro, the Dean of Peterborough, the Sub-dean of Lincoln, the former Chairman of the Westminster Hall Select Committee, and the architect Alfred Waterhouse. Among the mourners were Pearson's family and intimate circle including Caröe, who was to design his tombstone, and his assistant, John Codd. Numerous architects and artists came, some representing the Royal Academy and the Royal Institute of British Architects, the Architectural Association and other bodies; most, simply as friends. Among them were Sir Arthur Blomfield, T. G. Jackson, H. H. Armstead, Thomas Brock, W. W. Ouless, Norman Shaw, Hamo Thornycroft, Henry Tamworth Wells, Aston Webb,

James Brooks, William Emerson, J. P. Seddon, R. Phené Spiers, Alfred Gotch, John Slater, Paul Waterhouse, William White, Leonard Stokes and J. J. Stevenson.

After the choral funeral service, Pearson's massive oak coffin laden with wreaths and flowers was taken to the south side of the nave where a grave had been prepared beside those of Barry, Scott and Street. The concluding part of the service was read and Pearson's body was committed.

Deeply affected, Caröe wrote:

As he was being laid to rest by the side of the great ones of the past, under the canopy of the Abbey which he loved and served so well . . . the solemn office of the dead, rendered without pomp or undue ceremony as befitted his modest life and bearing, but with a perfection recalling his own strivings and ideals, seemed to speak of his attainments—the love of friends, the warm esteem of fellow-workers, the regret of all, and this—the nation's recognition—the most honoured of resting-places, which England bestows only upon her most worthy sons.

Frank Pearson was appointed in his father's place to complete the nave of Truro, and the work progressed rapidly. He completed churches at Hove, Bournemouth and Friern Barnet; he began two more of his father's masterpieces, a small one and a large one: the chapel at Woking and Brisbane Cathedral. He completed his father's plans for Chichester, Wakefield and Perth, and executed the work. He designed a church of his own, at Auckland, New Zealand, which with its Early English detail and massive oak roof supported by stone transverse arches rivals his father's church at Hove. He continued where his father had left off in supplying Astor's architectural requirements, and so it was with many of his father's other clients.

Early in 1898 Pearson's will was proved; apart from the legacies amounting to a few hundred pounds bequeathed to his sister, his sister-in-law, and John Codd, his fortune of nearly £52,000 was left to his son. It was less than half what Scott had left twenty years before, but a fortune no less, and some recompense to Frank for submerging his own personality in the furtherance of his father's work.

With Pearson's death the process of reappraising his work began. There already existed a body of criticism: from the start his churches had been commended in professional journals, and Eastlake had favourably commented on a handful of early works, recognizing especially the importance of St Peter, Vauxhall; but when he was writing, Kilburn was not yet built. Shortly before Pearson was chosen to design Truro, the *Architect* wrote:

There are few architects at the present day whose work evinces so much care, study, and attention to detail, as does that of Mr Pearson. We do not see silly caprices, or straying away into less pure styles such as Perpendicular or Flamboyant . . . one sees the evidence of a manly handling which culls the exquisite flowers of the best periods of Gothic architecture,

224

but arranges them in such a bouquet that it can scarcely be said that they are medieval at all.[5]

These are dated remarks, but perceptive.

Many fine words were spoken when Pearson was presented with the R.I.B.A. Gold Medal in 1880. Beresford Hope described his churches at Vauxhall, Kilburn and Red Lion Square as a 'noble trilogy of true and good work, subtly conceived and nobly carried out by an architect who held up the standard of traditionary art when as yet the future of traditionary art seemed hopeless'; and as for Truro, 'its architect's name would be famous in the annals of the land'.[6]

That was optimistic. Pearson's close associates made more modest claims. Newberry in 1896 restricted himself to describing his former employer's work, and, though he eulogised some of it, went no further than to say that it showed 'a vigorous and daring individuality'.

A week after Pearson's death the obituary notices of the *Builder* and the *Building News* appeared.[7] The *Building News* gave a comprehensive description of his career beginning, 'The rapidly dwindling school of Gothic Revivalists has lost its most distinguished exponent.' The *Builder*'s obituary was more analytical and exactly caught his conservatism.

> Without ever condescending to an eccentricity, or appearing to turn aside in the slightest degree to seek originality for its own sake, without ever even venturing perceptibly beyond the limits of precedent in the style he adopted, he succeeded in producing a series of monuments as interesting as they are beautiful.

Among the characteristics of his style, it singled out, 'His love of lofty proportions and of increasing their effect by every legitimate means, his unusual skill and thoughtfulness in making the most of the site and surroundings, and the insight and learning that he brought to bear upon the study of details.' To conclude,

> It is, no doubt, the vaulting and such features as triforium galleries and flying buttresses to which it leads, that have led to some of Mr Pearson's churches ... being called with some justice, miniature cathedrals, rather than simple churches ... More competent observers are, however, attracted rather by the carefully considered and learned detail, the skilfully adjusted proportions, and especially by the marked harmonious character of the whole.

Two notices were unable to rise above the bitterness caused by the restoration of the west front of Peterborough Cathedral. The *Antiquary* ignored him as a church designer;[8] the *Athenaeum* did not: 'A certain coldness amounting to timidity injured his vaultings, of which he was proud; while when mural painting and stained glass were introduced into his churches, they were never exhilarating or instructive.'[9] The latter comment is hardly true; the former is spiteful nonsense.

225

None appraised Pearson's work more perceptively than Caröe; he was not impartial, but in describing Pearson's ability to design vaulting he refuted the *Athenaeum*'s comments.

In Mr Pearson's case that innate power of appreciation and sympathy already alluded to had undoubtedly given him a keener insight than most of his fellows into the more abstruse causes and effects and methods of construction in which lies that indescribable factor 'quality' in architecture, quite apart from correctness of form or detail. In nothing is this more apparent than in his vaulting. The carefully studied plan of the ribs upon the cap, so primarily essential to a successful treatment, the best pitch of the diagonals and transverse ribs to give well-proportioned rise as viewed from below, their relative section and importance, differing so much in different surroundings, the awkward opposition of optical lines their conjunction is ever ready to set up if proper corrections are not warily introduced, and, not the least important of many intricacies, the constructional value and treatment without crudeness of the horizontal beds and springers—all the factors in successful vaulting—he had learned to control so readily that no space was too irregular or awkward to induce the least appearance of effort in the vault he threw across it.

The first completely impartial critic was Herman Muthesius, whose justly celebrated book, *Das Englische Haus*, has eclipsed its companion on churches. There he wrote:

A figure surpassing all others in the history of the new English church architecture and in whom one must perhaps find the high point of its development is the great church builder, J. L. Pearson. His activity as a church architect had begun at the start of the 1840s and stretched without a break until his death in 1897 which cut off this extraordinarily vigorous man in full career. Thus he had not only experienced the whole course of the development of the Gothic Revival from its beginning, but had also played one of the leading roles within it.[10]

So long as the Gothic Revival stood, Pearson's position was secure. In 1880 Beresford Hope realised that it was under attack; Muthesius saw its achievements as only partially successful, and Truro demonstrated its failures. The twentieth century gradually turned its back on the Gothic Revival and only occasional critics stood up for it. Some, like Maurice Adams, remembered its later phase. Like Butterfield, Pearson was 'also of a retiring temperament, was equally original, and produced buildings unsurpassed by any man of his time'; he was 'a master of the first degree'.[11]

Then came a new generation to whom the Gothic Revival was history. Goodhart-Rendel's *Index of Victorian Churches and Restorations* is full of illuminating aphorisms and complimentary remarks about his works. In 1933 E. Milner White reviewed the architecture of the Oxford Movement. 'A typical Pearson church is a thing wholly "sui generis",' he wrote, and their

226

architect, 'a pioneer with no followers save Bodley on occasions . . . [Pearson] never made a mistake with towers and spires. None but he again has been able to naturalise the apse.' Kilburn was 'daringly unconventional' and this and his other late churches were 'works of genius'.[12]

Just before the Second World War when the Gothic Revival was hardly considered seriously, a book appeared which was to renew interest in the subject, Basil Clarke's *Church Builders of the Nineteenth Century*. He recognized that Vauxhall was Pearson's 'first really fine church'; he described the later ones and concluded:

His planning and construction are characteristic. His churches are unmistakably late nineteenth century, in spite of their mediaevalisms. They may remind travelled ecclesiologists of churches in France; but in fact they are not like any others. They are English, in spite of certain features borrowed from abroad. They are churches designed for the carrying out of the services of the English Prayer Book in the manner that became customary in a large number of parishes during the second period of the Catholic revival, and for the accommodation of large Anglican congregations. And they are planned according to the good taste, common sense and deep ecclesiastical knowledge of one man.[13]

Since 1951 Pearson's buildings have found deserved recognition in Pevsner's *The Buildings of England*. He summarizes Pearson's work thus:

Essentially he is a church architect and a Gothicist. His best churches of the 1870s and 1880s are among the finest of their day not only in England but in Europe. Their style is C13 Franco-English, their decorative detail extremely sparing, and their spatial composition quite free and un-imitative.[14]

In some recent books on Victorian architecture Pearson has been omitted or misunderstood.[15] He is briefly mentioned for Holy Trinity, Bessborough Gardens, by Henry-Russell Hitchcock in his *Early Victorian Architecture in Britain*, and again in his monumental *Architecture: Nineteenth and Twentieth Centuries* where he notes Pearson's 'truly High Victorian love of grand and bold effects' continuing into his late work.[16] Hitchcock describes one of Pearson's buildings as 'an excellent example of the possibilities of free planning and free composition within the frame of medieval precedent. The detail is simple and related to the general structure, the composition is ingeniously studied, and there is very little extraneous ornament.'[17] This could apply to any of his great churches, yet it was written about Quar Wood. From its time, Pearson kept to these standards for forty years more; but despite that, his work never became stereotyped, as Hitchcock recognizes.

Butterfield seems to have frozen for life in the mode of his early maturity, and as a result produced ever feebler work after the mid sixties; Pearson was able to maintain a leading position with a younger generation grown chaster and more archaeological in its standards without forsaking his pursuit of those more abstractly architectonic values which gave distinction to his early work.[18]

As a church builder Pearson became a Gothicist by necessity; but inheriting the ideals of the last years of neo-classicism, he could give his Gothic buildings an instinctive sense of proportion seldom found in the work of his fellows. He was a slow developer and conservative; his innovations were personal, and unlike those of Pugin, Scott, Butterfield and Street were seldom copied. In recompense, his career was long; had it been as short as Street's, he would have designed nothing after St Augustine, Kilburn; had it been as short as Pugin's, it would have stopped with Holy Trinity, Bessborough Gardens.

As it was, Pearson was the only great Victorian church architect whose career extended through the three clearly marked phases of the Gothic Revival, and the only one to produce great works representative of each of them. In the early phase, apart from Holy Trinity, Bessborough Gardens, there are still the surviving churches at Llangasty Talyllyn and Eastoft; and there is Treberfydd House, a small masterpiece. Taste required an ideal; Pearson achieved it and in doing so, he stood alongside Pugin, Scott and R. C. Carpenter. He carried the ideal with him into his later works.

For the High Victorian phase there are Quar Wood and the fine series of churches from Scorborough to Appleton-le-Moors, full of the vigour of their time, but even these show reserve and a feeling for precedent. Here he expanded his horizons to stand alongside Butterfield and Street. At Vauxhall he perfected the town church providing a model for Brooks and a prototype for himself.

Lastly there are his late Victorian works, which appeared during the thirty years beginning with Sutton Veny and ending with the chapel at Woking. To his earlier characteristics he added a newly found mastery of space and an ability to create all the effects he wanted, soberly classical or ambiguously baroque, indissolubly unified by vaulting of the classical French type based on the structural logic of the quadripartite rib-vault. For this he stood at the head of his profession—a formidable achievement.

Nevertheless Pearson's faults cannot be ignored. His love of precedent and his extensive knowledge could lead to dullness. His sculptural decoration, however accurate, however hierarchical, often lacked one essential: a breath of life. He was at his best when he relied on sparing detail, though the result might be a little cold.

The combination of archaeological knowledge and reticent character led him to undertake restorations for determined clergy that ranged from the highly successful at Stow and Riccal to the rightly condemned at Westminster. His standards were those of his age; when they were overturned, he was at least partly able to adapt to them.

Muthesius found Pearson's greatest failure at Truro. The design was far more bound by precedent than those of his churches. It is a pity that Muthesius could not have seen Brisbane. Like the Church of England, Truro failed to be truly modern. How could it have been otherwise? It is for that failure, though, that the Victorians have been most strongly criticized. The roots of the modern style have been traced to the works of architects from Butterfield to Voysey, and the writings of others from Pugin to Morris. Some nineteenth-century architects sought deliberately to create a modern style and failed. Freed from contemporary architectural propriety, an engineer like Barlow and an estate manager like Paxton were able to respond to new requirements with new materials and new forms. This naturally was worrying; but, designing churches, houses and schools—buildings, that is, for age-old requirements—and steeped in a continuous tradition of eclecticism and an even older one of historicism, Pearson did not tackle such theoretical problems as the future of architecture in an industrial age. He never doubted his mission. He would neither philosophize nor innovate. Perhaps this reduces his stature; it probably accounts for his failure to produce a noteworthy school of followers.

Historians are rightly concerned with innovation; they will see Pearson as epitomizing an age, not leading it. Today's taste responds to nineteenth-century architects more as designers of surfaces than as designers of spaces, so Pearson has not yet received his due. Despite his failures and restricted practice, Pearson was a great Victorian architect. Architecture is concerned with space, mass and surface. It shares surface with painting and sculpture, mass with sculpture alone. Space is architecture's own special province. As a designer of surfaces Pearson was inconsistent. The poor decorative sculpture in his churches and his addiction to Bath stone have to be balanced against his happy use of local materials and the contrast he gave to ornate parts by areas left quite plain. As a designer of masses, Pearson was almost entirely successful. He took the greatest care in balancing the parts of his buildings, from the early suavity of Holy Trinity, Bessborough Gardens, to the bounding outlines of Truro. Perhaps it counts as failure that so many of his churches were intended to gain much from steeples that remained unbuilt. His massing shows the best elements of High Victorian vigour, never its elephantine ones; and this continues into his late churches, which are boldly modelled even when cheapness reduced their outlines to plain geometrical shapes.

As a designer of spaces, Pearson was supreme. His skill in vaulting allowed him to produce the spatial intricacies of Kilburn or Red Lion Square without the unity of the whole being jeopardized. Similarly he could provide delightful contrasts—as between the main body of Croydon and its side chapel, the one part classical, the other ambiguous and in a spirit which is quite baroque. Only second to this is his ability to proportion his churches, especially with his remarkable use of the Golden Section. This is architecture's special realm; and this is why Pearson has a special eminence among architects of whatever era and whatever type of building.

Within this framework Pearson indeed was an innovator: he produced a new architecture from old forms. The results do not startle, but this does not diminish their value. He dug deeply into the past and found inspiration in widely divergent places. That can be done by anyone: only genius can weld such material into an indivisible whole. Here lies his originality; here Pearson cheerfully and triumphantly accepted Ruskin. Let Ruskin have the last word: 'We want no new style of architecture. A man who has the gift will take up any style that is going, the style of his day, and will work in that, and be great in that, and make everything that he does in it look as fresh as if every thought of it had just come down from heaven.'[19]

153. John Pettie's portrait of Pearson early in the 1880s, commissioned by Alexander Macdonald, the Scottish connoisseur, as one of many Academicians whose friendship he esteemed.

NOTES TO THE TEXT

PROLOGUE

1. Based on accounts in *B* 1880 38 723–4 and *BN* 1880 38 678–9.
2. W. D. Caröe's anonymous memoir of Pearson in *Journal of the R.I.B.A.* 3rd s. 1897–8 5 113–21.

CHAPTER 1

1. The Bible along with most of Pearson's surviving personal papers is in the possession of his grand-daughter Mrs Marion Morgan, who has supplied the information for much of this chapter.
2. No record of Pearson's baptism has been found in any surviving Durham parish register; the registers of the embassy at Brussels survive only from 1818 (London, Guildhall Library Ms. 11199). The census returns at the Public Record Office show: 1841 (HO 107/320), aged 20, born foreign parts; 1851 (HO 107/1480), age 33, born Brussels; 1861 (RG 9/72), aged 43, born Brussels; 1871 (RG 10/157), age 53, born in Belgium, British subject.
3. Obituaries in *The Times* 13 December 1897, and *BN* 1897 73 866.
4. These books are listed in Part II of the Bibliography.
5. *CB* 1867 21 1–7.
6. The drawings are bound in a volume entitled *Tracings by J. L. Pearson, R.A. vol. II*; it is in the possession of Pearson's great-grandson, Mr M. N. Playford. The other five volumes are in the possession of Mrs Morgan.
7. Durham County Record Office D/Ch/C/1561.
8. *Ibid.* 1564.
9. *Ibid.* 1599 and 1602.
10. Caröe.
11. *Tracings* vol. 4.
12. Quoted by Caröe.
13. Durham County Record Office D/Ch/C/1613, 1619, 1620.
14. Diary 1842. In the Electoral Register for County Durham 1843 40 936, John Robson appears for the first time as the freeholder of a house in New North Road. He was the owner of a steam cornmill on the road, one hundred yards south of which lay the house. The cornmill has now gone and its site is occupied by a bus station; the house is used as the offices of the bus company.

CHAPTER 2

1. I am grateful to Dr Jill Allibone for letting me use information from her unpublished thesis on Salvin.
2. In *Tracings* vols 1, 2, 3.
3. Diary 1842.
4. *Proceedings of the R.I.B.A.* 1892 N.S. 8 191–2.
5. *B* 1845 3 521–2.
6. Eastlake 212.
7. R. Blomfield, *Memoirs of an Architect* (London, 1932) 39.
8. G. G. Scott, *Personal and Professional Recollections* (London, 1879) 88.

CHAPTER 3

1. A. W. N. Pugin *An Apology for the Revival of Christian Architecture* (London, 1843) 6.
2. *Ibid.* 25.
3. In the possession of Mrs Morgan.
4. The title of Plate 2 in A. W. N. Pugin, *The True Principles of Pointed or Christian Architecture* (London, 1841).
5. J. N. Summerson, *Victorian Architecture: Four Studies in Evaluation* (New York and London, 1970) 60.
6. ICBS 3200. Sources for details of individual buildings are to be found in the Catalogue of Works.
7. *E* 1842–3 2 165.
8. *B* 1848 6 375.
9. *E* 1852 13 409–12.
10. Recounted by John Whichcord, President of the R.I.B.A., at the presentation of the Royal Gold Medal to Pearson in 1880 *BN* 1880 38 679.
11. *BN* 1897 73 866.
12. *E* 1849–50 10 235.
13. *E* 1852 13 409–12.
14. *E* 1851 12 231–2.
15. H. Muthesius, *Die Neuere Kirchliche Baukunst in England* (Berlin, 1902) 34.
16. In his pamphlet written for the SPAB, *Concerning Westminster Abbey* (London, 1893).

CHAPTER 4

1. I am indebted for information about the Raikes family to the late Major-General Sir Geoffrey Raikes, the grandson of Robert Raikes of Treberfydd, and his nephew and daughter, Major and Mrs R. D. Raikes. This information has been

supplemented by J. R. Bailey in his enlargement of T. Jones, *A History of the County of Brecknock* vol. 3 (Brecknock, 1911) 219–21.

2. Pearson's Ledger B f. 1 (in the possession of Mrs Morgan).

3. In this letter, dated 8 February 1892, Pearson calls himself 'the friend you so freely made of me some 48 or 49 years ago'; he thus first met the Raikeses in 1843 or 1844. The letter and the gold cup referred to in it are at Treberfydd.

4. The information on Hippisley comes from A. E. Hippisley (edited and expanded by I. F. Jones), *Some Notes on the Hippisley Family* (Taunton, 1952) 48–55.

5. Newberry, Eastlake 382, and J. R. Bailey, *History of Brecknock*. See also Mark Girouard's account in *Country Life* 1966 140 276–9, 322–5; and his *The Victorian Country House* (Oxford, 1971) 82–4.

6. A. W. N. Pugin. *The True Principles of Pointed or Christian Architecture* (London, 1841) 50–52.

7. Ledger B f. 54.

8. *Ibid.* f. 2.

9. E. Christian, *Architectural Elevations of Skelton Church, Yorkshire* (London, 1846). Pearson had subscribed to the book and details of the church appear in his *Tracings* vols 2 and 4.

10. R. W. Billings, *Architectural Illustrations, History and Description of Carlisle Cathedral* (London, 1840). Bonomi subscribed to this volume and to the same author's *An Attempt to Define the Geometric Proportions of Gothic Architecture* (London, 1840). Pearson must have known them and he subscribed to Billings's *Illustrations of the Architectural Antiquities of the County of Durham* (Durham, 1846).

CHAPTER 5

1. C. J. H. Anderson, *A Short Guide to the County of Lincoln* 3rd edn (Lincoln, 1892) contains a memoir of Sir Charles Anderson by his friend Sir George Prevost.

2. *E* 1842 1 65; 1842–3 2 59.

3. E. E. Viollet-le-Duc, *Dictionnaire raisonné de l'architecture Française du XIme au XVIme siècle* vol. 8 (Paris, 1866). The translation quoted is by B. Bucknall in C. Wethered (ed.) *On Restoration* (London, 1875).

4. A. W. N. Pugin, *Contrasts* (London, 1836) 49.

5. ICBS 3758.

6. *CB* 1867 22 51–5.

7. Pearson's account of his work at Stinchcombe is in *CB* 1867 23 114–15.

8. G. W. G. L. Gower, in *Surrey Archaeological Collections* 1870 5 227–52.

9. This account is taken from G. Atkinson, 'On the Restoration in Progress at Stow Church' in Associated Architectural Societies: *Reports and Papers* 1850–1 1 315–26.

10. From Pearson's obituary notice in the *Antiquary* 1898 34 2.

11. *E* 1860 21 52.

CHAPTER 6

1. P. Thompson, 'All Saints' Church, Margaret Street, Reconsidered' in *Architectural History* 1965 8 73–94; the matter is considered more widely by Thompson in his *William Butterfield* (London, 1971). There is a contemporary account of the development of the High Victorian style in Eastlake, starting at Chapter 14, and modern accounts in H. R. Hitchcock, 'High Victorian Architecture' in *Victorian Studies* (Bloomington, Indiana) 1957 1 47–71; and S. Muthesius, *The High Victorian Movement in Architecture, 1850–1870* (London and Boston, 1972).

2. J. Ruskin, *The Seven Lamps of Architecture* (London, 1849) 77–8.

3. *Ibid.* 114.

4. *Ibid.* 174.

5. G. E. Street, *Brick and Marble in the Middle Ages: Notes on a Tour in North Italy* (London, 1855).

6. All four of Pearson's surviving sketchbooks are in the possession of Mrs Morgan. Although there may have been others, it is unlikely, especially as none were known to her father, Frank Pearson.

7. *Tracings* vol. 2.

8. J. Ruskin, *The Stones of Venice* vol. 1 (London, 1851) 199.

9. Ledger B f. 12.

10. *Ibid* f. 32.

11. Eastlake opp. 304.

12. *Ibid.* 303.

CHAPTER 7

1. H. S. Goodhart-Rendel in *Journal of the R.I.B.A.* 3rd s. 1949 56 251–8.

2. Ruskin, *Seven Lamps* 129–31.

3. *E* 1860 21 48–9.

4. East Riding County Record Office DDHO/48/235 and Ledger B f. 14.

5. East Riding County Record Office DDHO/48/235.

6. According to the Revd T. F. Simmons's funeral sermon for Lord Hotham published as *Christ Jesus Came into the World to Save Sinners* (Beverley, 1871) 10–11.
7. A. G. Dickens, *The East Riding of Yorkshire with Hull and York: a Portrait* (Hull, 1954) 37.
8. *E* 1862 23 60–1.
9. *BN* 1861 7 679.
10. Ledger B f. 53.
11. East Riding County Record Office DDHO/48/236.
12. Ruskin, *Stones of Venice* 336.
13. *BE* D. Verey, *Gloucestershire 1 The Cotswolds* (Harmondsworth, 1970) 207.
14. *BE* N. Pevsner and I. Nairn, *Surrey* (Harmondsworth, 1962) 409.
15. *E* 1860 21 49.

CHAPTER 8
1. In the possession of Mrs Morgan; the first entry is for 1853, the last for 1871.
2. Two volumes of photographs of foreign buildings are in the possession of Mrs Morgan together with a third volume of his own buildings.
3. Ruskin, *Stones of Venice* 17.
4. Most of the following account of Robert Gregory's work in Vauxhall comes from his *Autobiography of R. Gregory, 1819–1911* (London, 1912).
5. ICBS 5864.
6. *B* 1860 18 496.
7. I am grateful to Mrs Susan Beattie for information about the teachers and students at the Art School.
8. The portrait is in the possession of Mrs Morgan.
9. *B* 1865 23 626–7.
10. *Ibid*. The account of the Lancasters and St Peter's Home comes from Sister Rosamira, *The First Twenty-six Years of St Peter's Community* (privately published, 1917), and Mother Lisa, *Fifty Years' Memories of St Peter's Community* (privately published, 1944).
11. A. C. Benson, *The Life of Edward White Benson* vol. 2 (London, 1899) 640.
12. See the anonymous pamphlet *The Kilburn Sisters* (London, 1896).
13. Ruskin, *Stones of Venice* 200.
14. *E* 1862 25 272–4. *BN* 1861 7 427 was reminded somewhat of the Cologne churches which Pearson had seen. He may not yet have been to Italy but, even so, would have known of Italian apses from Ruskin and Street.

15. Pugin, *True Principles* 3.
16. Ruskin, *Stones of Venice* 168.
17. *Ibid*. 166–7.
18. *The Times* 11 December 1897.
19. *A* 1897 58 386.
20. *E* 1861 22 57.
21. Muthesius, *Neuere Kirchliche Baukunst* 34.
22. *E* 1861 22 57–8.
23. *BN* 1864 11 509 and 1865 12 707.
24. Eastlake 326.
25. Muthesius, *Neuere Kirchliche Baukunst* 34–6.
26. Eastlake 303–4.
27. Ruskin, *Seven Lamps* 131.

CHAPTER 9
1. Ledger B, in the possession of Mrs Morgan.
2. Ledger B f. 70.
3. *Ibid*. f. 20.
4. *Ibid*. f. 86.
5. Incorporated Church Building Society: *Annual Report* 1897.
6. Ledger B f. 87.
7. Information on the Sykes family comes from J. G. Hall, *A History of South Cave* (Hull, 1892) 195; *The Times* 23 March 1863; and *Illustrated London News* 1863 42 413.
8. Ledger B f. 55.
9. *B* 1861 19 39.
10. R.I.B.A. MS. Collection.
11. G. G. Scott, *Personal and Professional Recollections* (London, 1879) 189–90.
12. His anonymously written biography *Ewan Christian, Architect* (Cambridge, 1896) makes no mention of Pearson.
13. Jemima's surviving diaries are in the possession of Mrs Morgan.
14. In the possession of Mrs Morgan.
15. Ledger B ff. 98, 99, 104 and 105.
16. A. E. Street *Memoir of George Edmund Street, 1824–1881* (London, 1881) 183.

CHAPTER 10
1. P. Thompson, *William Butterfield* (London, 1971) 355.
2. Hertfordshire Record Office D/EQaQ3 has seven signed drawings dated May 1866 and a specification of works here quoted.
3. *E* 1861 22 330.
4. I am grateful to Dr Jill Allibone and Mr Andrew Saint for information on Devey and Shaw, some of which has appeared in the latter's *Richard Norman Shaw* (New Haven and London, 1976).

5. Eastlake 420.
6. *Ibid*. 382.
7. *Ibid*. 396.
8. *Ibid*. 420.

CHAPTER 11
1. *E* 1858 19 238.
2. Ruskin, *Stones of Venice* 237.
3. *BN* 1891 61 783–4.
4. Ledger B f. 110.
5. *B* 1880 38 724; after Pearson had been presented with the R.I.B.A. Royal Gold Medal.
6. *B* 1876 34 399.
7. Sister Rosamira, *St Peter's Community*.
8. R.I.B.A. MS. Collection.
9. *Ibid*.
10. B. Grueber, *Die Kunst des Mittelalters in Böhmen* (Vienna, 1871–9); the first volume was published a few months after Kilburn's design was made.
11. *A* 1871 5 229–30 (quoted) and *BN* 1871 20 894; the drawing, No. 854, was in the Royal Academy Summer Exhibition.
12. *A* 1871 5 229–30.
13. *CB* 1878 65 17–18.
14. H. R. Hitchcock, *Architecture: Nineteenth and Twentieth Centuries* (Harmondsworth, 1958) 189.
15. Muthesius, *Neuere Kirchliche Baukunst* 36.
16. *CB* 1878 65 17–18.
17. *A* 1878 19 387.
18. *CB* 1878 65 17–18.
19. Muthesius, *Neuere Kirchliche Baukunst* 36.
20. *BE London* vol. 2 (Harmondsworth, 1952) 297.

CHAPTER 12
1. In the possession of Mrs Morgan.
2. *B* 1887 52 755–8.
3. G. E. Street, *Some Account of Gothic Architecture in Spain* (London, 1865) 318–20, 510–13, Pl. 41, and Plan 18.
4. *B* 1878 36 501, and see *BN* 1878 34 209 and *A* 1875 13 315.
5. Muthesius, *Neuere Kirchliche Baukunst* 37.
6. *BE* N. Pevsner, and I. Nairn, *Surrey* (Harmondsworth, 1962) 159.
7. Ibid. 60.
8. *A* 1877 17 302.
9. *B* 1877 35 442.

CHAPTER 13
1. For the design of Stinchcombe church, see ICBS 4719.

2. Ledger B f. 42.
3. There is a letter written by Codd dated 22 February 1865 in ICBS 6316.
4. Sister Rosamira, *St Peter's Community*.
5. *Ibid*.
6. *BE Yorkshire: The West Riding* (Harmondsworth, 1959) 100; *B* 1891 61 52; the design was exhibited at the Royal Academy in 1897 (a year Pearson hung the architectural section) and illustrated in *BN* 1897 73 329.
7. A copy is in the possession of Mrs Morgan.
8. G. W. G. L. Gower, *Book of the Parish of Titsey* (London, 1869), and his obituary notice in *BN* 1882 42 647.
9. See Andrew Saint, 'Charles Buckeridge and his Family', *Oxoniensia* 1973 38 357–72.
10. *B* 1874 32 941–2 and *BN* 1874 27 546.
11. R.I.B.A. MS. Collection.
12. As far as the notes on the additional pages folded into the back of Ledger B mean anything.
13. In 1890 and '97; see *BN* 1890 58 612, 1897 72 621.
14. Where Reginald Blomfield remembered him; see his *Memoirs of an Architect* (London, 1932) 39.

CHAPTER 14.
1. Pearson's restoration is described in E. James, *The Parish Church of St Mary, Riccall* (York, 1947).
2. CCE 24675.
3. Reproduced by J. W. Kenworthy in 'St Michael's Church, Braintree', *Transactions of the Essex Archaeological Society* 1893 N.S. 4 264.
4. *BN* 1856 2 258.
5. *E* 1867 28 265–71.
6. *Ibid*.
7. *B* 1875 33 1022.
8. Sheffield Central Library, Bagshawe Papers 778 (xiii).
9. *BE Yorkshire: The North Riding* (Harmondsworth, 1966) 52.
10. ICBS 8456.
11. Lincoln Archives Office, The Ark 22/12.
12. *Ibid*. 22/13.
13. *Ibid*. 22/15.

CHAPTER 15
1. The refounding of the See of Truro and the building of its cathedral is recounted in *The Cornish See and Cathedral* (Truro, 1887); Pearson's copy is in the possession of Mrs Morgan.

2. E. W. Benson, *The Cathedral: Its Necessary Place in the Life and Work of the Church* (London, 1879) makes his hierarchical views clear.
3. Described in *BN* 1878 35 184.
4. On this and other architectural competitions in the nineteenth century see B. Kaye, *The Development of the Architectural Profession in Britain* (London, 1960) 105–16.
5. *A* 1878 20 128. Pullan's design is illustrated in *BN* 1880 38 368; St Aubyn's in *BN* 1879 36 144; Brydon's in *BN* 1878 35 584. *BA* 1878 10 86–7 lists the designs entered by each competitor.
6. *BN* 1878 34 624.
7. See the memoir of Bodley in *Journal of the R.I.B.A.* 3rd s. 1907–8 15 149–50.
8. Truro Cathedral Records.
9. The church is illustrated in ICBS 8573.
10. *BN* 1878 35 227.
11. *BN* 1881 40 591–2.
12. F. Bond *The Cathedrals of England and Wales* (London, 4th edn 1912) 19.
13. Truro Cathedral Records.
14. *A* 1880 23 373.
15. *BN* 1880 38 506 and 535.
16. *The Times* 21 May 1880.
17. *The Cornish See and Cathedral* (Truro, 1887).
18. The costs are given in *B* 1881 40 652.
19. The details are fully reported in *BN* 1881 41 263 and *B* 1881 41 482.
20. Benson, *Life of Benson* vol. 2 148.
21. *B* 1887 53 659.
22. *Ibid.*
23. *B* 1882 42 508.
24. Muthesius, *Neuere Kirchliche Baukunst* 37–8.
25. *B* 1882 42 508.
26. E. S. Prior, *The Cathedral Builders in England* (London, 1905) 107.
27. Bond, *Cathedrals* 483–6.
28. *Ibid.* 479–83.
29. *B* 1892 62 334.

CHAPTER 16.
1. *B* 1897 73 436.
2. *BE Northumberland* (Harmondsworth, 1957) 136.
3. *BN* 1883 45 745.
4. *BE South Lancashire* (Harmondsworth, 1969) 234.
5. *BE* N. Pevsner and D. Lloyd, *Hampshire and the Isle of Wight* (Harmondsworth, 1967) 125.
6. One or two clients noted that their commissions were delayed by Pearson's

work on Truro; for instance at St Peter, Manningford Bruce, Wiltshire, 'The numerous engagements of our architect ... have delayed the preparation of our plans' (ICBS 8638).
7. The restoration of the tower of All Saints, Bracebridge, Lincolnshire, in 1895; it was done by Hodgson Fowler of Durham (see CCE 49504); Pearson had previously restored the body of the church.
8. As Pearson described his St Barnabas, Hove, Sussex; see F. H. D. Smythe, *Forty Years of St Barnabas* (Hove, 1923) 5.
9. *B* 1896. 71 513.
10. In 'The Churches of Brighton and Hove', *AR* 1918 44 77–8.
11. In an unpublished lecture, 'The Churches of Brighton and the Gothic Revival' (1971).

CHAPTER 17.
1. These awards are in the possession of Mrs Morgan.
2. The occasion is fully reported in *B* 1880 38 723–4 and *BN* 1880 38 678–9; the exact words given by the two journals differ; those quoted are from the former.
3. Pearson attended the funeral on 26 April; see *B* 1881 40 532.
4. There is a letter of 9 May 1881 addressed from 46 Harley Street in ICBS 8618 and one of 11 May 1881 addressed from 13 Mansfield Street in ICBS 8573.
5. The Gothic bookcase is in the possession of Mr M. N. Playford, the other remaining pieces are Mrs Morgan's.
6. The following account from Street, *Memoir of Street* 272.

CHAPTER 18
1. The account of Pearson's office when Frank and Caröe were first there comes from Frank Pearson's obituary notice of Caröe in *Journal of the R.I.B.A.* 3rd s. 1938 45 558.
2. From evidence of his accounts of travels abroad in the 1880s; these are in books in the possession of his son Mr A. D. R. Caroe.
3. Recounted by Mrs Morgan.
4. Recounted by Mr A. D. R. Caroe.
5. *BN* 1896 70 256, 296 and 364.
6. *BE South Devon* (Harmondsworth, 1952) 148.
7. From his obituary notice in *B* 1951 180 18.
8. Illustrated in *B* 1892 62 62.
9. I am indebted to Mr G. L. Barnes for information on the younger Robson, to

Mr Ian Grant on Sidney Caulfield, and to the R.I.B.A.'s biographical files on members.

10. *B* 1891 60 395–6.
11. Benson, *Life of Benson* vol. 1 453.
12. A. J. Mason, *Memoir of George Howard Wilkinson* (London, 1909) vol. 2 120.
13. F. N. Heazell, *The History of St Michael's Church, Croydon* (London and Oxford, 1934) 24.
14. This account is based on J. S. Pollock, *Vaughton's Hole* (London, 1896).
15. But not Bordesley's unfortunate tower which was built in 1938 to the designs of E. F. Reynolds, according to the plaque in its base.
16. Recounted by Mr Ian Grant who was once Carvill's assistant.
17. *B* 1870 28 382.
18. Recounted by Mrs Morgan.
19. Ruskin, *Stones of Venice* 235.
20. *E* 1852 13 409–12.
21. R. J. Wood, *St Michael's, Headingley* (Shipley, 1957) 80–1.
22. Ruskin, *Stones of Venice* 215.
23. *Ibid.* 235; Clayton and Bell's wall painting at Kilburn is of a very high quality as is evident following the recent restoration and cleaning.
24. Benson, *Life of Benson* vol. 2 636.
25. *B* 1891 60 395–6.
26. *BN* 1887 53 458–9.
27. *B* 1882 42 363.
28. Building Committee Minutes in Parish Chest.
29. *B* 1892 62 16.
30. W. C. Monkhouse in his memoir of Pearson in *Pall Mall Magazine* 1898 15 92–110; Mrs Morgan says that Pearson was elected to the Athenaeum Club under the rule which empowered the committee to elect nine persons annually on the grounds of 'distinguished eminence in literature, science and the arts or for public service'.
31. According to George Aitchison; see *Journal of the R.I.B.A.* 3rd s. 1898 5 106–7.
32. Monkhouse, *Pall Mall Magazine* 92–110.
33. Frank Pearson gave some alabaster carvings collected by his father to the Victoria and Albert Museum. Some of the pictures are still in the possession of Mrs Morgan; she provided the information for this paragraph.
34. *B* 1880 38 724.

Chapter 19
1. Information from Mrs Morgan whose great-grandfather he was.

2. *B* 1878 36 501.
3. *BN* 1880 38 535.
4. I am indebted to Mrs Susan Beattie who has let me see her unpublished paper, 'The Schools of the London School Board (1872–1904) and the London County Council Education Department (1904–1910)', which describes the appearance in London of the 'Queen Anne' style in the 1870s and its application to the new schools.
5. *B* 1890 58 314.
6. *BN* 1890 58 612.
7. Girouard, *Victorian Country House* 199.

Chapter 20
1. Ruskin, *Seven Lamps* 179.
2. *Ibid.* 180.
3. Scott's attitude to restoration is discussed in N. Pevsner, *Some Architectural Writers of the Nineteenth Century* (Oxford, 1972) Ch. 17.
4. *The Athenaeum* 10 March 1877.
5. SPAB, *Annual Report of the Committee* 1879 9 and 17.
6. Kent County Record Office P 142/5/5.
7. SPAB, *Annual Report* 1883 19 and 22.
8. According to *B* 1885 48 57–8; Freeman's architectural writing is described in Pevsner, *Architectural Writers* 101–2.
9. Benson *Life of Benson* vol. 2 54.
10. SPAB, *Annual Report*, 1885 29.
11. The following account comes from *Report of the Select Committee on Westminster Hall Restoration* (London, 1885); there is a modern account in H. St G. Saunders, *Westminster Hall* (London, 1951) 302–9.
12. *Report on Westminster Hall Restoration* 11.
13. *Ibid.* 101.
14. *Ibid.* 90–91.
15. W. R. Lethaby, *Westminster Abbey and the Kings' Craftsmen* (London, 1906) 63; Ch. 3 deals with its restoration.
16. *Architecture* 1896 1 132–42.
17. In his SPAB pamphlet *Concerning Westminster Abbey* (London, 1893).
18. Burges's letter of reply is in the possession of Mrs Morgan.
19. A. D. Sharpe's account of Pearson's work on Westminster Abbey in *Journal of the R.I.B.A.* 3rd s. 1939 46 706–10.
20. Morris, *Concerning Westminster Abbey*.
21. *B* 1890 59 400.
22. SPAB, *Annual Report* 1890 40–2.
23. Lethaby, *Westminster Abbey* 76.
24. *B* 1890 59 400.
25. *B* 1892 62 11.
26. *BN* 1891 60 772.

27. M. B. Adams, *Architects from George IV to George V* (London, 1912) 8.
28. Morris, *Concerning Westminster Abbey*; a writer to the *Building News* (*BN* 1892 63 861) who signed himself 'M' praised Pearson's work and said Wren's towers (actually Hawksmoor's) should now be 'rectified'.
29. *B* 1892 62 247.
30. *Ibid.*
31. The controversy was fully described a dozen years later in W. D. Sweeting, *The Cathedral Church of Peterborough* (Peterborough, 1908) 71–81.
32. *B* 1895 68 252.
33. *B* 1896 70 5
34. *B* 1896 71 533–4.
35. *BN* 1897 72 78.
36. Quoted in Sweeting, *Peterborough* 71–81.
37. *B* 1896 71 533–4.
38. *B* 1897 72 69–71.
39. *B* 1897 72 49–50.
40. According to *B* 1897 72 59 the signatories included: Wollaston Franks (President of the Society of Antiquaries), Charles Read (its secretary), Thackerary Turner (Secretary of SPAB), William Lethaby, Detmar Blow, Philip Webb, J. T. Mickelthwaite, John Carruthers (a civil engineer), R. W. Schultz, F. W. Troup, E. S. Prior, F. Inigo Thomas, Halsey Ricardo, Mervyn Macartney, P. Morley Horder, J. A. Cossins (of Birmingham), H. Wilson, Ernest Newton, E. Guy Dawber, C. R. Ashbee, J. J. Stevenson, and Charles Mileham.
41. *B* 1897 72 69–71.
42. According to *BN* 1897 72 163 the signatories were: George Aitchison the younger, J. M. Brydon, William Fawcett, C. F. Hayward, B. Inglelow, John Slater, William Emerson, E. W. Mountford, Alexander Graham, Aston Webb, James Brooks, Henry Florence, Edward Grunning, Alfred Gotch, R. Reynolds Rowe, F. C. Penrose, and Ernest George.
43. *B* 1897 73 445.
44. *The Antiquary* 1898 34 2.
45. P. Ferriday, 'The Church Restorers', *AR* 1964 136 93, 95; the article does not fully recognize the dilemma.
46. *The Athenaeum* 18 December 1897.
47. Benson, *Life of Benson* vol. 2 636.

CHAPTER 21
1. Pearson's drawings of his proposals for this site are in the R.I.B.A. Drawings Collection.
2. Illustrated in *B* 1890 59 489–92.
3. *B* 1890 59 491.
4. SPAB's disapproval of the proposals was strongly expressed in its *Annual Report of the Committee* 1893 68.
5. *BE London* vol. 1 (Harmondsworth, 1957) 330.
6. The letter to the Dean and Chapter of Rochester Cathedral, which Pearson was then restoring, is in Kent County Record office DRC/Emp/26.

EPILOGUE
1. *B* 1897 73 514.
2. Information from Mrs Morgan.
3. *BN* 1897 73 858.
4. The account of his funeral comes from *The Times* 17 December 1897 and *BN* 1897 73 866.
5. *A* 1878 19 234.
6. *B* 1880 38 724; the account in *BN* 1880 38 679 is insignificantly different.
7. *B* 1897 73 514 and *BN* 1897 73 866.
8. *The Antiquary* 1898 34 2.
9. *The Athenaeum* 18 December 1897.
10. Muthesius, *Neuere Kirchliche Baukunst* 34.
11. Adams, *Architects* 10.
12. *Theology* 1933 27 27–8.
13. B. F. L. Clarke, *Church Builders of the Nineteenth Century* (London, 1938) 197–8.
14. J. Fleming, H. Honour and N. Pevsner, *The Penguin Dictionary of Architecture* (Harmondsworth, 1966) 167.
15. He is not included in P. Ferriday (ed.), *Victorian Architecture* (London, 1964), and the comments in R. F. Jordan, *Victorian Architecture* (Harmondsworth, 1966) are irrelevant; David Lloyd's more recent chapter in J. Fawcett (ed.), *Seven Victorian Architects* (London, 1976) is appreciative but idiosyncratic.
16. Hitchcock, *Architecture* 189.
17. In his 'Late Victorian Architecture, 1851–1900', *Journal of the R.I.B.A.* 3rd s. 1936–7 44 1032.
18. Hitchcock, *Architecture* 189.
19. Ruskin, *Seven Lamps* 187.

CATALOGUE OF WORKS

THE EARLIEST list of Pearson's works was given by Ernest Newberry at the end of his article in the first volume of the *Architectural Review* (*AR* 1896–7 1 80–2). It was compiled in 1896 and so does not include the work of Pearson's last year. Newberry admitted that his list was 'by no means exhaustive'; its intention, rather, was 'to give some idea of the nature and extent of Mr Pearson's large practice'. Nevertheless the list was full and has been the basis of all subsequent ones.

Newberry was concerned with the artistic side of Pearson's career. Pearson's own Ledger B shows the practical side as well; its survival has made it possible to include here all the work for which he charged a fee between 1854 and 1866, greatly amplifying the catalogue for this period. More important than the consequent numerical increase in his known works is the record of the amount of minor and even trivial work which occupied his time. Attention to dry rot appears equally in Ledger B alongside the making of new designs, and it does so below.

The catalogue is not subdivided in any way between major and minor works. Following Newberry, its order is topographical, though not county by county, as these have changed their names and boundaries since Pearson's time, but alphabetically by place. This avoids the need for a separate gazeteer. It does not show how Pearson's career developed over the years; for that a chronology of the more important events is given. The county names and boundaries used are those in force both at the time of the commission and at present.

Each entry is designed to give place, nature of work, client, principal dates of design and execution, a short description, builders and cost and artists employed, and major sources. The latter are given in the abbreviated form used in the Notes to the Text.

The destruction of the remainder of Pearson's ledgers has meant the loss of the only source for some works and made the retrieval of information about others practically impossible. I hope that such works were all minor. Others may be excluded through oversight, an inability to search all record repositories, and even to pursue all available clues. I shall naturally welcome any additions and amendments which readers may discover.

I have visited the majority of the surviving executed works in England and Wales, but none elsewhere.

ENGLAND

ALKBOROUGH (Lincs.) St John
Restoration, for Mrs Bentinck
Designed 1854, unexecuted
Source: Ledger B f. 6.

AMPNEY CRUCIS (Glos.) Holy Rood
Restoration of chancel, for J. Bravender of
    Cirencester
Designed 1854, probably unexecuted
New chancel roof proposed
Source: Ledger B f. 30

APPLETON-LE-MOORS (Yorks., N. Riding;
    N. Yorks.) Christ Church
New church, new site, for Mrs Joseph
    Shepherd
Designed 1862–3, built 1863–5, consecrated
    1866
Three-bay aisled nave with west narthex,
    chancel with semi-circular apse, north
    mortuary chapel and south tower with
    short pyramidal spire. Lancets, rose over
    west entrance. Early French and English
    Gothic details. Of local stone with bands
    and shafts of Rosedale firestone and red
    Mansfield stone, incised and coloured
    work around altar and in mortuary
    chapel. Timber roof with tie-beams,
    crown-posts and raking struts
Built by Smith and Tomlinson, cost £7,000.
    Glass by Clayton and Bell
Sources: Ledger B ff. 95, 107; *B* 1863 21 350–1,
    1864 22 327, 1866 24 636, 1869 27 652; *BN*
    1864 11 334, 1865 12 855, 1866 13 554; *CB*
    1867 21 1–7 (article initialled 'J.L.P.'); *E*
    1864 25 149–50; Eastlake 303, 408;
    Newberry

APPLETON-LE-MOORS (Yorks., N. Riding;
    N. Yorks.) Christ Church Parsonage (now
    Appleton Hotel)
New house incorporating former school and
    master's house, for Mrs Joseph Shepherd
Designed 1863, built 1865: damaged by fire
    1931, partly rebuilt and converted into
    hotel 1958
Two-storeyed, with gables and windows with
    pointed heads, stone mullions. Tudor
Built by Smith and Tomlinson, cost £1,500
Sources: Ledger B ff. 95, 107; *B* 1866 24 636;
    BN 1865 12 855; *CB* 1867 21 1–7 (article

initialled 'J.L.P.'); Eastlake 408; Newberry

APPLETON-LE-MOORS (Yorks., N. Riding;
    N. Yorks.) Christ Church Schools
New schools and master's house, to replace
    schools of 1854 incorporated into new
    parsonage, for Mrs Shepherd
Designed 1863, built 1865
School hall with plate tracery in end window,
    bellcote to east gable with two openings
    beneath octagonal steeple; to south, two-
    storeyed master's house with projecting
    bay with half-timbered upper storey and
    half-hipped roof
Built by Smith and Tomlinson, cost about
    £2,500
Sources: Ledger B ff. 95, 107; *B*1866 24 636;
    BN 1865 12 855; *CB* 1867 21 1–7 (article
    initialled 'J.L.P.'); Eastlake 408; New-
berry

ASCOT (Berks.) All Souls (All Saints until
    consecration), South Ascot
New church, new site, for Lord Stanmore
Designed 1894, eastern part including one bay
    of nave built 1896–7, remainder executed
    later by Frank Pearson
Aisled four-bay nave with north-west porch
    and south-west baptistery astride aisle
    wall, crossing with central tower and
    unbuilt spire, and transepts separated by
    double-arched arcades, single-bay chan-
    cel with south chapel and north organ
    chamber and vestry. Geometrical trac-
    ery. Chancel and south chapel have
    sexpartite rib-vaults, crossing quadripar-
    tite, baptistery octopartite. Nave has
    wooden, braced collar roof with tie-
    beams. Of red brick with Bath stone
    dressings, red tile roof.
Built by Cornish and Gaymer.
Sources: CCE 73687; *B* 1897 73 427; Newberry

ASHEN (Essex) St Augustine
Restoration and new chancel, for Revd Wil-
    liam John Deane
Designed 1853, new chancel built 1857–8,
    restoration continued until 1862
Chancel faced with knapped flint with po-
    lychromatic bands and dressings of red
    brick and yellow stone. Designs for new
    nave unexecuted. Unspecified repairs.
Sources: Ledger B f. 9; ICBS 5009; Essex
    Record Office D/P 366/8 (Vestry Min-
    utes); *CB* 1863 6 73; Newberry

ASHEN (Essex) St Augustine's Parsonage
Additions, for Revd William John Deane
Designed and presumably executed 1853
Cost about £280. No work by Pearson visible;
the parsonage has since been further
altered
Source: Ledger B f. 9

ASHEN (Essex) St Augustine's Schools
New schools, for Revd William John Deane
Designed 1853, unexecuted
Source: Ledger B f. 9

ASHFORD (Kent) St Mary
Pulpit
1897
Octagonal, mounted on drum with attached
shafts; each face has a niche with a
statuette. Of Hoptonwood stone
Source: N. M. G. Sharp, *St Mary's Church,
Ashford, Kent* (Gloucester, n.d.) 10–11

ATHERINGTON (Devon) St Mary
Restoration
1883–4
Renewal of masonry in arcades and window
tracery
Source: Newberry

AYLESBURY (Bucks.) St Mary
Reredos
1891
Gilded and painted triptych of wood
Probably made by Clayton and Bell
Source: Newberry

AYOT ST PETER (Herts.) St Peter
New church, old site, incorporating some of
previous building, for Revd Edwin Prodgers
Designed and built 1862–3; struck by lightning 1874, at first all but east end, now
entirely demolished
Aisled nave with west entrance, chancel with
semi-circular apse, vestry and organ
chamber on north, tower and spire. All
windows were lancets except for wheel
over west entrance. Of red brick with
stone dressings, floor with Minton's tiles,
open deal roofs. The church seems to
have been a brick version of Appleton-le-
Moors
Sources: Ledger B f. 62; ICBS 7774; *B* 1863 21
31; *CB* 1863 8 181; Newberry

AYOT ST PETER (Herts.) St Peter's Rectory
(now Old Rectory)
New House, for Revd Edwin Prodgers
Designed 1866, built 1866–7
Two-storeyed with many gables and complicated room plan, large mullioned windows, arched entrance in projecting half-
hipped block, prominent chimney-stacks.
Of red brick with darker red bands, half-
timbering in gablets, tile roof. Stables
and coach-house around yard on east
Sources: Hertfordshire County Record Office
D/EQaQ3 (seven signed drawings dated
May 1866 and specification); Ledger B f.
111, add. ff. 8, 9, and 11

BABWORTH (Notts.) All Saints
Restoration, for Revd William Bridgeman
Simpson and John Champion
Designed 1858, executed 1859–62, font 1878
Repairs to masonry including renewal of
tracery, new nave and chancel roofs with
arch-braced rafters, painting of east end
Cost about £1,200. East Window by Wailes
1859; west window by Kempe 1879
Sources: Ledger B ff. 60, 74; Lincoln Archives
Office (uncatalogued faculty for font,
1874); *B* 1858 16 280; Newberry

BANBURY (Oxon.) vicarage
New house, not found, probably not in Ban-
bury, but nearby
Source: Newberry

BARNET VALE (Herts., London, Barnet) St
Mark, Potters Road
New church, new site
Designed 1896, nave built 1897–9, remainder
unexecuted
Four-bay aisled nave with south porch. Transepts, chancel and north vestries were
designed, a tower was contemplated;
none executed. Perpendicular. Of flint
with dressings of Little Casterton stone,
chequer-work in west gable, arch-braced
roofs covered in red tile (nave) and
copper (aisles)
Executed by Frank Pearson, built by Henry
Wilcock and Co. of Wolverhampton, cost
about £3,000
Sources: Parish Chest (eight drawings signed
and dated June 1896); CCE 76723; *B* 1897
73 355, 1899 76 205

BECKENHAM (Kent; London, Bromley)

Crystal Palace District Cemetery, Elmers End Road
Memorial Cross
Dedicated 1894
Square base, octagonal shaft, crucifix with canopy over it. Stone
Source: H. W. Bateman, *A Short History of the Church of St John the Evangelist, Upper Norwood* (London and Oxford, 1937) 24

BEVERLEY (Yorks., E. Riding; Humberside) Minster
New vestry, for trustees and Revd John B. Birtwhistle
Two designs 1859, unexecuted
Source: Ledger B f. 80
Supervision of addition of statues by Nathaniel Hitch and mosaics based on originals by Powells, to Percy screen, 1897
Source: C. Hiatt, *Beverley Minster* (London, 1898) 90–1

BISHOP BURTON (Yorks., E. Riding; Humberside) All Saints
Restoration, for Francis Watt
Designs for chancel 1859–64, executed 1864–5; designs for remainder 1866, executed 1866
Chancel: south wall repaired and parapet removed, east wall repaired and upper half rebuilt, north wall entirely rebuilt, five original windows rebuilt or repaired, new window added to match. Vestry largely rebuilt, given new east window, new chancel arch. Nave and aisles repaired, floors lowered and nave arcade underpinned. Tower repaired, new spire unexecuted. New roofs throughout. New seating
Builders were Simpson and Malone of Hull, cost about £3,000
Sources: Ledger B f. 77; Sketchbook of 1859 (notes on back papers dated September 1859 listing work to chancel); *B* 1865 23 839–40; *CB* 1865 17 40

BISHOP WILTON (Yorks., E. Riding; Humberside) St Edith
Restoration, for Sir Tatton Sykes (fourth Bart); new windows and tomb, for Christopher Sykes and Miss Sykes in memory of Sir Tatton Sykes (fourth Bart)
Designed 1857–8, executed 1858–9; east window designed 1863; memorial window and tomb designed 1864

New north vestry, new roofs, hammerbeam to nave, new pulpit, masonry repaired
Cost nearly £4,000
Sources: Ledger B ff. 8, 56; *B* 1858 16 183; *BN* 1858 4 281; Newberry

BISHOP WILTON (Yorks., E. Riding; Humberside) St Edith's Schools
New boys', girls' and infants' schools and master's house, for Sir Tatton Sykes (fifth Bart)
Designed 1864, to cost £1,825, unexecuted
Source: Ledger B f. 99

BISLEY (Glos.) All Saints
Restoration for Revd Thomas Keble
Designed 1858, unexecuted
'Preparing Elevations & Sections of Bisley Ch.: to show how it may be restored with high pitch roofs to nave and south aisle & lean-to to North aisle. Elevation & Sections showing the effect of adding a high pitched roof to N. aisle.'
Source: Ledger B f. 65

BLECHINGLEY (Surrey) St Mary
Restoration
Designed 1869, executed 1869–70
East window formerly late Perpendicular rebuilt as triple lancets using reset stones; three windows on north side of chancel restored; plastered chancel roof opened up and restored, crown-posts added; south aisle roof repaired, roughcast removed, brick embattled parapet replaced in stone; gallery removed from tower and tower arch opened up; new seating, new stone pulpit and low chancel screen
Builder was Carruthers of Reigate, cost about £1,800
Sources: Ledger B add. ff. 7–9; *A* 1870 3 283; *B* 1870 28 431; *BN* 1869 17 197; *Surrey Archaeological Collections* 1870 5 227–52; Newberry

BOOTHBY PAGNELL (Lincs.) St Andrew
Restoration, for Mrs Thorold of Boothby Hall
Executed 1896–7
Walls of nave, aisles and chancel raised; new parapets and roofs; tower repointed, new pinnacles, new vault in ground storey; new tracery in windows; new north vestry; new stone facing to much of interior; new floors; new heating; new

furnishings: carved oak pulpit on stone base, carved oak chancel screen with crucifix and figures of Our Lady and St Andrew, carved oak choir stalls, altars, bishop's chair, font cover; lychgate and churchyard walls

Builder was John Thompson, windows by Clayton and Bell, carving by Nathaniel Hitch and Thomas Nicholls; cost about £6,000

Sources: *B* 1896 70 876, 1897 73 224, 244; *BN* 1896 70 876

BORDESLEY (Birmingham; West Midlands) St Alban

New church, new site, for Revd James Samuel Pollock and Revd Thomas Benson Pollock

Designed 1879, built 1879–81

Four-bay aisled nave with fifth west bay with entrances under gallery, unfinished tower and spire to south of west end of south aisle; crossing and unequal transepts, two bays to north, one to south; two-bay chancel with semi-circular apse and passage ambulatory, three-bay south chapel divided into nave, chancel and sanctuary, north organ chamber and vestries. Two-storeyed interior elevation with passage below clerestory; proportions based on Golden Section; vaulted throughout. Lancets, a little plate tracery, rose windows especially at west end. Red brick exterior with Bath stone dressings, brick interior with stone dressings, vaulting entirely of stone. Tower finished to new design by E. F. Reynolds in 1938

Built by John Shillitoe, cost over £20,000. Light iron chancel screen made by White and Son, 1897

Sources: R.I.B.A. Drawings Collection (seven drawings dated March 1879); CCE 33960; *B* 1881 40 811, 1897 73 436, 446; *BA* 1880 13 70; *BN* 1881 40 592, 1897 73 604; J. S. Pollock, *Vaughton's Hole* (London, 1896) 38–9; Newberry

BORDESLEY (Birmingham; West Midlands) St Patrick

New church, new site, for Revd James Samuel Pollock and Revd Thomas Benson Pollock

Designed 1895, nave and aisles built 1895–6, east parts built 1906, demolished *c.* 1960

Five-bay nave with north and south passage aisles, second south aisle of three bays

extending from south-west tower, west entrance porch; two-bay chancel narrower than nave with polygonal apse, north organ chamber and vestry. Of red brick with stone dressings, vaulted chancel, wooden roof to nave. Only lower part of tower was built

Sources: ICBS 10641 (plan signed by Frank Pearson); CCE 76010; J. S. Pollock, *Vaughton's Hole* (London, 1896) 94–5; Newberry

BOURNEMOUTH (Hants; Dorset) St Stephen

New church, new site, for Revd Alexander Sykes Bennett in memory of his father

Designed 1881–3, nave built 1883–5, chancel built 1897–8, north-west tower built 1907–8, spire unexecuted

Six-bay nave with inner and outer aisles, crossing and transepts, apsidal chancel with passage ambulatory, tower at west end of outer north aisle, south-east organ chamber, vestries and clergy room. Two-storey interior elevation with passage below clerestory; vaulted throughout. Of brick faced in white Swanage stone outside and Bath stone inside, Bath stone dressings

Built by E. Abley and Co. of Salisbury; decorated by Clayton and Bell; reredos by Moos Brothers, carving by Nathaniel Hitch. East parts and tower executed by Frank Pearson

Sources: CCE 62110; *B* 1883 44 596, 1885 49 75, 1898 74 619; *BA* 1883 19 244; *BN* 1883 44 616, 1884 46 286, 292–3, 1885 48 991, 1897 73 242; Newberry

BRACEBRIDGE (Lincs.) All Saints

Restoration and new north aisle, transept and chapel, for Revd Charles Christopher Ellison

Executed 1874–5

Restoration included new roofs, floors and seating; cleaning and repointing of body of church and east face of tower. New north arcade to match existing south arcade; new north aisle incorporating window and door openings from previous north wall, and new lancet windows. New stone pulpit and reredos

Builder was R. Young of Lincoln, cost about £2,100

Sources: CCE 49504; ICBS 7759; *B* 1875 33 581; Newberry

BRADFORD (Yorks., W. Riding; W. Yorks.)
St Peter (now Cathedral)
Consultation with T. H. and F. Healey for extension and restoration 1896–7, the Healeys' work was executed 1899
Source: *B* 1896 71 430, 525

BRAINTREE (Essex) St Michael
Restoration for Revd J. D. Browne and others
Designed 1855–66; nave, north aisle, tower and spire restored 1857–60, south aisle restored, chancel refurnished 1866–7
Restoration included removal of north and west galleries and other fittings, repair and renewal of stone and brickwork, new nave clerestory and windows, widening of north nave aisle and provision of new north porch, new nave and aisle roofs, new floors, widening chancel arch, new east window, widening north chancel aisle to same width as north nave aisle, new chancel and aisle roofs, new furnishings and fittings, tower and spire repaired and reshingled
Builder was Parmenter and Son of Bocking, east window by Clayton and Bell
Sources: Ledger B ff. 42, 61, 75, 97, add. ff. 3–11; Essex Record Office D/CF/25/2 (Faculty Papers); *B* 1857 15 565, 1858 16 318, 1860 18 500, 516; *BN* 1856 2 258, 1858 4 337, 446; J. W. Kenworthy in *Transactions of the Essex Archaeological Society* N.S. 1893 4 254–77; Newberry

BRAINTREE (Essex) St Michael's Parsonage
New house, new site, for Ralph Lindsay of Biggin Lodge, Norwood (he was patron of Pirton, Herts.)
Designed 1853–5, built 1855
Two-storeyed, of red brick with black brick bands and diaper, red gauged brick heads and relieving arches to windows, red tile roof. Vernacular.
Cost perhaps £1,535
Source: Ledger B ff. 18, 19

BRAINTREE (Essex) St Michael's Schools
New boys' and girls' schools, for Revd J. D. Browne and others
Design of 1855, to cost £850; subsequent design 'to suit the altered ground' 1857, unexecuted
Source: Ledger B f. 38

BRAYTON (Yorks., West Riding; N. Yorks.)
St Wilfrid

Restoration, for Revd Robert Lamatt Crossthwaite
Designed 1876, executed 1877–8
Repair of masonry, new nave roof of increased pitch, new aisle roofs, floors lowered and remade in flags and Staffs. tiles, bases of piers repaired, parapets of nave and aisles repaired, some window tracery renewed, modern window in south aisle replaced to match old ones, new seating and pulpit, new heating, new vestry and organ chamber. The roofs were rotten; the chancel roof was only twenty years old. In his report, Pearson explained: 'The present roof is out of character with the architecture, and is so injurious to the effect of this very unusually fine feature of the church, that it ought to be taken off, and a new roof put on, in harmony with the style of architecture'
Cost £2,350
Source: CCE 54995

BRISTOL (Avon) All Saints, Clifton
Pulpit, given by Clement George, and Memorial Cross
1888 and 1890–1 respectively; pulpit destroyed during Second World War
Pulpit, of dark red marble standing on ten short columns and with alabaster panels carved by Nathaniel Hitch, cost about £440. Cross on tall shaft, of stone
Source: Mr Gordon Barnes; Church Guide

BRISTOL (Avon) Cathedral
Completion of west towers to Street's designs, restoration, re-arrangement of choir
Towers completed 1887–8, restoration 1890–1900, the main work 1893–5. Restoration of Lady chapel, north transept, central tower, north walk of cloister, St Augustine's Gateway. New tracery to north transept window with glass by Powell and Son, east window with glass by Hardman. New choir fittings include choir screen, reredos, sedilia, marble floor
Builder was Cowlin and Son, cost at least £8,000, fittings over £4,000; work completed by Frank Pearson
Sources: R.I.B.A. Drawings Collection (drawings for reredos and choir screen, sedilia and screen); *B* 1892 62 313, 1893 64 98, 495, 1894 66 58, 242, 1894 67 28, 339, 1895 68 14, 157, 1895 69 105, 1896 70 242, 1896 71 143, 1897 72 529, 1898 74 208, 1900 78 14; *BN* 1890

58 927, 1890 59 671, 1891 61 170, 1892 62 551, 586, 815, 882, 1893 64 150, 392, 885, 1893 65 28, 668, 1894 66 68, 416–7, 519, 908, 1894 67 60, 304, 339, 1895 68 318, 653, 1896 70 401, 695, 1896 71 394, 1897 72 621; Newberry

BRISTOL (Avon) St James
Survey, for ICBS
1861
Source: Ledger B f. 86

BRISTOL (Avon) St Mark (Mayor's Chapel)
Restoration and additions, for Bristol City Council
Designed 1884, approved 1887, executed 1888–9
General repair, reconstruction of western entrance, alterations to nave and chancel, new north transept with communicating north vestry on east side, and new north cloister between new transept and west end of nave
Cost £4,000. North transept glass designed by W. G. Bailey, made by Edwin Howard of Frome
Sources: R.I.B.A. Drawings Collection (seven signed drawings dated March 1884); *B* 1889 56 69; *BN* 1881 40 294 (illustrating former west entrance of 1777–8), 1887 53 165, 1889 57 542, 1890 59 132, 344; W. R. Barker, *St Mark's; or, The Mayor's Chapel, Bristol* (Bristol, 1892) 103–34; Newberry

BROADHEMPSTON (Devon) St Mary
Restoration, for Revd Fitzhenry Hele
Designed 1853–4, executed 1854 or '55
New east window
Source: Ledger B f. 15

BROADWELL (Glos.) House
Alterations, new stables and other offices, for Capt. Leigh RN
Designed 1854, probably unexecuted
Source: Ledger B f. 16

BROOMFLEET (Yorks., E. Riding; Humberside) St Mary
New church, for Mrs Elizabeth Mary Barnard of Cave Castle
Designed and built 1859–61
Two-cell: nave with north tower and pyramidal spire and entrance porch in base, chancel with south vestry. Of local stone

with slate roof, interior plastered with arch-braced rafter roof
Sources: Ledger B f. 79; Newberry; J. G. Hall, *A History of South Cave* (Hull, 1892) 177–8

BROOMFLEET (Yorks., E. Riding; Humberside) St Mary's Parsonage
New house, for Mrs Elizabeth Mary Barnard, of Cave Castle
Designed 1861, built 1862
Two-storeyed, L-plan with coach-house in projecting wing, gabled entrance porch. Of brown brick with bands and diaper in darker brick, slate roof. An unexecuted design had a two-storeyed porch and a detached coach-house
Sources: Ledger B f. 83; Parish Chest (engraving of unexecuted design); J. G. Hall, *A History of South Cave* (Hull, 1892) 177–8

BROOMFLEET (Yorks., E. Riding; Humberside) St Mary's Schools
New schools and master's house, for Mrs Elizabeth Mary Barnard of Cave Castle
Designed 1861, unexecuted
For site west of church. Master's house in front, of two storeys, projecting gable at one end; school hall attached at rear
Sources: Ledger B f. 82, add. f. 4; J. G. Hall, *A History of South Cave* (Hull, 1892) 177–8

BURGHWALLIS (Yorks., W. Riding; S. Yorks.) St Helen
Restoration
1883–5
New vestry and organ chamber, new tracery to windows of chancel and north side of nave, new buttresses to north nave wall, new gables and crosses, new roofs, new altar cross, candlesticks and reredos. Lychgate
Cost £1,300
Source: Parish Chest (plan and accounts)

BURLEY-ON-THE-HILL (Rutland; Leics.) Holy Cross
Restoration, for the Hon. George Henry Finch
Designed 1868, executed 1869–70
Renewed tracery to nave aisle windows, new oak seats, pulpit and chancel screen, new three-bay aisled chancel with passage linking it to Burley House
Sources: Ledger B add. ff. 6–11; *BN* 1870 18 401; Newberry

BURSTWICK (Yorks., E. Riding; Humberside) All Saints
Survey, for Revd Charles Hotham
October 1861
Source: Ledger B f. 87

BURTON PIDSEA (Yorks., E. Riding; Humberside) St Peter
Survey, for Revd Charles Hotham
October 1861
Source: Ledger B f. 87

CALNE (Wilts.) St Mary
Restoration
Designed 1890, executed 1890–1
Chancel roof raised three feet, east window raised, new reredos and low chancel screen
Sources: Salisbury Diocesan Record Office, bundle 32/2 (plan of reredos); CCE 986

CAMBRIDGE (Cambs.) Emmanuel College
Emmanuel House and extension of hostel in Parker Street 1892–4
Irregular square building of two storeys and attic with projecting bays, shaped gables and curved battlements. Jacobean. Red brick with stone dressings, red tile roof. The extension to an adjacent building (by W. H. Fawcett) is two-storeyed, in red brick, and similar in style
Sources: Newberry: RCHM, *City of Cambridge* (London, 1959) 63

CAMBRIDGE (Cambs.) King's College
Design for east end of chapel
1889, unexecuted
Decorated style
Source: RCHM, *City of Cambridge* (London, 1959) 115

CAMBRIDGE (Cambs.) Old Schools
Completion of West Range
Designed 1886, executed 1887–90
The West Range was begun in the mid fifteenth century but left unfinished; the South Range is by Scott, 1863; the North Range by C. R. Cockerell, 1836–42. Pearson completed the medieval block in Perpendicular style linking Scott's and Cockerell's buildings, in three storeys with embattled parapet, including gatehouse and angle turrets
Built by Luscombe and Son

Sources: R.I.B.A. Drawings Collection (eleven drawings dated 1886); *B* 1889 56 328, 464, 491; *BN* 1887 53 599, 1889 56 610; Newberry; RCHM, *City of Cambridge* (London, 1959) 12, 17

CAMBRIDGE (Cambs.) Sidney Sussex College
New range and designs for new chapel
Designed 1888–9, new range built 1890–1
Three-storeyed with arcaded cloisters on north and west sides, segmental projecting bays, shaped gables. Jacobean. Red brick and stone.
Sources: Sidney Sussex College (drawings); *B* 1890 58 314; *BN* 1890 58 612; Newberry; RCHM, *City of Cambridge* (London, 1959) 204, 206

CANTERBURY (Kent) Cathedral
Restoration of St Anselm's chapel, for Canon Francis Holland 1888–90
The chapel survived the fire of 1174 and predates the choir of William of Sens to which it is attached. Pearson strengthened the walls of the chapel by inserting iron girders and masonry; this enabled him to take down the buttress wall built across the chapel apse to support the choir roof; behind was found a fresco of St Paul
Sources: *BN* 1890 58 784; SPAB, *Annual Report of the Committee* 1888 70; Newberry; J. C. Cox in the *Archaeological Journal* 1897 54 241

CASTLE HOWARD (Yorks., N. Riding; N. Yorks.) Reformatory (now Farm School)
New chapel
Designed and built 1868
Single-cell with porch at west end of south side under continuation of roof, Geometrical tracery, flèche begun but not carried above ridge of roof. Of local stone with slate roof. The *Building News* commented: 'The style is plain and unpretending and in accordance with the reformatory itself'
Cost £750. East window dedicated to seventh Earl of Carlisle by Mary, Lady Taunton, 1876; according to Mr Gordon Barnes it is by William Morris
Sources: Ledger B add. ff. 3–5; *BN* 1868 15 335; Mr Gordon Barnes

CATHERSTON LEWESTON (Dorset) St
Mary
New church, old site, for Revd Richard C.
Hildyard
Designed 1857, built 1857–8
Two-cell, nave and chancel with north organ
chamber and vestry. West doorway be-
neath bellcote containing bell captured at
Sebastopol. Decorated tracery. Of knap-
ped flint with Bath stone dressings, red
tile roof; interior faced with Bath stone,
open arch-braced pine roof with two
stages of cusped wind-braces
Built by H. Poole of Westminster, cost £2,600.
Carving by M. Barnes of Clifton and S.
Poole of London superintended by John
Herley; floors paved with Minton's tiles;
glass by Clayton and Bell
Sources: Ledger B f. 53; *B* 1858 16 318, 361,
667; *E* 1860 21 49

CAVERSWALL (Staffs.) St Peter
Restoration, for the Hon. E. S. Parker Jervis
1867–8
New south vestry; restoration of chancel roof
and east wall with new gable
Source: Ledger B add. ff. 3–6

CHAGFORD (Devon) St Michael
Restoration
1888
Reredos in memory of Hayter George Hayter
Haines, new stained glass in east window
Source: Newberry

CHARLTON (Near Upavon, Wilts.) St Peter
New church, old site, for Thomas Everett
Fowle of Durrington House, and Frederick Fowle
Designed 1856–7, built 1857–8
Two-cell: nave and chancel attached to
Perpendicular north tower and chapel of
former church. Geometrical tracery.
Faced in knapped flint with stone bands
and dressings, red brick arches to windows, interior plastered, wooden arch-
braced roof with wind-braces to nave,
red-tiled exterior. Break in roof line
between nave and chancel but no arch
Cost £1,620
Sources: Salisbury Diocesan Record Office:
bundle 6/18 (drawings dated 1857); Ledger B f. 48; *B* 1858 16 508; Newberry

CHARMOUTH (Devon) St Andrew
Alterations to seating and new seats, for Revd
Edward Rose Breton
Designed and presumably executed 1858–60
Plain wooden benches
Source: Ledger B f. 61

CHESWARDINE (Salop.) St Swithin
Rebuilt, for Charles Donaldson Hudson and
Revd J. E. Hughes
Designed 1884–6, rebuilding complete 1889
West tower restored, pinnacles increased in
height (since lowered); thirteenth-
century north chapel rebuilt 13 feet to
east. Rest of church (rebuilt 1808–10)
replaced by new nave and chancel with
some details based on, and reusing,
medieval remains; nave arcades with
pointed arches to north, round to south;
chancel floor based on design of old tiles;
nave clerestory and aisle walls new, nave
arcade increased from three to four bays.
New pulpit and font. Charles Buckeridge
made designs for rebuilding in 1872
Cost about £4,000. Windows by Kempe
Sources: ICBS 7442; Newberry; R. H. Hudson
*An Historical Survey of the Parish of
Cheswardine* (Shrewsbury, 1939)

CHICHESTER (Sussex; W. Sussex) Cathedral
Rebuilding of north-west tower
Designed 1896, executed by Frank Pearson
1897–1901
Designed both to stabilize the nave and
complete west end; based on south-west
tower. Proposals to raise wooden lead-
covered spires on both west towers were
unexecuted
Cost over £8,000
Sources: *B* 1897 73 387–8, 1901 80 423; SPAB,
Annual Report of the Committee 1896 16,
23; Newberry

CHIPPENHAM (Wilts.) Kington House
Enlargement, lodges and entrance gates, for
Revd Herbert Prodgers
Designed 1862–3, probably unexecuted
Not found
Source: Ledger B f. 92

CHISWICK (Mddx; London, Hounslow) St
Nicholas
New church, old site, incorporating medieval

west tower, and chancel east wall by William Burges, for Henry Smith

Designed 1882, built 1883–4

Four-bay nave and aisles wider than their length, with north porch and south *porte-cochère*; chancel with three-bay arcade between it and south chapel, north vestry and organ chamber. Perpendicular. Of Kentish rag, with wooden barrel-vault roof to chancel, open roof to nave with tie-beams, crown-posts and arch-braced collars, copper covered exterior. H. S. Goodhart-Rendel called it 'One of the best churches imagineable of its type—in rich refined "Perpendicular". General effect of interior exceptionally pleasing and very reminiscent of old churches' (Index of Victorian Churches and Restorations at R.I.B.A.)

Built by Goddard and Son of Farnham, cost £12,780. Stained glass by Clayton and Bell and by Powell

Sources: *B* 1882 43 541, 1883 44 361; *BA* 1882 18 490; *BN* 1883 44 253, 1887 53 645; Newberry

CHUTE (Wilts.) Chute Lodge

Repairs and alterations, for Thomas Everett Fowle

Repairs 1866, alterations 1869–71

Source: Ledger B f. 99, add. ff. 3–11

CHUTE (Wilts.) St Nicholas

New chancel and vestry, for Thomas Everett Fowle, restoration, for Revd S. Cosway

Chancel designed and built 1868–9, restoration 1869–72

Chancel of two bays with north vestry, all tracery in nave renewed, west wall rebuilt, new arch-braced, scissor-rafter roofs, tower restored, new slated broach spire. Plate and Geometrical tracery. Knapped flint with brick and stone dressings, slate roofs. Previous church was modern but in disrepair

Built by Salmon and Chivers of Devizes, cost (excluding chancel) about £1,700. Windows by Clayton and Bell

Sources: Salisbury Diocesan Record Office: bundle 17/12 (plans dated 1868); ICBS 6993 (plan): ledger B add. ff. 7–11; *BN* 1869 16 512; Newberry

CHUTE FOREST (Wilts.) St Mary

New church, new site, for Thomas Everett Fowle

Designed 1870, completed 1875

Two-bay aisled nave with south-west entrance porch, two-bay chancel with north aisle and south transept in base of tower attached to western bay, north vestry to eastern bay. No chancel arch but transverse arches carrying timber roof between each bay. Lancets. Tower with pyramidal spire. Of knapped flint with red brick and stone dressings outside, red brick with stone dressings inside. Red tile roof with flattened pitch over aisles

Cost about £1,700. Minton's tiles in chancel

Sources: Ledger B add. ff. 9–11; CCE 39762; ICBS 7123; *B* 1875 33 605; Newberry

CLIVEDEN (Bucks.) Cliveden House

Interior decoration and refitting, conversion of gazebo into chapel, for William Waldorf Astor

1893–7

Main hall panelled and given fluted Corinthian columns, incorporating antique furnishings collected by Astor, new staircase with figures on balusters, new panelling in sabicu in library

Mosaics and stained glass in gazebo by Clayton and Bell

Sources: Newberry; *Country Life* 1912 32 808–18, 854–9

COATES-BY-STOW (Lincs.) St Edith

Restoration

1883–4

Norman windows in chancel opened up, repairs

Source: Parish Chest (report)

COTTESMORE (Rutland; Leics.) St Nicholas

Restoration for Revd Andrew Godfrey Stuart

1866–7

Repairs. Cost £600

Sources: Ledger B f. 114, add. ff. 4–8; Newberry

COWLEY (Oxon.) St John's Home

Additions to buildings started by Charles Buckeridge in 1873, 1889–90

Irregular, two-storeyed block with attic in gabled roof, embattled tower at rear, projecting north wing at front, windows with mullions and transoms. Tudor. The design is an extensive modification of Buckeridge's original. Of Cotswold stone with red tile roof

Sources: *BN* 1870 18 406, 1873 24 574; Newberry; Mr Peter Howell

CROWCOMBE (Somerset) Holy Ghost
Restoration, for Revd Edward Hotham
Designed 1854–6, executed 1856
Plans were for repairs to cost £1,084; executed work cost £470
Source: Ledger B f. 13

CROWLAND (Lincs.) Croyland Abbey
Restoration
Executed in stages 1887–99
1888: north-east and south-east piers at end of old nave, Norman arch, stone screen, south arcade and interior of west front repaired, strengthened and secured; 1889: south and east sides of part used as parish church repaired, and south jamb of south pier of tower rebuilt, all four tower piers underpinned; 1890: west buttresses underpinned and south-west wall of west front repaired; 1891: squinch arches supporting steeple rebuilt, tower gutter replaced in lead, spiral staircases in screen in tower rebuilt, and west window reglazed; 1892: parvis partly rebuilt, bell chamber repaired and new floor laid; 1893: west front repaired and buttresses repointed; 1895–9: chancel built, north wall underpinned and partly rebuilt. The roof of the north aisle was rebuilt after Pearson's death
Sources: CCE 45539; SPAB, *Annual Report of the Committee* 1885 28, 1889 54, 1890 66, 1891 39; W. D. Sweeting, *The Abbeys of Crowland and Thorney* (Peterborough, 1908)

CROWTON (Cheshire) Christ Church
New church, new site, for Revd Charles Spencer-Stanhope
Designed 1869, built 1870–1
Two-cell, nave with south porch, and chancel with north organ chamber and vestry; western bellcote with three bells, a single one over pair. Geometrical tracery. Of local red sandstone with tile roof; plastered interior with open timber roof
Built by S. Drinkwater of Northwich, cost £2,000
Sources: ICBS 7041 (signed plan dated August 1869); Ledger B add. ff. 7–9, 11; CCE 37174: *A* 1870 3 156; *B* 1871 29 932

CROWTON (Cheshire) Christ Church Schools
New schools, for Revd Charles Spencer-Stanhope

Proposed 1870, Built 1871–2 presumably to Pearson's design; enlarged 1880, D. Forster the builder, demolished 1965
Sources: Ledger B add. ff. 9–11; National Society file

CROWTON (Cheshire) Christ Church Vicarage (Crowton House)
New house, for Revd Charles Spencer-Stanhope
Designed 1871, begun 1872 and occupied by January 1875; demolished 1970
Two-storeyed, entrance porch on east, semicircular bay on south, plain and half-hipped gables, tall chimney-stacks. Old English style. Red brick ground storey with part half-timbered and part tile-hung upper storey, some stone dressings, tile roof
Sources: Ledger B add, ff. 10–11; CCE 37174; Newberry

CROYDON (Surrey; London, Croydon) St Michael and All Angels
New church, new site, for Revd Richard Whitehead Hoare
Designed 1876–7, built 1880–1, vestries 1894–5
Nave of four aisled bays and fifth west bay with side entrances under gallery, porch in base of unfinished tower at west end of south aisle, crossing and equal transepts treated as two bays to south and as one bay to north, two-bay chancel with semicircular apse and passage aisles and ambulatory, south chapel divided into one-bay nave and one-bay chancel with polygonal apse, square north chapel with organ chamber over. Three-storeyed elevation with blank triforium; proportions probably based on Golden Section; vaulted throughout. Most windows are tall lancets, fine rose to north transept. Of red brick outside, yellow brick inside, Bath stone dressings, brick vaulting cells, stone ribs.
Built by Goddard and Sons of Dorking, cost over £16,000. Glass (some destroyed 1939–45) by Lavers, Westlake and Barraud, and by Clayton and Bell, later glass by Kempe. Font, pulpit and organ case by Bodley, font cover and nave seats by Frank Pearson, choir stalls by Temple Moore, hanging rood and lectern by Cecil Hare
Sources: Parish Chest (Perspective exhibited at Royal Academy 1877); CCE 41921; ICBS 8435; *A* 1877 17 302; *B* 1877 35 442;

BA 1881 16 551, 1883 20 165; *BN* 1877 32 157, 451; *CB* 1879 71 189, 1883 80 109; F. N. Heazell, *The History of St Michael's Church, Croydon* (London and Oxford, 1934)

CULLERCOATS (Northumberland; Tyne and Wear) St George
New church, new site, for sixth Duke of Northumberland
Designed 1878–81, built 1882–4
Six-bay nave with west porches and aisles, crossing with single-bay transept to north, tower and spire to south, single bay chancel and polygonal apse. Three-storeyed interior elevation with blank triforium; proportions probably based on Golden Section; vaulted throughout. Of local sandstone
Built by Walter Scott of Newcastle. Stained glass by Kempe and Tower, designed 1906
Sources: CCE 5641; *B* 1882 43 290; *BN* 1882 43 182; Newberry

DALTON HOLME See under South Dalton

DARLINGTON (Durham) St Hilda, Parkgate
New church, new site, for Revd Alfred Boot
Designed probably 1886–7, built 1887–8
Four-bay nave and aisles; narrower two-bay chancel with north chapel, south organ chamber and vestries, and single-bay sanctuary. North tower unexecuted. Two-storey nave elevation with arcade of alternating round and octagonal piers. Chancel arch probably based on Golden Section. North chapel with canted east bay to fit encroaching boundary of site. Very tall lancets to west window, clerestory and, especially, east window. Of local red brick with a minimum of stone dressings, open pitch-pine roof with tie-beams, exterior slated
Cost £4,500
Sources: ICBS 9172 (copy plan dated 1888); *BN* 1888 55 325

DARTINGTON (Devon) St Mary
Restoration, for Revd Richard Champernowne
Designed 1851–3, executed probably 1853–5
Cost about £1,600
Sources: Ledger B f. 8; *BA* 1879 12 57
New church, new site but replacing old church, for Revd Richard Champernowne
Designed 1877–8, built 1878–80
New church closely follows design of old Perpendicular one, and reuses much of its fabric including window tracery, granite copings, nave and chancel arcades, roofs and rood screen. Tower is a new design (old tower is all that is left standing on old site): a Devon type with belfry stage with single large openings on each face with reticulated tracery, ornate embattled parapet with central and corner pinnacles. Newly designed tracery for aisle windows. North-east vestry. Of local limestone with Bath stone dressings
Built by Jonathan Marshall of Plymouth, cost about £12,000. East window by Clayton and Bell, carving by Harry Hems of Exeter
Sources: CCE 60941; *B* 1879 37 894, 1880 38 588; *BA* 1879 12 57, 1880 13 238; *BN* 1879 37 200; 1880 38 556; Newberry

DARTINGTON (Devon) St Mary's School
New school, for Revd Richard Champernowne
Designed 1853, unexecuted
To cost £600
Source: Ledger B f. 8

DARTINGTON (Devon) St Mary's School, schoolmaster's house
New house for Revd Richard Champernowne and others
Designed 1853, built presumably to later design 1880
Two-storeyed, gabled, of local limestone
Sources: Ledger B f. 8; *B* 1880 38 588

DAYLESFORD (Worcs., Glos.) St Peter
New church, old site, for Harman Grisewood of Daylesford House
Designed 1857–9, built 1859–63
Cruciform, aisleless, south-west porch, north-east vestry and organ chamber, central tower with pyramidal spire and north-west newel turret. Of local stone, with brown bands and red Mansfield shafts outside, with polished grey marble shafts inside; open timber roof with braced collars to nave and south transept, wood herring-bone patterned barrel-vault to north transept, stone barrel-vault to

chancel; all roofs covered with local brown stone tiles

Glass by Clayton and Bell

Sources: Ledger B ff. 1, 50, add. ff. 5–9; *B* 1861 19 342, 1863 21 393; *BN* 1861 7 449, 1863 10 374–5, 1866 13 275; *CB* 1864 9 33; *E* 1860 21 48, 1861 22 162; *Illustrated London News* 1861 38 419; Eastlake 400; Newberry

DEVORAN (Cornwall) St John and St Petroc

New church, new site, for Revd Thomas Phillpotts

Designed 1854, built 1855–6

Nave with south tower and adjacent porch, chancel with polygonal apse and north vestry. Tower with pyramidal spire. Of granite with slate roof; interior plastered, open rafter roof to nave, with wooden ribs and boarded vault to chancel

Cost £1,425

Sources: ICBS 4789 (signed plan dated April 1854); Ledger B f. 21

DULAS (Herefs.; Herefs. and Worcs.)

Unspecified work, unknown client

1869–70, probably unexecuted

Source: Ledger B add. ff. 7–9

DURHAM (Durham) Market Place

Plan, for the mayor

1841–2

Source: Diaries 1841 and 1842

DURHAM (Durham) House in North Road

New house, for John Robson of Durham

Designed and built 1842

Rectangular, symmetrical, two-storeyed, three-window front, central doorway, sashes. Of stone, hipped slate roof

Source: Diary 1842

DURHAM (Durham)

Plan of 'the property belonging to the Corporation and Smith's Charity'

1841, November 15–18

Source: Diary 1841

DURHAM (Durham)

Unspecified plans, for R. J. Shafto (who was acquainted with Salvin)

1841. April 27 'Received £2. 7. 0.'

Source: Diary 1841

EASINGTON (Yorks., E. Riding; Humberside) All Saints

Survey, for Revd Charles Hotham

October 1861

Source: Ledger B f. 87

EAST FARLEIGH (Kent) St Mary

Restoration, for Revd W. M. Hitchock, at cost of Herbert Ellis

Designed 1890, executed 1890–1

New nave arcade with one more arch on each side, nave floor lowered 'to what must have been its original level', nave roof repaired, new aisle windows and roofs, new seating; new chancel east window, roof repaired; tower opened up to church; new vestry and organ chamber on north side of chancel; new lychgate. Previous nave arcade was only fifty years old

Builder was Pryor and Co. of Maidstone, cost £7,534. East window by Powell and Son

Sources: Kent Archives office P142/5/5, 6 and P142/6/1, 2, 5–7; SPAB, *Annual Report of the Committee* 1890 22; Newberry

EASTLEIGH (Hants) Resurrection

Additions to church by Street, for Revd W. A. Longlands

Designed 1883, built 1883–5

New north aisle with new arcade of four bays with octagonal piers and arches of two orders; north transept and choir vestry to its east. Decorated style

Source: ICBS 8846 (signed plan)

EASTOFT (Yorks., W. Riding; Humberside) St Bartholomew

New church, new site, for Lady Strickland

Designed 1853–4, built 1855

Four-bay nave and aisles under same roof, south-west porch, chancel with north vestry. Bellcote over crossing with single opening over pair. Tall lancets, wheel in west gable. Quatrefoil piers to nave arcade. Of local stone with Bath stone dressings, interior plastered, arch-braced collar roof covered with red tiles

Cost £3,900

Sources: Ledger B f. 25; *BN* 1855 1 1239; Newberry

EASTOFT (Yorks., W. Riding; Humberside) St Bartholomew's Vicarage

New house, for Lady Strickland

No date, design may not have been begun, unexecuted

Source: Ledger B f. 41

ELLERKER (Yorks., E. Riding; Humberside) St Ann's Chapel

New chapel of ease, old site, for Revd George Townsend and Revd George Fyler Townsend

Designed 1843, built 1843–4

Two-cell: nave with south porch, chancel with north vestry. Western bellcote. Geometrical tracery. Of local stone, plastered inside, slate roof. Pearson's first church, attributed by the *Ecclesiologist* to W. H. Dykes, subsequently retracted

Cost £600

Sources: Diary 1842; ICBS 3200; University of Durham, Department of Palaeography and Diplomatic (Durham Chapter Acts, 1840–4); *B* 1843 1 475; *BN* 1897 73 866; *E* 1842–3 2 165; 1843–4 3 29; *The Times* 13 December 1897; Newberry; J. G. Hall, *A History of South Cave* (Hull, 1892) 203

ELLERTON (Yorks., E. Riding; Humberside) St Mary and St Lawrence

New church, old site, for Revd William George Wilkinson

Designed 1846, built 1846–8

Two-cell: nave and south porch, chancel and north vestry. West bellcote. Decorated tracery. Of local stone, plastered inside, arch-braced rafter roof, slated.

Cost £1,200

Sources: ICBS 3089 (signed plan dated 26 June 1846): *B* 1846 4 381, 1848 6 224; Newberry

ELLESMERE (Salop.) St Mary

Restoration

1889

East wall rebuilt keeping original Perpendicular window

Source: Mr Peter Howell

ELLOUGHTON (Yorks., E. Riding; Humberside) St Mary

Restoration, for Revd Thomas Williams

Designed 1844, executed 1845

Church fell down in 1843. Pearson rebuilt it on old foundations, incorporating south door to nave and old masonry. Very tall lancets. Boarded roof with arch-braces resting on corbels

Sources: *B* 1845 3 Supp. 11; Newberry; J. G. Hall, *A History of South Cave* (Hull, 1892) 208–9

ELTON (Hunts.; Cambs.) All Saints

Restoration, for Earl of Carysfort

Completed 1886

Aisle roofs replaced by ones of lower pitch, allowing blocked clerestory then discovered to be opened up; porch restored; new organ case

Builder was John Thompson, cost £1,500

Source: *B* 1886 51 108

EMMINGTON (Oxon.) St Nicholas

Completion of restoration by Charles Buckeridge, for Revd Greville Henry Lambert

Completed 1874

Nave and tower rebuilt, chancel rebuilt to new design by Buckeridge

Builder was Giles Holland of Thame

Sources: B 1874 32 548, *VCH Oxfordshire* vol. 8 (Oxford, 1964) 96–7

ETON (Bucks.; Berks.) College Chapel

New organ case, for John Wilder, Vice Provost

1885–8

Organ is mounted on Street's screen of 1882

Source: Newberry

ETTON (Yorks., E. Riding; Humberside) St Mary

Restoration, for Revd William Peete Musgrave

Three designs for restoration of west tower, unexecuted; designs for restoration of whole church 1861–2, partly executed at most, possibly unexecuted

The chancel was rebuilt 1844–5, the tower was restored and a new nave and tower roof were designed and built by Simpson and Malone of Hull in 1868. Pearson's designs for the tower were to cost £450, £550 and £600, his later designs were to cost £2,000. In 1862 he charged Musgrave £68 15 0 for his work, but agreed to accept only £43 in 1865. None of his plans may have been executed; perhaps he was responsible for setting up the Norman panels. The chancel arch has label-stops decorated with masks and could be his restoration; the tower has them too, and certainly is not his

Sources: Ledger B f. 73; *BN* 1868 15 832

EXETER (Devon) Cathedral
Rebuilding of south-east angle of cloister and formation of library over
Designed 1884–6, built 1887
The cloister was destroyed in the seventeenth century; the restoration of one corner was based on surviving fragments with large glazed Perpendicular window to each bay and a star-vault inside; the library over is of one further storey and has a two-storeyed tower, each bay has a Perpendicular window in the style of those below. Of Doulting stone
Built by Luscombe and Son, cost £5,000
Sources: *B* 1887 53 599; *BA* 1884 27 104; *BN* 1885 49 673, 1887 52 140, 181; Newberry

EXETER (Devon) St Pancras
Restoration
1887–9
Chancel taken down and rebuilt using old stones in former positions; chancel arch largely new, masonry stripped of plaster and repaired, new roofs, new floors, new altar table and dossal, western belfry refaced. Criticising Micklethwaite's objection to an old font being 'thoroughly restored', 'G' asked in a letter to the *Builder* (*B* 1889 56 209): 'What would he think of the chancel of St Pancras, Exeter, which has been pulled down to the foundations and "restored" so cleverly that even an expert may be excused if he thinks the building is of original Early English work with Decorated additions?'
Builder was Luscombe and Son, cost £5,000
Sources: CCE 68639; *BN* 1889 56 887

EXMINSTER (Devon) Spurfield
New house, for Revd Stephen Willoughby Lawley (formerly of Escrick)
Built 1887–9
Two-storeyed with attics, projecting bays, gables, large mullioned windows. Red brick with tile-hanging, half-timbering. Tall chimney-stacks. Red tile roof. Old English style
Built by Luscombe and Son
Sources: *BN* 1887 53 599; Newberry

EXTON (Rutland; Leics.) St Peter and St Paul
Restoration, for Revd Leland Noel
Church was struck by lightning in 1843; designed 1852–3 executed 1853–4

Much of the church was rebuilt from the ground upwards. New east window, and hammer-beam roof to nave
Sources: Ledger B ff. 31, 83; ICBS 4655; *B* 1854 12 575; *CB* 1867 22 51–5; *E* 1844 3 155; Newberry

FAIRFORD (Glos.) St Mary
Restoration, for Revd Francis William Rice
Designed and executed 1854, new west door designed 1858
Repairs to floor, and masonry of tower piers, arches and interior. New nave seats with bench ends similar to those of medieval choir stalls
Cost about £1,100
Source: Ledger B f. 23

FAVERSHAM (Kent) 21 East Street
Repairs, for Dr Thomas Charles Spyers
1865
No doubt part of Dr Thomas Spyers's plan to start Pearson working again after the death of his wife
Source: Ledger B f. 108

FEN DITTON (Cambs.) St Mary
Restoration
1878–81
West tower rebuilt
Source: Newberry

FLEDBOROUGH (Notts.) St Gregory
Restoration, for Revd Charles Nevile
1857, designs for rebuilding chancel, probably unexecuted
The chancel was rebuilt in 1891, not by Pearson
Source: Ledger B f. 48

FREELAND (Oxon.) St Mary
New church, new site, for the Raikes and Taunton families
Designed 1865–6, built 1866–9
Three-bay nave with south porch and chamber over, connecting door to parsonage; two-bay chancel with semi-circular apse and north tower with saddleback roof and organ chamber in base. Lancets and plate tracery. Vaulted chancel and apse. Of local stone with Bath stone dressings and interior facing, wooden nave roof, tiled outside. Robert and Frances Raikes and Lady Taunton are buried here

Built by Bartlett of Witney, cost about £2,500 exclusive of fittings

Sources: Ledger B f. 109, add. ff. 3–11; CCE 39260; *A* 1870 3 263; *B* 1869 27 592, 1870 28 358; Eastlake 412; Newberry; T. Jones, *A History of the County of Brecknockshire* (enlarged from the notes by J. R. Bailey,) vol. 3 (Brecknock, 1911) 219–21

FREELAND (Oxon.) St Mary's Parsonage

New house, for the Raikes and Taunton families

Designed 1865–6, presumably completed with church in 1869

Irregular, two-storeyed, with lancets and plate tracery as well as casements and large mullioned windows. Private chapel in projecting south wing. Roofline broken by gables and chimney-stacks. Of local stone with Bath stone dressings, half-timbering, red tile roof

Sources: Ledger B f. 109, add. ff. 3–9; Eastlake 412; Newberry

FREELAND (Oxon.) St Mary's School

New school, for the Raikes and Taunton families

Designed 1865–6, opened 1871

School hall with flèche at east end, gabled cross wing on south side, two-storeyed master's house at rear on north side. Lancets and plate tracery for school, casements for house. Of local stone with Bath stone dressings, the upper storey of the house half-timbered, tile roofs

Source: Ledger B f. 109, add. ff. 3–11

FRIERN BARNET (Mddx; London, Barnet) St John

New church, new site, for Revd Frederick Hall (former curate at Kilburn)

Designed 1889, chancel built 1890–1, remainder executed (except tower) by Frank Pearson to modified design 1899–1901, 1911

Three-bay chancel with polygonal apse, passage aisles and ambulatory; three-bay south chapel with semi-circular apse; second north aisle, vestry and organ chamber, part in base of tower; aisled five-bay nave planned (six bays with entrances in transepts built). Two-storeyed interior, vaulted throughout. Of Weldon stone

Designed to cost about £12,000

Sources: Greater London Record Office, Middlesex Records DRO12 II/B1/16 (nine drawings, some showing Frank Pearson's modifications, signed and dated 1898 and 1901); Newberry

FRINDSBURY (Kent) All Saints

Restoration, for Revd W. H. Jackson

Designed 1882, executed 1883–4

New north aisle, new vestry and organ chamber, new north wall of chancel, new roof and windows in south nave aisle; Norman work uncovered in chancel including triplet of windows in east wall with paintings on their soffits; gallery removed and tower arch opened out; new seats. Pearson reported: 'I look upon the church as one that especially requires restoration. Both internally and externally it has a most forlorn and unsightly appearance.'

Cost £3,582 exclusive of chancel

Sources: CCE 63352 (report); ICBS 8861; SPAB, *Annual Report of the Committee* 1884 42; *Archaeologia Cantiana* 1883 15 331–2, 1884 16 225–6; Newberry

GAINSBOROUGH (Lincs.) All Saints

Pulpit and furnishings

1869

Pulpit has fat Corinthian column as base, marble inlaid band and gilded wrought-iron superstructure. Prayer desk, of wood

Source: Ledger B add. f. 9

GAINSBOROUGH (Lincs.) Holy Trinity

Alterations and fittings, for George Laughton Hodgkinson 1871

Church cleaned and repaired, chancel extended five feet into nave, new oak screen with seven arches with trefoiled heads and pierced spandrels, new oak pulpit

Sources: Ledger B add. ff. 9–10; *B* 1871 29 612; *BN* 1871 21 57

GARTON-IN-HOLDERNESS (Yorks., E. Riding; Humberside) St Michael

Survey, for Revd Charles Hotham

October 1861

Source: Ledger B f. 87

GARTON-ON-THE-WOLDS (Yorks., E. Riding; Humberside) St Michael

Restoration, for Sir Tatton Sykes (fourth Bart)

Designed 1856, executed 1856–7; reredos 1870s

Chancel rebuilt in Norman style using old foundations and existing remains. Three round-headed windows in east end with zigzag decoration to heads. Reredos like Vauxhall's executed by Ratee and Kett

Cost £2,300

Sources: Ledger B f. 44; *E* 1860 21 52

GLOUCESTER (Glos.) Cathedral

Consulting architect, repairs to Lady Chapel 1896–7

Cleaning and repair of masonry

Sources: *A* 1897 58 386; J. C. Cox in the *Archaeological Journal* 1897 54 263

GLOUCESTER (Glos.)

Designs for a parsonage near Gloucester, for Revd J. A. Addison of Borthwaite Abbey, Windermere

Designed 1853, unexecuted

Source: Ledger B f. 5

GREAT RISSINGTON (Glos.) St John

Proposed restoration, and two designs for new church on new site, for Revd Henry Rice (brother of F. W. Rice of Fairford)

1856 and 1859, unexecuted

Source: Ledger B f. 47

GREAT WARLEY (Essex) Fairstead

New house, new site,

Dated 1889

Ten bedrooms, bathroom, principal and secondary staircases, entrance and lounge halls, three reception rooms, four kitchen offices; lavish interior decoration with oak, mahogany and teak panelling; galleried hall with fat, Mannerist Ionic columns. Two-storeyed, irregular, gabled exterior, Jacobean shaped gables to main front. Of red brick, some half-timbering at rear, red tile roof. Engine house, entrance lodge with three bedrooms, stables

Sources: Newberry; Essex Record Office A 67 (Sale Catalogue of 1923: 'erected some thirty years ago')

GREAT YARMOUTH (Norfolk) St Nicholas

Restoration

Consulted 1882, reports 1883–9. Church was ruinous in eighteenth century, restored by J. H. Hakewill (1852) and J. P. Seddon (1864). Pearson's restoration begun 1889, completed by Frank Pearson 1898–9. Church was gutted 1942 and rebuilt

Rebuilding of south chancel aisle parapet in stone, restoration of east window using ancient jambs and arch, repair and part rebuilding of roof, lowering of floors; similar repairs to north chancel aisle, repairs to nave and north aisle roofs; repair of tower; provision of new heating.

Cost expected to be over £7,000

Sources: CCE 40821 (1889 report); *BA* 1882 18 412; *BN* 1883 44 253; Newberry

HALSHAM (Yorks., E. Riding; Humberside) All Saints

Survey, for Revd Charles Hotham

October 1861

Source: Ledger B f. 87

HAMBLETON (Yorks., W. Riding; N. Yorks.) St Mary

New church, new site, for Revd Robert Jarrow Crossthwaite

Designed 1881, built 1881–2

Three-bay aisled nave with south porch, chancel with north organ chamber and vestry. Aisles under same roof as nave with pitch reduced. Western bellcote with quatrefoiled openings and pyramidal spire. Decorated tracery. Round piers. Of red brick with stone dressings, arch-braced rafter roof to nave, wagon roof to chancel, red tiles

Cost over £1,700

Sources: ICBS 8618 (plan): CCE 30092, 62273

HAMPSTEAD (Mddx; London, Camden) St Peter's Home, Mortimer Road, Kilburn

Conversion and enlargement of two neighbouring houses, and additions including chapel, for Mr and Mrs Benjamin Lancaster

1867–71; demolished by bombing in 1944

1867–9: first house converted and chapel built; 1871, second house converted and linked to first. Five-bay chapel with triple lancets in east window, open timber roof, painted stencilled decoration based on Italian models

Paintings and glass by Clayton and Bell

Sources: St Peter's Convent, Woking (two

drawings and photographs); Ledger B add. ff. 4–10; *BN* 1870 18 370; Newberry; Sister Rosamira, *The First Twenty-six Years of St Peter's Community* (1917); Mother Lisa, *Fifty Years Memories of St Peter's Community* (1944)

HASELBECH (Northants.) St Michael
Restoration, for Lady Milton
1858–9 three designs, none executed
Sources: Ledger B f. 59; ICBS 5369; *E* 1859 20 293

HASTINGS (Sussex; E. Sussex) St Matthew, Silverhill, St Leonard's
New church, new site but replacing smaller church of about 1860, for Revd Francis Edward Newton
Designed 1883–4, built 1884–5, pulpit 1888, steeple designed later, base built 1896, remainder unexecuted
Newton chose Pearson after seeing St Barnabas, Hove, and rejecting several local architects. This is a very similar design: five-bay nave and aisles with south porch later replaced by entrance in base of tower, north and south transepts flanking east bay of nave, chancel with polygonal apse, south chapel, north organ chamber and vestry; nave and aisles under same roof; two-storeyed interior with blind foiled oculi for clerestory; shafting round apse; flèche over chancel arch; tall lancets. Of red brick with Bath dressings outside, of yellow brick with red diaper and Bath dressings inside, aisles have cement groin-vaults, nave has arch-braced roof with tie-beams and crown-posts, chancel has wagon roof with tie-beams and crown-posts, red tiles
Built by John Shillitoe, cost £11,000. Reredos by Aston Webb 1900
Sources: Parish Chest (Building Committee Minutes 1883–6, signed elevation of steeple); CCE 40977; ICBS 8910; *BA* 1887 27 398, 416 436; *BN* 1884 46 426; Newberry

HAUGHTON (Staffs.) St Giles
Restoration, for Revd Gilbert Twemlow Royds and others
Designed and executed 1887
The original thirteenth-century church was rebuilt in the eighteenth century in a plain style, and after repairs in 1841 was in a very bad state. Pearson rebuilt

chancel and lengthened it by nine feet, rebuilt the nave south wall on same lines as previous, leaving medieval tower and nave north wall. New nave wall is Early Decorated with three triple-light windows with tracery in square heads; the chancel is Early English with triple lancets in east wall. New arch-braced roofs. New reredos and pulpit, both of Caen stone, the pulpit with red marble shafts, carved by Nathaniel Hitch
Built by G. J. Muirhead, cost about £2,000. Glass by Gibbs and Howard
Sources: ICBS 9163 (signed plan dated 1887); *BN* 1887 53 881; Newberry

HEDON (Yorks., E. Riding; Humberside) St Augustine
Survey, for Revd Charles Hotham
October 1861
Source: Ledger B f. 87

HEMINGBOROUGH (Yorks., E. Riding; Humberside) St Mary
Restoration, for Revd William Henry Wright followed by Revd James Paton
Report on church between 1865 and 1880, restoration probably 1884–5
Repair of south chancel aisle roof starting at Turnham Hall chantry and continuing as far as crossing
Source: T. Burton, *The History and Antiquities of the Parish of Hemingborough in the County of York* (York, 1888) 17 and 125–6

HEMSWORTH (Yorks., W. Riding; W. Yorks.) St Helen
Restoration, for Revd Arthur Bland Wrightson
Designs 1864–5, executed 1865–7
Tower, south aisle and porch rebuilt, clerestory removed, new roof to both nave and aisles, interior scraped, floor lowered, new bases to south piers to match those on north, new seating.
Sources: Ledger B f. 102, add. f. 3; *E* 1867 28 265–71; Newberry

HERSHAM (Surrey) St Peter
New church, old site, for Revd William F. Fagan
Designed 1883–5, built 1885–7
Five-bay nave with aisles, tower and spire

attached to west end of south aisle, transepts opening off east end of nave, three-bay chancel with south chapel and vestries beyond. Windows are mostly groups of lancets, a few with plate tracery. Of rough-dressed buff stone, interior plastered. Arch-braced wood roofs, red tiles. Previous church was of 1839; Fagan wrote to ICBS: 'The chief reason for building a new church is the extreme poorness of the present one, and its unsuitableness for reverent and orderly worship and services. It is also not large enough.'
Cost about £8,500
Sources: ICBS 9049; Newberry

HICKLETON (Yorks., W. Riding; S. Yorks.) St Wilfrid
Restoration, for Viscount Halifax
Designs 1866, presumably executed 1866–7
The work was to cost £2,000. Pearson's charge of £94 was promptly paid. No work is visible though the vestry might be his; otherwise the work must have been confined to repairs
Source: Ledger B f. 103, add. f. 3

HIGHWORTH (Wilts.) St Michael
Report for ICBS
1861
Source: Ledger B f. 86

HILSTON (Yorks., E. Riding; Humberside) St Margaret
New church, old site, for Sir Tatton Sykes (fourth Bart)
Designed and built 1859–62, destroyed 1939–45
Nave and west tower and spire, chancel with north sacristy. Of stone with bands of red Mansfield stone. Lancet windows. Open timber roof to nave, boarded to chancel. Tower with pair of shafted lancets to belfry
Windows by Clayton and Bell
Sources: Ledger B ff. 78, 80; CB 1863 5 37; E 1862 23 181; Newberry

HOLBORN (Middx; London, Camden) Lincoln's Inn
New Hall and Library
Design of details, and executed for Philip Hardwick 1842–4
Sources: Diary 1842; B 1843 1 39, 416;

Gentleman's Magazine 1843 N.S. 19 517–8; Proceedings of the R.I.B.A. N.S. 1898 8 191–2; Newberry

HOLBORN (Mddx; London, Camden) St John, Red Lion Square
New church including clergy house, new site, for Revd William Thomas Thornhill Webber
Designed 1874, built 1875–8; bombed 1941 and subsequently demolished
Aisled chancel with south chapel, clergy house to north; nave as wide as chancel and its aisles, inner and outer nave aisles, partly executed south tower with entrance in base. Interior elevation of three storeys with tribune; vaulted throughout. Chancel arch based on Golden Section. Red brick exterior, white brick interior, stone dressings
Sources: R.I.B.A. Drawings Collection (ten drawings, some dated 1874): CCE 34473; ICBS 7889; A 1875 13 315, 1888 40 209; B 1874 32 595, 1875 33 382, 1877 35 190, 1878 36 227, 501; BA 1874 2 28, 1878 9 101; BN 1875 28 535, 1877 32 206, 1878 34 209, 1879 36 6; CB 1878 66 69–73; Newberry

HOLLYM (Yorks., E. Riding; Humberside) St Nicholas
Survey, for Revd Charles Hotham
October 1861
Source: Ledger B f. 87

HOLMPTON (Yorks., E. Riding; Humberside) St Nicholas
Survey, for Revd Charles Hotham
October 1861
Source: Ledger B f. 87

HOOTON PAGNELL (Yorks., W. Riding; S. Yorks.) All Saints
Restoration, for William Wright Warde-Aldam
1885–6
East wall of chancel rebuilt with three lancets, new north organ chamber, south wall repaired, lancets opened up, new Y-tracery in west end of south wall, two similar new windows to south wall of nave, new tracery in west window, upper storey of windows in nave removed, new nave roof with braced collar, raking struts and upper collar, new south porch, new seating

Sources: C. E. Whiting (revised by H. R. Wilson), *All Saints' Church, Hooton Pagnell, Yorkshire* (Dewsbury, 1967)

HORNBY (Yorks., N. Riding; N. Yorks.) St Mary
Restoration, for Duke of Leeds
1877
Chancel largely rebuilt with three round-headed windows in east wall and rose over them, new north organ chamber and vestry, new south porch, new pulpit, organ case, seats and doors
Sources: Newberry; H. B. MacCall, *Richmondshire Churches* (London, 1910) 44–5

HORSFORTH (Yorks., W. Riding; W. Yorks) St Margaret
New church, new site, for W. Spencer Stanhope
Designed 1874–6, built 1877–83
Five-bay aisled nave with north-west and south-west porches, two outer aisle bays at east end of north aisle, chancel with organ chamber in base of south-west tower, north chapel and vestries to east of it. Severe Early English style with tall lancets and Y-tracery. Two-storeyed interior elevation. Tower with tall belfry stage; designed with pyramidal spire with lucarnes (executed to a different design as a broach by J. B. Fraser, 1901). Of local gritstone, interior plastered, arch-braced rafter roofs, red tiles. 'There is something expressively clear and crisp in the architectonic outlines and forms of this church' (*BN* 1877 32 457)
Built by B. Whitaker and Sons of Horsforth, cost £13,000 without tower
Sources: R.I.B.A. Drawings Collection (perspective); CCE 24246; *A* 1877 17 302; *BN* 1877 32 451, 457, 1877 33 22; Newberry

HOTHAM (Yorks., E. Riding; Humberside) St Oswald
Restoration, for Revd William Sabine
Designed 1866, completed 1871
Probably included extensive repairs to tower and renewal of many of the windows. Pearson's fee was £30; works were therefore small
Source: Ledger B f. 118, add. ff. 4–10

HOVE (Sussex; W. Sussex) All Saints, Eaton Road
New church, new site, for Revd Thomas Peacey

Designs of 1880 rejected, new designs of 1887, one of which was built in modified form; nave and aisles 1889–91, chancel and south chapel executed by Frank Pearson 1898–1901, west narthex and stump of tower 1924
Five-bay nave with north aisle and wider south aisle with unfinished tower at west end, west narthex, crossing and single-bay transepts, three-bay chancel with two-bay south chapel with apse, northern organ chamber and vestries. Sanctuary bay of chancel, south chapel, interior of tower and west end bay of north aisle are vaulted. Interior elevation of two storeys; nave arcade with clustered piers carries stone transverse arches supporting timber roof. Chancel arch based on Golden Section. Chancel narrower than nave with internal buttressing. Windows have traceried heads, north transept has rose. Of Paddockhurst stone, oak roofs
Built by John Shillitoe, first part cost about £14,000, total cost about £40,000. Stained glass by Clayton and Bell
Sources: Parish Chest (Building Committee Minutes for 1880–90 and nineteen drawings by Pearson and Frank Pearson signed and dated variously from December 1887 to 1898); ICBS 9236, 9957; *A* 1909 82 8; *B* 1901 81 199, 322; Newberry

HOVE (Sussex; W. Sussex) All Saints' Vicarage, Eaton Road
New house, for Revd Thomas Peacey
Designed by 1882, built 1882–3
Corner site. Two-storeyed with attics in gables. Irregular, projecting bays and oriels. Windows with Perpendicular tracery. Of red brick with Bath stone dressings, red tile roof
Built by John Shillitoe, cost over £4,400
Sources: Parish Chest (accounts): CCE 50428; Newberry

HOVE (Sussex; W. Sussex) St Barnabas, Sackville Road
New church, new site, for Revd Thomas Peacey
Designed 1881–2, built 1882–3, pulpit 1884, choir stalls 1893
Five-bay nave and aisles with transepts at east end, chancel with polygonal apse, south chapel, north organ chamber and vestry. Nave and aisles under same roof. Two-storeyed interior with blind triple

257

openings in clerestory; shafting round apse. Flèche over chancel arch. Lancets, Geometrical tracery in north transept. Of flint with red brick and Bath stone dressings outside, yellow brick (now painted) inside. Aisles have groin vaults, nave and chancel have arch-braced roof with tie-beams and crown-posts, red tiles. Steeple unexecuted

Built by John Shillitoe, cost £8,000. Apse windows by Clayton and Bell. Reredos by Bodley

Sources: Parish Chest (signed plan dated February 1882); All Saints' Parish Chest (Building Committee Minutes for 1881–4); ICBS 8703 (signed plan dated 1883); Newberry; F. N. D. Smythe, *Forty Years of St Barnabas, Hove* (Hove, 1923)

HULL (Yorks., E. Riding; Humberside) Royal Infirmary

New chapel, for Christopher Sykes

Designed 1864, probably unexecuted

Pearson charged twelve guineas for the design and seems to have been paid in 1869; there is no record of the design being executed. According to Sheahan, Sykes gave £100 towards a new operating theatre at this time; there already was a chapel

Sources: Ledger B f. 103, add. ff. 4–6; J. J. Sheahan, *History of the Town and Port of Kingston-upon-Hull* (Beverley, 1866) 609

HUMBLETON (Yorks., E. Riding; Humberside) St Peter and St Paul

Survey and restoration, for Revd Charles Hotham

Survey 1861, restoration 1888–90

Repairs included releading of tower roof, new font cover and lectern

Sources: Ledger B f. 87; Parish Chest (accounts)

HYTHE (Kent) St Leonard

Restoration of chancel, for Dr H. C. Wildash, D. West and Revd Thomas Guppy Hall

Designed 1886, executed 1886–8

Completion of chancel and aisle vaults to thirteenth-century plan; new north triforium and clerestory to match those of south wall; blocked clerestory opened on south side

Builder was Cornish and Gaymer, cost £2,900

Sources: ICBS 7737 (signed plan of chancel and crypt); *BN* 1887 52 418, 1891 60 328; *Archaeologia Cantiana* 1889 18 403–20, 1914 30 263–70; Newberry

IDMISTON (Wilts.) All Saints

Restoration, for Revd Alfred Robinson and Revd William Dowding

Designs 1857–8, unexecuted; designs 1862–3, executed 1866–7

New north doorway to chancel, new chancel arch, new window in centre of south aisle, repairs to tower, and perhaps new belfry stage, new pyramidal spire. Churchyard wall

Cost over £1,700

Sources: ICBS 6316 (signed plan); Ledger B ff. 58 and 68; Newberry

IDMISTON (Wilts.) All Saints' Schools

New schools, for Revd Alfred Robinson

Plan 1858, unexecuted. According to National Society, a school was built for Dowding in 1868–9, apparently not by Pearson

Sources: Ledger B f. 58; National Society file

IRCHESTER (Northants.) St Katherine

Restoration, for Revd Henry Slater, and Lord and Lady Wantage

Designed 1886, executed 1887–8

The church was thought 'almost ruinous'; restoration included new roofs, repairs to masonry, and perhaps some new tracery, new floors, new seating

Sources: ICBS 9076; *B* 1887 52 165; SPAB, *Annual Report of the Committee* 1886 49, 1888 72; Newberry

IWERNE MINSTER, (Dorset) St Mary

Restoration and new south chapel, for Lady Wolverton (in memory of Lord Wolverton, died 1887)

Designed 1889, built 1889–90

South transept wall restored. Chapel of three bays extends from south transept beside chancel; the arcade between it and chancel has clustered shafts with secondary shafts of Purbeck marble. Filling arcade is a Decorated teak screen. Lierne-vault with prominent bosses. Decorated tracery. Of local stone

Sources: Salisbury Diocesan Record Office: bundle 31/12 (plans dated 1889); Newberry

KENSINGTON (Mddx; London, Kensington and Chelsea) Thorpe Lodge, Campden Hill
Studio, for Henry Tanworth Wells R.A.
Wells first occupied Thorpe Lodge in 1877; evidence from the Ordnance Survey suggests that the studio was added to south-west. The house was remodelled c. 1900 and the studio obliterated
Source: Newberry

KEYINGHAM (Yorks., E. Riding; Humberside) St Nicholas
Survey and report, for Revd Charles Hotham September 1860
Source: Ledger B f. 87

KILBURN, see under Hampstead and Paddington

KINGSBURY (Mddx; London, Brent) St Andrew
See under Westminster

KINGSTON-UPON-HULL, see under Hull

KINGSTON-UPON-THAMES (Surrey; London, Kingston-upon-Thames) All Saints
Restoration, for Revd A. S. Winthrop Young
Designed 1884, executed 1884–6
Galleries removed, north and south transepts extended, aisles refaced, clerestory repaired, plaster removed from aisle roofs, new hammer-beam roof to nave; attempt to raise north and south arches of crossing to match east and west caused cracks to appear in south-west pier, so abandoned
Sources: B 1886 50 185; BN 1886 50 157; Newberry

KIRDFORD (Sussex; W. Sussex) Roundwyck House
New house, old site, for Capt. Penfold
Designed and built 1868–70
Irregular, two-storeyed, entrance hall running from west to east, living accommodation to south, services to north grouped round yard with farm buildings beyond. Ground storey of stone and brick, upper storey half-timbered and tile-hung, red tile roof, tall chimney-stacks. Old English style

Cost about £4,200
Sources: Ledger B add. ff. 5–8; Eastlake 420; Newberry

KIRKBURN (Yorks., E. Riding; Humberside) St Mary
Restoration, for Sir Tatton Sykes (fourth Bart)
Designed 1856, executed 1856–7
Extra bay added to east end of nave, chancel taken down and rebuilt further east in Norman style to match original and the nave; new north vestry, new south porch to nave, new nave roof, new chancel arch with triple lights above archway, new seating, pulpit, floors
Builders were Simpson and Malone of Hull, cost £2,600
Sources: Ledger B f. 45; ICBS 5095; B 1857 15 613; E 1860 21 52

LAMBETH (Surrey; London, Lambeth) Norwood
'Surveying at various times sundry houses in Norwood and making plans of ditto', for Ralph Lindsay of Biggin Lodge, Norwood 1853
Source: Ledger B f. 18

LAMBETH (Surrey; London, Lambeth) St Mary the Less
Alterations and refurnishing, for Revd Robert Gregory 1854–64; demolished about 1967
1854: new font, pulpit, seating, iron-work and heating, redecoration, costing £700; 1856: alterations to east end to form chancel; 1858: painting of east wall; 1861: chancel stalls; 1864: parclose screens
Sources: Ledger B f. 11; ICBS 4743; Newberry; R. Gregory, Autobiography of R. Gregory, 1819–1911 (London, 1912) 56

LAMBETH (Surrey; London, Lambeth) St Mary the Less Parsonage, Prince's Road (later Black Prince Road)
New house, for Revd Robert Gregory
Designed 1854, built 1855; demolished 1967
Built at end of terrace, cost about £1,900
Sources: Ledger B f. 10; ICBS 4743; R. Gregory, Autobiography of R. Gregory, 1819–1911 (London, 1912) 56

LAMBETH (Surrey; London, Lambeth), St
Mary the Less Schools
See St Peter's Schools

LAMBETH (Surrey; London, Lambeth), St
Peter, Vauxhall
New church, new site, for Revd Robert
Gregory and Revd George William Herbert
First design 1860, modified design built 1863–4
Nave and aisles with entrance in western
narthex and baptistery at west end of
south aisle, apsidal chancel with
southern organ chamber and northern
chapel and vestries. Tower planned beside
north aisle but unexecuted. Interior of
three storeys with blank triforium stage.
Proportions extensively based on Golden
Section. Vaulted throughout. Of yellow
brick with decoration in red and black
brick, stone dressings; brick vaults with
stone ribs.
Built by Longmire and Burge, cost about
£8,000. Painted decoration partly executed by Clayton and Bell. Stained glass
by Clayton and Bell and by Lavers and
Barraud
Sources: R.I.B.A. Drawings Collection (seven
drawings of original design, some dated
November 1860, and of unexecuted designs for exterior of narthex); Parish
Chest (Building Committee Minutes);
Ledger B ff. 93–4, add. ff. 7–10; CCE 20728;
ICBS 5864; A 1872 7 235, 1872 8 232, 1878
19 234, 1897 58 386; B 1860 16 856, 1864 22
327, 1865 23 626–7, 1870 28 382, BN 1861 7
427, 1865 11 509, 1865 12 581, 707, 715, 748
755, 847, 1870 19 3, 1875 29 696; CB 1864 12
186, 1871 37 11; E 1861 22 56–8, 162, 1864 25
272–4; Eastlake 326, 410; Newberry; The
Times 13 December 1897; R. Gregory,
Autobiography of R. Gregory, 1819–1911
(London, 1912) 65

LAMBETH (Surrey; London, Lambeth) St
Peter's Orphanage (now Herbert House),
Kennington Lane
New orphanage, for Revd Robert Gregory
Designed 1860, finished 1862
Three-storeyed, sash windows in openings
with pointed heads or under pointed
relieving arches. Of yellow brick with red
brick and stone decoration; slate roof
with plain and half-hipped gables
Cost about £2,000
Sources: Ledger B f. 7, add. f. 5; B 1865 23 626;

CB 1862 4 173; R. Gregory, Autobiography of R. Gregory, 1819–1911 (London,
1912) 65

LAMBETH (Surrey; London, Lambeth) St
Peter's Parsonage, Kennington Lane
Addition of upper storey to house, for Revd
Robert Gregory and Revd George Wil-
liam Herbert
1862
Gable end to street in yellow brick with red
brick bands and diaper, three-light win-
dow under pointed head; slate roof
Sources: Ledger B f. 93; E 1862 25 274; R.
Gregory, Autobiography of R. Gregory,
1819–1911 (London, 1912) 65

LAMBETH (Surrey; London, Lambeth) St
Peter's Schools
New National School, art school and soup
kitchen, for Revd Robert Gregory
Designed 1857–60, built 1860–1, soup kitchen
built 1863–4; modern upper storey added
to art school, other minor alterations
Group of two-storeyed buildings loosely arranged around two yards. Pointed heads
or relieving arches to windows and doorways. Of yellow brick with red brick and
stone decoration. Gabled roofs and pyramidal turret roof all slated.
Built by Colls and Son, cost over £4,000
Sources: Ledger B ff. 21, 25, 40, 57; A 1872 8
232; B 1860 18 413–4, 496–7; BN 1860 6
525; E 1861 22 330; Newberry; R. Gregory,
Autobiography of R. Gregory, 1819–1911
(London, 1912) 56–9, 65

LAMBETH (Surrey; London, Lambeth) Sal-
amanca Schools (St Saviour's or St Mary
the Less infants' school), Randall Row
New schools, for Revd Robert Gregory
Designed 1863–5, built 1865–6; demolished
1960
L-shaped, single-storeyed building of yellow
brick with red brick and stone decoration
Built by Colls and Son, cost £1,460
Sources: Greater London Record Office
RO/Y/SP/1916 A–F (six signed drawings
dated 1865): Ledger B ff. 10, 41, add. ff.
9–10; National Society file; R. Gregory,
Autobiography of R. Gregory, 1819–1911
(London, 1912) 65

LAMBETH (Surrey; London, Lambeth)
South London Cemetery, West Norwood

260

Tomb, for George Field in memory of his parents
Designed 1855, presumably executed, not found, 3 guineas charged
Source: Ledger B f. 40

LANDSCOVE (Devon) St Matthew
New church, new site, for Miss Champernowne
Designed 1849, built 1849–51
Four-bay nave with three-bay south aisle and south-east tower, south porch; chancel with north vestry under same roof. Geometrical tracery. Steeply pitched roofs, tall spire with three stages of lucarnes. Of Dunstone, with Bath stone dressings. Churchyard cross
Built by John Mason of Exeter, cost about £3,000. Reredos carved by Harry Hems of Exeter, 1895
Sources: Ledger B f. 7; CCE 17472; *B* 1849 7 389, 1896 70 22; *BN* 1895 69 940; *Illustrated London News* 1851 19 620; Eastlake 384; Newberry

LANDSCOVE (Devon) St Matthew's Parsonage
New house, for Miss Champernowne
Completed 1851
Presumably by Pearson. Two-storeyed; gabled entrance block with oratory in upper storey, galleried hall; coach-house round court. 'Harmonizing with character of church'
Source: *Illustrated London News* 1851 19 620

LASTINGHAM (Yorks., N. Riding; N. Yorks.) St Mary
Restoration, for Dr Ringer
Possibly first designed 1872, completed 1879
Alterations of 1835 removed; new clerestory to nave, new groin vault to nave, short tunnel vault to chancel, both based on crypt vault, in stone, rough dressed
Sources: Newberry; E. R. Mowforth, *Lastingham: A Brief History* (Hull, n.d.)

LAVERSTOKE (Hants) St Mary
New church, new site but replacing former parish church
Designed 1893, built 1893–5, consecrated 1896
Five-bay nave with north aisle, south-west porch and south-east tower, chancel with north organ chamber and vestry. Tower with broach spire. Plate tracery. Interior arcade of round, octagonal and clustered piers. Dormer windows over spandrels of arches. Double tracery for south chancel window. Of flint with stone dressings; interior plastered, braced collar roof to nave, wagon roof to chancel.
Sources: CCE 74734; Newberry

LEA (Lincs.) Lea Hall
Alterations and additions, for Sir Charles Anderson
Designed 1854, executed 1855–7; demolished 1972
Complete extent unknown: plaque over west entrance dated 1857; stair turret in re-entrant angle of south front must have been Pearson's
Cost £525
Source: Ledger B f. 4

LEA (Lincs.) St Helen
Restoration, for Sir Charles Anderson (senior) and Sir Charles Anderson
1847–9
Chancel repaired, east window and chancel arch rebuilt, new south organ chamber and vestry, new sanctuary rails, new arch-braced rafter roof
Sources: *B* 1848 6 461; Newberry

LECHLADE (Glos.) Manor House (now St Clotilde's Convent)
New house, for George Milward of Lechlade
Designed 1871–2, built 1872–3
Asymmetrical domestic block of two storeys and attic, attached service wing of one and two storeys. Jacobean. Of local stone
Contract cost about £6,000
Sources: R.I.B.A. Drawings Collection (twelve signed drawings dated January 1872); Ledger B add. f. 11; *B* 1873 31 359; *BN* 1873 24 571; Newberry; *AR* 1896–7 1 135

LEDBURY (Herefs.; Herefs. and Worcs.) St Michael
Restoration, for Revd Charles Maddison Green
Designed 1894, executed 1894–6
South chancel aisle fitted out as morning chapel, new heating, new seating, new floors, restoration of some tracery. Pearson reported: 'I have examined your fine old church with very deep interest. For

size alone it claims an important place among the churches of this country. The spaciousness of the internal effect is very striking and it possesses much variety of detail worth study.' To criticisms of heating the church by hot-water pipes under the floor, he replied to ICBS: 'to limit the heating of old churches to stoves with all their dirt, dust and fumes, with the addition of smoke pipes going up through the roofs, windows &c and perhaps the addition of brick or stone chimneys outside to improve! the external appearance as in our grandfathers' time, seems to me to be altogether wrong.'

Sources: ICBS 9780; SPAB, *Annual Report of the Committee* 1894 33–7; Newberry

LEEDS (Yorks., W. Riding; W. Yorks) St Michael, Headingley

New church, old site, for Revd Frederick John Wood

Designed 1882, built 1884–6, spire and north porch completed 1890, fittings added up to 1897

Incorporates foundations and parts of R. D. Chantrell's former church. Three-bay nave with unequal aisles, west tower with side chambers to north and south, north entrance porch, crossing and unequal transepts, three-bay chancel with south chapel, north organ chamber and vestries. Severe Early English with lancets and Y-tracery. Two-storeyed interior elevation. Interior of tower vaulted; nave and chancel with stone transverse arches carrying timber roof, transepts with herringbone-boarded roofs, south chapel with collar-braced roof. Fine tower with two stages of openings, the upper ones very tall, and broach spire with corner spirelets and lucarnes between. Of Horsforth sandstone, red tile roof

Executed in conjunction with C. H. Chorley, architect, of Leeds, built by Wilson and Son of Headingley, cost about £15,000. Stained glass by John Powell executed by Hardman & Co.

Sources: *B* 1896 71 512; *BN* 1883 44 949, 1884 46 227, 1884, 47 563, 1886 51 114; Newberry; R. J. Wood, *St Michael's, Headingley* (Shipley, 1957)

LEICESTER (Leics.) St Martin (now Cathedral)

Restoration of outer south aisle

1896–8

Repair and renewal of masonry and roof

Source: Newberry

LEWES (Sussex; E. Sussex) St Michael

Restoration

1884–5

Perhaps minor repairs and renewal of tracery

Source: J. Phillips, 'J. L. Pearson, R.A.' (unpublished R.I.B.A. thesis, 1953)

LEWISHAM (Kent; London, Lewisham) Westwood House, Sydenham

Remodelling of house, for Henry Littleton

Designed 1878, slightly modified design built 1880–1; demolished 1950s

Symmetrical, three-storeyed elevations with projecting and recessed, gabled and turreted blocks. Mixture of French Renaissance and Elizabethan details. Of red brick. Interior with large, panelled music-room

Carving by Thomas Nicholls

Sources: R.I.B.A. Drawings Collection (two drawings); *Builders' Journal and Architectural Record* 1897 5 73; *B* 1878 36 501, 1880 39 252; *BN* 1880 38 506, 535, 1880 39 732, 1881 40 85; Newberry

LICHFIELD (Staffs.) Cathedral

Report on restoration by John Oldrid Scott, new reredos

1892

Recommendation of Scott's restoration of transepts, crossing tower, north nave aisle, nave vaulting, and chapter house, which were undertaken 1881–1908. Alabaster reredos in north transept east chapel (St Stephen's chapel)

Sources: *B* 1892 53 306; *BN* 1892 63 581; J. C. Cox, *Archaeological Journal* 1897 54 248–9

LIMPSFIELD (Surrey) St Peter

Restoration, for William Leveson Gower of Titsey Park

Designed 1870, executed 1870–2

Plaster removed from walls, pews and west gallery removed and replaced by oak benches, belfry windows restored to original length, blocked north and west tower arches opened, new windows in south wall, three-light Perpendicular east window removed and replaced by triple lancets, sills and jambs of which were discovered, similar replacement of window in north chapel

Sources: Ledger B add. ff. 9–11; *B* 1872 30 290; *BN* 1872 22 121; *Surrey Archaeological Collections* 1871 6 70–7; Newberry

LINCOLN (Lincs.) Cathedral
Restoration
1870–93
Appointed architect to cathedral 1870. Apart from minor repairs, major works were: north transept 1870–91; securing south-west tower 1877–80; chapter house 1880 and 1888–92; cloister 1888–92; investigation of St Hugh's apse 1886–7; unexecuted proposals for Wren library 1892; north-west tower 1892–3. Queen Eleanor's tomb was restored; tracery inserted in Angel Choir reredos

Sources: Lincoln Archives Office: D&C CC 2/5/10/1–6 (letters), The Ark 22/12–20 (reports): ledger B add. ff. 9–11; *Archaeological Journal* 1887 44 194–202, 1897 54 246; *A* 1871 6 161, 1875 14 292, 1877 18 154; *Architecture* 1896 1 288; *BN* 1871 21 15, 222, 1875 29 574, 1877 33 293, 1880 39 719, 1883 44 807, 1891 60 58, 1892 62 456, 751, 1896 71 590; SPAB *Annual Report of the Committee* 1883 29, 1885 42, 1890 33, 1891 41, 1892 26–30, 1893 50; Newberry

LINCOLN (Lincs.) Archdeaconry, Cathedral Close
Additions to house, and new stables and coach-house
Designed 1870–1, presumably complete soon after
Three-storeyed extension at rear of house for library, bedroom and attic bedroom; stabling across small yard. Sash windows with straight skew-back heads. Of red brick
Cost £910
Sources: Lincoln Archives Office MGA 533 (survey, specification, estimate and signed drawings dated 11 August 1871); Ledger B add. ff. 9–11

LINCOLN (Lincs.) the Deanery, Cathedral Close
Additions to house
Designed 1870–2, completed 1873
New two-bay, two-storeyed front with entrance under four-centred arch, five-light

window over with mullions and transoms; slightly projecting bay to left with four-light window to each storey; plain parapet. Of grey stone
Cost £755
Sources: Lincoln Archives Office MGA 572 (survey, specification, estimate and drawings signed and dated 21 February 1872); Ledger B add. ff. 9–11

LINCOLN (Lincs.) Stonebow
Restoration and alterations, for City Council
1885–7
Western side of north face largely rebuilt. Alterations to ground storey and creation of new archway to west
Sources: Lincoln Archives Office (letters); Mr Timothy Ambrose

LINCOLN (Lincs.)
Examination of plans for cemeteries competition and reporting thereon, for Lincoln Burial Board
1855
Source: Ledger B f. 36

LIVERPOOL (Lancs.; Merseyside) Cathedral
Competition design
1884–5, incomplete and not submitted
Sources: *BN* 1884 46 810, 1884 47 51, 300, 1885 49 348, 848

LIVERPOOL (Lancs.; Merseyside) St Agnes, Sefton Park
New church, new site, for Howard Douglas Horsfall
Designed 1882, built 1883–5
Four-bay aisled nave; western crossing with two-bay transepts and western bay with entrances at each side; main crossing with two-bay transepts; chancel with polygonal apse and semi-circular passage ambulatory; south chapel. Two-storeyed elevation with passage below clerestory; vaulted throughout. Of red Ruabon brick with Runcorn sandstone dressings, inside faced in Bath stone
Built by John Shillitoe, cost £28,000
Sources: CCE 63475; *A* 1883 29 56; *BN* 1883 45 745, 1885 48 187; Newberry

LONDON (City of London) All Hallows, Barking by the Tower
Restoration and additions
1884–95; largely destroyed 1939–45
New north porch with room over, new high-

pitched nave roof, new aisle roofs, alterations to organ gallery, repair of masonry
Built by Cornish and Gaymer
Sources: R.I.B.A. Drawings Collection (eight drawings dated February 1892, one dated March 1893); SPAB, *Annual Report of the Committee* 1889 56, 1892 47, 1894 12–18 ('it will become a commonplace modern church'); Newberry; *Survey of London* vol. 12 *The Parish of All Hallows, Barking* Part 1 (London, 1919)

LONDON (City of London) St Helen, Bishopsgate
Restoration, for Charles Matthew Clode
Designed 1891, executed 1892–3
New south vestries; new nave, north aisle, chantry and east chapel roofs, remainder repaired; parapets repaired; nave and north aisle floors lowered to original level; masonry repaired; new chancel screen, sedilia and reredos
Cost £11,000
Sources: R.I.B.A. Drawings Collection (five drawings dated 1891); *A* 1891 46 68; *B* 1892 62 155, 1893 65 17; *BN* 1891 61 169; SPAB, *Annual Report of the Committee* 1888 92, 1889 56, 1892 30–1 ('the work muddled twenty-five years ago is to be redone at a cost of £11,000 but it is a waste of money'); Newberry; *Survey of London* vol. 9 *The Parish of St Helen, Bishopsgate* Part 1 (London, 1924)

LONDON
See also under
Barnet Vale	Lambeth
Beckenham	Lewisham
Chiswick	Paddington
Croydon	Pinner
Friern Barnet	St Marylebone
Hampstead	St Pancras
Holborn	Southwark
Kensington	Upper Norwood
Kingston-upon-Thames	Westminster

LOWICK (Northants.) St Peter
Restoration, for Revd Henry George Middleton Pretyman
Designs 1855, unexecuted
Sources: Ledger B f. 39; ICBS 6906

LOWICK (Northants.) St Peter's Parsonage

New house, for Revd Henry George Middleton Pretyman
Designed 1855, unexecuted
Source: Ledger B f. 37

LUDGERSHALL (Wilts.) St James
Restoration, for Revd Thomas Everett of Biddenden House, Andover
Designs for chapel and new seats 1858–9, chancel 1874
New seating, oak pulpit and lectern, perhaps general repairs and new roof
Builder was David Hunt of Ludgershall
Sources: Ledger B f. 68; *B* 1875 33 61

LUDLOW (Salop.) St Lawrence
Consultant for restoration by A. W. Blomfield 1889
Source: J. Phillips, 'J. L. Pearson, R.A.' (unpublished R.I.B.A. thesis, 1953)

MAIDSTONE (Kent) All Saints
Restoration, the roof as a memorial to Archdeacon Dealtry
Designed 1884, completed 1885, rood screen 1886, reredos 1896
Previous modern roof was 'substantial but defective' with eaves in place of parapets; replaced by new oak roofs to nave and chancel with tie-beams, king- and queen-posts to principal rafters with tracery in intervening spaces; aisle parapets repaired, new nave and chancel parapets; new heating; new floors, altar table and rails, choir seats, rood screen, reredos
Builder was J. W. Bunning, cost over £10,500
Sources: CCE 44181; *BN* 1886 50 438

MAIDSTONE (Kent) St Paul
Unspecified work, probably spurious, perhaps given in error for All Saints
Source: Newberry

MANNINGFORD BRUCE (Wilts.) St Peter
Restoration, for Revd James Bliss
Designed 1881, executed 1881–2
New nave wagon-roof with pitch restored to original, new wooden bellcote with pyramidal lead roof, west wall raised, plaster removed and masonry repaired, new floors, new chancel roof following original externally, internally boarded in herringbone pattern, new chancel fit-

tings, seating, painted decoration of walls
Cost £1,460. Reredos and painting by Clayton and Bell
Sources: ICBS 8638 (undated plan); Newberry

MIDDLETON-ON-THE-WOLDS (Yorks., E. Riding; Humberside) St Andrew
Restoration and fittings, for Revd Henry Dacre Blanchard
'For plans for altar rails, advice about restoration of roof of a chancel of a church and drawings, drawings of stalls, and replying to various letters giving advice upon various subjects', Pearson charged Blanchard, curate at Middleton and later Rector, 6 guineas in 1854 and was paid in 1858. The seating might be Pearson's
Source: Ledger B f. 33

MILTON LILBOURNE (Wilts.) St Peter
Restoration, for Revd J. Henry Gale
Designed 1874, executed 1874–5
South wall rebuilt exactly as before with old windows re-instated and repaired, new heating and seating
Cost £700
Sources: Salisbury Diocesan Record Office: bundle 22/9 (plans); ICBS 7825 (signed plans dated July 1874)

MINSTER LOVELL (Oxon.) St Kenelm
Restoration and fittings, for William Elias Taunton
Designs 1853, 1861 and 1867, executed 1868–9, pulpit 1870, reredos 1876
Plaster removed, masonry and roof repaired. Pulpit and reredos both of stone, the pulpit octagonal with pairs of foiled openings on each face, the reredos with five niches with figures beneath canopies
Sources: ICBS (signed plan dated December 1867); Ledger B f. 27, add. ff. 2–11; BN 1890 59 242

MOSS (Yorks., W. Riding; S. Yorks.) All Saints
Execution of design for new church, new site, by Charles Buckeridge, for Scholes Birch 1873–5
Buckeridge died soon after work began. According to a letter to CCE, 'The vicar is the laughing stock of the locality for

siting the church so far from the centre of the congregation.'
Built by Shillitoe and Morgan of Campsall, cost about £3,000. East window by Clayton and Bell
Sources: CCE 47535; B 1875 33 536; Guardian 12 November 1873

MOWSLEY (Leics.) St Nicholas
Restoration, for Revd John Henry Green
Designed 1877, executed 1882
Old furnishings removed; parapets repaired and gables rebuilt to original height, the west one with a bellcote; new roof with tie-beams and crown-posts, slated; new floor lowered to former level; plaster removed from walls; window tracery repaired and renewed. According to Green, the west end of the church was screened off and contained rubbish, the pews were so high that the congregation was invisible. Pearson told him: 'The proportions are perfect. I can make the church a place which will lend itself to worship.'
Builder was Mr Bunning, cost about £1,200. Glass by Burlison and Grylls
Sources: ICBS 8725 (signed copy plan); J. H. Green, Notes on Mowsley and Knaptoft (n.d.)

NETHER WALLOP (Hants) Labourers' Cottages
New cottages, for Dr Thomas Spyers
1854. Presumably executed, not identified
To cost £850
Source: Ledger B f. 24

NETHER WALLOP (Hants) Wallop Lodge (Old Lodge)
Additions and alterations to house, for Dr Thomas Spyers
Various works designed and executed between 1850 and 1871; demolished 1915
House apparently largely remodelled and given a chapel. Two-storeyed; of flint with brick diaper bands and dressings; tiled, gabled roof; mullioned windows. Coach-house
Sources: Ledger B ff. 24, 31, add. ff. 4–11; Mrs Morgan (three photographs)

NEWBOLD PACEY (Warwicks.) St George
New church, old site
Designed probably 1879–80, built 1880–1 (Buckeridge made a design in 1870)

Four-bay nave with south aisle and transept, north-west tower with entrance in base, three-bay chancel and south organ chamber and vestry. Two twelfth-century doorways reused in nave. Lancets. Of local limestone with Warwick stone dressings, interior plastered, nave roof with arch-braced collars and ogee windbraces, red tiles. Tower with saddleback

Built by James Kibler of Wellesbourne, cost £2,500

Sources: *BA* 1881 16 348, 360; *BN* 1870 18 406, 1881 41 152

NORLEY (Cheshire) St John
New church, old site
Designed and built 1875–9
Five-bay nave with north aisle and south porch, choir beneath tower with attached north organ chamber and vestry, chancel. Plate and Y-tracery. Of local red sandstone, tile roof, interior with open arch-braced collars, panelled under tower
Source: Newberry

NORTHAM (Devon) St Margaret
Restoration
1871
Presumably small works; Pearson's charge was 10 guineas
Sources: Ledger B add. ff. 10–11; CCE 62897

NORTH DALTON (Yorks., E. Riding; Humberside) All Saints
Designs for monument and window, for Mrs Henry Woodall
1859, only monument executed
Tomb-chest with overhanging cruciform roof with gables to ends and arms, carried by stout red marble columns
Source: Ledger B f. 82

NORTH FERRIBY (Yorks., E. Riding; Humberside) All Saints
New church, old site, for Revd Thomas Dikes and W. W. Wilkinson
Designed 1845–6, built 1846–8
Four-bay aisled nave with north and south entrance porches and west tower, chancel with north vestry. Geometrical tracery. Some reused stone. Of local stone with Mexborough stone dressings, plastered inside; arch-braced roof

Built by Firby and Co. of Swanland or Simpson and Malone of Hull or both of them, cost £3,039. East window by Wailes, Minton's tiles.
Sources: ICBS 3806 (signed plan dated 1 November 1848); Ledger B f. 35; *B* 1845 3 23, 1847 5 185, 1848 6 368, 375; Eastlake 380; Newberry; J. G. Hall, *A History of South Cave* (Hull, 1892) 234–6

NORTH NEWNTON (Wilts.) St James
Restoration, for Frederick Fowle and Thomas Everett Fowle
Designed 1861–2, executed 1862–3
Nave north wall rebuilt, new south porch, new nave roof, removal of western gallery, repairs to chancel and vestry
Sources: Salisbury Diocesan Record Office: bundle 11/6 (plans); ICBS 5895 (signed plan dated March 1862); Ledger B ff. 88, 91; Newberry

NORTH NIBLEY (Glos.) St Martin
Restoration and additions, for Revd David Edwards
Additions designed 1859, built 1859–60, restoration, decoration and fittings 1873
Rebuilding of chancel with new, south organ chamber and vestry under same roof. Restoration of south aisle including repair of three windows in south wall, new east wall and window
Painting of chancel and glass by Clayton and Bell, gold mosaic reredos by Powell and Son
Sources: Ledger B f. 76; *B* 1861 19 45, 1873 31 1036, 1874 32 512–3; *E* 1860 21 52; Newberry

NORWICH (Norfolk) Cathedral
Report on restoration and new bishop's throne
Report 1892, throne designed 1893, finished 1895
Wood throne with much tabernacle work
Sources: *B* 1892 62 66, 1893 65 389, 418; R.I.B.A. Drawings Collection (one drawing dated 1893): *BN* 1895 68 784; Newberry

NOTTINGHAM (Notts.) St Bartholomew, Blue Bell Hill
New church, new site, for Revd W. G. Spearing

Designed 1894, nave built by Frank Pearson 1900–3 to slightly lengthened design, remainder unexecuted; demolished c. 1970

Four-bay nave with south-west porch and provision for north-west tower, three-bay chancel, south chapel with polygonal apse, north chapel with organ chamber over, and north vestries. Two-storeyed interior. Early English. Of local stone with Bath stone dressings, plastered inside, arch-braced timber roofs. Nave and aisles to seat 650

Built by J. Hutchinson of Nottingham, cost £3,500

Sources: Nottinghamshire Record Office (eight signed drawings dated August 1894); CCE 5188; ICBS 9834; B 1900 78 621

NOTTINGHAM (Notts.) St Paul, Daybrook

New church, new site, for Sir Charles Seeley

Built by 1892 except for steeple, consecrated 1896, steeple later

Four-bay nave and aisles with north porch and south tower and spire, three-bay chancel with south chapel and north organ chamber and vestries. Two-storeyed interior. Decorated tracery. Of local stone, timber roof with tie-beams to nave, wagon-roof to chancel. Tower and spire with corner turrets and one stage of lucarnes

Source: CCE 53063

OAKHILL (Somerset) All Saints

New church, new site, for Richard Charles Strachey of Oakhill and Mr Dickenson of Shepton Mallet

Designed 1860–2, built 1862–3

Two-cell: nave and south porch, chancel with north organ chamber and vestry; western bellcote. Lancet windows. An 'unworthy' design, according to ICBS, 'unsatisfactory in its general architectural character' was made by Wainwright and Heard, surveyors, of Shepton Mallet, in April 1860. Pearson was asked to make a design and sent one in June. He visited the site for the first time in July and later made plans for the churchyard. ICBS suggested that he add a buttress to the north wall; he did not agree that it was necessary, but nevertheless included it

Sources: Ledger B f. 85; ICBS 5563; CB 1862 4 169

ODDINGTON (Glos.) St Nicholas

Additions, for Revd William Wiggin

'Drawings for organ case' 1854, 'plans for corbels to chancel arch and superintending' 1856, probably unexecuted

The church was built to designs by S. Dawkes of 1850, and subscribers included Robert Raikes, Robert Hippisley, and F. W. Rice of Fairford

Sources: Ledger B f. 34; ICBS 4240

ODDINGTON (Glos.) St Nicholas's Parsonage

New house, for Revd William Wiggin

'House to be built as a parsonage next the Ch', and 'Plan for laying out the ground and planting' 1856, unexecuted

Source: Ledger B f. 34

OTTRINGHAM (Yorks., E. Riding; Humberside) St Wilfrid

Survey, for Revd Charles Hotham

October 1861

Source: Ledger B f. 87

OTTRINGHAM (Yorks., E. Riding; Humberside) St Wilfrid's Parsonage

New house, for Revd Miles Mackereth

Designed 1862, unexecuted

Source: Ledger B f. 91

OVER WALLOP (Hants) St Peter

New chancel and restoration, for Revd Henry John Fellowes

Designed 1864–5, executed 1865–7

Chancel has triple lancets to east window, side windows with plate tracery. Of flint with brick quoining and stone dressings, tile roof. Interior has panelled oak wagon roof. Restoration of nave, aisles, porch, tower largely new with twin bell openings and saddleback

Sources: Ledger B ff. 69, 103, add. ff. 4–11; CB 1866 20 166; Newberry

OWSTON (Yorks., W. Riding; S. Yorks) All Saints

Restoration

1897–8, continued by Frank Pearson

Rebuilding top part of tower and west wall from twenty feet above ground with stones replaced in original positions

Source: B 1898 74 527

OXFORD (Oxon.) New College Chapel
Completion of upper part of reredos and
    addition of figures to niches, new sedilia
    to each side of chancel
1888–91
Carved by Nathaniel Hitch
Source: Newberry

OXFORD (Oxon.) Society of the Holy Trinity
    Convent (now St Anthony's College)
Addition of chapel to modified design in
    completion of scheme by Buckeridge of
    1866–70
1891–3
Plan lengthened by one bay to five bays with
    polygonal apse. Single lancets to each
    bay. Of local stone, interior of brick
    including cells of vault with stone ribs
Sources: Newberry; Mr Peter Howell

OXFORD (Oxon.) Society of the Holy Trinity
    School
New school
1875; demolished
Source: Mr Peter Howell

PADDINGTON (Mddx; London, Westmin-
    ster) Catholic Apostolic Church
New church, new site
Designed and built 1891–3
Five-bay nave and aisles, crossing and two-
    bay transepts, chancel with polygonal
    apse and passage aisles and ambulatory,
    apsidal south chapel with vestigial aisles
    and ambulatory, north chapel, vestries to
    south, linked south-west steeple only
    partly built, and north-west caretaker's
    house and meeting room. Interior eleva-
    tion of three storeys with blank trifor-
    ium stage; vaulted throughout. Of red
    brick with stone dressings outside, of
    Stamford and Weldon stone inside
Source: Newberry

PADDINGTON (Mddx; London, Westmin-
    ster) St Augustine, Kilburn
New church, new site, for Revd Richard Carr
    Kirkpatrick
Designed 1870, eastern part built 1871–2,
    western part with one extra bay to nave
    1876–8, steeple 1897
Five-bay nave with inner and outer aisles and
    two further bays screened off from tran-
    septs by gallery over inner aisle carried
    across on bridges, three-bay chancel with

single aisles, apsidal south chapel open-
    ing off transept, north sacristy and
    vestry, north-west steeple with entrance
    in base. Two-storeyed interior elevation
    with open gallery beneath clerestory;
    vaulted throughout. Exterior of red
    brick, interior of yellow brick, stone
    dressings
Built by Colls and Son, cost over £13,000.
    Stone carving by Thomas Nicholls, paint-
    ing on brickwork, and stained glass by
    Clayton and Bell
Sources: R.I.B.A. Drawings Collection
    (twenty-five drawings, some dated De-
    cember 1870); Parish Chest (building
    committee minutes); Ledger B add. ff.
    9–11; CCE 40118; ICBS 7301; A 1871 5
    229–30, 1872 7 235, 1878 19 387, 1897 58 408;
    B 1871 29 339, 1872 30 359, 571, 1874 32 386,
    1897 72 303; BN 1871 20 894, 1872 22 332,
    402, 532, 1872 23 242, 1874 26 549, 1875 28
    536, 1884 46 663, 1891 60 55–6, 1897 73 242;
    CB 1878 65 17–18; Newberry

PADDINGTON (Mddx; London, Westmin-
    ster) St Augustine's School, Kilburn
    Park Road
New school
Built 1872–5; demolished 1969. Architect
    unknown, but style of building and un-
    signed drawings very similar to
    Pearson's
Large two-storeyed hall of six bays with
    attached blocks at north and east cor-
    ners. Pointed heads and relieving arches
    to windows. Of red brick with stone
    dressings
Cost £4,100
Sources: National Society file (plan); Sister
    Rosamira, The First Twenty-six years of
    St Peter's Community (1917)

PAUL (Cornwall) Parsonage
Alterations and enlargement to house, for
    Revd John Garrett
Designed 1858–9 to cost £1,100, unexecuted
Source: Ledger B f. 70

PAULL (Yorks., E. Riding; Humberside) St
    Mary and St Andrew
Survey, for Revd Charles Hotham
October 1861
Source: Ledger B f. 87

PETERBOROUGH (Northants.; Cambs.),
    Cathedral

Rebuilding of crossing, rearrangement and refurnishing of choir, monuments, restoration of west front

1883–97

Crossing rebuilt in replica 1884–90; designs for restoration to original Norman form and new spire unexecuted; rearrangement of choir with new fittings including baldachino and marble floor complete 1894; memorials to Mary Queen of Scots and Catherine of Aragon; cenotaph monument to Dr Magee, Archbishop of York (died 1891); restoration of west front included taking down north-west gable and arch below

Builder was John Thompson

Sources: R.I.B.A. Drawings Collection (five drawings dated 1882–92); *A* 1897 58 386; *Architecture* 1896 1 56–7; *B* 1883 44 33, 59, 71, 106, 110, 1884 46 695, 709, 1885 48 57–8, 95, 126, 573, 610, 684, 1888 55 178, 1890 59 53, 314, 1891 60 271, 1892 62 108, 1893 64 117, 1893 65 342, 1894 66 192, 204, 393, 1894 67 4, 1895 68 235, 247, 252, 404–5, 412, 1896 70 5, 10, 240, 1896 71 206, 463, 513, 533–4, 1897 72 49–50, 69–71, 103, 1897 73 44–5, 74, 91, 447; *BA* 1883 20 165; *BN* 1883 44 33, 55, 148, 271, 340, 1883 45 746, 1884 46 205, 732, 1884 47 801, 888, 1018, 1885 48 50, 105, 152, 640, 673, 1886 51 1004, 1887 52 540, 1888 54 187–8, 584, 1889 56 530, 1889 57 95, 1890 58 222, 536, 1890 59 558, 1893 65 473, 493, 880, 1894 66 658–9, 1895 68 463, 784, 797, 1895 69 832, 1896 70 739, 1896 71 247, 288, 394, 829, 867, 1897 72 47, 78, 114, 163, 309, 401, 1897 73 45, 326, 832; SPAB, *Annual Report of the Committee* 1883 19, 1884 22, 1885 29, 1886 50, 1890 23, 1892 48, 1895 53–5, 1896 16, 1897 54–5; Newberry; J. C. Cox in the *Archaeological Journal* 1897 54 260–2; W. D. Sweating, *The Cathedral Church at Peterborough* (Peterborough, 1908) 71–81

PETERBOROUGH (Northants., Cambs.) St John

Restoration, for Revd Henry Syers

Designed 1880, executed 1882–3

1819 restoration 'brutally swept away' old features and added clerestory and galleries. Pearson provided new roofs, new clerestory, aisle parapets, tracery; galleries removed, east window unblocked and raised, floors lowered, new pulpit

Builder was John Thompson, cost £11,000

Sources: R.I.B.A. Drawings Collection (six drawings dated 1880); CCE 11941; ICBS 8720; Newberry

PINNER (Mddx; London, Harrow) St John

Restoration, for William Arthur Tooke of Pinner Hill 1879–80

Tower repaired; chancel gable and south porch rebuilt; windows and doors, capitals and bases of piers renewed; nave and chancel re-roofed, new dormers being substituted for eighteenth-century attic windows; south chancel chapel of 1859 raised and lengthened; new north vestry; new floors and seating. Old materials reused; new lead roofs for aisles and south porch.

Builder was Wall and Cook of Stroud

Sources: *BN* 1879 36 679; 1880 38 556, 1881 40 643; SPAB, *Annual Report of the Committee* 1880 17; Newberry

PIRTON (Herts.) St Mary

Restoration, for Revd Ralph Lindsay Loughborough (apparently a relation)

Survey 1851, restoration designs 1874, executed 1876–7

Tower rebuilt

Builder was Bates of Stevenage, cost £1,200

Sources: Ledger B f. 17, add. ff. 2, 4, 7–11; *B* 1877 35 140; Newberry

PIRTON (Herts.) St Mary's School

Enlargement of schools, for Revd Ralph Lindsay Loughborough

Designed 1860–70, unexecuted

Conversion of school (by James Jeeves, 1841) and extension to rear providing two new classrooms, two yards, coal sheds and lavatories. New boundary wall and gateway

Sources: Hertfordshire County Record Office D/E S1/62 (signed plan dated December 1870, site plan and drawings of boundary wall); Ledger B f. 1, add. ff. 9–11

PIRTON (Herts.) St Mary's Vicarage

Survey, for Revd Ralph Lindsay Loughborough

1851

Source: Ledger B f. 17

POOLE (Dorset) St Peter, Parkestone

Alterations and additions to new church, for Canon Ernest Edward Dugmore (former curate at Vauxhall)

Executed in stages 1877–92, and completed 1900–1 by Frank Pearson

The chancel of a new church was built to design of Frederick Rogers 1876–8; it was structurally unsound. Pearson's first work was design of wrought-iron screen in 1877. Beginning in 1881 he added transverse arches to chancel aisles and doubled triforium arcade; organ chamber and vestries were added at same time. Three bays of nave and aisles were added by 1892, following chancel design with clustered piers with stiff-leaf capitals and a wooden octopartite rib-vault. The aisles have stone quadripartite rib-vaults, adapted opposite north entrance opposite a pier by insertion of a triangular cell with three ribs meeting at centre, between two quadripartite cells with inner sides canted to receive it. A steeple was designed but not built. Of local stone

Builder was S. Clarke of Parkestone

Sources: *A* 1876 15 310; *B* 1876 34 175, 1881 41 31; Newberry

PORTON (Wilts.) St Nicholas

New church, new site but replacing nineteenth-century chapel of ease, for Revd William Dowding

Designed 1876, built 1876–7

Two-cell: nave with south porch, chancel with north organ chamber and vestry; west bellcote. Geometrical tracery. Flint with stone dressings, tile roof, cemented interior with stone dressings, rafter roof with tie-beams to nave, polygonal wagon roof to chancel

Built by John Grace of Lower Wallop, cost about £1,500

Sources: Salisbury Diocesan Record Office: bundle 24/17 (plans); ICBS 8000 (signed plan dated April 1876); *B* 1877 35 941; *BN* 1877 33 91; Newberry

PRESTON (Yorks., E. Riding; Humberside) All Saints

Survey, for Revd Charles Hotham

October 1861

Source: Ledger B f. 87

PYRFORD (Surrey) St Nicholas

Restoration, for Revd Harry Almack Spyers

Designed 1864, unexecuted

Pearson's charge of £15. 4. 6 was unpaid by 1871

Source: Ledger B f. 30, add. ff. 3–11

QUEEN CAMEL (Somerset) St Barnabas

Restoration

Designed 1886, executed 1887–8

Removal of eighteenth-century fittings including west gallery, pews and pulpit; repair of masonry; new north sacristy; new lead roof to south aisle; new seating

Sources: Bath and Wells Diocesan Registry: bundle 1880–83 (faculty papers and drawings); Newberry

REDHILL (Surrey) St John

Remodelling of old church, for Revd J. M. Gordon

New nave and chancel 1889–91, new steeple 1895

Removal of nave (by J. T. Knowles, 1840–3) and addition of new one of five bays with west entrance under vaulted gallery, its timber roof supported by stone transverse arches carried on shafts attached to arcades (by Robert Hesketh, 1860), and a three-bay chancel, narrower than nave with extra space forming passage aisles for west two bays. South-west tower with shallow set-back buttresses, short octagonal spire with corner spirelets and single lucarnes. Of brick with stone dressings outside, entirely stone within

Source: Newberry

RICCALL (Yorks., E. Riding; N. Yorks.) St Mary

Restoration, for Revd John Rotherford Farrow, Revd Stephen Willoughby Lawley of Escrick and others

Designed 1864, executed 1864–5

Tower rebuilt, clerestory rebuilt from nave arcade upwards, south aisle rebuilt except for Norman doorway which was pushed vertical. New south porch, new roofs to nave and aisles. All stones replaced in original positions

Builders were Lilley and Cawthorne of Retford, cost over £3,000

Sources: ICBS 6294 (signed plan dated December 1865); Ledger B f. 100; CCE 24675; *B* 1865 23 753; *BN* 1865 12 705; *CB* 1866 17 41; Newberry

RIMSWELL (Yorks., E. Riding; Humberside) Church

Survey, for Revd Charles Hotham

October 1861

Source: Ledger B f. 87

270

ROCHESTER (Kent) Cathedral
Restoration of west front, new stone screen between nave and choir
Designed 1888, executed mainly 1889–94
Underpinning west front and lowering ground level; partial rebuilding of all but south nave tower; rebuilding west ends of north and south aisles; discovery and opening of blocked niches beside tympanum over west door, and placing statues in them; refacing of decayed masonry. Choir screen with statues in niches carved by Nathaniel Hitch
Sources: Kent Archives Office DRC/Emf/65–71, DRC/Emp/26 (correspondence); *BN* 1889 56 300; 1890 59 308, 1891 61 922, 1892 62 730, 1892 63 232, 617, 1897 72 901; SPAB, *Annual Report of the Committee* 1889 56, 1892 39; Newberry; J. C. Cox in *Archaeological Journal* 1897 54 258–9; W. H. St J. Hope, *History of the Cathedral Church and Monastery of St Andrew at Rochester* (London, 1900) 31–2, 92–3

ROMALDKIRK (Yorks., N. Riding; Durham) St Romald
Restoration, for Revd Gilbert Beal
1890–4
Repair of chancel, south aisle west window opened out, inlaid floor laid
Cost £1,600
Source: Newberry

ROOS (Yorks., E. Riding; Humberside) All Saints
Survey to assess for repairs, for Revd Charles Hotham
1860, no work executed
Source: Ledger B f. 87

ROYSTON (Yorks., W. Riding; S. Yorks) St John
Restoration, for Revd William Francis Wilberforce
Designed 1862, executed 1867–9
New timbers to chancel roof, releaded; paint scraped off internal masonry, two new windows by Wailes, new oak seating, new stone pulpit, new doors, new east window
Sources: Ledger B f. 18, add. ff. 3–9; *BN* 1869 16 490

RUSTINGTON (Sussex; W. Sussex) Rustington Manor
New house
After 1880

Irregular, two-storeyed, projecting gabled blocks each side of entrance, the one to right with embattled canted bay and crow-stepped gable; arched entrance, mullioned windows; long roof lines broken by tall chimney-stacks. Tudor. Of brick, channelled on ground storey, stone dressings, tile roof
Source: Newberry

RYHOPE (Durham; Tyne and Wear)
New church, new site, for Revd William Wilson
Designed 1864–65, unexecuted
Sources: Ledger B f. 35 ('Design prepared by direction of Mr E. Christian'); ICBS 6693

ST BRIAVELS (Glos.) St Mary
Survey, for ICBS
1860
Source: Ledger B f. 86

ST MARYLEBONE (Mddx; London, Westminster) 12 Bryanston Square
Studio, for Walter William Ouless R.A.
Probably 1880 when Ouless first occupied the house; destroyed
Source: Newberry

ST MARYLEBONE (Middx; London, Westminster) Middlesex Hospital
New chapel
Built 1890–1, decorated 1891–1929
Narthex, western crossing with unequal transepts, three-bay nave and two-bay chancel with semi-circular apse. Of red brick with stone dressings, interior faced in marble and mosaic. Groined
Source: Newberry

ST MARYLEBONE (Mddx; London, Westminster) St Andrew, Wells Street
Font cover, in memory of Eden Upton Edis (died 1885); sedilia, in memory of Benjamin Webb (joint founder of Cambridge Camden Society, vicar of St Andrew, died 1885)
Sedilia 1888, font cover presumably the same
Font cover, a wooden octagonal pinnacle with nodding arches; sedilia, on north and south sides of sanctuary, each of three bays with a nodding arch to each bay and a segmental arch overall. The

church was removed to Kingsbury (Mddx) in 1933

Source: Newberry

ST PANCRAS (Mddx; London, Camden) Holy Cross, Cromer Street

New font

Heavy drum with carved sides

Source: *Survey of London* vol. 24 *King's Cross Neighbourhood: The Parish of St Pancras* pt 4 (London, 1952) 95

SAUNDBY (Notts.) St Martin

Restoration, for Revd George Townshend Hudson

1865–6, but possibly 1885–6

New east window, refacing of exterior of chancel and repair of interior

Sources: Ledger B f. 106; *B* 1892 62 213; Newberry

SCORBOROUGH (Yorks., E. Riding; Humberside) St Leonard

New church, old site, for James Middleton Hall

Designed 1857, built 1857–9

Nave and chancel, west tower, south-west porch, north vestry. Lancets, plate and Geometrical tracery. Arcading before windows and shafting between. Of grey stone with coloured bands and marble shafts. Interior of tower vaulted, nave and chancel with arch-braced rafter roof with cusped wind-braces

Cost about £5,500. Stained glass by Clayton and Bell

Sources: Ledger B f. 51; East Riding Record Office DDHQ/48/235; *B* 1862 20 343; *BN* 1859 5 796; *E* 1860 21 48–9; Eastlake 394; Newberry

SETTRINGTON (Yorks., E. Riding; N. Yorks.) All Saints

Restoration, for the Ven. Charles Maitland Long

First design 1861, unexecuted, second design 1867, executed 1867–8

Chancel largely rebuilt, Geometrical tracery, new roof with herringbone boarding, chancel arch, fittings

East window by Clayton and Bell. East end decorated by J. W. Knowles of York 1872

Sources: Ledger B f. 90, add. ff. 2–5; *BN* 1872 22 21

SHENINGTON (Oxon.) Holy Trinity

Restoration, for Revd Arthur Blythman

Designed 1878, executed 1879

Norman chancel arch removed to north side of chancel and replaced by new Early English one with capitals to match those in nave, new organ chamber and vestry to north of chancel, new nave roof, new seating, new tiles for chancel floor, new heating

Builder was G. Bartlett of Bloxham, cost £1,400

Sources: ICBS 8374 (plan): *B* 1879 37 1219: *VCH Oxfordshire* vol. 9 (Oxford, 1969) 149

SHIPLEY (Sussex; W. Sussex) St Mary

Restoration, for Sir Robert Loder and Lady Burrell

Design perhaps begun 1889, restoration completed 1893

Plaster removed and masonry repaired, new nave roof; north aisle (of 1830) replaced by new one with arcade of alternate round and octagonal piers, plain lancets, plate tracery at west to match nave window, new north vestry; new doors throughout, new seating, oak pulpit, brass lectern

Builder was Cornish and Gaymer. East window by Kempe

Sources: *B* 1893 65 495; SPAB, *Annual Report of the Committee* 1889 57, 1890 69, 1891 42

SHREWSBURY (Salop.) Abbey of the Holy Cross

Restoration

Designed 1886, modified design executed 1886–7

The church, ruinous in seventeenth century, was badly restored 1862–3. First design was to include a new east end with apse, ambulatory and projecting Lady Chapel. Executed design has square east end and new end walls to transepts, new clerestory to nave; chancel is vaulted with one quadripartite bay and east bay with two extra ribs springing from divisions between triple lancets. Of red Shelvoke and Harmer stone

Built by Luscombe and Son, cost about £10,000

Sources: Parish Chest (first design, three drawings dated 1886); *B* 1886 51 289; *BN* 1887 53 599; Newberry

SIGGLESTHORNE (Yorks., E. Riding; Humberside) St Lawrence

Restoration, for Archdeacon William Henry
  Edward Bentinck
1848 and 1862–3
Restoration of 1848 included removal of
  gallery from tower and box pews from
  nave, repair of masonry, renewal of
  tracery and new windows by Wailes.
  1862–3, directing and supervising design
  of new window made by Clayton and Bell
Sources: Ledger B f. 32; *B* 1848 6 489

SIGGLESTHORNE (Yorks., E. Riding; Hum-
  berside) St Lawrence's School
New school, for Archdeacon William Henry
  Edward Bentinck
1864, unexecuted
Three elevations and one plan, cost £12. 16. 0
Source: Ledger B f. 32

SKEFFLING (Yorks., E. Riding; Humber-
  side) St Helen
Survey, for Revd Charles Hotham
October 1861
Source: Ledger B f. 87

SKIPWITH (Yorks., E. Riding; N. Yorks) St
  Helen
Restoration, for Revd Charles E. Gray
Complete 1877
Repair of external masonry, new south
  porch, probably new pulpit, south door
  and tiled floor
Source: *BN* 1877 32 453

SLEAFORD (Lincs.) St Denys
Consultant to Messrs Kirk for restoration
Source: J. Phillips, 'J. L. Pearson, R.A.'
  (unpublished R.I.B.A. thesis, 1953)

SLEDMERE (Yorks., E. Riding; Humberside)
  Cottages
New cottages, for Sir Tatton Sykes (fifth Bart)
Designed 1864–5, unexecuted
Pearson designed three groups of Gothic
  cottages
Sources: Sledmere Estate Office (drawings);
  Ledger B f. 98

SOUTH CAVE (Yorks., E. Riding; Humberside) All Saints
Restoration, for Revd Edward William Still-
  ingfleet and Henry Gee Barnard of Cave

Castle, George Baron of Faxfleet Hall,
  Blanchard Buckland, and Mrs Elizabeth
  Mary Barnard of Cave Castle
Chancel was rebuilt 1845–8 for Barnard, the
  patron, who had east window filled with
  old glass; the south transept was simultaneously rebuilt for Baron; Mrs Barnard commissioned a memorial window
  to her husband in 1858, when the south
  porch was added; north aisle was restored 1859–60; and Buckland paid for
  repair of tower roof and bellframes
  1860–2
Sources: Ledger B ff. 66–7; *BN* 1858 4 461;
  Newberry; J. G. Hall *A History of South
  Cave* (Hull, 1892) 41, 61, 139–40

SOUTH CAVE (Yorks., E. Riding; Humber-
  side) Cave Castle
Alterations, for Mrs Elizabeth Mary Barnard
Proposed 1858, unexecuted
Source: Ledger B f 67

SOUTH DALTON (Yorks., E. Riding; Humberside) St Mary, Dalton Holme
New church, replacing old church nearby, for
  third Baron Hotham
First design 1857–8, unexecuted, subsequent
  design 1858, built 1858–61, additions
  1868–70, vestries after 1872 for fifth
  Baron Hotham
Aisleless nave with west tower and spire and
  south porch, crossing and transepts,
  chancel with south mortuary chapel,
  north organ chamber and vestry.
  Geometrical tracery, much lavish carving, blank arcading and foiled friezes,
  vaulted interior of tower and south
  porch, rest with wooden roofs. Tower and
  tall spire and corner pinnacles. Exterior
  of Steetley stone, interior of Holdenby
  stone, slate roof
Built by George Myers of Lambeth, cost about
  £25,000. Glass by Clayton and Bell,
  wrought-iron screen by Skidmore
Sources: Ledger B ff. 14, 81, add. ff. 6–9; East
  Riding Record Office DDHO/48/235–8; *A*
  1872 8 232; *BN* 1858 4 1099, 1861 7 679; *E*
  1862 23 60–1; Eastlake 303, 398; Newberry

SOUTH ORMSBY (Lincs.) Schools
New schools and Master's house, for Revd
  Francis Charles Massingberd
Designed 1854–7, probably unexecuted

Pearson was paid £10 for a design but did not execute it, schools were built by Massingberd but their designer is unknown
Sources: Ledger B f. 32; National Society file

SOUTHWARK (Surrey; London, Southwark) Guy's Hospital
Design for 'improving entrance to chapel to give it more a Chapel appearance', for Thomas Turner, Treasurer
1866–7, unexecuted
Source: Ledger B f. 49

SPEKE (Lancs., Merseyside) All Saints
New church, new site, for Mr Sprot
Designed 1872, built 1872–5
Four-bay nave with north aisle and transept, entrance in south-west tower, chancel with north organ chamber. Decorated tracery. Of local red sandstone, plastered inside. False hammer-beam, collar-truss roof to nave, arch-braced collar-truss roof to chancel, tiled. Lychgate. Church hall to west of church probably by Pearson
Cost over £4,000
Sources: CCE 49506; B 1876 34 912; Newberry

SPROATLEY (Yorks., E. Riding; Humberside) St Stephen
Survey, for Revd Charles Hotham
October 1861
Source; Ledger B f. 87

STEETLEY (Derbys.) All Saints' Chapel
Restoration, for Revd George Edward Mason of Whitwell
Designed 1876–80, executed 1880
Outer order of colonettes and upper part of south porch, some of corbel cornice of nave, and nave and chancel roof renewed
Sources: Sheffield City Libraries: Bagshawe Papers 778 xiii (letters); G. E. Mason, *Steetley Chapel* (Worksop, 1883); B 1875 33 1022, 1068, 1113; BA 1876 5 279; BN 1868 15 36, 1880 39 544; Newberry

STINCHCOMBE (Glos.) St Cyr
New church, old site, incorporating west tower and north porch of previous church, for Revd Sir George Prevost
Designed 1852–4, built 1854–5
Nave and south aisle with four-bay arcade,

chancel and south vestry. Decorated tracery. Of local stone, plastered inside. Scissor-brace and collar roof, stone tiled. Lychgate
Cost £2,100. Chancel windows by Wailes, south aisle windows by Clayton and Bell. Chancel floor with Minton's tiles reproducing old ones
Sources: CB 1867 23 114–5 (description initialled J. L. P.); Ledger B f. 6, 22, add. ff. 3–8; ICBS 4719; Newberry

STOKE POGES (Bucks.)
New house, for A. Easson
Designed 1864–5
Probably built, not located
Source: Ledger B f. 33, add. ff. 4–11

STOKE PRIOR (Worcs.; Herefs. and Worcs.) St Michael
Restoration, for John Corbett of Chateau Impney
Designed 1891–4, executed 1894–5
There were heavy restorations in 1825 (after part had fallen) and 1848. Pearson underpinned all walls, lowered floors, inserted three lights in north aisle (of 1825) and uncovered a Norman doorway, provided new south porch and north vestry and heating chamber, repaired masonry, especially of parapets and belfry, covered spire with shingles, repaired roofs. SPAB wrote: 'There seems every reason to fear that one of those restorations is contemplated which leaves a *new* church in place of an old one.' Corbett, it continued surprisingly in view of its general disapproval of Pearson, 'has certainly done all a reasonable man, not professing any special knowledge of the the subject, could do, by employing one of the first architects of the day'; but it was discouraged that he would not submit his plans for criticism
Built by Cornish and Gaymer, cost £4,500
Sources: B 1895 69 140; BN 1895 69 318; SPAB, *Annual Report of the Committee* 1891 42, 1893 52, 1894 46–7

STOW-IN-LINDSAY (Lincs.) St Mary
Restoration for Revd George Atkinson and Canon Charles Nevile
Chancel restored 1850–2, crossing, transepts and nave 1864–7
Repair of chancel side walls, new east wall,

new vault based on remains, new roof. Removal of Norman stair tower to north-west angle of crossing from inside nave against west side of crossing pier, with several Saxon window frames salvaged from elsewhere used to light stairway. Masonry repaired, and benches designed for nave. Proposals to raise tower to provide space for bellringers, to place new screen across chancel, and provide new organ unexecuted

Sources: Parish Chest (faculty papers of 1865); Ledger B f. 3, add. ff. 4–11; CCE 6498; ICBS 6209; *B* 1849 7 165, 1850 8 487, 1863 21 728, 1864 22 361; *E* 1851 12 235; G. Atkinson in Associated Architectural Societies, *Reports and Papers* 1850–1 1 315–26, 1852–3 2 xxix; Newberry

STOW-ON-THE-WOLD (Glos.) Quar Wood
New house, for Revd Robert William Hippisley
Designed 1856–7, built 1857–9; drastically altered 1954
Massive four-storeyed stair tower with saddleback roof at south-east corner, entrance front with projecting porch to east, gabled garden front to south. French Gothic. Of local stone
Sources: Mrs Morgan (perspective); Ledger B ff. 12, 52; Eastlake 303, 306, Plate opp. 304

STOW-ON-THE-WOLD (Glos.) St Edward
Restoration, for Robert William Hippisley
Design complete by 1846, largely executed 1846–7
Eradication of dry rot, new seating and chancel fittings. Restoration of east window 1854, new nave roof 1859
Total cost £1,225
Sources: Ledger B ff. 12, 72; ICBS 3809; Newberry

STOW-ON-THE-WOLD (Glos.) St Edward's Schools
Alterations, for Revd Robert William Hippisley
1854, presumably executed
'Plans for alterations to schools' and for 'Grammar Schools' founded by Hippisley *c.* 1844 and closed 1908
Sources: Ledger B f. 12; National Society file

STREATLEY (Berks.) St Mary
Reredos
1893

Stone, three canopies with figures under, tabernacles between
Source: *BE Berkshire* (Harmondsworth, 1966) 230

STURTON-BY-STOW (Lincs.) St Hugh of Avalon
New church, new site
1879
Two-cell: Nave and narrower chancel with semi-circular apse; north organ chamber; west narthex with vestry at north end. Of brick with crown-post roof, tiled. Wooden pulpit and screen, stone font. Churchyard house, lychgate
Source: Coates-by-Stow Parish Chest (drawings)

SUNK ISLAND (Yorks. E. Riding; Humberside) Holy Trinity
Survey, for Revd Charles Hotham
October 1861
Source: Ledger B f. 87

SUTTON VENY (Wilts.) St John
New church, new site but replacing ruinous one nearby, for Capt. and Mrs W. Everett of Greenhill House
First design 1865–6, second design 1866, built 1866–8
Three-bay aisled nave with south-west porch, crossing and single-bay transepts, two-bay chancel with north organ chamber and vestry. Decorated tracery, rose to north transept. Crossing tower with broach spire behind parapet. Interior of crossing and chancel with quadripartite rib-vaults. Of Frome and local stone with Bath stone dressings. Nave roof with arch-braced collars supporting crown-posts and scissor braces; aisles with stone transverse arches supporting wooden roofs, transepts with wooden barrel-vaults, red Staffordshire tiles
Built by Rogers and Booth of Gosport, cost over £7,000. Windows by Clayton and Bell
Sources: Ledger B f. 110; add. ff. 3–10; *B* 1866 24 455, 1867 25 384, 1868 26 362; Newberry

SUTTON VENY (Wilts.) St John's Schools
New schools, for Revd George Powell
Designed 1867–72, built 1872–3
Very ecclesiastical, as though with nave and

275

chancel, south transept and south-east chapel, all gable ends with large windows with Geometrical tracery. Tower in south-west angle over entrance, three-storeyed with saddleback and bell-gable attached like a lucarne; so unlike Pearson's style that probably an addition of 1885. Further additions of 1898

Sources: Ledger B add. ff. 4–11; National Society file

SWIMBRIDGE (Devon) St James

Restoration, for W. B. Vere Stead and Revd J. N. Pyke

Designed 1878, executed 1878–9

North and south aisle walls lowered and parapets rebuilt, masonry repaired, nave dormer removed, new transept roof, new floors, new seats, repairs to screen, new screens to match old for sides of chancel, new heating

Sources: Devon Record Office 1621A/PW 4 (Restoration Account Book 1879–82); CCE 57714; ICBS 8456; *B* 1880 39 543; Newberry

THEDDINGWORTH (Leics.) All Saints

Reredos, for Revd Frederick Heathcote Sutton

Designed 1864, apparently unexecuted

Source: Ledger B f. 97

THIXENDALE (Yorks., E. Riding; Humberside) Epiphany

New church, new site, for Sir Tatton Sykes (fifth Bart)

Designed 1865, unexecuted

Source: Ledger B f. 105

THURSTASTON (Cheshire; Merseyside) St Bartholomew

New church, new site, replacing former church nearby, for Mrs Grace Ellen Kennard and Mrs Agnes Kennard, and Thomas Henry Ismay of Dawpool

Designed 1883, complete 1886

Three-bay nave with north porch, choir with south organ chamber and vestry, two-bay chancel. Vaulted. Tower over choir with corner spirelets and broach spire. Early Decorated tracery. Of local red sandstone

Sources: CCE 63897; *BN* 1886 50 277; Newberry

TITSEY (Surrey) St James

New church, old site, for William Leveson Gower of Titsey Park

Designed 1859, built 1860–1, furnishings added up to 1869

Four-bay nave with south-west porch and transeptal space in base of south-east tower; chancel with north organ chamber and vestry at west end of north side and a mortuary chapel adjoining them to east. Lancets and plate tracery to window openings, highly decorated arched openings between chancel and mortuary chapel with cusped roundels containing statues. Of Limpsfield sandstone with Bath stone dressings. Interior faced in Bath stone with bands and patterns of green Godstone firestone, red Devonshire and green Galway marbles. Mortuary chapel has two bays of vaulting, nave roof has arch-braced scissor rafters, chancel roof is boarded. Tomb-chest in mortuary chapel; altar tombs to south of nave, lychgate. Former church of 1776 replaced medieval church nearby

Built by Carruthers of Reigate, cost about £6,000. Glass by Clayton and Bell; encaustic tiles by Minton; oak seats, reading desk, and pulpit by Ratee and Kett

Sources: Ledger B ff. 71–2, 98, add. ff. 3–7; *B* 1861 19 849; *E* 1860 21 49; Eastlake 400; G. W. G. L. Gower, *Book of the Parish of Titsey* (London, 1869); Newberry

TOCKWITH (Yorks., W. Riding; N. Yorks.) Epiphany

New church, new site, for Mrs Penelope Beatrice York of Wighill Park

Designed 1862, unexecuted

Source: Ledger B f. 94

TORQUAY (Devon) All Saints, Bamfylde Road, Torre

New church, new site, for Revd Henry William Majendie

First design 1880–1, design for new site 1883, eastern part built 1885–6, remainder 1889

Western crossing with entrance from narthex with open arcade of three arches, single-bay transepts, aisled four-bay nave, main crossing with single-bay transepts, two-bay chancel and polygonal apse, north and south chapels, vestries to north. Crossing tower planned but removed from design before completion. Two-storeyed interior elevation. Geometrical tracery. Nave aisles vaulted, nave divided by major and minor piers, the major ones and the crossing piers carrying stone transverse arches. Of local limestone outside, red sandstone inside, with Bath stone dressings. Timber wagon roofs

Built by F. Matthews of Babbacombe, cost £11,000 (original design was for £12,500). Bishop's throne carved by Harry Hems of Exeter

Sources: Parish Chest (drawing of proposed crossing tower); CCE 36326; *B* 1889 56 341; *BN* 1890 58 222

TORQUAY (Devon) St Mary, Union Street, Chelston
Alterations
1894–5
New west front to church built 1846 by Salvin
Source: J. Phillips, 'J. L. Pearson, R.A.' (unpublished R.I.B.A. thesis, 1953)

TORQUAY (Devon) St Matthias, Ilsham
Alterations and remodelling of nave of church by Salvin of 1857–8. Lengthening of sanctuary 1882–5; new nave arcade and clerestory, extension of nave by one bay with new west wall and north-west porch 1894
Sanctuary extended by five feet and given new marble floor and reredos to lowered altar
Builder was J. W. Bunning of London, cost £4,737. Pulpit, oak screen before western entrance carved by Harry Hems of Exeter. West window by Powell and Son
Sources: CCE 12124; *B* 1894 67 419, 1895 68 14; *BN* 1894 67 802; Newberry

TOWCESTER (Northants.) St Lawrence
Restoration, for Revd W. E. Lee
1882–3
Repair and reseating of nave
Sources: ICBS 8769; *BN* 1883 44 33; SPAB, *Annual Report of the Committee* 1883 30

TRURO (Cornwall) Cathedral
New cathedral, partly on site of former parish church, for Bishop Benson and Building Committee (Chairman, Earl Mount Edgcumbe)
Designed 1878–9, east parts built 1880–7, nave and crossing tower 1897–1903, west

towers 1910, part of cloister 1935, remainder unexecuted
Nave and aisles with west towers; main crossing with transepts and central tower; choir with single north aisle and triple south aisles, outer one being old parish church south chancel aisle; eastern transepts and retro-choir; three-storeyed interior elevation with tribune; crypt under choir; baptistery in re-entrant angle of nave and south transept; unexecuted cloister and chapter house to north. Entirely vaulted except parish church aisle. Of local granite with Bath dressings
First part built by John Shillitoe, cost £96,000 with £19,000 for fittings by Clayton and Bell, Nathaniel Hitch, Luscombe and Son, and others
Sources: Truro Cathedral Records (drawings, reports); CCE (nine drawings probably now at Truro); R.I.B.A. Drawings Collection (seven drawings); ICBS 8573 (details of parish church); *The Cornish See and Cathedral* (Truro, 1887); *A* 1878 20 128, 238, 1879 21 370–1, 1879 22 79, 1880 23 373, 376, 1881 25 358, 384, 388, 1881 26 253, 275, 1882 28 211, 284, 1883 29 16, 1887 38 275; *B* 1878 34 922, 1879 37 898, 1880 38 554, 570, 576, 676, 1880 39 120, 486, 1881 40 652, 1881 41 482, 805, 1882 42 508, 1883 44 809, 1886 50 390, 693, 1887 52 629, 1887 53 560, 626, 657–60, 1888 54 9, 11, 1892 62 334, 1892 63 356, 1893 64 54, 1896 71 360, 379, 1897 72 71, 1897 73 515, 1898 75 389, 1899 76 122, 1901 80 541, 1910 136 56; *BA* 1876 5 353, 1881 16 515, 1882 17 208, 1887 28 318, 334–7, 348, 410, 425; *BN* 1878 34 624, 1878 35 184, 227, 236, 519, 584, 631, 640–3, 1879 36 144, 552, 706, 1879 37 173, 1880 38 368, 506, 535, 560, 570, 642, 1880 39 91, 256, 441, 1881 40 215, 591–2, 606–7, 635–6, 1881 41 263, 491, 823, 1882 42 371, 499, 647, 711, 1882 43 461, 1883 45 387, 1002, 1884 46 852, 1884 47 69, 1885 48 69, 1886 50 400, 600, 727, 887, 1886 51 150, 603, 1887 53 458–9, 675, 678–9, 881, 932, 1888 54 632, 634, 1890 59 633, 1892 62 592, 885, 1893 65 636, 1896 71 590–1, 896, 1897 72 434, 808, 1897 73 328, 866, 941; *The Times* 21 May 1880, 4 November 1887; Newberry

TUNBRIDGE WELLS (Kent) Trinity (or Old) Cemetery, Woodbury Park
Mausoleum of Sydney Smirke (died 1877)
Tomb-chest with overhanging cruciform roof with gables to ends and arms, carried by

stout red Devonshire columns with foliated capitals; exposed sides of chest have inscriptions or symbols within cusped foils

Source: Newberry

TUNSTALL (Yorks., E. Riding; Humberside) All Saints
Survey, for Revd Charles Hotham
October 1861
Source: Ledger B f. 87

UPPER NORWOOD (Surrey; London, Croydon) St John, Auckland Road
New church, new site, for Revd William Fairbairn Latrobe Bateman
Designed 1878, choir and aisles and part of nave built 1881–2, Lady chapel, base of tower, north transept, western bays of nave built 1886–7, upper part of tower and spire unexecuted
Five-bay nave with inner and outer aisles to four eastern bays and open western narthex with entrances all under western gallery across west end bay, crossing with three-bay north transept and single-bay south transept opening into base of tower, three-bay chancel with aisles to two western bays, organ chamber over northern aisle and vestries beyond, two-bay chapel with semi-circular apse. Two-storeyed interior elevation with triforium reduced to passage beneath clerestory. Vaulted throughout. Windows are lancets or have Y-tracery, rose to north transept. Of red brick outside, yellow inside, Bath stone dressings
Built by John Shillitoe. Windows by Clayton and Bell, Kempe, and Powell destroyed 1944 when church was severely damaged. Rose by Comper survives. Chancel screen by Thomas Nicholls. Unfinished organ case by Frank Pearson
Sources: Parish Chest (nine signed drawings dated November 1878); CCE 22480; BN 1882 42 647; Newberry; H. W. Bateman, A Short History of the Church of St John the Evangelist, Upper Norwood (London and Oxford, 1937)

WAKEFIELD (Yorks., W. Riding; W. Yorks.) Cathedral
Enlargement at east end
Design completed by Frank Pearson 1897–8, executed by him 1901–5
Addition of retro-choir and east chapel, north and south transepts, north organ chamber; vestry, muniment room and chapter house beneath north transept. Perpendicular
Sources: B 1897 73 524, 1898 75 465, 1899 76 72, 1901 80 612 BN 1897 73 886; F. S. Gray and F. W. Walker A History of Wakefield Cathedral (Wakefield, 1905)

WALKERINGHAM (Notts.) St Mary
Restoration, for Revd George Martyn Gorham
Designed 1858, unexecuted
Source: Ledger B f. 62; ICBS 5525

WALSALL (Staffs.; W. Midlands) St Paul
New church, old site, for Revd E. H. Fitzgerald
Design 1890, second design 1892, built 1892–3
First design for nave and aisles, chancel and south-west tower. Executed design has four-bay nave with aisles, north porch, west porch in unfinished tower, crossing and transepts, chancel with semi-circular apse, south chapel with semi-circular apse, organ chamber over double north aisle, attached vestries at north-east. Decorated tracery. Of Codsall stone, timber roofs with tie-beams to nave, wagon roof to chancel. Previous church of 1826 in the 'Ionic style'
Built by H. Wilcock of Wolverhampton, cost over £11,000
Sources: ICBS 9466; B 1892 63 288, 1893 65 268; BN 1892 62 487, 1893 65 527; Newberry

WANSFORD (Yorks., E. Riding; Humberside) St Mary
New church, new site, for Sir Tatton Sykes (fifth Bart)
Designed 1865, unexecuted
Like Scorborough but with central tower
Sources: Sledmere Estate Office (drawings); Ledger B f. 109

WANTAGE (Berks.) St Mary's Convent, Farringdon Road
New chapel
Designed 1885, built 1887–9
Six continuous bays with north-west entrance, south-west subsidiary chapel, vaulted throughout. Lancets and plate tracery. Of stone, red tile roof

Sources: R.I.B.A. Drawings Collection (five drawings dated 1885); Newberry; Convent Record

WAULDBY (Yorks., E. Riding; Humberside) Chapel of Ease to Elloughton
New chapel, old site, for Mrs Anne Raikes of Welton House
Designed 1844, probably built 1844, complete before 1847
Two-cell: nave and chancel, south entrance porch, polygonal bell-turret with twin openings. Narrow windows with Geometrical tracery, pulpit approached through separate opening in chancel arch
Built by Firby and Co. of Swanland
Sources: *B* 1847 5 185; Newberry; J. G. Hall, *A History of South Cave* (Hull, 1892) 206, 218

WELLS (Somerset) Cathedral
Monument to Lord Arthur Hervey, Bishop of Bath and Wells (died 1894)
Unveiled 1897
Alabaster tomb on red marble plinth; five foliated and crocketed arches on each side, two at ends, separated by traceried panels and buttresses with canopies and crockets. Effigy by Brock
Source: *BN* 1897 73 204

WELTON (Yorks., E. Riding; Humberside) Eastdale
New farm buildings, for Robert Raikes of Eastdale
Designed 1845, unexecuted
Source: Ledger B f. 1

WELWICK (Yorks., E. Riding; Humberside) St Mary
Survey, for Revd Charles Hotham
October 1861
Source: Ledger B f. 87

WENTWORTH (Yorks., W. Riding; S. Yorks.) Holy Trinity
New church, new site, replacing church nearby, for Lord Fitzwilliam
Designed 1866–72, built 1872–7
Five-bay nave with north porch, crossing with two-bay transepts, central tower, two-bay chancel with north organ chamber and vestries. Geometrical tracery.

Two-storeyed elevation, vaulted throughout. Of Durnford Bridge stone with Darfield stone for ashlar, slate roofs
Built by G. W. Booth of London, cost about £25,000. West window by Kempe, east window by Clayton and Bell
Sources: Ledger B f. 117, add. ff. 3–7; CCE 47972; *A* 1872 8 163, 1873 9 244, 1876 15 286, 1877 18 63; *B* 1872 30 731, 1873 31 339, 1877 33 115; Newberry

WESTMILL (Herts.) St Mary
Restoration, for Revd John Aiken Ewing
1865
Restoration of chancel roof and aisle windows; design for new west window apparently unexecuted.
Source: Ledger b f. 36

WESTMINSTER (Mddx; London, Westminster) Abbey
Restoration, organ cases and monuments, 1879–97
Followed Scott as Surveyor to the Abbey in 1879 and was responsible for three major works: the completion of north porches to Scott's design and the rebuilding of the rest of the transept façade to new design based on archaeological evidence and old prints, the work being completed in 1890; the repair of the side of the nave from the south transept as far west as the organ screen, largely complete by 1886; repair of the clerestory walls and buttresses of the east limb, completed about 1896. Additionally in 1884 or before design of three organ cases executed 1895–7, and three monuments: to Lord John Thynne (died 1880) erected 1884; to Dean Arthur Penrhyn Stanley (died 1881) erected 1884; and to the seventh Earl of Shaftsbury (died 1885) erected 1887; Boehm was the sculptor of the Stanley and Shaftsbury monuments, Armstead of the Thynne monument. Pearson also supervised the Siemens memorial window
Sources: R.I.B.A. Drawings Collection (drawing of Stanley monument); *A* 1891 46 145; *Architecture* 1896 1 132–42; *B* 1879 37 312–3, 1884 46 776, 1884 47 622, 724, 726, 1885 49 773, 1886 509 39, 1890 59 400, 1892 62 11, 415, 1899 76 537; *BA* 1881 16 620; *BN* 1883 44 147, 1884 47 489, 1885 48 1, 1885 49 914, 1886 50 940, 1886 51 115, 150, 712, 1888 54 450, 1890 58 891, 1891 60 500, 772, 1892 62 592, 1892 63 805, 861, 897, 1893 65 539;

SPAB, *Annual Report of the Committee*
1883 30, 1884 32–3, 1885 44, 1888 42–3, 1890
40–2, 1891 41, 1892 31–2, 1893 64, 1894 61;
W. Morris, *Concerning Westminster Abbey* (London, 1893); Newberry; W. R.
Lethaby, *Westminster Abbey and the Kings' Craftsmen* (London, 1906) Ch. 3;
A. D. Sharpe in *Journal of the R.I.B.A.*
3rd s. 1939 46 706–10

WESTMINSTER (Mddx; London, Westminster) Abbey precinct
Proposed monumental chapels
Various designs 1888–92
Sources: R.I.B.A. Drawings Collection (seven
drawings dated 1888–92); *A* 1891 46 98; *B*
1884 42 227, 284, 320, 354, 389, 1885 48 358,
1889 56 157–9, 159, 188, 1890 59 474,
489–92, 1891 61 6, 60, 81, 1894 66 167; *BN*
1889 56 324, 1890 58 818, 1890 59 909–11,
1891 61 4, 132, 206, 1892 62 498; *Journal of the R.I.B.A.* 1890–1 7 119–20, SPAB,
Annual Report of the Committee 1889 47,
1893 68

WESTMINSTER (Mddx; London, Westminster) Abbey precinct, 1 and 2 Abbey
Garden
Two new houses for canons
1882
Two-storeyed with basements and attics in
gabled roofs, projecting bays, large mullioned windows. Tudor Gothic. Of red
brick with stone dressings, slate roofs.
No. 1 more ornate, with more stonework,
twin chimney-stacks linked at top by
stone bridges with blank tracery
Source: Newberry

WESTMINSTER (Mddx; London, Westminster), Abbey precinct
Railings for east and north of Abbey Close
Designed 1882, partly executed (designed by
W. D. Caröe, according to his son Mr A.
D. R. Caroe)
To cost £2,700
Source: CCE 34858

WESTMINSTER (Mddx; London, Westminster) Abbey precinct, Little Dean's Yard
Building, for Westminster School, east of
Ashburnham House (Turle's House)
1884
Three-storeyed with basement and attic,
mullioned windows, with arched heads to
ground floor. Tudor Gothic, red brick,
stone dressings
Source: Newberry

WESTMINSTER (Mddx, London, Westminster), 18 Carlton House Terrace
Alterations and redecoration, including formation of library, for William Waldorf
Astor
1895
The library has mahogany-panelled walls
with fluted pilasters with a variety of
Serlian Corinthian capitals. New sanitary arrangements
Sources: Crown Estate Office file 14723;
Newberry

WESTMINSTER (Mddx; London, Westminster) Dean Street, Soho
Unspecified work for Henry Littleton, chairman of Novello's
1868–71
Source: Ledger B add. ff. 4–10

WESTMINSTER (Mddx; London, Westminster) Holy Trinity, Bessborough Gardens
New church, new site, for Archdeacon Henry
Edward Bentinck
Designed 1849, built 1849–52, reredos and
furnishing of chancel 1867–71; demolished 1950s
Cruciform. Five-bay nave and aisles with
north and south porches, crossing and
transepts, chancel wider than nave,
vestry in north-east angle, chapel in
south-east angle, crossing tower.
Geometrical tracery. Of Bargate stone
with Bath stone dressings. Hammerbeam, collar-truss roof to nave, archbraced collar roof to chancel, vaulted
crossing, brown Staffordshire tiles
Cost about £12,000. Glass by Wailes
Sources: Ledger B f. 75, add. ff. 3–11; *A* 1878 19
234, 1880 23 397; *B* 1849 7 557, 1858 16 632;
BN 1882 42 647; *E* 1849 10 235, 1851 12
231–2, 1852 13 409–12, 1864 25 273;
Graphic 1874 9 442; Eastlake 303; Newberry

WESTMINSTER (Mddx; London, Westminster) Holy Trinity Schools, Dorset Place
New National and commercial schools, for
Archdeacon William Henry Edward Ben-

280

tinck and Revd Charles Frederick Sec-
retan (vicar of Holy Trinity)
1856 design for schools including master's
house to be built beside church; 1857
design omitting master's house, to cost
about £2,000; 1860 sketch plan for present site for school to hold 600 without
classrooms; 1861 final design for same
site for school to hold 400 with classrooms, built about 1861–3; closed c. 1939,
damaged, altered and now in light industrial use
Three-storeyed, irregular block with windows with pointed heads and relieving
arches. Of yellow brick with red and
black brick and stone decoration. Pros-
pectus (at CCE) states: 'The boys are
instructed in the usual branches of a
sound Commercial Education, including
the rudiments of LATIN, FRENCH,
Vocal Music, DRAWING, and
ALGEBRA'; charges were one guinea
per quarter plus one shilling for sta-
tionery, books extra, giving 'a sound
Commercial Education at such terms as
to be within the reach of the majority of
tradespeople, and of professional men of
moderate income'
Cost about £3,100
Sources: Greater London Record Office
Y/SP/5353 A–G (seven drawings); Ledger
B ff. 26, 49; CCE 17959; Newberry

WESTMINSTER (Mddx; London, Westmin-
ster) Sackville Street
Additions to premises, for Thomas Price,
tailor, of Suffolk Street
Designed 1865, unexecuted
Source: Ledger b f. 5

WESTMINSTER (Mddx; London, Westminster) St Margaret
New west and south-east porches
Designed by 1891, presumably built 1892–4
Both Perpendicular. West porch with three
openings and embattled parapet, fan-
vaulted inside. South-east porch very
simple
Source: BN 1891 60 772

WESTMINSTER (Mddx; London, Westmin-
ster) St Michael, Burleigh Street
Designs for rearranging church, for Revd
George Fyler Townsend
1862, execution unknown
Source: Ledger B f. 15

WESTMINSTER (Mddx; London, Westminster) 2 Temple Place
New estate office, for William Waldorf Astor
Designed 1892–3, finished 1895; altered and
restored after damage 1944
Two-storeyed, rooms arranged around central staircase, great hall on upper floor
across main front. Tudor. Of Portland
stone, interiors lavishly decorated with
rare woods and much carving
Artists included Sir George Frampton, W. S.
Frith, J. Starkie Gardner, Thomas Nicholls, Clayton and Bell
Sources: R.I.B.A. Drawings Collection (nineteen drawings dated 1892–5); Architecture 1896 1 404; Newberry

WESTMINSTER (Mddx; London, Westminster) Westminster Hall
Addition of cloister to north side with committee rooms over, and proposal to raise
north towers
Designed 1883–4, modified design executed
1888
Cloister with range of rooms above on flank of
hall. Decorated. Of Ketton stone, teak
roofs
Sources: R.I.B.A. Drawings Collection (two
drawings); Report from the Select Committee on Westminster Hall Restoration
(London, 1885); B 1884 47 78, 115, 809, 1885
48 181, 216, 358, 760, 1885 49 1–3, 72, 804,
1886 51 332, 1890 59 114, 368–9; BN 1885 48
1, 673; Newberry

WEST MOLESEY (Surrey) church
Advice on dry rot, for Revd Tresilian George
Nicholas
1851
Source: Ledger B f. 20

WESTON (Lincs.) St Mary
Restoration of nave
Designed 1882, completed 1885
Restoration of clerestory, part new on north
side, all new on south; new roof with
braced crown-posts, new aisle roofs.
Existence of former steeply pitched roof
was found on side of tower, existing
fifteenth-century roof had flat pitch.
Pearson's was to match Scott's and
original. An SPAB member who had only
seen roof from passing train complained
that it 'completely dwarfed' west tower.
It does dwarf it, but is a fine roof

Sources: CCE 64016; SPAB, *Annual Report of the Committee* 1883 30, 1884 34, 1886 37–8

WESTOW (Yorks., East Riding; N. Yorks.) St Mary's Vicarage
New house
Newberry records the building of a new vicarage here, but existing one is by Ewan Christian 1868–70
Sources: Newberry; CCE 23893

WEYBRIDGE (Surrey) House (probably Halstain House)
Additions and alterations, for Dr Thomas Spyers
Design 1862, new design 1862, further design presumably executed 1865
Cost about £400
Source: Ledger B ff. 16, 37

WEYBRIDGE (Surrey) St James
New church, new site but replacing old church nearby, for Revd William Giffard
Designed 1845, built 1846–8, tower and spire 1853–5, additions 1856–9, enlargements 1864–70
Church originally had five-bay aisled nave with west tower and north and south porches, three-bay chancel with north vestry. After extension it has five-bay nave with north and south aisles, the north one with porch, second wider aisle to south with porch, west tower and spire, chancel with south chapel, north vestry and organ chamber and second vestry. Decorated tracery. Of Guildford stone, plastered inside, chancel faced with marble. Arch-braced collar and rafter roof to nave, pointed wagon roof to chancel
First church cost £5,000, additions cost further £4,600. Designed in association with Arthur Johnson
Sources: ICBS (plan signed by Pearson and Johnson dated November 1848); Ledger B ff. 15, 29, 43, 46, 63, 101, add. ff. 7–10; CCE 21452; *B* 1846 4 211; *E* 1859 9 369; Eastlake 380; Newberry

WEYBRIDGE (Surrey) St James's School
Additions or alterations or both, for Revd Edward Joseph Rose
Designed and presumably executed 1865–6
Cost over £1,200
Sources: Ledger B f. 20; National Society file

WEYBRIDGE (Surrey) Vigo House
Survey, for Revd Harry Almack Spyers 1864
Source: Ledger B f. 17

WHITWELL (Derbys.) St Lawrence
Restoration, for Revd George Edward Mason
Executed 1885–6
Restoration of nave and aisles, west tower, south porch and transepts. New drainage, new floors, walls replastered, dressings repointed, new parapets to aisles, new pine roofs to nave and aisles, new oak roofs to transepts, exterior lead-covered, box pews and gallery in tower removed, tower arch repaired, new pitch-pine benches, windows repaired and fitted with cathedral glass. Proposed restoration of chancel abandoned
Builder was Morgan and Cowper of Campsall, cost £2,200
Sources: *BN* 1885 49 953, 1886 50 885

WHITWELL (Derbys.) St Lawrence's (now Old) Parsonage
New house, for Revd George Edward Mason
Completed 1885
Of local stone with Bath dressings and brown tile roof
Built by Morgan and Cowper of Campsall, cost over £2,000
Sources: *BN* 1885 49 953; Newberry

WHITWELL-ON-THE-HILL (Yorks., N. Riding; N. Yorks.) St John
New church, new site, for Louisa Rosamond Haigh of Whitwell Hall and Arthur Stephens
Designs 1857–8, unexecuted
Source: Ledger B ff. 55, 69

WHITWELL-ON-THE-HILL (Yorks., N. Riding; N. Yorks.) Whitwell Hall
Enlargement, for Louisa Rosamond Haigh of Whitwell Hall and Arthur Stephens
Designed 1857–8, unexecuted
To cost £1,125
Source: Ledger B f. 55

WIGGINTON (Oxon.) St Giles
Restoration
1886
Continuation of restoration begun by William White. Plaster removed from south

aisle, stone floor replaced by tiles, new doors and seating. Designs for screens and reredos unexecuted

Cost £1,300

Sources: SPAB, *Annual Report of the Committee* 1886 51; *VCH Oxfordshire* vol. 9 (Oxford, 1969) 168–9

WILLESBOROUGH (Kent) St Mary

Restoration and new north aisle, for Revd Sydenham Francis Russell

Designed 1866, executed 1867–8

New chancel east window, repair of south aisle and restoration of windows, resetting chancel arch; new north aisle with crown-post roof to match medieval one in south aisle, Decorated tracery, arcade of circular and octagonal piers; new north vestry; new fittings and furnishings

Cost about £1,825

Sources: Ledger B f. 116, add. ff. 3–5; CCE 31342; ICBS 6607; *BN* 1868 15 367; Newberry

WIMBOURNE MINSTER (Dorset) St Cuthberga

Restoration

Executed 1890–1 in association with Walter J. Fletcher of Wimbourne

Restoration of transepts: walls raised two feet and repaired, dressings of Tissbury stone renewed with Doulting, new oak roofs raised to pitch of Norman roofs, traces of which were uncovered, plaster removed from walls, and altar recesses and fresco found in north transept, remains of single-light window found in south transept, new access to central tower

Builder was Merrick and Son of Glastonbury on tender of £1,689. Glass by Clayton and Bell, except for south window by Powell and Sons

Source: *B* 1892 62 16

WINCHESTER (Hants) All Saints, Chilcomb, Petersfield Road

New church, new site, for Revd Ninian H. Barr

Designed 1885–9, two west bays of nave built 1889–90, remainder of nave built 1890–1, chancel 1896–7, vestry and tower unexecuted

Four-bay nave with north aisle. Lancets and

plate tracery. Of chalk faced in flint outside, brick angles and buttresses, stone dressings. Arch-braced collar roofs with tie-beams, red tiles

Built by John Shillitoe, cost £5,000

Sources: ICBS 9370 (signed plan dated 1897); *B* 1897 72 465; *BN* 1897 72 665; Newberry

WINDSOR (Berks.) Castle, St George's Chapel

Restoration, new altar cross, font, and memorials

Restoration 1878–86

Restoration of buttresses with new figures inserted into niches below pinnacles on south side, restoration of parapets, gargoyles, and bosses. Altar cross presented by Queen Victoria on her Jubilee 1887, alabaster font in memory of Canon Frederick Anson (died 1885) in south aisle, carved by Thomas Nicholls; brass wall tablets to sculptor Sir Joachim Edgar Boehm (died 1890) 1891, and to Canon Charles Leslie Courtenay (died 1894) 1896–7. In Albert Memorial Chapel, white marble tomb of Prince Leopold, Duke of Albany (died 1884), figure by Boehm

Sources: plaster casts of panels in altar cross in possession of Mrs Morgan; SPAB *Annual Report of the Committee* 1883 21, 1884 45; Newberry; S. M. Bond (ed.), *The Monuments of St George's Chapel, Windsor Castle* (Windsor, 1958) 5–6, 19, 48, 233

WINESTEAD (Yorks., E. Riding; Humberside) St German

Survey, for Revd Charles Hotham

October 1861

Source: Ledger B f. 87

WINNINGTON (Cheshire) St Luke

New church, new site

Built 1896–7

Nave with north porch, chancel with south organ chamber and vestry, parish room beneath nave. North tower unexecuted. Lancets and plate tracery. Of brown brick with stone dressings, timber roofs, arch-braced in nave, braced collars in chancel, boarded in sanctuary, tiled.

Built by Beckett and Co. of Hartford, cost £5,000

Sources: CCE 89885; *B* 1897 73 57; *BN* 1897 73 10; Newberry

WOKING (Surrey) St Peter's Convent, May-
bury Hill
New convent buildings, including chapels,
for Benjamin Lancaster
Domestic buildings designed 1882–3, first part
built 1883–5, lodge 1886, entrance tower
and porch 1889, main chapel designed
1897, built by Frank Pearson 1898–1900
Irregular, two-storeyed blocks with attics in
gables. Tudor, of red brick with stone
dressings; entrance tower with attached
porte-cochère and two-storeyed canted
bay with embattled parapet, clock in
tower. Small vaulted mortuary chapel,
Early English. Main chapel has five
aisled bays, single unaisled bay and
canted bay with apses to east and to
north and south. Crypt chapel under
three eastern bays and apses. Tall lancets. Vaulted throughout. Of red brick
with stone dressings, interior faced in
stone, crypt chapel faced in marble and
mosaic.
First building cost £17,000; main chapel built
by Luscombe, cost £9,000
Sources: Convent (eight drawings for chapel,
four drawings for additions, dated 1897);
BN 1885 48 673; Sister Rosamira, *The
First Twenty-six Years of St Peter's Community* (1917); Mother Lisa, *Fifty Years
Memories of St Peter's Community* (1944)

WOODLANDS (Somerset) St Katherine
Rebuilt largely to new design using west
tower of 1712. Chancel 1872, nave and
aisles 1880
Aisled nave with south porch, chancel with
north organ chamber and vestry. Decorated tracery. Wagon roof with tie-
beams to nave, scissor-rafter roof to
chancel
Sources: CCE 46122; *B* 1880 39 340

WOOLLEY (Yorks., W. Riding; W. Yorks) St
Peter
Restoration, for Revd Frederick Fawkes and
G. H. Wentworth
Designed 1868–70, executed 1870–1
Removal of box pews, gallery in tower; north
nave aisle wall rebuilt, new east window
and flanking buttresses, new doorway to
north chancel aisle, new south doorway
to nave aisle and window to west of it,
chancel floor raised, masonry repaired,
new seats, new collar-braced roofs to
nave and chancel, new font and cover

Builders were Simpson and Malone of Hull,
cost about £2,300. Old glass reworked by
Clayton and Bell, south choir window by
Lavers, Barraud and Westlake, two other
windows by Morris and Co.
Sources: Ledger B add. ff. 6–10; CCE 40748;
ICBS 7127; *B* 1871 29 190–1; Newberry

YORK (N. Yorks.) St Philip's and St James's
School and Parish Room, Clifton
New school and parish room, for Revd H. G.
Hopkins
Built 1877–8
L-Plan. Plate and Geometrical tracery. Bell
turret to north. Red brick with stone
dressings, slate roof
Built by Shillitoe and Morgan
Sources: National Society file; *BN* 1877 33 345

YORK (N. Yorks.) St Philip's and St James's
Vicarage, Clifton
New House, for Revd G. M. Straffen
Designed 1877–8, built 1878–9
Two-storeyed, with projecting square and
semi-circular bays, large mullioned windows, gabled and hipped roofline with
prominent chimney-stacks. Red brick
ground storey, parts of upper storey with
coved jetties, tile-hung, red tile roof
Sources: CCE 37319; Newberry

WALES

ABEREDW (Radnors.; Powys) School
New school, for Archdeacon Henry de Winton
Designed 1869, built 1869–70
Simple hall with windows with trefoiled
heads. Large gable end window above
entrances with cat-slide roof, belfry in
roof
Sources: Ledger B add. f. 7; National Society
file

CAERPHILLY (Glamorgan; Mid Glamorgan) St Martin
Execution of church designed in 1870 by
Buckeridge, for Revd Thomas Jenkins
1874–9
Additions including fifth nave bay and west
tower made in 1910
Sources: ICBS 7647 (plan); *BN* 1870 18 406,
1879 37 814

CAPEL-Y-FFIN (Brecons.; Powys) Llanthony Monastery
Completion of monastery church by Buckeridge
Source: A. Saint, 'Charles Buckeridge and his Family', *Oxoniensia* 1973 38 357–72

CARMARTHEN (Carmarthens.; Dyfed) St Mary
Restoration for Revd Francis William Rice, Lord Dynevor
1867
New pew and prayer desk, restoration of tomb of Sir Rhys ap Thomas
Source: *E* 1867 28 314

CILCAIN (Flints.; Clwyd) Vicarage
Survey for enlargement, for Revd Brabazon Hallowes
1866, probably unexecuted
Source: Ledger B f. 106

CRICKHOWELL (Brecons.; Powys)
New house
1873
Design exhibited at Royal Academy in 1873 was described as 'castellated' and 'medieval'. A house to west of Crickhowell, Maes Celyn, was built at that time for R. Townley Woodman; though neither castellated nor medieval, it has many characteristics of Pearson's designs, especially its windows; its lodges, dated 1888, are similar to ones at Fairstead, Great Warley.
Sources: *B* 1873 31 359; *BN* 1873 24 571; Mr Gordon Barnes

CRICKHOWELL (Brecons.; Powys) St Edmund
According to *Hereford Times* the spire was rebuilt to designs by Pearson in 1861, the work being executed by Daniels, a local architect. The cost was £400; Daniels said he could have done it unaided for £80. There is no entry in Ledger B and report may be inaccurate
Source: Mr Gordon Barnes

GWYSANEY (Flints.; Clwyd) Gwysaney House
Enlargement and alterations, for Philip B. Davies Cooke

Designed 1863, reduced design executed 1863–5; altered 1910
First designs for building a set of reception rooms and extensive service quarters on site of wing demolished *c.* 1820, restoring Jacobean hall to original size, providing access through new staircase. More modest executed design for extension of house westward, two storeys, five bays, L-shaped plan, details following original such as two-light mullioned and transomed windows, to include guest rooms and servants' quarters
Sources: At house (signed plans dated December 1863 for unexecuted design); Ledger B f. 96; Mr Edward Hubbard

HEYOPE (Radnors.; Powys) St David
New church, old site, for Archdeacon Henry de Winton and others
Designed 1876, built 1880–2
Continuous nave and chancel with southwest porch, north-east organ chamber and vestry, west tower from previous church given new belfry and broach spire. Square windows with groups of lights with trefoiled heads, based on ones in previous church. Of local stone, plastered inside, arch-braced rafter roof, tiled
Cost about £1,150
Source: ICBS 8542

KNIGHTON (Radnors.; Powys) St Edward
New chancel, to church rebuilt by S. Pountney Smith 1875–7
1896–7
Three bays with south organ chamber. Tall lancets, triplet in east window. Of local stone, arch-braced collar roof, slated
Sources: *B* 1897 73 155; *BN* 1897 73 960

LLANBEDR (Brecons.; Powys) Church
Restoration, for Revd Thomas Augustus Davies
1896–7
Many features dated from restorations of 1864 and 1883. Church rearranged so that aisle reverted to south side. Modern nave windows rebuilt to be more in keeping with those of south aisle, and one added. Chancel arch rebuilt, floors renewed and sanctuary floor raised. Plaster removed from walls and a diaper fresco uncovered. New pulpit
Builder was Luscombe and Son
Sources: *B* 1897 72 228; Newberry

LLANDAFF (Glamorgan; South Glamorgan)
Cathedral
Consultant to Prichard and Seddon during
their restoration
Source: Mr Donald Buttress

LLANFIHANGEL-NANT-BRAN (Brecons.;
Powys) St Michael
Rebuilt except for tower, for Archdeacon
Henry de Winton
Proposed 1870, design completed 1880, re-
building 1880–2
Former church was ruinous and consisted of
nave, chancel and west tower without
distinction. Pearson rebuilt nave and
chancel and added a south porch. Paired
windows to sides, triplet at east
Cost £1,300
Sources: ICBS (signed plan): Ledger B add. ff.
9–11; T. Jones, *A History of the County of
Brecknock* (enlarged from the notes by J.
R. Bailey) vol. 2 (Brecknock, 1909) 209

LLANFRECHFA (Mon.; Gwent) Church
Rebuilding by Buckeridge, completed 1873
Source: A. Saint, 'Charles Buckeridge and his
Family', *Oxoniensia* 1973 38 357–72

LLANGASTY TALYLLYN (Brecons.;
Powys) St Gastayn
New church, old site, for Robert Raikes of
Treberfydd
Designed 1848, built 1848–50, fittings added to
1856, vestry 1862
West tower using foundations and part of
former tower, nave with south porch,
chancel with south organ chamber, north
vestry. Lancets, belfry with plate tracery,
plain exterior of local stone, interior with
painted texts and decorative patterns.
Complete fittings including screens, can-
delabra, choir stalls, pulpit, reading and
prayer desks, altar, organ case
Sources: Ledger B ff. 2, 4; Newberry; T.
Jones, *A History of the County of Brecknock* (enlarged from the notes by J. R.
Bailey) vol. 3 (Brecknock, 1911) 219–20

LLANGASTY TALYLLYN (Brecons.;
Powys) St Gastayn's School
New school and master's house
1848–50
School hall, and master's house of ground
storey and attic in gabled roof. Windows
with trefoiled heads single or in groups.

Of Bwlch stone with Bath stone dress-
ings, red tile roof
Sources: T. Jones, *A History of the County of
Brecknock* (enlarged from the notes by J.
R. Bailey) vol. 3 (Brecknock, 1911) 219–20

LLANGASTY TALYLLYN (Brecons.;
Powys) Treberfydd House
New house incorporating parts of previous
one, for Robert Raikes of Treberfydd
Designed and built 1848–52, alterations 1854,
entrance gates 1856, gardener's house
and furnishings to main house 1857
Two storeys and attics, irregular design with
living rooms separated from dining-room
and servants' quarters by hall extending
across building, entrance porch in base of
embattled tower, gabled roofline with
many prominent chimney-stacks. Of
Bwlch stone with Bath dressings, red tile
roofs. Tudor
Gardens laid out by W. A. Nesfield
Sources: At Treberfydd (drawings); Ledger B
ff. 2, 54; Eastlake 303, 382; Newberry; T.
Jones, *A History of the County of Brecknock* (enlarged from the notes by J. R.
Bailey) Vol. 3 (Brecknock, 1911) 219–21

MERTHYR TYDFIL (Glamorgan; Mid Glamorgan) St Tydvil
Rebuilt except for tower
Designed 1894, executed 1895–1901
Nineteenth-century church rebuilt in a Bur-
gundian Romanesque style, with four-
bay aisled nave, and transepts projecting
no further than aisles, semi-circular
apse. West tower retained. Round-
headed windows, nave arcade with
water-leaf capitals and round arches,
stone transverse arches to nave and
groined aisles, groined chancel, flat cemented ceiling to nave. Of local stone,
interior plastered, slate roof. An uncharacteristic design except for apse
Built by Cowlin and Son, cost £4,000
Sources: ICBS 9780; *B* 1895 69 317, 1901 80 612

PEMBROKE (Pemb.; Dyfed) St Mary
Execution of restoration planned by Buckeridge, for Revd Charles Coddington
1877–84
Removal of plaster from ceilings, gallery,
sash windows and pews; repairing masonry; new floors, tracery, chancel arch,
and tower
Sources: ICBS 8187; *CB* 1879 71 187

PORT TALBOT (Glamorgan; West Glamorgan) St Theodore
New church, new site, for Miss Emily Talbot
Designed and built 1895–7
Four-bay aisled nave with unfinished west tower, north and south porches, crossing and transepts, three-bay chancel with south chapel of two bays and semicircular apse, north organ chamber and vestries. Lancets, some plate tracery. Two-storeyed interior. Wooden roof with tie-beams and arch-braced collars supporting crown-posts and secondary collars; tower, aisles, chancel and chapel quadripartite rib-vaulted. Bell turret over chancel arch. Of local stone
Sources: Parish Chest (plan signed by Frank Pearson dated 1898); Newberry

PRESTEIGN (Radnors.; Powys) St Edward
Restoration, for Charles E. Maddison Green 1889–91
Repair of nave, new floor and roofs to nave and aisles; Saxon remains, and frescoes over north nave arcade uncovered. Brass crucifix and candlesticks probably by Pearson, teak chancel screen, stone pulpit, doors, west windows of aisles
Sources ICBS 9350; BN 1890 58 222; Newberry

RHYDYMWYM (Flints.; Clwyd) St John
New church, new site, for Revd Brabazon Hallowes and Philip B. Davies Cooke
Designed 1860, built 1860–3
Two-cell: nave with north porch, chancel with south organ chamber and vestry. Western bellcote with twin openings. Plate tracery. Of local stone with bands and dressings of Bath stone, interior of Bath stone with bands of darker stone in chancel. Foliated bands to chancel. Reredos with Last Supper in red incised work between green Irish marble shafts. Arch-braced timber roof. Pulpit of Caen stone on marble shafts
Cost about £2,400
Sources: Ledger B f. 84; B 1863 21 759–60

RHYDYMWYM (Flints.; Clwyd) St John's Parsonage
New house, for Dr Reynolds
Designed 1866, unexecuted
Pearson charged and was paid ten guineas
Source: Ledger B f. 113

RHYDYMWYM (Flints.; Clwyd) St John's Schools
New Schools, for Dr Reynolds
Designed 1866, unexecuted
Pearson charged and was paid twenty guineas
Source: Ledger B f. 113

SOLVA (Pemb.; Dyfed) St Aidan, Upper Solva
New church, new site, for Revd Rees Williams
Designed 1875–6, built 1877–8
Continuous nave and chancel with north-west entrance porch, south-west organ chamber and vestry. Western bellcote. Lancets. Of local stone, brick and Doulting stone dressings, plastered inside, arch-braced collar roof with tie-beams, slated
Cost £1,600
Sources: ICBS 8069 (signed plan); Newberry

TREHARRIS (Glamorgan; Mid Glamorgan) St Matthias
New church
Designed 1894, built 1895–6
Continuous nave and chancel of five bays with north aisle, north-west entrance porch, and north-east organ chamber and vestry. West bellcote. Lancets and plate tracery. Wood screen between nave and chancel. Of local stone, plastered inside, wagon roofs, slated
Built by Cowlin and Son, cost £3,000
Sources: ICBS 9780; B 1894 67 86, 1895 69 89, 1896 71 15

TRETOWER (Brecons.; Powys) St John
New church, old site, for Harry Russel Taylor and Sir Joseph Russel Bailey
Built 1877
Two-cell: nave with south porch, chancel with north organ chamber and vestry. Bellcote over chancel arch with two cross-gabled openings. Tall lancets. Of local stone, Bath stone dressings, interior plastered. Arch-braced roof with cusped wind-braces to nave, rafter roof to chancel, red Broseley tiles
Cost £2,400
Sources: BA 1877 8 264; BN 1877 33 550; Newberry; T. Jones A History of the County of Brecknock (enlarged from the notes by J. R. Bailey) vol. 3 (Brecknock, 1911) 183

TRETOWER (Brecons.; Powys) St John's Parish Room (now a school)
New parish room, for Sir Joseph Russel Bailey
1887–8
Hall with entrance under hip of roof, projecting semi-circular bay at other end. Groups of lancets and trefoiled openings. Of local stone with Bath dressings, red tile roof, half hipped at one end, gabled at entrance end
Source: T. Jones, *A History of the County of Brecknock* (enlarged from the notes by J. R. Bailey) vol. 3 (Brecknock, 1911) 183

WHITCHURCH (Pemb.; Dyfed), Church
Completion of restoration planned by Buckeridge in 1872, for Revd Rees Williams
Executed 1872–4
Church largely rebuilt
Source: ICBS 7459

SCOTLAND

AYR (Ayr.) Holy Trinity
New church, old site, for Revd J. M. Lester
The east parts completed 1888, the remainder built by Frank Pearson 1898–1900
Five-bay aisled nave with unfinished north west tower, narthex in sixth bay of nave under west gallery; three-bay chancel with south chapel and north organ chamber and vestries. Lancets. Of local stone. Two-storeyed interior elevation with shafts rising from capitals of nave piers to support stone transverse arches and wooden roof, similar roofs to aisles. Chancel has polygonal wagon roof
Built by Cowlin and Son, cost over £11,000
Sources: *B* 1898 75 155, 1900 79 469; *BN* 1888 54 272; Newberry

GLENALMOND (Perthshire) Trinity College
New infirmary, for Dr John Hannah
Designed 1861, built 1861–2
Cost £1,300
Cources: Ledger B f. 89; Newberry

PERTH (Perthshire) Cathedral
Alterations and extension of choir, for Bishop Wilkinson
Designed 1896–7, executed by Frank Pearson 1899–1901
The cathedral was begun to designs by Butterfield in 1849. Alterations included removal of stump of tower, extension of chancel, provision of vaulted south chapel with polygonal apse, and arcade between it and chancel with tomb beneath, cloister leading from south transept to new chapter house
Source: A. J. Mason, *Memoir of George Howard Wilkinson* (London, 1909) vol. 2 242

ISLE OF MAN

DOUGLAS, St Matthew
New church, new site but replacing old church, for Revd J. A. Taggart
Designed 1895, nave and aisles built 1895–7, remainder built by Frank Pearson about 1901
Five-bay aisled nave with unfinished north-west tower and transepts at east, chancel with south organ chamber and vestries. Early English
Built by Kelly and Preston of Douglas, cost over £5,000
Sources: ICBS 9871 (plan signed by Frank Pearson dated May 1901); *B* 1897 73 155; *BN* 1895 69 318; Newberry

KIRKBRADDAN, St Braddan
New church, new site but replacing old church
Designed 1871, built 1872–4, consecrated 1876, tower and spire built 1883–6
Four-bay aisled nave with north-west porch and smaller porch at east end of north side, chancel with semi-circular apse, south tower and transeptal chapel. Lancets, triple lights in apse. Tower with broach spire. Of local stone with Bath stone dressings, slate roof
Built by Wall and Hook of Brinscombe, cost £4,300
Sources: ICBS 7402 (signed plan dated June 1871); Ledger B add. ff. 10–11; *A* 1873 9 244; *B* 1873 31 339; *BA* 1876 6 153; *BN* 1872 22 21, 423, 1873 24 571, 1876 31 248; *The Manx Notebook* 1886 2 42; Newberry

MALTA

VALETTA, Ta Braxia Protestant Cemetery, Floriana
New memorial chapel, for Lord Stanmore in memory of his wife (died 1889)
Probably 1894
Octagonal central space with arcade of eight piers carrying drum and dome, surrounded by double aisles with arcade between, western entrance in projecting gabled doorway, eastern chancel with semi-circular apse. Byzantine. Interior vaulted
Sources: Newberry; Mrs Morgan

AUSTRALIA

BRISBANE (Queensland) Cathedral
New cathedral, for Dr William Thomas Thornhill Webber, Bishop of Brisbane
Designed 1887–9, alterations made before 1897, further alterations by Frank Pearson, east parts built 1901–10, west parts begun 1955
Six-bay nave with inner and outer aisles with seventh bay flanked by towers containing entrance and projecting porch; crossing with central tower and spire, three-bay transepts, aisled four-bay choir and semi-circular apse and ambulatory with projecting east chapel, chapter house in north-east angle with polygonal apse. Two-storeyed interior with very tall arcade. Lancets and Geometrical tracery, Vaulted throughout. Of pink porphyry with dressings of Pyrmont stone, interior of Brown Helidon sandstone.
Designed to cost £100,000, the east parts to cost £35,000
Sources: Truro Cathedral Records (drawings including plan, north elevation dated 1889, perspective dated 1897); R.I.B.A. Drawings Collection (Frank Pearson's revised drawings); B 1901 80 541

GOULBURN (New South Wales) Cathedral
Design for new cathedral, for Mesac Thomas, Bishop of Goulburn
Designed 1869–71, unexecuted
Sources: Ledger B add. ff. 7, 10–11; B 1871 31 284

SYDNEY (New South Wales) Cathedral
Reredos
Source: Mrs Morgan (photograph)

CHRONOLOGY OF EVENTS

1817   July 5: born, probably in Brussels, but brought up in Durham

1831   Enters Bonomi's office in Durham

1836   October: visits Hamburg

1840   *Studies and Examples of Modern Architecture* left nearly complete; letters to Sir William Chaytor about Clervaux Castle

1841   Further letters to Chaytor
September 28: last payment of salary by Bonomi

1842   January 20: gives plans and specification of house to Robson
January 24: starts work for Pickering in Sunderland
February 21–3: journey to London
March 14: starts work for Salvin
August 23–6: leaves Salvin and visits Durham
October 21: starts work with Hardwick on Lincoln's Inn

1843   February–November: Ellerker chapel designed and started
April 20: foundation stone of New Hall and Library of Lincoln's Inn laid

1844   Wauldby chapel designed for Mrs Raikes of Welton
Befriended by Robert Raikes of Treberfydd
August 8: Ellerker chapel consecrated
Finished work at Lincoln's Inn

1845   January: design of North Ferriby church begun
July: plans for farm buildings for Robert Raikes of Eastdale
October: restoration of Elloughton church complete
Designs for Weybridge church begun

1846   Designs completed and work begun on churches at Ellerton, North Ferriby, Stow-on-the-Wold and Weybridge
April 21: Ann Pearson (sister) dies at Truro

1847   Restoration of Lea church begun for Sir Charles Anderson
July 5: thirtieth birthday

1848   Work begun on Treberfydd and Llangasty Talyllyn church for Robert Raikes, and restoration of Sigglesthorne church for Archdeacon Bentinck
April 26: Ellerton church consecrated
June 17: Weybridge church consecrated
July 20: North Ferriby church consecrated

1849   August 7: foundation stone laid of Landscove church
November: design of Holy Trinity, Bessborough Gardens, complete
November 19: William Pearson (father) dies

1850   January 1: visit to Dr Spyers at Wallop Lodge
Restoration of Stow chancel begun
Holy Trinity, Bessborough Gardens, complete

1851 July 2–5: visits to Dartington to see about restoration of church
      Landscove church completed
1852 February 25: begins first work for Robert Gregory at St Mary the Less
      March 3–4: visit to Stinchbombe to see about rebuilding church
      June 8: visit to Exton to see about restoring church
      September 14: Pugin dies
      Holy Trinity, Bessborough Gardens, and restoration of Stow chancel
          completed: Treberfydd largely complete
1853 March 8: visits Braintree to see about new parsonage
      June 16: elected Fellow of the Society of Antiquaries
      July: travels in France—Amiens and Beauvais
      August 12: visits Eastoft to see about new church
      September 22 to about October 11: travels in Belgium and up Rhine
          from Cologne to Mainz
      Ashen chancel designed
1854 April 15: design of Devoran church completed
      July 24–6: first visit to Lord Hotham at South Dalton, and to Sir
          Charles Anderson about Lea Hall on return
      Stinchcombe church begun
1855 July 26: Stinchcombe church consecrated
      August: possible visit to France
      Braintree parsonage built
1856 March 12–14: surveys of Kirkburn and Garton churches for re-
          storation for Sir Tatton Sykes
      Devoran church completed
      June 21: fixing site for Quar Wood
1857 January 2: first visit to Daylesford
      January 12–13: further visits to Kirkburn and Garton, first visit to
          Scorborough
      March: Quar Wood set out
      April 27: first visit to Catherston Leweston
      May 23: Devoran church consecrated
      June 23: Scorborough church set out
      July 5: fortieth birthday
      September 25: examines site for Dalton Holme church
1858 Extensive journeys to Gloucestershire, Wiltshire and Yorkshire to
          inspect work in progress
      June: design of Dalton Holme church completed, work begun
      Catherston Leweston church completed
1859 January 26–7: first visit to Titsey
      February 8: design for Daylesford church completed
      July: elected a member of the Ecclesiological Society
      September 6: starts travels of about three weeks in Normandy and
          northern France from Le Havre
      Quar Wood and Scorborough church completed

1860	February 26: foundation stone of Titsey church laid
	March 19: elected Fellow of the R.I.B.A.
	June: extensive work on Vauxhall church and schools
	June 27: foundation stone of schools laid by Prince of Wales
	November: first design of St Peter, Vauxhall, completed
1861	February 13: Broomfleet parsonage design completed
	May: Daylesford church completed
	August 6: Dalton Holme church consecrated
	October 1–5: survey of nineteen churches in Holderness
	October 28: becomes engaged to Jemima Christian
	November 27: Titsey church consecrated
1862	June 5: marries Jemima Christian
	December 6: first visit to Appleton-le-Moors
1863	April 16: foundation stone of St Peter, Vauxhall, laid
	Appleton-le-Moors church begun, school designed
1864	January 14: Frank Pearson born
	April 26: first visit to Riccall
	May 19: Riccall designs completed
	June 28: St Peter, Vauxhall, consecrated
	August 4: Appleton-le-Moors church consecrated
1865	March 23: Jemima dies of typhoid fever aged 35
	April 1: visit to Dr Spyers at Wallop Lodge
	October: Riccall church restoration completed
	October 26: paid off by Sir Tatton Sykes V
	November: Freeland church design begun
	November 22: first visit to Sutton Veny
1866	May 7: Sutton Veny church set out
	May: Ayot St Peter rectory plans completed, building started
	June 5: visit to Freeland to choose site for church
	June 27: Freeland church set out
	November 21: first visit to Wentworth
1867	July 5: fiftieth birthday
	Ayot St Peter rectory finished
	St Peter's Home, Kilburn, begun
1868	April 17: Sutton Veny church consecrated
	Roundwyck House begun
1869	May 14: Ann Pearson (mother) dies
	June: Freeland church completed
	July 3: attends consecration of Freeland church
1870	Appointed architect to Lincoln Cathedral
	Design of Chute Forest church begun
	December: design of St Augustine, Kilburn, completed
	Roundwyck House completed
1871	First visit to see about Lechlade Manor House
	Crowton vicarage designed

July 12: foundation stone laid of St Augustine, Kilburn

August 31: sets out for tour of France from Etretat

1872 January: design of Lechlade Manor House completed

June: east parts of St Augustine, Kilburn, completed

Plans to restore Lastingham church begun

Wentworth church begun

1873 September: Charles Buckeridge dies

Lechlade Manor House completed

1874 January 29: elected Associate of the Royal Academy

April 14: sets out from Turin on tour of Italy lasting three weeks

November 2: receives Street's R.I.B.A. Gold Medal on his behalf

December 15: design of St John, Red Lion Square, completed

1875 June 10: Chute Forest church consecrated

June 23: second report on Lincoln Cathedral dealing especially with
south-west tower

St John, Red Lion Square, started

1876 May 27: foundation stone laid of nave of St Augustine, Kilburn

Plans for restoration of Steetley chapel begun

Design of St Michael, Croydon, begun

1877 May: design of St Michael, Croydon, exhibited at Royal Academy

July 5: sixtieth birthday

November 6: nave of St Augustine, Kilburn, completed

Work to secure south-west tower of Lincoln Cathedral begun

Wentworth church completed

1878 January 28: design of Clifton vicarage completed

February 23: St John, Red Lion Square, consecrated

March 27: Scott dies (funeral April 6)

May: designs of Westwood House exhibited at Royal Academy

August 20: accepts appointment as architect of new cathedral for
Truro

November: design of St John, Upper Norwood, completed

Design of Cullercoats church begun

1879 March: design of St Alban, Bordesley, completed

August 4: design of Truro Cathedral completed and approved

September: St Alban, Bordesley, begun

Appointed Surveyor of Westminster Abbey

Clifton vicarage and restoration of Lastingham church completed

1880 April 20: foundation stone of St Michael, Croydon, laid

May 20: foundation stone of Truro Cathedral laid

June 7: receives R.I.B.A. Gold Medal

November 27: elected Royal Academician

December: restoration of south-west tower of Lincoln Cathedral
completed

Westwood House begun

Restoration of Steetley chapel completed

1881   March 2: William Nesfield dies
        March 7: Dr Spyers dies
        April 20: Burges dies (funeral April 26)
        May 3: St Alban, Bordesley, opened
        May 6: St John, Upper Norwood, begun
        May 10: removes to 13 Mansfield Street
        August: goes with Street to St Gervais to take the waters
        September: stays on in France with Ewan Christian at Aix-les-Bains
            and is rejoined by Street
        October 27: St Michael, Croydon, dedicated
        December 17: Salvin dies
        December 18: Street dies (funeral December 29)
        Westwood House completed
1882   April: design of Headingley church completed
        May 17: James Bubb dies of typhoid fever at Truro and is succeeded as
            clerk of works by Robert Swain
        May 22: east parts of St John, Upper Norwood, dedicated
        August 4: foundation stone of Cullercoats church laid
        December 6: design of St Agnes, Sefton Park, completed
        St Peter's Convent, Woking, begun
        Design of St Stephen, Bournemouth, begun
        Frank Pearson and W. D. Caröe in the office
1883   January 3: crossing of Peterborough Cathedral in danger of imminent
            collapse
        February: design of Thurstaston church completed
        June 22: design of St Stephen, Bournemouth, completed and church
            started
        October 1: St Michael, Croydon, consecrated
        October 17: foundation stone of St Peter's Convent, Woking, laid
        Cullercoats church completed
1884   Restoration of north transept of Westminster Abbey begun
        May 7: corner stone of crossing of Peterborough Cathedral laid
        September 24: designs for restoration of crossing of Peterborough
            Cathedral laid before Restoration Committee
        September 29: foundation stone of Headingley church laid
        November 19: first appearance before Westminster Hall Select
            Committee
1885   January 21: St Agnes, Sefton Park, consecrated
        March 19: appears for last time before Westminster Hall Select
            Committee
        July 6: St Peter's Convent, Woking, occupied
        July 6: signs will
        July 11: nave of St Stephen, Bournemouth, opened
        August: invited (together with Bodley, Brooks and Emerson) to
            prepare a design for new cathedral at Liverpool

November: abandons design through ill health
Whitwell rectory completed
1886 January 7: Thurstaston church consecrated
July: plans to restore Hythe church completed, work begun
July 8: Headingley church consecrated
Designs for completion of Old Schools, Cambridge
1887 February: elected member of the Athenaeum Club
March 26: designs of St Hilda, Darlington, completed
April 30: St John, Upper Norwood, consecrated
June 14: foundation stone of Wantage Convent chapel laid
July 5: seventieth birthday
November 3: east parts of Truro Cathedral consecrated
New design for All Saints, Hove, made
Asked to make design for new cathedral for Brisbane
1888 Restoration of Rochester Cathedral begun
August 13: restoration of chancel of Hythe church completed
August 30: St Hilda, Darlington, consecrated
Additions to Westminster Hall completed
1889 Rebuilding of Redhill church begun
February 2: Wantage Convent chapel dedicated
February: Brisbane Cathedral designs completed
April 25: foundation stone of All Saints, Hove, laid
May: portrait by W. W. Ouless exhibited at Royal Academy
July 11: choir of Peterborough Cathedral opened
Design of St John, Friern Barnet, completed
1890 St John, Friern Barnet, begun
Old Schools, Cambridge, completed
Middlesex Hospital chapel designed
April: responsible for hanging Royal Academy Summer Exhibition
architectural section
November: north transept of Westminster Abbey completed
1891 Catholic Apostolic Church begun
May 1: nave of All Saints, Hove, consecrated
October 10: east parts of St John, Friern Barnet, consecrated
Redhill church completed
1892 February 8: letter of congratulation and gold cup sent to Mr and Mrs
Raikes for their golden wedding
Proposals to remove Wren library from Lincoln Cathedral cloister
June 13: plan to restore Bristol Cathedral approved
July 5: seventy-fifth birthday
Design of Astor Estate Office begun and largely completed
1893 Astor Estate Office begun
Catholic Apostolic Church completed
1894 December: design of Bristol Cathedral choir furnishings completed
1895 February: Ewan Christian dies (funeral February 25)

March 24: gale brings down pinnacle from west front of Peterborough cathedral

May 6: choir of Bristol Cathedral opened

May 28: report on west front of Peterborough Cathedral

Port Talbot church begun

1896 Controversy over plans to restore west front of Peterborough Cathedral

1897 January 12: work begun on west front of Peterborough Cathedral

January 17: visits St Peter's Convent, Woking, to see about new chapel

March 12: rebuilding of Peterborough Cathedral begun

April: responsible for hanging architectural section of Royal Academy Summer Exhibition

May 20: work on west parts of Truro Cathedral begun

July 1: design of new chapel for St Peter's Convent, Woking, completed and accepted

July 5: eightieth birthday

July 5: rebuilding at Peterborough Cathedral completed

August 5: Port Talbot church consecrated

December 3: taken ill

Spire of St Augustine, Kilburn, completed

December 11: dies

BIBLIOGRAPHY

For a complete bibliography of the Gothic Revival one should refer to the Victorian Library edition of Eastlake's *A History of the Gothic Revival* (Leicester, 1970) edited by J. Mordaunt Crook.

Frank Pearson disposed of most of his father's library during the Second World War, but Mrs Morgan kept some books, and others are known. These are listed in part I. In part II come those which Pearson referred to but is not known to have owned: books which are listed in his diaries or from which he made copies of illustrations when he was too poor to purchase them himself. Part III includes those books with substantial information on Pearson.

Part I

Billings, R. W. *Architectural Illustrations and Description of the Cathedral Church of Durham* (London, 1843)

——*Illustrations of the Architectural Antiquities of the County of Durham* (Durham, 1846)

Burges, W. *Architectural Drawings* (London, 1870)

Christian, E. *Architectural Elevations of Skelton Church* (London, 1846)

Christian, M. *The Resolutions of Mary Christian upon the Day of her Marriage* (details unknown)

Codd, J. *A Legend of the Middle Ages, and other Songs of the Past and Present* (London, 1890)

The Cornish See and Cathedral (Truro, 1887)

Gotch, J. A. *The Buildings Erected in Northamptonshire by Sir Thomas Tresham 1575–1605* (Northampton, 1883)

Gwilt, J. *An Encyclopaedia of Architecture* (London, 1842)

Pearson, W. *Rural Beauties* (details unknown)

——*Antiquities of Shropshire* (Shrewsbury, 1807)

Scott, G. G. *Gleanings from Westminster Abbey* (Oxford and London, 1861)

Sharpe, E. *The Mouldings of the Six Periods of British Architecture from the Conquest to the Reformation (1050–1550)* (London, 1879)

——*The Architecture of the Cistercians* (London, 1874)

Shaw, H. *The Encyclopaedia of Ornament* (London, 1842)

——*Dresses and Decorations of the Middle Ages* (London, 1843)

——*Alphabets, Numerals and Devices of the Middle Ages* (London, 1845)

——*The Handbook of Medieval Alphabets and Devices* (London, 1853)

Smith, J. T. *Antiquities of Westminster: The Old Palace; St Stephen's Chapel* (London, 1807)

Part II

Billings, R. W. *Architectural Illustrations Historical and Description of Carlisle Cathedral* (London, 1840)

Britton, J. *Architectural Antiquities of Great Britain* (London, 1807–26)

Britton J. and Pugin, A. C. *Historical and Descriptive Essays Accompanying a Series of Engraved Specimens of the Architectural Antiquities of Normandy* (London, 1828)

Darwin, C. R. *Journal of Charles Darwin* (London, 1839)

de Vries, J. V. *Architectura* (Antwerp, 1563)

Eustace, H. M. *Philosophy of Human Nature* (details unknown)

Fitzroy, R. *Narrative of the Surveying Voyages of His Majesty's Ships Adventure and Beagle between the Years 1826 and 1836* (London, 1839)

Grueber, B. *Die Kunst des Mittelalters in Böhmen* (Vienna, 1871–9)

Hallam, H. *Introduction to the Literature of Europe in the Fifteenth, Sixteenth and Seventeenth Centuries* (London 1837–9)

Hunt, T. F. *Exemplars of Tudor Architecture* (London, 1830)

Klenze, L. von. *Anweisung zur Architectur des Christlichen Cultus* (Munich 1834)

Krafft, J. C. *Portes cochères et portes d'entrées de maisons et d'édifices publics de Paris* (Paris, 1838)

Lane, E. W. *An Account of the Manners and Customs of the Modern Egyptians* (London, 1836)

Letters on Paraguay: Nine Years in the Republic under the government of the Dictator Francia (details unknown)

Neale, J. P. *The History and Antiquities of the Abbey Church of St Peter, Westminster* (London, 1818)

Parker, C. *Villa Rustica* (London, 1832)

Petit, J. L. *Remarks on Church Architecture* (London, 1841)

Pugin, A. C. *Gothic Ornaments* (London, 1831)

——*Examples of Gothic Architecture* (London, 1831–8)

Pugin, A. W. N. *Timber Houses of the Fifteenth Century* (London, 1835)

——*Designs for Iron and Brass Work in the Style of the Fifteenth and Sixteenth Century* (London, 1836)

Retrospect of a Military Life (details unknown)

Richardson, C. J. *Studies from Old English Mansions* (London, 1841)

Rubens, P. P. *Palazzi di Genova* (1622)

Shaw, H. *Examples of Ornamental Metal Work* (London, 1836)

——*Details of Elizabethan Architecture* (London, 1839)

Simpson, F. *Baptismal Fonts* (London, 1828)

Stephens, J. L. *Incidents of Travel in Central America, Chiapas and Yucatan* (London, 1841)

Suys, T. F. and Haudebourt, L. P. *Palais Massimi à Rome* (Paris, 1818)

Tanner, T. *Notitia Monastica* (Oxford, 1695)

Venables, R. L. *Domestic Scenes in Russia* (London, 1839)

Viollet-le-Duc, E. E. *Dictionnaire raisonné de l'architecture Française du XIme au XVIme siécle* (Paris, 1854–68)

Widmore, R. *An Enquiry into the Time of the First Foundation of Westminster Abbey* (London, 1743)

Part III

Adams, M. B. *Architects from George IV to George V* (London, 1912)

Bond, F. *The Cathedrals of England and Wales* 4th edn (London, 1912)

Clarke, B. F. L. *Church Builders of the Nineteenth Century* (London, 1938)

——*Anglican Cathedrals outside the British Isles* (London, 1958)

Dixon, R. and Muthesius, S. *Victorian Architecture* (London, 1978)

Fawcett, J. (ed.) *Seven Victorian Architects* (London, 1976)

Girouard, M. *The Victorian Country House* (Oxford, 1971)

Hitchcock, H.-R. *Early Victorian Architecture* (London, 1954)

——*Architecture: Nineteenth and Twentieth Centuries* (Harmondsworth, 1958)

Howell, P. *Victorian Churches* (London, 1968)

Lethaby, W. R. *Westminster Abbey and the Kings' Craftsmen* (London, 1906)

Muthesius, H. *Die Neuere Kirchliche Baukunst in England* (Berlin, 1901)

Muthesius, S. *The High Victorian Movement in Architecture 1850–1870* (London and Boston, 1972)

Pevsner, N. *The Buildings of England* 46 vols (Harmondsworth, 1951–74)

Prior, E. S. *The Cathedral Builders in England* (London, 1905)

Saint, A. *Richard Norman Shaw* (New Haven and London, 1976)

Summerson, J. N. *Victorian Architecture: Four Studies in Evaluation* (New York and London, 1970)

——(ed.) *Concerning Architecture* (London, 1968)

Sweeting, W. D. *The Cathedral Church of Peterborough* (Peterborough, 1908)

White, J. T. *The Cambridge Movement* (Cambridge, 1962)

INDEX

Numbers in italic refer to plates.